MW00710614

Consumer Reports

BEST BUYS
FOR YOUR
HOME

2003

THE EDITORS OF CONSUMER REPORTS

Published by Consumer Reports ◆ A Division of Consumers Union ◆ Yonkers, New York

A Special Publication from Consumer Reports

Managing Editor Bette LaGow
Contributing Editor Duncan C. Stephens
Special Publications Staff Merideth Mergel, Joan Daviet
Design Manager Rosemary Simmons
Designer Kimberly Shake
Illustrator Trevor Johnston
Technology Specialist Jennifer Dixon
Page Composition William Breglio

Consumer Reports Technical Division

Vice President and Technical Director Jeffrey A. Asher
Director, Product Research Operations Frank Iacopelli
Director, Appliances and Home Environment Mark Connelly
Director, Consumer Sciences Geoff Martin
Director, Electronics Evon Beckford
Testing Director, Recreation, Power & Auto Equipment John Galeotafiore
Associate Technical Director Alan Lefkow
Manager, Home Improvement James Nanni
Director of Product and Market Analysis Julie Levine
Director of Product Information Celeste Monte
Products Director, Product Tracking Carolyn Clifford-Ferrara

Consumer Reports

Vice President and Editorial Director Julia Kagan
Editor/Senior Director Margot Slade
Executive Editor/Associate Editorial Director Eileen Denver
Design Director, Consumers Union George Arthur
Creative Director, Consumer Reports Tim LaPalme
Products Director Paul Reynolds
Director, Production Operations David Fox
Vice President, Multimedia Publishing John Sateja
Senior Director, ConsumerReports.org and New Media Jerry Steinbrink
**General Manager, Multimedia Information Products & Senior Director
    Market Development** Paige Amidon
Product Manager, Special Publications Carol Lappin
Director, Information Services and Survey Research Charles Daviet
Associate Director, Survey Research Mark Kotkin
Manufacturing/Distribution Ann Urban

Consumers Union

President James A. Guest
Executive Vice President Joel Gurin
Senior Vice President, Technical Policy R. David Pittle

First printing, December 2002
Copyright © 2002 by Consumers Union of United States, Inc., Yonkers, New York 10703.
Published by Consumers Union of United States, Inc., Yonkers, New York 10703.
All rights reserved, including the right of reproduction in whole or in part in any form.
ISSN: 1528-4743
ISBN: 0-89043-972-9

Manufactured in the United States of America.

TABLE OF CONTENTS

PART TWO: NUTS & BOLTS

Chapter 8 Heating, Cooling, Filtering

PART THREE: REFERENCE SECTION

Best Buys for Your Home covers, in a convenient format, the latest buying tips and product Ratings from CONSUMER REPORTS. Published by the non-profit Consumers Union, CONSUMER REPORTS is a comprehensive source of unbiased advice about products and services, personal finance, health and nutrition, and other consumer concerns. Since 1936, the mission of Consumers Union has been to test products, inform the public, and protect consumers. Our income is derived solely from the sale of CONSUMER REPORTS magazine and our other publications and services, and from nonrestrictive, noncommercial contributions, grants, and fees. We buy all the products we test. We accept no ads from companies, nor do we let any outside entity use our reports or Ratings for commercial purposes.

OTHER BUYING GUIDES FROM CONSUMER REPORTS

- ◆ Digital Buying Guide
- ◆ New Car Buying Guide
- ◆ Used Car Buying Guide
- ◆ Consumer Reports Buying Guide

OTHER PUBLICATIONS FROM CONSUMER REPORTS

- ◆ Sport-Utility Special
- ◆ New Car Preview
- ◆ Used Car Yearbook
- ◆ Road Tests
- ◆ Travel Well for Less
- ◆ Consumer Drug Reference
- ◆ Guide to Baby Products
- ◆ How to Clean and Care for Practically Anything

All around the house

If there's an upside to recent sobering world events or the faltering stock market, it might be that people are finding that putting time, energy, and money into their homes is a worthwhile and satisfying investment. Home is not only where the heart is, but these days, it's also where the body and soul—and wallet—reside as well. This book is designed to give you an in-depth look at the home-products marketplace so you can get the most for your investment, whether you're buying new products or upgrading existing ones. Generally, what you'll find is that appliance manufacturers are working to satisfy a consumer's desire for kitchen and laundry equipment that is quick, convenient, and "smart," with sensors and other controls—with varying degrees of success—for easier and more precise operation. The home-entertainment industry continues its race toward making everything digital, which can greatly enhance audio and video performance. Out in the yard, equipment is getting safer, quieter, and friendlier to the environment.

Despite the excitement over the Internet and the popularity of catalog sales, the principal shopping arena is still the retail store, from the neighborhood hardware purveyor to Home Depot and Wal-Mart. One thing that hasn't changed is the need for informed decision making. CONSUMER REPORTS provides an invaluable service in that regard, delivering information that can help consumers shop smart in today's world.

USING THIS BOOK

Best Buys for Your Home is designed to help you sort through the myriad choices faced by shoppers for home products. It's divided into three parts. In "Feathering Your Nest," the chapters focus on how a home can be equipped in a way that is functional and often fun, from a step-by-step guide to setting up a home theater and choosing key components such as TV sets and DVD players to advice on appliances for the kitchen and laundry, equipment and tools for the yard, gear that keeps your home clean or safe such as vacuums and smoke detectors, and home "software" such as bedding and carpeting.

In "Nuts & Bolts," you'll find information on home-remodeling, followed by chapters on decorative products, such as paint and wallpaper; building components, such as countertops and windows; and important home equipment, such as air conditioning.

In the back of the book you'll find a comprehensive 107-page reference section that includes CONSUMER REPORTS Ratings of more than 700 brand-name products, as well brand-repair histories for many product categories.

HOW CONSUMER REPORTS TESTS PRODUCTS

For nearly 70 years, CONSUMER REPORTS has bought products and tested them so consumers can make informed decisions. From methodical, scientific tests of products that we buy at retail, we develop our Ratings. (Reliability information for key products, such as TV sets, lawn mowers, and washing machines, comes from surveys of readers of CONSUMER REPORTS magazine, who report their actual experience with specific brands.)

To determine what to test, our engineers, market analysts, and editors attend trade shows, read trade publications, and look at what's in the stores to spot the latest products and trends. They also pay attention to letters from readers. Our market analysts query manufacturers about product lines and update in-house databases listing thousands of models. Eventually, staff shoppers anonymously visit dozens of stores or go online to buy the selected models. A test plan is then prepared to evaluate performance and other aspects of the product, such as safety, energy and water consumption, noise, and convenience. For every product tested, the technical staff records a "pedigree," a thorough accounting of all features and idiosyncrasies.

A microphone is used in assessing loud-speaker performance in an echo-free chamber at CONSUMER REPORTS headquarters.

Measurements are made by computers and by various sensitive instruments, including the most important instruments of all—human eyes, ears, noses, and hands. Much of the work we do in our labs mimics how a product would be used at home, albeit more systematically. Testers read and try out the buttons on the controls. They turn the knobs on the receivers and washing machines and flip through channels on the TV sets. A panel of testers systematically compares everything from TV pictures to vacuum-cleaner handling, sewing-machine ease of use, and more. For some products, we have to test away from our headquarters in Yonkers, N.Y. We test lawn mowers, for instance, in Florida, where a large lawn of winter rye is specially prepared for five to six weeks of tests every January through March in order to have results by spring. Sometimes our tests are supplemented by the real-life experiences of engineers and volunteers who use the products in their homes.

HOW HOT? For ranges, we determine heating speed by bringing measured amounts of water to a near boil, over and over, model after model. Cooking performance is gauged in various ways: by melting chocolate in a saucepan, by baking cakes and broiling burgers in an oven, and by reheating food in a microwave. To evaluate a range's self-cleaning feature, we bake on and then remove our own special blend of gunk, consisting of cherry pie, tomato puree, egg yolk, mozzarella, cheese spread, tapioca, and lard. To help us evaluate whether irons heat uniformly or have hot spots, we use a thermal camera, which represents different temperatures on the soleplate of each iron as different colors.

HOW COLD? We test refrigerators and room air conditioners in an environmental chamber—a large, heavily insulated room that allows us to control temperature and humidity. To see how readily refrigerators respond to changes in room temperature, we heat up the test chamber from 70° F to 90°, cool it back down to 70°, and then take it down further to 55°. To measure the reserve power a refrigerator might need for torrid weather, we set the room at 110°. Sensors inside each refrigerator monitor how evenly the unit keeps cold.

To test room air conditioners, we mount them in a room within the environmental chamber to create an "outside" and an "inside." Can they maintain a comfortable temperature and humidity level in the room when the outside temperature is 95°? How level do they keep humidity? The chamber's instruments tell the tale.

HOW CLEAN? We feed vacuum cleaners measured amounts of fine sand and talcum powder that we sprinkle onto and then grind into a medium-pile carpet. After a vacuum is passed back and forth over the carpet eight times, we weigh and measure what's left on the carpet and what's inside the machine. To see how much dust spews back into the air, we vacuum fine sawdust from carpeting and use instruments to detect dust in the air.

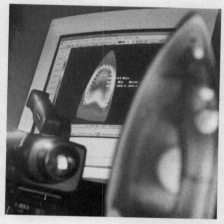

A thermal camera helps determine how evenly heat is distributed on the soleplate of an iron.

With dishwashers, we wash dozens of place settings, all systematically soiled with tenacious foods such as chili, spaghetti, mashed potatoes, egg yolk, peanut butter, raspberry jam, cheese spread, cornflakes and milk, oatmeal, stewed tomatoes, and coffee. With washing machines, we assess performance by washing several specially soiled fabric swatches in a load of bed sheets, dress shirts, pillowcases, T-shirts, towels, boxer shorts, and a washcloth.

HOW GREEN? Environmental factors are taken into consideration. For big energy users such as refrigerators, we measure electricity consumption. For washing machines and dishwashers, we measure usage of hot water—typically more costly than the electricity used to run the machine. For room air conditioners, we note energy efficiency. Noise is an important concern when it comes to equipment such as power blowers and wet/dry vacs. It's also a consideration for items that might be located near a living area, such as washing machines, dishwashers, clothes dryers, toilets, room air cleaners, and room air conditioners.

HOW EASY TO USE? No matter how well a product performs its task, if it isn't convenient to use and live with, it isn't a useful product. Small inconveniences on a product that is used every day—the shelf arrangement in a refrigerator, the design of the loading racks in a dishwasher, the arrangement of buttons on a remote control—can become annoying. We carefully examine every product to see how thoughtfully it was designed. We also try out all the built-in menus and prompts to make sure they're logical and not irksome. And we read and evaluate all product instructions.

For updates on the products in this book, check out monthly issues of CONSUMER REPORTS or our web site, Consumer Reports.org.

Kitchen & Laundry

1

Today's appliances are smarter, more capable, and more energy efficient than yesterday's. New technologies and tightened government energy standards have sparked the change. A bonus is that today's appliances, large and small, are likely to be more stylish than the appliances you currently own. Here's a rundown on current trends:

ADDED INTELLIGENCE. Everything from dishwashers to mixers has been embellished with electronic sensors, controls, and monitors. "Smart" products are supposed to minimize the guesswork of knowing when the clothes are dry, the food is cooked, the dishes are washed, or the toast is browned. This technology can use water and energy more efficiently, as with a washer that automatically fills to the water level the load requires, and a refrigerator that defrosts only as necessary rather than at set intervals.

But such advances are only the first wave. Ready to debut: microwave ovens that scan bar codes on packaged-food labels and automatically set the precise cooking time and power level; Internet-connected refrigerators that scan labels and automatically reorder provisions when you're running low; and self-diagnosing appliances that can convey information to a repair center by computer, allowing a technician to make a preliminary diagnosis before a service call. Whether these products will truly fill a consumer need—or merely serve a manufacturer's need to spark sales—remains to be seen.

FASTER COOKING. Consumers seem to want food cooked ever faster, or at least manufacturers say they do. Titans such as GE, Maytag, and Whirlpool have introduced appliances that claim to reduce cooking times by as much as 60 percent over conventional means by combining various methods—microwave, convection, and halogen or quartz light bulbs. Such hybrid devices may offer another advantage: no preheating. The perceived desire for speed has even fueled a resurgence in a category from another era—pressure cookers—in more consumer-friendly and safer designs.

IMPROVED EFFICIENCY. Over the next several years, the U.S. Department of Energy is mandating that new washing machines be 35 percent more efficient. Based on recent CONSUMER REPORTS tests, many top-loading models now on the market won't pass muster, so expect innovative designs in the future. Perhaps in anticipation of DOE regulations, manufacturers have introduced more front-loading machines, inherently more frugal because they tumble clothes through water instead of submerging them. Front-loaders consume about two-thirds less water than most top-loaders, though new top-loaders are narrowing the gap.

THE APPLIANCE NAME GAME

Who makes what?

Despite all the nameplates, only a handful of companies actually make refrigerators, ranges, washing machines, dryers, and dishwashers. They typically sell products under their own brand and also produce specific models for other manufacturers. From our laboratory inspections, we know, for example, that GE's front-loading washer comes off Frigidaire's assembly line. Sears' Kenmore brand, the biggest name in appliances, isn't made by Sears at all. Kenmore products are made entirely by others, the identities of which change from time to time. Here's a rundown of the key players and the familiar names they sell, listed alphabetically:

Frigidaire The company, owned by Sweden's Electrolux, also makes Gibson, Kelvinator, and Tappan appliances. The Frigidaire line is typically higher priced, especially in the tony Frigidaire Gallery and Gallery Professional series. Tappan is a significant force in gas ranges. Kelvinator and Gibson are harder to find, and the products sold under those names are generally less expensive with fewer features.

General Electric One of the two biggest U.S. appliance makers (along with Whirlpool), GE is particularly strong in the cooking categories. The GE name is considered a midrange brand; GE Profile and GE Profile Performance are geared toward more affluent consumers. GE Monogram, focusing on high style and a commercial look with both freestanding and built-in products, competes with boutique names like Thermador (owned by Bosch) and Viking and is distributed separately. Hotpoint is GE's value brand.

Kenmore The nation's biggest source of major appliances, Sears has its store-brand Kenmore models made to order by companies such as Whirlpool, long a manufacturer of many Kenmore laundry machines. A few Kenmore washing machines and dryers are also made by Frigidaire. Kenmore Elite is Sears' high-end brand of kitchen and laundry products.

Maytag The company that made its name in washing machines and dryers cultivates a premium image, with many of its products bearing the flagship name. Maytag Neptune is a line of premium laundry machines. Performa is the company's low-priced line. Jenn-Air, best known for modular cooktops and ranges, is Maytag's upscale kitchen brand. Admiral and Magic Chef are budget brands. Maytag purchased Amana in 2001. The company will continue to market appliances under the Amana brand name. (Amana had been the fifth-largest appliance maker, and was known mostly for its refrigerators.)

Whirlpool Also strongly positioned in the laundry room, the nation's other major appliance maker sells products under its corporate name in a wide variety of prices. Whirlpool Gold products are a notch up from the mainstream Whirlpool line; KitchenAid is the company's upscale brand; Roper is the bargain brand.

European and boutique brands Small on market share but often leaders in design and styling, brands such as Asko, Bosch, and Miele were among the first to showcase water-efficient engineering and clean-looking controls for dishwashers and washing machines. Viking is the leading manufacturer of pro-style kitchen appliances and outdoor grills. Sub-Zero is gaining market share with products sold under its own name and the Wolf brand. KitchenAid sells pro-style appliances under the KitchenAid Architect moniker. Other makers of pro-style ranges include DCS, Dacor, and Dynasty.

Refrigerators, which typically devour more electricity than any other kitchen appliance, have, over the years, been subject to energy-efficiency constraints. For instance, in 2001, manufacturers were required to reduce energy consumption once again. In general, side-by-side units are less space- and energy-efficient than either top- or bottom-freezer models. Over the long run, a pricier model with a low annual energy cost may be less expensive than a cheaper model that uses more electricity.

EASIER CLEANING. More products are designed with flat, seamless surfaces, fewer buttons, and touchpad controls, making them easier to clean. Smoothtop electric ranges continue to rise in popularity. And manufacturers are offering a new stainless-steel look-alike finish known as VCM that hides the smudges and fingerprints that seem to multiply on stainless-steel surfaces.

Gas ranges are cleaning up their act, too, as companies such as GE unveil gas smoothtops: Burners and grates sit atop a solid-glass surface, eliminating pesky nooks, crannies, and dripbowls—although you do have to use a special cleansing cream. Nearly all refrigerators now feature movable glass shelves bound by a lip to retain spills.

SLEEKER STYLING. Just about every major appliance maker now offers stylish kitchen appliances with curved doors, sleek-looking hardware and controls, and a flashy logo or nameplate. Such equipment can cost twice as much as mainstream products, but it may come with plenty of extra features to go with the high styling to help justify the price tag.

Some dishwashers relocate controls from the front panel to the top lip of the door, where they're out of sight. With a front panel that matches kitchen cabinets, this design can help the dishwasher blend in with its surroundings.

Color choices are proliferating as well. Stainless steel debuted in "professional" and "semi-pro" high-end models. And brushed aluminum finishes are now widely available in mass-marketed products, along with the traditional white and black. Biscuit, bisque, or linen are replacing almond. If you prefer a splashier color for your appliance—such as cobalt blue or hunter green—look to premium brands such as Jenn-Air, KitchenAid, or Viking.

FAMILY-FRIENDLY FEATURES. Manufacturers are using child lockouts to keep curious fingers out of potentially hazardous places. Some microwave ovens let you punch in a code to prevent accidental activation. A lockout button disables the knobs on a gas range or keeps the dishwasher from shutting down midcycle if curious little fingers start poking at the keypad. Such niceties are still relatively new and not yet found on many products.

MORE POWER. Sales of powerful commercial-

CRACKING THE KENMORE CODE

The model number you'll find on a major Sears Kenmore appliance is much longer than what you'll see in Sears ads and CONSUMER REPORTS Ratings. On the appliances, you'll see a three-digit prefix, which indicates the manufacturer and is separated from the rest of the model number by a period. (Sears manufactures none of the products it sells.) The five digits after the period—the item number—are what you'll see in Sears ads and CONSUMER REPORTS Ratings. The fifth digit, which Ratings put in brackets, refers to the appliance's color: for example, white, black, bisque, stainless steel. (Other appliance brands use letters to code color.) On a Kenmore appliance there are three more digits of the model number, which reflect "engineering changes"—small changes in a product that occur when, say, the manufacturer decides to use a different vendor for its nuts and bolts.

SEARS BY THE NUMBERS

Item number in a Sears ad; the '2' refers to the color white

987.65432100

Model number on appliance; the first three digits refer to the manufacturer.

The last three digits indicate any 'engineering change.'

style, stainless-steel ranges—with four or more high-output burners rated at maximum outputs of 15,000 British thermal units per hour, or Btu/hr.—continue to rise. More typical upscale stoves come with an assortment of burners with maximum outputs from 5,000 to 14,000 Btu/hr. Microwaves continue to get more powerful, too, with 1,300 watts the benchmark, up from around 800 watts a few years ago.

MORE SHOPPING OPTIONS. Frigidaire, GE, Maytag, Sears, and Whirlpool sell almost three-quarters of all major appliances. In some categories, Sears alone sells more than some of its biggest competitors combined, and the company is trying to strengthen its position by selling white goods online. But the competitive landscape is changing. Deep-discount warehouse-membership clubs such as Costco have expanded their selection of refrigerators, ranges, and the like. Home Depot and Lowe's, the nation's biggest home-center chains, have publicly announced they want to dethrone Sears as the leading appliance marketer. While the Internet has become a popular way to buy books and get travel deals, it's not much of a factor in the appliance category. Still, e-commerce experts predict online appliance sales could reach $2 billion by 2004—about 6 percent of sales.

BRAND BATTLES IN SMALL APPLIANCES. Coffeemakers, toasters, and blenders rule the countertop, with consumers buying more of them every year than any other countertop appliance. Three brands account for nearly three-quarters of small-appliance sales: Black & Decker, Hamilton Beach/Proctor-Silex, and Sunbeam/Oster.

Major mass retailers, where most of the products are sold, are trying to grab an even larger share of the business by gaining exclusive rights to established national brands. Hamilton Beach/Proctor-Silex, for example, makes products under the GE name (via a licensing agreement) for sale at Wal-Mart. Philips markets a line under its own name through Target. Black & Decker has partnered with chains such as Kmart. Sears sells small appliances under its Kenmore name.

BREADMAKERS

Machines costing $50 or less can turn out white bread and raisin bread that is comparable in texture, color, and taste to loaves kneaded by hand and baked in an oven.

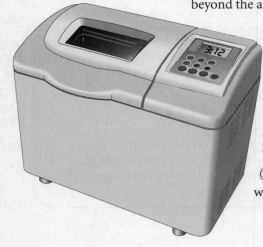

Breadmakers allow virtually anyone to bake bread with just minutes of effort and few skills beyond the ability to measure ingredients and push buttons. What's more, they produce bread that is better than respectable in quality. And they allow you to control what goes into your bread, which might appeal to people with food allergies or gluten intolerance.

What's available

There are fewer brands today than there were 10 years ago, when this product was introduced. Salton, owner of the Breadman and Toastmaster brands, dominates the market. Salton also makes Kenmore (Sears) and Williams-Sonoma breadmakers. They can be found everywhere from specialty kitchen shops to Wal-Mart.

An increasing number of machines have a rectangular bread pan, which produces a more traditional-looking loaf than did the tall, squarish pan common in the past. Most machines produce one 2-pound traditional-shaped loaf, which typically measures about 7x5 inches and yields about 13 inch-thick slices. One brand, Welbilt, makes two 1-pound loaves. Price range: $40 to $200.

Key features

With a typical machine, you place the ingredients in the **pan,** insert the pan in the machine, close the cover, and push buttons to select the right cycle. A **paddle** fitted on a shaft in the pan's base mixes the ingredients and kneads the dough, stopping at **programmed times** to allow for rising before kneading again. An **electric heating coil** in the machine's base then bakes the bread. The time required for each step depends on the type of bread. For example, whole-wheat dough needs more time to rise and bake than white.

The typical breadmaker has **cycles** for basic white, whole-wheat, sweet, or fruit-and-nut bread, plus "dough" (to be used when you want to shape the dough by hand and bake it in the oven). Most machines have specialty cycles for, say, French bread and pizza dough. On their regular white-bread cycle, breadmakers can take as long as 3½ hours.

Most machines have one or two **rapid cycles,** which increase heat during mixing to prepare loaves in as little as an hour. Recipes for rapid bread often call for more yeast than recipes for regular bread.

Convenience features let you bake without constantly having to supervise the machine. A **delay-start timer,** available on most machines, lets you postpone when your bread is done—typically 13 hours from the time you press the button. **A temperature-warning signal** lets you know when the kitchen temperature isn't optimal for yeast growth. An **add-in signal** tells you when to add fruit, nuts, or other extras so they don't get chopped during kneading.

Crust control adjusts baking time so you get the crust color of your choice. A **keep-warm/cool-down function** keeps the bread from getting soggy for at least an hour if you're not there to take it out right away. **Power-outage protection** ensures that when the electricity comes back on after a power outage, the breadmaker will pick up where it left off. Some machines can withstand an hour-long outage; others, an outage of only a few seconds.

How to choose

PERFORMANCE DIFFERENCES. Very good bread is symmetrical and evenly baked, with an interior that's somewhat soft, moist, and airy and a crust that's crisp but not too thick or hard. All the breadmakers that CONSUMER REPORTS tested made very good white bread on their regular (not rapid) cycle (at a cost of about 90 cents per loaf). They also made very good raisin bread. Testing found differences, however, in the quality of whole-wheat bread. CONSUMER REPORTS also found that most machines produced short, dense loaves when set on the rapid cycle.

RECOMMENDATIONS. If you're looking for a breadmaker that will turn out very good white or raisin bread, opt for the least expensive model. The largest selection can be found in mass-marketing outlets and discount stores. Don't base your decision on the availability or speed of a rapid cycle; you're likely to be disappointed in the results.

Consider your counter space. Breadmakers typically require a lot of it. Most are 12 to 13 inches high and 10 to 11 inches deep, but they vary in width from 10 inches to 19 inches.

Should you need to replace a bread pan or dough blade after the warranty expires, it might make more sense to buy a new machine. We found that replacing those parts could cost up to 65 percent of the original purchase price.

COFFEEMAKERS

You don't need to spend a lot to get a machine that makes good coffee. But you may want to spend a bit more for a model with convenience features and styling that appeals.

The profusion of Starbucks and other specialty coffee shops appears to be driving demand for a new generation of coffeemakers that seek to replicate the coffeehouse experience at home. Customized brewing, water filtration, and thermal carafes are a few of the features manufacturers are hoping will encourage consumers to trade up. Truth is, virtually any model can make a good cup as long as you use decent beans.

What's available

Manual-drip systems, coffee presses, and percolators are available, but consumers buy more automatic-drip coffeemakers than any other small kitchen appliance: 17 million per year. Mr. Coffee and Black & Decker are the two largest brands, along with well-known names such as Braun, Krups, Melitta, and Proctor Silex.

Coffeemakers come in sizes from single-cup models to machines capable of brewing up to 12 cups at a time. Ten- and 12-cup units account for more than 80 percent of the market, although manufacturers are trying to expand sales by pushing fully featured 4-cup models.

Models range from bare-bones coffeemakers with a single switch to start the brewing and a plain metal hotplate to those with programmable starting and stopping, a water filter, frothing capability, and a thermal carafe. Most consumers opt for plainer models. Black and white remain the standard colors for coffeemakers, but some brands are adding other hues. Price range: $15 to more than $90.

Key features

The easiest models to load with coffee have a **removable filter** basket; baskets that sit inside a pullout drawer are messy. **Paper filters**—usually "cupcake" or cone-shaped—absorb oil and keep sediment from creeping through. Models with a **permanent mesh filter** need to be cleaned after each use, but can save you money over time. Neither type of filter detracted from coffee flavor in CONSUMER REPORTS tests. The simplest way to pour water is into a **reservoir** that has a big flip-top lid with lines that mark the number of cups in large, clearly visible numbers. Some reservoirs are removable—so you can fill up at the sink—and dishwasher safe. **Transparent fill tubes** with **cup markings** let you check the water level while pouring.

A **thermal carafe** helps retain flavor and aroma longer than a glass pot on a hotplate. Other niceties: a **small-batch setting** to adjust brew time when you make fewer than 5 cups; **temperature and brew-strength controls;** and a **drip-stop feature** that lets you pour a cup before the whole pot's done. A **programmable**

timer lets you add ground coffee and water the night before, so you can wake up to a freshly brewed pot in the morning. A **clock-timer** automatically turns off the hotplate at a specified or programmed time after brewing. New models frequently have a more **compact footprint,** and **flat electronic-touchpad controls.** Some high-end models feature a **built-in bean grinder.** A **built-in water filter** may cut chlorine and, sometimes, mineral buildup. (But a filter can harbor bacteria if you don't regularly change it.)

How to choose

PERFORMANCE DIFFERENCES. In CONSUMER REPORTS tests, just about any drip coffeemaker made good-tasting coffee. The differences among machines mostly pertain to convenience. Some models have hard-to-clean nooks and crannies or unclear markings; some easily show stains.

Some programmable models were much tougher to set than others. Brewing time for a full pot took from 9 to 11 minutes; models designated as "restaurant" type—which keep a full reservoir of hot water at the ready—brewed 8 cups in less than 4 minutes.

RECOMMENDATIONS. If all you want is a good cup of java, there are plenty of coffeemakers from which to choose, starting at around $15. A few dollars more buys a machine that's easier to fill with water and carafes that are easier to pour. At higher prices, you get luxuries such as programmability, sculptural style, and extras such as a drip stop or a grinder.

COFFEEMAKERS ◆ **Ratings:** Page 209

DISHWASHERS

Models selling for $300 to $500 can excel at washing dishes, but they may not measure up to costlier models in quietness, water or energy usage, or features.

Spend $300 to $500, and you'll get a dishwasher that cleans dirty dishes without prerinsing but is a little noisy. To get the best of everything—cleaning prowess plus the quietest operation, convenience features, water and energy efficiency, and designer styling—you'll have to spend $800 or more.

A dirt sensor, once a premium feature, has made its way down to lower-priced models. That's not necessarily a plus. Machines with dirt sensors have been less energy efficient in CONSUMER REPORTS tests than the federal government's EnergyGuide stickers and Energy Star designations suggest. That's because these stickers and Energy Star designations for dishwashers are calculated using completely clean loads. When washing very heavily soiled loads, these models can use much more hot water and thus more energy.

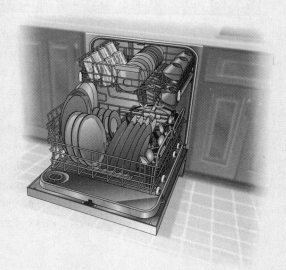

What's available

GE, Maytag, and Whirlpool make most dishwashers and sell them under flagship and associated brands, including Kenmore. Whirlpool makes the high-end KitchenAid and the cheaper Roper; Maytag, the high-end Jenn-Air and the low-end Magic Chef; and GE, the upscale GE Monogram and the value-priced Hotpoint. Kenmore dishwashers are made by Whirlpool, CONSUMER REPORTS has determined in recent tests. Asko, Bosch, and Miele are high-end European brands.

Most models fit into a 24-inch-wide space under the kitchen countertop, attached to a hot-water pipe, a drain, and an electrical line. Compact models require less width. Portable models in a finished cabinet can be rolled over to the sink and connected to the faucet. A "dishwasher in a drawer" design from Fisher & Paykel, a New Zealand–based company, has two stacked compartments that can be used simultaneously or individually. Price range: domestic brands, $250 to $1,200; foreign-made brands, $700 to $1,400.

Key features

Most models offer a choice of at least three **wash cycles**—Light, Normal, and Heavy—which should be enough for the typical dishwashing jobs in most households. **Light** is a shorter cycle that uses less water than the others and may be suitable for most dishes. **Rinse/Hold** lets you rinse dirty dishes before using the dishwasher on a full cycle. Other cycles offered in many models—none of which we consider crucial—include **Pot Scrubber, Soak/Scrub,** and **China/Crystal.** Dishwashers often distribute water from multiple places, or "levels," in the machine. Dishwashers also typically offer a choice of drying with or without heat.

Some models use two **filters** to keep wash water free of food: a coarse outer filter for large bits and a fine inner filter for smaller particles. In most such models, a spray arm cleans residue from the coarse filter during the rinse cycle, and a food-disposal grinder cuts up large food particles. These tend to be rather noisy. Some of the more expensive models have a filter that you must pull out and clean manually; these are quieter than those with grinders.

Dirt sensors in "smart" dishwashers determine how dirty the dishes are and provide the appropriate amount of water. Some brands use **pressure sensors** that respond to the actual soil removed from the dishes. Other brands use **turbidity sensors** that work by measuring the amount of light that passes from the sender to the receiver in the sensor. In CONSUMER REPORTS tests with very dirty dishes, models with sensors didn't clean noticeably better than those without sensors. The sensor models also tended to use significantly more energy for heavily soiled loads than did nonsensor models.

A **sanitizing wash or rinse** option that raises the water temperature above the typical 140° F doesn't necessarily mean improved cleaning. Routine use could cost a small amount

ENZYMES IN DISHWASHER DETERGENTS

Enzymes in dishwasher detergents aren't new, but they're a growing trend. More and more dishwasher detergents use them. CONSUMER REPORTS confirmed their dirt-busting ability in recent tests. While two of the eight enzyme detergents we tested cleaned poorly, the other six cleaned far better than all of the other detergents tested.

Curiously, manufacturers seem reluctant to brag about the use of enzymes. To determine whether a dishwasher detergent contains them, you'll usually have to squint at the list of ingredients buried in the label's fine print. While there have been reports of factory workers becoming allergic to enzymes, CONSUMER REPORTS research has turned up no evidence to suggest that ordinary household use of enzyme-containing detergent poses a health risk. If problems do occur, stop using the product. As for enzymes and the environment, the U.S. Environmental Protection Agency says it has seen no evidence that enzymes adversely affect water quality. It's also important to keep all dishwasher detergents away from children because most are highly alkaline and can burn skin; they can also pose an ingestion hazard. And you should never use dishwasher detergent to hand-wash dishes.

more a year in electricity. Remember that as soon as you touch a dish while taking it out of the dishwasher, it's no longer sanitized.

Better **soundproofing** is a step-up feature in many lines. You'll also pay more for **electronic touchpad** controls, some of them "hidden" in the top lip of the door. Less expensive models have mechanical controls, usually operated by a dial and push buttons. Touchpads are easier to clean. **Dials** indicate progress through a cycle. Some electronic models digitally display time left in the wash cycle. Others merely show a "clean" signal. Some models with mechanical controls require you to set both dial and push buttons to the desired setting for the correct combination of water quantity and temperature. A **delayed-start** control lets you run the washer at night, when utility rates may be lower. Some models offer **child-safety features,** such as a door and controls that can lock.

Most models hold cups and glasses on top, plates on the bottom, and silverware in a basket. Features that enhance flexibility include **adjustable and removable tines,** which flatten areas to accept bigger dishes, pots, and pans; **slots for silverware** that prevent "nesting"; **removable racks,** which enable loading and unloading outside the dishwasher; **stemware holders,** which steady wine glasses; **fold-down shelves,** which stack cups in a double-tiered arrangement; and **adjustable and terraced racks,** for tall items. Stainless-steel tubs may last virtually forever, whereas plastic ones can discolor or crack. But most plastic tubs have a warranty of 20 years—much longer than most people keep a dishwasher. In our tests, stainless-steel-lined models had a slightly shorter drying time but didn't wash any better.

How to choose

PERFORMANCE DIFFERENCES. Most dishwashers tested by CONSUMER REPORTS have done an excellent or very good job, with little or no spotting or redepositing of food. Manufacturers typically make a few different wash systems, with different "levels" and filters. Avoid the lowest-priced models—those without a filtering system. They tend to redeposit tiny bits of food. Otherwise, according to our tests, the main differences are in water and energy use and noise level. The quietest models are so unobtrusive you might barely hear them. Cycle times in recent tests varied from about 75 to 135 minutes. Several machines that did an excellent job at washing dishes had cycle times of about 90 minutes or less.

A dishwasher uses some electricity to run its motor as well as its drying heater or fan. But about 80 percent of the energy is used to heat water, both in the home's water heater and in the machine. Long-term water efficiency differences can noticeably affect the cost. Models in recent tests used between 5 and 11 gallons in a normal cycle. The annual cost of operation might range from about $25 to $67 with a gas water heater or $30 to $86 with an electric water heater.

Concerning water-adjusting dirt sensors, CONSUMER REPORTS has found that for very dirty loads the feature significantly increases energy use over the values shown on the Department of Energy's EnergyGuide stickers. That's because these stickers and Energy Star designations for dishwashers are calculated using completely clean loads. That can make dishwashers with dirt sensors less efficient than advertised, particularly if you don't prerinse, since these models can use much more hot water and thus energy to wash heavily soiled loads than clean loads. The DOE has said it is aware of the problems, but changes have been delayed. Any dishwasher can be made to use less water and less energy to heat the water by simply running it at its lightest cycle.

RECOMMENDATIONS. The best-performing dishwashers aren't always the most expensive ones, but high-priced models offer styling and soundproofing that appeal to some buyers. Foreign brands are often more energy efficient and quieter, but they're also pricier. Some have spray arms that may hamper loading large dishes and filters that require periodic manual cleaning. You can get fine performance at a low price if you don't insist on the quietest operation and the most flexible loading; for $500 or a bit more, you can get less noise and more features. Compare prices of delivery and installation and expect to pay about $100; removing your old dishwasher may cost an extra $25 to $50.

DISHWASHERS ♦ **Ratings:** Page 217 ♦ **Reliability:** Page 297

DRYERS

It's hard to find a clothes dryer that can't, at the very least, dry clothes. The more sophisticated models do the job with greater finesse.

Dryers are relatively simple. Their major distinctions are how they're programmed to shut off once the load is dry (thermostat or moisture sensor) and how they heat the air (gas or electric). Both affect how much you'll pay to buy and run your machine. CONSUMER REPORTS has found that machines with a moisture sensor tend to recognize when laundry is dry more quickly than machines that use a traditional thermostat. Since they shut themselves off sooner, they use less energy. Sensors are now offered on many models, including some relatively low-cost ones. In our most recent tests, some $400 models had sensors.

Gas dryers typically cost more than electric ones but are cheaper to operate.

What's available

The top four brands—GE, Maytag, Kenmore (Sears), and Whirlpool—account for about 80 percent of dryer sales. Other brands include Amana (owned by Maytag), Frigidaire (owned by Electrolux), Hotpoint (made by GE), and KitchenAid and Roper (both made by Whirlpool). You may also run across smaller brands such as Crosley, Gibson, and White-Westinghouse, all of which are made by the larger brands. Asko, Bosch, and Miele are European brands.

FULL-SIZED MODELS. These generally measure between 27 and 29 inches in width—the critical dimension for fitting into cabinetry and closets. Front-mounted controls on some let you stack the dryer atop a front-loading washer. Full-sized models vary in drum capacity from about 5 to 7½ cubic feet. The larger the drum, the more easily a dryer can handle bulky items. Price range: electric, $200 to $800; gas, $250 to $850. Buying one of the more expensive models may get you more capacity and a few extra conveniences.

SPACE-SAVING MODELS. Compacts, exclusively electric, are typically 24 inches wide, with a drum capacity roughly half that of full-sized models—about 3½ cubic feet. Aside from their smaller capacity, they perform much like full-sized machines. They can be stacked atop a companion washer, but shorter users may have

HOW TO VENT YOUR DRYER SAFELY

Dryers vent their exhaust, including some lint, through a duct that must attach to the machine. Four types of ducts are available, but two of those types may be dangerous. Flexible ducts made of plastic or foil, far right, may sag over time and lead to a buildup of lint in the duct. That lint could catch fire. Rigid or flexible metal ducts, near right, are much safer choices.

Types to choose

Rigid metal duct (the best choice)

Flexible metal duct (holds its shape if bent)

Types to avoid

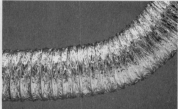

Flexible plastic duct

Flexible foil duct (doesn't hold its shape if bent)

difficulty reaching the dryer controls or the inside of the drum. Some dryers operate on 120 volts, others on 240 volts. Price range: $380 to more than $1,400.

Another space-saving option is a laundry center, which combines a washer and dryer in a single unit. Laundry centers come with gas or electric dryers. Those can be full-sized (27 inches wide) or compact (24 inches wide). The dryer in a laundry center typically has a somewhat smaller capacity than a full-sized dryer. Models with electric dryers require a dedicated 240-volt power source. Price range: $700 to $1,900.

Key features

Full-sized dryers often have two or three **auto-dry cycles,** which shut off the unit when the clothes reach desired dryness. Each cycle might have a **More Dry** setting, to dry clothes completely, and a **Less Dry** setting, to leave clothes damp and ready for ironing. Manufacturers have refined the way dryers shut themselves off. As clothes tumble past a **moisture sensor,** electrical contacts in the drum sample their conductivity for surface dampness and relay signals to electronic controls. Dryers with a **thermostat,** by contrast, measure moisture indirectly by taking the temperature of exhaust air from the drum (the temperature rises as moisture evaporates). Moisture-sensor models are more accurate, sparing your laundry unnecessary drying—and sparing you energy bills that are needlessly high.

Most dryers have a separate **temperature control** to use a lower heat for delicate fabrics, among other things. A **cool-down feature,** such as Press Care or Finish Guard, helps to prevent wrinkling when you don't remove clothes immediately. Some models continue to tumble without heat; others cycle on and off. An **express-dry cycle** is meant for drying small loads at high heat in less than a half hour. Large loads will take longer. **Touchpad electronic controls** found in higher-end models tend to be more versatile and convenient than mechanical dials and buttons—once you figure them out. Maytag recently introduced a computer screen with a progression of menus that enable you to program specific settings for recall at any time.

A **top-mounted lint filter** may be somewhat easier to clean than one inside the drum. Some models have a **warning light** that signals when the lint filter is blocked. It's important to clean the lint filter regularly to minimize any fire hazard. It's also advisable to use metal ducting (either rigid or flexible) rather than plastic or flexible foil, which can create a fire hazard by trapping lint. (See "How to vent your dryer safely," on the preceding page.)

Most full-sized models have a **drum light,** making it easy for you to spot stray items. You may be able to raise or lower the volume of an **end-of-cycle signal** or shut it off. A **rack** included with many machines attaches inside the drum and keeps sneakers or other bulky items from tumbling. Models with **doors that drop down** in front may fit better against a wall, but **side-opening doors** may make it easier to access the inside of the drum.

How to choose

PERFORMANCE DIFFERENCES. CONSUMER REPORTS has found that nearly all machines dry ordinary laundry loads well. Models with a moisture sensor don't overdry as much as models using a thermostat, saving a little energy as well as sparing fabric wear and tear. If the dryer will go near the kitchen or a bedroom, pay attention to the noise level. Some models are quiet, but others are loud enough to drown out normal conversation. Virtually all dryers can accommodate the load from a typical washer, so capacity isn't an issue unless you want to dry bulky items such as comforters.

RECOMMENDATIONS. It's worthwhile to spend the $30 to $50 extra for a moisture-sensor model. More efficient drying will eventually pay for the extra cost. Buy a gas dryer if you can. Although priced about $50 more than an electric model, a gas dryer usually costs about 25 cents less per load to operate, making up the price difference in a year or two of typical use. The extra hardware of a gas dryer, however, often makes it more expensive to repair.

DRYERS ✦ **Ratings:** Page 224 **Reliability:** Page 297

FREEZERS

Chest freezers cost the least to buy and run, but self-defrost uprights are the winners for convenience.

If you buy box-loads of burgers at a warehouse club or like to keep a few weeks' worth of dinner fixings on hand, the 4- to 6-cubic-foot freezer compartments in most refrigerators may seem positively lilliputian. A separate freezer might be a good investment.

What's available

Two companies make most freezers sold in the U.S.: Frigidaire, which makes models sold under the Frigidaire, GE, and Kenmore labels; and W.C. Wood, which makes models sold under its own name as well as Amana, Danby, Magic Chef, Maytag, and Whirlpool. There are two types of freezers: chests, which are essentially horizontal boxes with a door that opens upward; and uprights, which come in self-defrost and manual-defrost versions and resemble a single-door refrigerator.

CHESTS. These freezers vary most in capacity, ranging from 4 to 25 cubic feet. Aside from a hanging basket or two, chests are wide open, letting you put in even large, bulky items; nearly all the claimed cubic-foot space is usable. The design makes chests more energy efficient and cheaper to operate than uprights. Cooling coils are built in to all four walls, so no fan is required to circulate the cold air. Because the door opens from the top, virtually no cold air escapes when the door is opened. But a chest's open design makes it hard to organize the contents. Finding something can require bending and, often, moving around piles of frozen goods. If you're short, it can be difficult to extricate an item buried at the bottom (assuming you can remember that it's stashed there). A chest also takes up more floor space than an upright: A 15-cubic-foot model is about 4 feet wide by 2½ feet deep; a comparable upright is just as deep but only 2 to 2½ feet wide.

Defrosting a chest can be a hassle, especially if it's fully loaded or has a thick coating of ice. All chests are manual-defrost, meaning you have to unload the food, store it somewhere at 0° F until the ice encrusting the walls has melted, remove the water that accumulates at the drain, then put back the food. Price range: $140 to $400.

SELF-DEFROST UPRIGHTS. These models (sometimes called frost-free) have from 11 to 25 cubic feet of space. Like a refrigerator, they have shelves in the main compartment and on the door; some have pullout bins. That lets you organize and access contents but reduces usable space by about 20 percent. Interior shelves can be removed or adjusted to fit large items. When you open the door of an upright, cold air spills out from the bottom, while warm, humid air sneaks in at the top. That makes the freezer work harder and use more energy to stay cold, and temperatures may fluctuate a bit.

Self-defrost models compensate by using a fan to circulate cold air from the cooling coils, which are in the back wall. Self-defrosting, which involves heaters that turn on periodically to remove excess ice buildup, eliminates a tedious, messy chore but uses extra energy—a self-defrost model costs about $20 a year more to run than a similar-sized chest. For many people, the convenience might be worth the extra cost. Self-defrosting models are also a bit noisier than other types—an issue only if they're located near a living area rather than in the basement or garage. While freezers of old weren't recommended for use in areas that got very hot or cold, current self-defrost models should work fine within a wide ambient temperature range—typically 32° F to 110° F. Price range: $350 to $750.

MANUAL-DEFROST UPRIGHTS. These freezers have a capacity of 5 to 25 cubic feet, of which some 15 percent isn't usable. They cost less to buy and run than self-defrost models but aren't as economical as chests. Unlike their self-defrost counterparts, these uprights don't have a fan to circulate cold air, which can result in uneven temperatures. Defrosting is quite a chore. The metal shelves in the main space are filled with coolant, so scraping ice from them is risky: You can damage the shelves and cause the coolant to leak. What's more, ice tends to cling to the wires on the shelves, so defrosting can take up to 24 hours. Because the shelves contain coolant, they can't be adjusted or removed to hold large items. Price range: $160 to $600.

Key features

While freezers have fewer features than some other major appliances, there are several features worth looking for. **Interior lighting** makes it easier to find things, especially in dimly lit areas. A **power-on light,** indicating that the freezer has power, is helpful. A **temperature alarm** lets you know when the freezer is too warm inside, such as after a prolonged power outage. (If you lose power, don't open the freezer door; food should remain frozen for about 24 to 48 hours.) A **quick-freeze** feature brings the freezer to its coldest setting faster by making it run continuously instead of cycling on and off; that's handy when you're adding a lot of food. A **flash-defrost** feature on manual-defrost models can speed defrosting by circulating hot gas from the compressor through the cooling tubes in the walls.

How to choose

PERFORMANCE DIFFERENCES. CONSUMER REPORTS has found that most models of a type are similar in terms of performance, efficiency, and convenience. The usable capacity of chest freezers is generally the same as the labeled capacity; the capacity of some manual-defrost and self-defrost uprights is somewhat less than what is labeled. Operating a new 15-cubic-foot freezer costs $30 to $55 a year at typical electric rates, depending on the type. That's in the same ballpark as a new refrigerator's annual energy cost.

RECOMMENDATIONS. A chest freezer gives you the most space, with room for bulky items, and the best performance for the lowest purchase price and operating cost. But you'll have to defrost it periodically. For freedom from defrosting and ease of access, go with a self-defrost upright. It will cost a little more to buy and operate than a chest, but the convenience may be worth it. We don't see a compelling reason to buy a manual-defrost upright when comparable self-defrosting units perform better and cost about the same. Manual models, however, do offer more usable space for the money than self-defrost models.

IRONS

Many new irons are bigger, more colorful, more feature-laden, and more expensive. But you can still get a fine performer for $25 or so.

Many business people are hanging up their business suits and dresses in favor of casual attire, often made of washable fabrics such as cotton. That means fewer trips to the dry cleaner and more time spent pressing machine-washed garments so they look presentable. If you're in the market for an iron, you've got plenty of choices, ranging from budget models to fancy irons with features galore.

What's available

GE, Kenmore, and Toastmaster have started selling irons, joining familiar names such as Black & Decker and Proctor-Silex, which together account for more than half of all iron sales. More consumers are springing for a higher-priced iron than in years past, but three out of four still spend less than $40. Budget-priced doesn't necessarily mean bare-bones. Features such as automatic shutoff, burst of steam, and self-clean are now standard on most $25 to $40 models. Irons priced at $40 and up tend to be larger, with innovations such as vertical steaming, antidrip steam vents, and even anticalcium systems designed to prevent mineral buildup. Price range: $10 for plain vanilla to $150 for top of the line models.

Key features

Steam makes a fabric more pliable so the heat and pressure of the iron can set it straight. Many new irons release more steam than earlier models. Most produce the best steaming during the first 10 minutes of use and then gradually taper off as the water is used up. You can usually adjust the amount of steam or turn it off, but models with **automatic steam** produce more steam at higher temperatures. A few won't allow you to use steam at low settings, since the water doesn't get hot enough and simply drips out. An **antidrip feature,** usually on higher-priced models, is designed to prevent leaks when using steam at lower settings.

Burst of steam, available on most new irons, lets you push a button for an extra blast to tame stubborn wrinkles. If steam isn't enough for something such as a wrinkled linen napkin, dampen it using the **spray function,** available on virtually all irons today. On some models, burst of steam can be used for vertical steaming to remove wrinkles from hanging items.

An iron should have an easy-to-see **fabric guide** with a list of settings for common fabrics. A temperature control that's clearly marked and easily accessible, preferably on the front of the handle, is a plus. Most irons have an **indicator light** to show that the power is on; a few also indicate when the iron reaches or exceeds the set temperature.

Automatic shutoff has become standard on most irons, but a few still lack this must-have feature. Some irons shut off only when they're left motionless in a horizontal or vertical position. Those with three-way shutoff also lose power when tipped on their side. Shutoff times vary from 30 seconds to 60 minutes.

Water reservoirs in general are getting larger. Some are a small, vertical tube; others are a large chamber that spans the saddle area under the handle. Transparent chambers, some brightly colored, make it easy to see the water level.

A growing number of irons have a **hinged** or **sliding cover** on the water-fill hole. The idea is to prevent leaking, but it doesn't always work. Also, the cover may get in the way or can be awkward to open and close. Most convenient is a **removable tank.** Some irons come with a handy plastic **fill cup.** Almost all new irons can use tap water, unless the water is very hard. An **anticalcium system,** usually on more expensive irons, is designed to reduce calcium deposits.

Most models now offer a **self-cleaning feature** to flush deposits from vents, but it's not always effective with prolonged use of very hard water. The burst of steam feature also cleans vents to some extent.

Many models have a nonstick **soleplate.** Some more expensive irons have a stainless-steel soleplate, while some budget irons have an aluminum one. We didn't find any difference in glide among the various types of soleplate when ironing with steam. Nonstick soleplates are generally easier to keep clean, but they may be scratched by something such as a zipper, and a scratch could create drag over time. You should clean the soleplate occasionally to remove residue, following the manufacturer's directions, especially if you use starch.

The **power cord** on many irons pivots down or to the sides during use, which keeps it out of the way. A retractable cord can be convenient, but be careful so that it doesn't whip when retracted. Cordless irons eliminate fumbling with the cord but must be reheated on the base for 90 seconds or so every couple of minutes, which can be time-consuming.

Weight is more critical to comfort than performance. Managing a heavy iron can be

SOLEPLATES

Soleplates of steam irons are made of different materials, all of which performed well in CONSUMER REPORTS tests.

Aluminum

Nonstick

Enamel-coated

Stainless steel

an arm workout you might prefer to have at the gym. Some handles might be too thick for smaller hands; others provide too little clearance for larger hands.

How to choose

PERFORMANCE DIFFERENCES. Many of the irons on the market will do a fine job of removing wrinkles from clothing. The most significant differences come in ease of use. Some controls are easier to see and use, for example. For everyday pressing, a $20 or $25 iron should have the performance and basic features to do the job. Models selling for $10 or $15 are less likely to satisfy. A $30 to $50 model will generally have more bells and whistles but won't necessarily offer better performance. A price more than that is likely to get you the most (and the newest) features but may not result in better ironing.

    RECOMMENDATIONS. Features differ from model to model, so determine what is important to you—and be sure to include automatic shutoff on your must-have list. Try handling an iron that's on display in a store to see if its size and shape feel right to you.

IRONS ◆ **Ratings:** Page 232

KITCHEN KNIVES

Expensive forged knives that require regular honing generally cut the best. But some moderately priced alternatives do a fine job.

Whether you routinely whip up gourmet meals or rarely rise above making sandwiches, good knives are essential kitchen equipment. With them, you can work more efficiently and safely. Without them, even slicing a tomato can be tricky. While top-notch kitchen knives can cost hundreds, there are less expensive options that would be good choices for most home cooks.

What's available

Ekco, Farberware, and Oxo are among the less expensive brands. High-end brands include Calphalon, Cuisinart, Emerilware, Henckels, KitchenAid, and Wüsthof. Starter sets of kitchen knives typically cost less than the same knives sold individually. Price range for sets: $10 to $200 or more. There are often seven or nine pieces in a set that includes a storage block, a sharpening steel, and the following four basic knives:

    CHEF'S KNIFE. Perhaps the most versatile, it's used for chopping, dicing, slicing, and mincing, often with a rocking motion. The blade is wide for extra heft. Typical blade length: 8 to 10 inches.

    SLICING KNIFE. The thin, flexible blade of this knife is especially appropriate for carving beef, poultry, and pork. Typical blade length: 8 to 10 inches.

    UTILITY KNIFE. Probably second to the chef's knife in usefulness, it's good for similar but somewhat smaller cutting tasks. The blade is narrower than the blade of a chef's knife. Typical blade length: 5 to 6 inches.

PARING KNIFE. Handy for peeling, coring, paring, cleaning (shrimp, say), and slicing. It's also good for creating garnishes and fine work. Like a utility knife, it has a thin blade, but it's even shorter. Typical blade length: 3 to 4 inches.

Key features

Most expensive knives are forged from stain-resistant and rust-resistant high-carbon steel. Forged blades are created by pounding a steel slab into shape with a mechanical hammer that exerts tons of force. They demand regular honing, but the payoff is a razor-sharp edge.

Many cheaper kitchen knives, and a few expensive ones, are stamped from a single sheet of steel, creating a relatively thin, light blade. Some require regular honing; some don't.

There are three main types of knife blades: **fine-edged blades** that require sharpening; fine-edged that don't require sharpening; and **serrated blades,** with teeth along part or all of the edge, which don't require sharpening. Serrated knives are especially good at cutting through bread and tomatoes.

Most knives have a hard-plastic **handle**. Restaurants favor plastic for sanitary reasons and because it stands up to hot water and soaking in the dishwasher. A bare-wood handle may be vulnerable, although a waterproof coating can help it resist moisture. Riveted handles might appeal to traditionalists, but our tests uncovered no drawbacks to molded handles. A **sharpening steel,** used to keep a fine-edged knife in top shape, is a good addition to your kitchen.

How to choose

PERFORMANCE DIFFERENCES. Knives that need routine sharpening generally cost more but do perform best, according to CONSUMER REPORTS tests. While stamping can produce a top-notch blade, stamped knives generally don't perform as well as forged ones. Blades that don't require sharpening typically cut unexceptionally, but they're usually cheaper and require little upkeep.

RECOMMENDATIONS. You generally get what you pay for. But there are some decent sets for $60 or less. When shopping, hold a knife in your hand. It should feel balanced, neither too heavy nor too light. Check to ensure that the handle is attached securely, without gaps that can trap food residue.

CONSUMER REPORTS advises that kitchen knives be hand-washed, since dishwasher detergent can pit the blades.

KITCHEN KNIVES ♦ **Ratings:** Page 234

MICROWAVE OVENS

You'll see larger capacities, added power, sensors that detect doneness, and stylish designs. Countertop models start at under $100.

Microwave ovens, which built their reputation on speed, are also showing some smarts. Many models automatically shut off when a sensor determines that the food is cooked or sufficiently heated. Such sensors are also used to automate an array of cooking chores, with buttons labeled for frozen entrées, baked potatoes, popcorn, and other items. Design touches include softer edges for less boxy styling, stainless steel, hidden controls for a sleeker look, and for a few, translucent finishes.

What's available

Sharp leads the countertop microwave-oven market with almost 25 percent of sales, followed by GE, Panasonic, Emerson, Samsung, and Kenmore. GE sells the most over-the-range models.

Microwaves come in a variety of sizes, from compact to large. Most ovens sit on the countertop, but a growing number sold, about 25 percent, are mounted over the range. Manufacturers are working to boost capacity without taking up more counter space by moving controls to the door and using recessed turntables and smaller electronic components. They also tend to tally every cubic inch, including corner spaces where food on the turntable can't rotate, to gauge capacity.

CONSUMER REPORTS has found that the diameter of the turntable is a more realistic measurement, and bases the calculation of usable capacity on that.

Microwave ovens also vary in the power of the magnetron, which generates the microwaves. Midsized and large ovens are rated at 900 to 1,300 watts, compact ovens at 600 to 800 watts. A higher wattage may heat food more quickly, but differences of 100 watts are probably inconsequential.

Price range: countertop models, $80 to $300; over-the-range, $300 to $700; convection countertop or over-the-range, $330 to $600.

Key features

A **turntable** rotates the food so it will heat more uniformly, but the center of the dish still tends to be cooler than the rest. Most turntables are removable for cleaning. With some models (especially over-the-range ovens), you can turn off the rotation when, say, you're using a dish too large to rotate. But results won't be as good.

You'll also tend to find similarities in the controls from model to model. A **numeric keypad** is used to set cooking times and power levels. Most ovens have **shortcut keys** for particular foods, reheating, or defrosting; some start immediately when you hit the shortcut key, and others require you to enter the food quantity or weight. Some models have an **automatic popcorn feature** that makes popcorn at the press of a button. Pressing a **1-minute** or **30-second key** runs the oven at full power or extends the current cooking time. Microwaves typically have several **power levels,** though six are more than adequate.

Most automatic sensors are **moisture sensors,** which gauge the steam that food emits when heated and use that information to determine when the food is cooked. An alternative is an **infrared sensor,** which detects a food's surface temperature to determine doneness. CONSUMER REPORTS believes that the small premium you pay for a sensor (about $10 to $30) is worth it. A few ovens have a **crisper pan** for frying eggs or crisping pizza, since microwave cooking leaves food hot but not browned or crispy. A relatively new category known as

speed cookers use a combination of heating technologies to cook food quickly and make it crisp or browned.

Over-the-range ovens have at least two **vent-fan speeds;** often, the fan turns on whenever heat is sensed from the range below. Exhaust can go outside or into the kitchen. If you want the oven to vent inside, you'll need a charcoal filter (sometimes included). An over-the-range microwave generally doesn't handle ventilation as well as a hood-and-blower ventilation system because it doesn't extend over the front burner.

How to choose

PERFORMANCE DIFFERENCES. CONSUMER REPORTS has found that most microwave ovens are very good overall. Most are easy to use and competent at the main tasks of heating and defrosting. We found a few ovens that left large icy chunks while defrosting ground beef, however. Be skeptical about special technologies claimed to improve cooking evenness. All but a few microwave ovens heated a baking dish full of cold mashed potatoes to a fairly uniform temperature in our tests.

RECOMMENDATIONS. Look for the size that best fits your kitchen. A large or midsized countertop model is a good choice. Compact models, though less expensive, typically have lower power ratings and don't heat as fast. Your kitchen layout may dictate an over-the-range microwave, which ventilates itself and the range. But these models cost about two to three times as much as large countertop models, are heavy, and may take two people to install. Properly installing an over-the-range model may also require an electrician.

MICROWAVE OVENS ◆ **Ratings:** Page 244 ◆ **Reliability:** Page 299

MIXING APPLIANCES

You need to choose the right machine for the way you prepare foods.
Depending on your needs, you may want more than one machine.

Which food-prep appliance best suits your style and the foods you prepare? Blenders usually excel at mixing icy drinks. Stick-shaped immersion blenders are handy mostly for stirring powdered drinks. Food processors are versatile machines that can chop, slice, shred, and puree many different foods. Mini choppers are good for small jobs such as mincing garlic and chopping nuts. Hand mixers can handle light chores such as whipping cream or mixing cake batter. And powerful stand mixers are ideal for committed cooks who make bread and cookies from scratch.

What's available

BLENDERS. Rugged construction and increased power are driving blender sales. Ice-crushing ability is the key attribute consumers look for in a blender, manufacturers say. But appearance counts as well, since consumers are more likely to store the appliance on the countertop than in the cupboard. As a result, you'll see more colors and metallic finishes. Hamilton Beach and Sunbeam account for more than 60 percent of countertop-blender sales. Other makers include Cuisinart, KitchenAid, Krups, Vita-Mix, and Waring, a product pioneer. Braun controls the handheld segment of the market. Price range: $20 up to $400 for high-end machines.

Immersion blenders—stick-shaped handheld devices with a swirling blade on the bottom—are on a power trip, with models juiced up to 200 watts or more. With these devices, though, power does seem to make a difference. An immersion blender in the 100-watt range didn't have the energy to mince onions in CONSUMER REPORTS tests. These blenders, popular for stirring soups and pureeing and chopping vegetables, are increasingly paired with accessories such as beaters, whisks, and attachments to clean baby bottles.

FOOD PROCESSORS. With food processors, the trend is toward multifunction capability, with one piece doing the job of two appliances. Cuisinart's Smart Power Duet comes with an interchangeable food-processor container and a glass blender jar and blade. Either attachment fits on the motorized base. Another design trend is a mini-bowl insert that fits inside the main container for smaller tasks. Newer designs tend to be sleeker, with rounded rather than squared-off corners.

Among food processors, the dominant brands are Cuisinart and Hamilton Beach. Black & Decker is the foremost name in mini-choppers, most of which sell for less than $20, with more powerful, fully featured models costing considerably more. Price range: $20 to $250

STAND AND HAND MIXERS. As with blenders, the big push in mixers is for more power, good for handling heavy dough. Stand mixers come in varieties from heavy-duty (offering the most power and the largest mixing bowls) to light-service machines that are essentially detachable hand mixers resting on a stand. Models typically vary in power, from about 200 to 525 watts. Sales of light-duty, convenient hand mixers have held their own in recent years.

KitchenAid owns half the stand-mixer market; Sunbeam is the next best-selling brand. Black & Decker, Hamilton Beach, and Sunbeam are the predominate brands among hand mixers. The majority of stand mixers sell for more than $100, some up to several times as much. Price range: $10 (for hand mixers) to $150 and up.

Key features

WITH BLENDERS. Three to 16 speeds are the norm; power ratings are from 330 to 525 watts. Manufacturers claim that higher wattage translates into better performance, but in recent CONSUMER REPORTS tests, lower-wattage models often outperformed beefier ones, turning out icy drinks faster and leaving them smoother in consistency. Three well-differentiated speeds are adequate; a dozen or more closely spaced ones are overkill.

Containers are glass, plastic, or stainless steel, and come in sizes from about a quart to a half-gallon. A glass container is heavier and more stable. In tests, the blenders with glass jugs tended to perform better because they didn't shake. Glass is also easier to keep clean. Plastic may scratch and is likely to absorb the smell of whatever is inside. A stainless-steel container makes it difficult to know whether the mixture is the right consistency.

A wide mouth makes loading food and washing easier; big and easy-to-read markings help you measure more accurately. A **pulse setting** lets you fine-tune blending time. A power boost offers a momentary burst of higher speed, useful for demanding jobs such as pulverizing ice. **Touchpad controls** are easy to wipe clean. A blade that's permanently attached to the container (typical of the Warings) is harder to clean than a removable blade.

WITH FOOD PROCESSORS. All have a clear-plastic **mixing bowl** and lid, an S-shaped metal **chopping blade** (and sometimes a duller version for kneading dough), and a **plastic food pusher** to prod food through the feed tube. Some tubes are wider than others, so you don't have to cut up vegetables—such as potatoes—to fit the opening. One speed is the norm, plus a **pulse setting** to precisely control processing. Bowl capacity ranges from around 1 cup to 14 cups (dry). Also standard on full-sized processors: a **shredding/slicing disk.** Some also come with a **juicer** attachment. **Touchpad controls** are becoming more commonplace, too. Mini-choppers may look like little food processors, but they're for small jobs only, like chopping a clove of garlic or an onion half.

WITH MIXERS. Stand mixers have one or two different-sized **bowls,** a **beater** or two, and a **dough hook.** Some mixers offer options such as **splash guards** to prevent flour from spewing out of the bowl, plus **attachments** to make pasta, grind meat, and stuff sausage. Stand mixers generally have 5 to 16 speeds; CONSUMER REPORTS thinks three well-spaced settings is enough. You should be able to lock a mixer's power head in the Up position so it won't crash into the bowl when the beaters are weighed down with dough and, conversely, in the Down spot to keep the beaters from kicking back in stiff dough.

Just about any hand mixer is good for nontaxing exercises such as beating egg whites, mashing potatoes, or whipping cream. The **slow-start** feature on some mixers prevents ingredients from spattering when you start the mixer, though it's no big deal to manually step through the three or so speeds. An indentation on the underside of the motor housing allows the mixer to sit on the edge of a bowl without taking the beaters out of the batter.

How to choose

PERFORMANCE DIFFERENCES. With blenders, power, performance, and price don't always go hand in hand. Recent CONSUMER REPORTS tests revealed modestly powered, inexpensive blenders that turned out smooth-as-silk mixtures, while some bigger and fancier ones left food pulpy or lumpy.

Most food processors we've tested can shred cheese, puree baby food, and slice tough, fibrous produce such as ginger and celery without missing a beat. Kneading dough takes power, and large models handled the job with aplomb. Smaller machines force you to split the dough into batches, and, even after doing so, some labored while performing the task.

Heavy-duty stand mixers can tackle tough baking tasks such as kneading large quantities of dense dough. In tests, light-duty, less powerful models strained and overheated under a heavy load.

RECOMMENDATIONS. Choose the right machine for your cooking tasks. Blenders excel at pureeing soup, crushing ice, grating hard cheese, and making fruit smoothies.

A food processor is better at grating cheddar cheese and chopping meat, vegetables, and nuts. A processor can also slice and shred. Neither machine can match a mixer's prowess at mashing potatoes or whipping cream to a light, velvety consistency. For those kinds of tasks, you can buy a perfectly adequate hand mixer for as little as $10.

A midsized processor is probably the best choice for basic tasks. Bigger models are geared toward cooking enthusiasts who want to create picture-perfect salads and knead large quantities of pasta dough. Mini-choppers save space but aren't too versatile.

Not everyone needs a stand mixer. But if you're a dedicated baker, a stand mixer is useful and convenient. It will weigh more than 20 pounds or so, however; keep that in mind if you're planning to store the mixer in a cabinet.

Spending more will typically get you touchpad controls, sculpted styling, extra speeds and power, and perhaps colors to match your kitchen's decor. You'll pay more for a blender with a thermal, copper, or stainless-steel jar than a plastic or glass one; a food processor with a bigger container; and a more powerful, capacious mixer.

POTS & PANS

Nonstick pots and pans are easy to clean. Uncoated cookware is often more durable. Your best bet might be some of each.

Is boiling water the extent of your kitchen prowess or do you routinely take on much more challenging tasks? Could you work in the kitchen of a five-star restaurant or are you a culinary klutz? How you answer those questions is a good gauge of the price range for the cookware you need.

A basic set of 7 to 10 pieces, typically one or two pots, a skillet, a stockpot, and lids, can be had for $50. At the other end of the spectrum is a set of stylish and sturdy commercial-style cookware for as much as $600. And there are lots of good choices in between.

What's available

Farberware, Mirro/Wearever, Revere, and T-Fal are the most widely sold brands. Commercial-style brands include All-Clad and Calphalon. TV's celebrity chef Emeril Lagasse is mixing it up in the cookware market with Emerilware (made by All-Clad). Other recent entrants in the cookware field include the appliance maker KitchenAid and the knife maker Henckels.

Choices abound: aluminum, stainless steel, copper, cast iron, tempered glass, or porcelain on carbon steel; nonstick, porcelain-coated, or uncoated; lightweight or heavy-duty commercial-style; handles of metal, plastic, or wood.

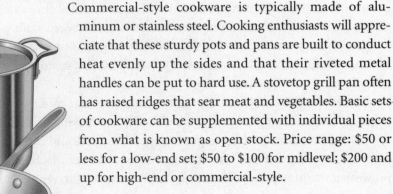

Commercial-style cookware is typically made of aluminum or stainless steel. Cooking enthusiasts will appreciate that these sturdy pots and pans are built to conduct heat evenly up the sides and that their riveted metal handles can be put to hard use. A stovetop grill pan often has raised ridges that sear meat and vegetables. Basic sets of cookware can be supplemented with individual pieces from what is known as open stock. Price range: $50 or less for a low-end set; $50 to $100 for midlevel; $200 and up for high-end or commercial-style.

Key features

The most versatile materials for pots and pans are the most common ones: aluminum and stainless steel.

Aluminum, when it's sufficiently heavy-gauge, heats quickly and evenly. Thin-gauge aluminum, besides heating unevenly, is prone to denting and warping. **Anodized aluminum** is an excellent heat conductor and is relatively lightweight. Matte, dark-gray, anodized aluminum is durable but easily stained and not dishwasher-safe. **Enamel-coated aluminum,** typically found in low-end lines, can easily chip.

Stainless steel goes in the dishwasher, but it conducts and retains heat poorly. It's usually layered over aluminum or comes with a copper or aluminum core on the bottom.

Copper heats and cools quickly, ideal when temperature control is important. It's good for, say, making caramel sauce. Provided that it's kept polished, copper looks great hanging on a kitchen wall. Because copper reacts with acidic foods such as tomatoes, it's usually lined with stainless steel or tin, which may blister and wear out over time. Solid-copper cookware, thin-gauge or heavy-gauge, is expensive.

You might want some **cast-iron** or **tempered-glass** pieces. Cast iron is slow to heat and cool, but it handles high temperatures well and it's great for stews or Cajun-style blackening. Tempered glass breaks easily and cooks unevenly on the stove, but it can go from the freezer to the stove, oven, broiler, or microwave—and to the table.

Most Americans opt for **nonstick** pots and pans to reduce the need for elbow grease when cleaning up. The first nonstick coatings, introduced on cookware more than 30 years ago, were thin and easily scratched. Nonsticks have greatly improved but still shouldn't be used with metal utensils or very high heat. To improve durability, some manufacturers use a thicker nonstick coating or create a gritty or textured surface before applying a nonstick finish. Many nonstick pots and pans aren't meant for the dishwasher, but they are easy to wash by hand.

There are some advantages to **uncoated** cookware. It's dishwasher-safe, it can handle metal utensils, and it's good for browning. It's also better when you want a little food to stick—say, when you want particles of meat left behind in a pan after sautéing so you can make a flavorful pan sauce. **Porcelain coatings** are easy to maintain and tough (although they can be chipped).

Handles are typically made from tubular stainless steel, cast stainless steel, heat-resistant plastic, or wood. **Solid metal handles** can be unwieldy but are sturdy. Solid or **hollow metal handles** can get hot but go from stovetop to broiler without damage. (But check labels; some can warp or discolor.) **Lightweight plastic handles** won't get as hot but can't go in ovens above 350° F, plus they can break. **Wooden handles** stay cool but don't go in the oven or dishwasher and may deteriorate over time. Handles are either welded, screwed, or riveted onto cookware. **Riveted handles** are the strongest. Some sets have removable handles that are used with different pieces, but they may fit with some pieces better than others.

Cookware with a specific shape simplifies certain cooking tasks. A skillet with **flared sides** aids sautéing or flipping omelets. **Straight sides** are better for frying. **Flat bottoms** work well on an electric range, especially a smoothtop.

How to choose

PERFORMANCE DIFFERENCES. Most people now opt for nonstick, which requires little or no oil and cleans easily. But uncoated cookware is better for browning and can stand up to metal utensils better. Commercial-style sets are sturdy, but they're relatively heavy and their metal handles get hot. "Hand-weigh" pieces as you shop, and imagine how they will feel when full. You might be more comfortable using lightweight pots and pans with comfortable plastic handles that stay better-insulated from the heat. Cast iron and copper are great for making certain dishes, but they may not be practical as basic cookware.

RECOMMENDATIONS. Choose a set with pots and pans that best match your cooking style. Over time, you can supplement your set by buying from open stock. Some people prefer individual pieces in different styles—a nonstick frying pan, say, and an uncoated stockpot.

COOKWARE SETS ◆ Ratings: Page 213

RANGES, COOKTOPS & WALL OVENS

Choices can be confusing, but you don't have to spend top dollar for impressive performance with high-end touches.

If you're in the market for a stove, you must first decide whether you want a freestanding range (with oven included) or a separate cooktop and wall oven. A cooktop/wall oven combo may offer you more flexibility with your kitchen design, although ranges can be less expensive. You'll also need to decide on gas, electricity, or both. Gas, of course, is only possible if you have access to a gas hookup.

Electric ranges now include traditional coil and newer smoothtop models, in which a sheet of ceramic glass covers the heating elements. Both types of cooktop elements offer quick heating and the ability to maintain low heat levels.

Gas ranges use burners, which don't heat as quickly as electric elements. Even high-powered burners tend to heat more slowly than the fastest electric coil elements, sometimes because the heavy cast-iron grates slow the process by absorbing heat. But you can see how high or low you are adjusting the flame, and you can instantly shut off the burners. Many high-end gas stoves are "professional-style" models with beefy knobs, heavy cast-iron grates, stainless-steel construction, and four or more high-powered burners. These

high-heat behemoths can cost thousands, and typically require a special range hood and blower system. They may also need special shielding and a reinforced floor.

You'll also find more and more shared characteristics between electric and gas ranges. For example, some gas models have electric warming zones, and a growing number of high-end gas ranges pair gas cooktop burners with an electric oven. Fortunately, you don't have to spend top dollar for top cooking performance.

What's available

GE and Whirlpool are the leading makers of ranges, cooktops, and wall ovens. Other major brands include Kenmore (Sears), Amana, Frigidaire, Maytag, Jenn-Air, and KitchenAid. Mainstream brands have established high-end offshoots, such as Kenmore Elite, GE Profile, and

Whirlpool Gold. High-end, pro-style brands include Bosch, Dacor, DCS, GE Monogram, Thermador, Viking, and Wolf.

FREESTANDING RANGE. These ranges can fit in the middle of a kitchen counter or at the end. Widths are usually 20 to 40 inches, although most are 30 inches wide. They typically have controls on the backguard. Slide-in models eliminate the backsplash and side panels to blend into the countertop, while drop-ins rest atop toe-kick-level cabinetry and typically lack a storage drawer. Ovens can be self-cleaning or manual-clean, although most mainstream ranges and a growing number of pro-style models now include a self-cleaning feature. Price range: $400 to $1,500.

PRO-STYLE RANGE. Bulkier than freestanding ranges, these can be anywhere from 30 to 60 inches wide. Larger ones include six or eight burners, a grill or griddle, and a double oven. Many have a convection feature, and some have an infrared gas broiler. But you usually don't get a storage drawer or sealed burners, which keep crumbs from falling beneath the cooktop. Price range: $2,500 to $8,000.

COOKTOP. You can install a cooktop on a kitchen island or anywhere else where counter space allows. As with freestanding ranges, cooktops can be electric coil, electric smoothtop, or gas. Paired with a wall oven, a cooktop adds flexibility, since it can be located separately. Most cooktops are 30 inches wide and are made of porcelain-coated steel or ceramic glass, with four elements or burners. Some are 36 or 48 inches wide and have space for an extra burner.

Modular cooktops let you mix and match parts—removing burners and adding a grill, say—although you'll pay more for that added flexibility. Preconfigured cooktops are less expensive. Price range: electric cooktop, $200 to $1,200; gas cooktop, $300 to $1,750.

WALL OVEN. These can be electric or gas, self-cleaning or manual, with or without a convection setting. Width is typically 24, 27, or 30 inches. Best of all, you can eliminate bending by installing it at waist or eye level, although you can also nest it under a countertop. Price range: $400 to more than $3,500 for double-oven models. The convection option typically adds $400 to the price.

BURNER TYPES COMPARED

There's no such thing as a perfect burner. Here is a look at the performance, cost, and maintenance advantages of smoothtop, coil, and gas.

ADVANTAGE	SMOOTHTOP	COIL	GAS
Easier to clean	✓		
More options for burner sizes, features	✓		
Better low-temperature performance	✓		
Less repair-prone	✓		
Easier to clean	✓	✓	
Heats food faster		✓	
Less expensive to buy		✓	
Less expensive to repair		✓	
Works well with all pots and pans		✓	✓
Faster temperature adjustment			✓
Visual feedback for temperature adjustment			✓
Less expensive to operate			✓

Key features

ON ALL RANGES. Look for easy-cleaning features such as a glass or porcelain backguard, instead of a painted one; seamless corners and edges, especially where the cooktop joins the backguard; and a raised edge around the cooktop to contain spills.

ON ELECTRIC RANGES AND COOKTOPS. Consider where the **controls** are located. Slide-in ranges have the dials to the front panel, while freestanding models have them on the backguard. Some models locate controls to the left and right, with oven controls in between, giving you a quick sense of which control operates which element. But controls clustered in the center stay visible when tall pots sit on rear heating elements. On most electric cook-tops, controls take up room on the surface. Some models have electronic touchpads, however, allowing the entire cooktop to be flush with the counter.

Coil elements, the most common and least expensive electric option, are easy to replace if they break. On an electric range with coil elements, look for a **prop-up top** for easier cleaning, and deep **drip pans** made of porcelain to better contain spills and ease cleaning.

Spending $200 more will buy you a **smoothtop** model; most use radiant heat, though halogen is a niche segment. **Halogen elements** redden immediately when turned on, while radiant elements take about six seconds. Some smoothtops have **expandable elements**, which allow you to switch between a large, high-power element and a small, low-power element contained within it. Some smoothtops also include a **low-wattage element** for warming plates or keeping just-cooked food at the optimal temperature. Some have an elongated "bridge" element that spans two burners—a nicety for accommodating rectan-gular or odd-shaped cookware. And many have at least one **hot-surface light**—a key safety feature, since the surface can remain hot long after the elements have been turned off. The safest setup includes a dedicated "hot" light for each element.

Most electric ranges and cooktops have one large, **higher-wattage burner** in front and one in back. An **expanded simmer range** in some electric models lets you fine-tune the sim-mer setting on one burner for, say, melting chocolate or keeping a sauce from getting too hot.

ON GAS RANGES AND COOKTOPS. Most gas ranges have four burners in three sizes, measured in British thermal units per hour (Btu/hr.): one or two medium-power burners (about 9,000 Btu/hr.), a small burner(about 5,000 Btu/hr.), and one or two large ones (about 12,500 Btu/hr.). We recommend a model with one or more 12,000 Btu/hr. burners for quick cook-top heating. On a few models, the burners automatically reignite.

For easier cleaning, look for **sealed burners** and removable **burner pans** and **caps.** Gas ranges typically have **knob controls**; the best give you 180 degrees or more of adjusting room. Try to avoid knobs that have adjacent "off" and "low" settings and that rotate no more than 90 degrees between High and Low.

Spending more on a gas stove or cooktop gets you heavier **grates** made of porcelain-coated cast iron, a low-power **simmer burner** with an extra-low setting for delicate sauces, an easy-to-clean **ceramic surface**, and **stainless-steel accents.**

ON PRO-STYLE RANGES. These models have six or more brass or cast-iron burners, all of which offer very high output (usually about 15,000 Btu/hr.). The burners are usually non-sealed, with hard-to-clean crevices, though sealed burners are appearing on some models. Large knobs are another typical pro-style feature, as are continuous grates designed for heavy-duty use. The latter, however, can be unwieldy to remove for cleaning.

ON OVENS. Electric ovens used to have an edge over gas ovens in roominess, but recently CONSUMER REPORTS has found roomy ovens among both types. Note, though, that an oven's usable capacity may be less than what manufacturers claim, because they don't take protruding broiler elements and other features into account.

A **self-cleaning cycle** uses high heat to burn off spills and splatters. Most ranges have it, although many pro-style gas models still don't. An **automatic door lock**, found on most self-cleaning models, is activated during the cycle, then unlocks when the oven has cooled. Also useful is a **self-cleaning countdown** display, which shows the time left in the cycle. Higher-priced ranges and wall ovens often include a **convection mode,** which uses a fan and, sometimes, an electric element to circulate heated air. CONSUMER REPORTS tests have shown that the convection mode shaved cooking time for a large roast and baked large cookie batches more evenly because of the circulating air. But the fan can take up valuable oven space. A few electric ovens have a low-power **microwave feature** that works with bake and broil elements to speed cooking time further. Another cooking technology, found in the GE Advantium over-the-range oven, uses a **halogen heating bulb** as well as microwaves.

A **variable-broil** feature in some electric ovens offers adjustable settings for foods such as fish or thick steaks that need slower or faster cooking. Ovens with **12-hour shutoff** turn off automatically if you leave the oven on for that long. But most models allow you to disable this feature. A **child lockout** allows you to disable oven controls for safety.

Manufacturers are also updating oven controls across the price spectrum. **Electronic touchpad controls** are a high-end feature now showing up in a growing number of lower-priced ranges. A **digital display** makes it easier to set the precise temperature and keep track of it. A **cook time/delay start** lets you set a time for the oven to start and stop cooking; remember, however, that you shouldn't leave most foods in a cold oven very long. An **automatic oven light** typically comes on when the door opens, although some ovens have a switch-operated light. A **temperature probe,** to be inserted into meat or poultry, indicates when you've obtained a precise internal temperature.

Oven windows come in various sizes. Those without a decorative grid usually offer the clearest view, although some cooks may welcome the grid to hide pots, pans, and other cooking utensils typically stored inside the oven.

How to choose

PERFORMANCE DIFFERENCES. Almost every range, cooktop, or oven CONSUMER REPORTS has tested cooks well. Differences are in the details. An electric range may boil a pot of water a bit more quickly than a gas range, while a gas model can sometimes be adjusted with more precision. CONSUMER REPORTS tests have also shown that the powerful burners on some pro-style gas ranges may not simmer some foods without scorching them. Among electric ranges, smoothtops are displacing coil-tops, but they aren't necessarily better or more reliable. A smoothtop's glass surface eases cleaning, but you need to wipe up sugary spills immediately to avoid pitting the surface.

Be aware that the doors and windows of some ovens can become fairly hot during self-cleaning, while others are left with a permanent residue.

RECOMMENDATIONS. Decide on the type you want, then consider the features, price, and brand reliability. Cabinetry, floor plan, and whether you have access to a gas hookup will also factor into your decision. A freestanding range generally offers the best value; a very basic electric or gas range costs $400 or less. Smoothtop electric ranges cost a few hundred dollars more than those with coil elements. Spending more than $1,000 buys lots of extras, including electronic controls and pro-style touches such as stainless-steel trim. Pro-style ranges cost thousands. In wall ovens, the convection feature adds hundreds of dollars to the price.

COOKTOPS, RANGES, WALL OVENS ◆ **Ratings:** Page 211, 253, 255, 288 ◆ **Reliability:** Page 299

RANGE HOODS

Several brands offer matching hood-and-blower ventilation systems to whisk heat, smoke, odor, and combustion gases out of the kitchen. An alternative is an over-the-range microwave oven, which also handles ventilation, when vented outside, but not as well. Manufacturers of pro-style ranges and cooktops recommend a hood-and-blower system capable of moving at least 1,000 cubic feet of air per minute.

REFRIGERATORS

Top-freezer and bottom-freezer refrigerators generally give you more usable space for your money than comparable side-by-sides. And they cost less to run.

If you're shopping for a refrigerator, you are probably considering models that are fancier than your current one. The trend is toward spacious fridges with flexible, more efficiently used storage space. Useful features such as spill-proof, slide-out glass shelves and temperature-controlled compartments, once only in expensive refrigerators, are now practically standard in midpriced models. Stainless-steel doors are a stylish but costly extra. Built-in refrigerators appeal to people who want to customize their kitchens, but they're expensive. Some brands offer less-expensive, built-in-style models.

Replacing an aging refrigerator may reduce your electric bill, since refrigerators are more energy efficient now than they were a decade ago. The Department of Energy toughened its rules in the early 1990s and imposed even stricter requirements in July 2001 for this appliance, which is the top electricity user in the house.

What's available

Frigidaire, GE, Kenmore (Sears), and Whirlpool account for almost 60 percent of top-freezer refrigerator sales. For side-by-side models, these brands and Amana account for more than 80 percent of sales. Brands offering bottom-freezer models include Amana, GE, Kenmore, and KitchenAid. Mainstream manufacturers have launched high-end sub-brands such as GE Profile and Kenmore Elite. Two brands that specialize in built-in refrigerators, Sub-Zero and Viking, have been joined in that market by Amana, GE, and KitchenAid. Only a handful of companies actually manufacture refrigerators. The same or very similar models may be sold under several brands.

TOP-FREEZER MODELS. Accounting for half the refrigerators sold, models of this type are generally less expensive to buy and run—and more space- and energy-efficient—than comparably sized side-by-side models. Width ranges from about 24 to 36 inches. The eye-level freezer offers easy access, but you have to bend down to reach the bottom refrigerator shelves. Nominal labeled capacity ranges from about 10 to almost 26 cubic feet. (Our measurements show that a refrigerator's usable capacity is typically about 25 percent less than its nominal capacity.) Price range: typically $600 to $800, but can exceed $1,300 depending on size and features.

SIDE-BY-SIDE MODELS. This type puts part of both the main compartment and the freezer at eye level, where it's easy to reach. The narrow doors are handy in tight kitchens. High, narrow compartments make finding stray items easy in front (harder in the back), but they may not hold a sheet cake or a large turkey. Compared with top- and bottom-freezer models, a higher proportion of capacity goes to freezer space. Side-by-sides are typically large—30 to 36 inches wide, with nominal capacity of 19 to 30 cubic feet. They're more expensive than similar-sized top-freezer models and less space- and energy-efficient. Price range: typically $1,000 to $1,600 but can exceed $2,150).

BOTTOM-FREEZER MODELS. A small but fast-growing part of the market, these put frequently used items such as milk and cheese at eye level. Fairly wide refrigerator shelves provide easy access. You must bend to locate items in the freezer, even with a pull-out basket. Bottom-freezers are a bit pricier than top-freezer models and offer a bit less capacity for their external dimensions. Price range: usually $800 to $1,000, but can exceed $2,100.

BUILT-IN MODELS. These are generally side-by-side models, though some bottom-freezers are available. Built-ins show their commercial heritage, often with fewer standard amenities and less sound-proofing than less expensive "home" models. Usually about 25 inches front to back, they fit flush with cabinets and counters. Their compressor is on top, making them about a foot taller than regular refrigerators. Some can accept front panels that match the kitchen's décor. Price range: $4,000 and up.

BUILT-IN-STYLE MODELS. Sometimes called cabinet-depth models, these free standing refrigerators stick out only a few inches beyond standard cabinets. Price range: typically $1,700 to $2,200.

Key features

Interiors are ever more flexible. **Adjustable door bins** and shelves can be moved to fit tall items. Some shelves can be cranked up and down without removing the contents. Some **split shelves** can be adjusted to different heights independently. To provide clearance, the front half of some shelves slides under the rear portion, or one side folds up. **Sliding brackets** on door shelves secure bottles and jars.

A few models have a **wine rack** that stores bottles horizontally. **Glass shelves** are easier to clean than wire racks. Most glass shelves have a **raised rim** to keep spills from dripping over. Some shelves slide out. Pullout shelves or bins in the freezer give easier access; some bottom freezers have a sliding drawer.

A **temperature-controlled drawer** can be set to be several degrees cooler than the rest of the interior, useful for storing meat or fish; some models maintained meat-keeper temperatures more precisely than others in CONSUMER REPORTS tests.

Crisper drawers have controls to maintain humidity. CONSUMER REPORTS tests have shown that in general, temperature-controlled drawers work better than plain drawers; results for humidity controls were less clear-cut. **See-through drawers** let you tell at a glance what's inside. **Curved doors** give the refrigerator a distinctive profile and retro look. Many manufacturers have at least one curved-door model in their lineup.

Step-up features include a variety of finishes and colors. Every major manufacturer has a **stainless-steel** model that typically costs significantly more than one with a standard **textured finish.** Another alternative is a smooth, **glasslike finish.** New color choices are emerging: biscuit, bisque, or linen instead of almond. Several lines include black models, and KitchenAid has a cobalt-blue finish that matches its small appliances.

Most models have an **icemaker** in the freezer (or the option of installing one yourself). Typically producing 3 or 4 pounds of ice per day, an icemaker reduces freezer space by about a cubic foot. The ice bin is generally located below the icemaker, but some new models place it on the inside of the freezer door, providing a bit more usable volume in the compartment itself. Some models can make more ice in less time.

A through-the-door **ice and water dispenser** is common in side-by-side refrigerators; a **child lockout button** in some models disables it. An icemaker adds $70 to $100 to the price of a refrigerator; an in-door water dispenser adds about $100. Some top-freezer models offer a water dispenser in the refrigerator.

With many models, the icemaker and water dispenser include a **water filter,** designed to reduce lead, chlorine, and other impurities, a capability you may or may not need. An icemaker or water dispenser will work without a filter. You can also have a filter installed in the tubing that supplies water to the refrigerator. An unusual premium feature is a **refreshment center,** a small, fold-out door in the main door that gives access to bottles in a chiller.

Once a refrigerator's controls are set, there should be little need to adjust temperature. Still, accessible controls are an added convenience. Digital controls and displays have replaced temperature-setting dials on a few side-by-sides.

Top- and bottom-freezer models have **reversible hinges** so they can open to either side. The doors on side-by-side models require the least amount of front clearance space.

How to choose

PERFORMANCE DIFFERENCES. Most refrigerators, even the least expensive, keep things cold very well. Many models are pretty quiet, too; some are very quiet. Energy efficiency, configurations, and convenience features vary considerably from model to model. Less expensive refrigerators usually lack niceties such as simple-to-use crispers and chillers or easily arranged shelves.

Energy efficiency can vary significantly, according to CONSUMER REPORTS tests. A highly efficient model that costs more than an inefficient model may be a better buy in the long run. Since a refrigerator can account for up to one-fifth of a household's annual electricity costs, the savings can be substantial. Models made as of July 2001 are required to meet efficiency standards up to 30 percent more stringent than those before. By 2003, new models must be made without hydrochlorofluorocarbons, which can harm the earth's ozone layer (though less so than chlorofluorocarbons, which are not used in current models).

RECOMMENDATIONS. Top-freezer models give you the most refrigerator for the money. But personal preference or kitchen layout may point toward another type. Once you choose a type, assess models for convenience features and accessible, flexible storage. Before going shopping, take measurements not only of the space the refrigerator is to fit in but of your doorways and hallways. If you need to place your new fridge with the door opening against your kitchen's side wall, look for a model with a door hinge that lets it open flat against the wall.

REFRIGERATORS ✦ **Ratings:** Page 259 ✦ **Reliability:** Page 300

SEWING MACHINES

Sewing is easier than ever. Mechanical machines under $200 have many features. Spend more for an electronic model, and you get more convenience and hundreds of stitches.

New electronic sewing machines are almost like robots. They can recommend the proper presser foot, divine the right thread tension and stitch length, size and sew a buttonhole, and automatically cut the thread. Combination embroidery/sewing machines, introduced about nine years ago, combine those features with superior sewing and the ability to produce professional-quality embroidery.

What's available

Singer, Brother, and Kenmore sell about 70 percent of all units. Brands such as Bernina and Husqvarna Viking are gaining as the market shifts to more expensive, feature-laden machines.

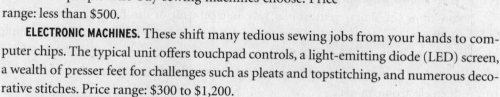

MECHANICAL MODELS. These require you to manipulate most controls by hand, generally cost less than electronic or sewing/embroidery models, and handle the basics—repairs, hems, simple clothing, and crafts projects. They're what most people who buy sewing machines choose. Price range: less than $500.

ELECTRONIC MACHINES. These shift many tedious sewing jobs from your hands to computer chips. The typical unit offers touchpad controls, a light-emitting diode (LED) screen, a wealth of presser feet for challenges such as pleats and topstitching, and numerous decorative stitches. Price range: $300 to $1,200.

SEWING/EMBROIDERY UNITS. These combine the talents of a stand-alone embroidery machine with a sewing machine. The machine holds a hoop under its needle and moves the hoop in four directions as the needle sews. You push a start button, watch, and periodically change thread colors. Embroidery machines require a link to a home computer to access all their capabilities. Price range: $1,000 to more than $6,000.

Key features

Among the most convenient features is an **automatic buttonholer** that sews in one step instead of making you continually manipulate selector dials or the fabric itself.

Setting up the machine is made easier by several innovations. A needle threader, for instance, reduces eyestrain and frustration. A **top-load bobbin,** available on both mechanical and electronic models, lets you drop the bobbin directly into the machine without fiddling; most top-load bobbins have a see-through **window**. A **bobbin thread lift** function on some electronic models brings the bobbin thread to the sewing surface so you don't have to insert your fingers under the presser foot. Some electronic machines have an **"adviser"** program on their LED screens; it can recommend the stitch and presser foot to use, and it gives other handy advice.

A number of features help you avoid mistakes. A **feed-dog adjustment** lets you drop the toothy mechanism (which moves the fabric along) below the sewing surface so you can do freehand work or keep from damaging sheer fabrics. On some electronic models, automatic tension adjustment for the upper thread helps avoid loopy stitches and annoying "birds' nests" that can jam the machine or bend the needle. An **adjustable presser foot** allows you to regulate how tightly the machine holds fabric while sewing; it prevents puckering in fine fabrics and ensures that knits don't stretch out of shape.

Among the especially helpful features are **speed control,** which lets you determine sewing speed with a button instead of with the foot pedal. It can be useful when teaching a child to sew. **A stop/start switch,** auxiliary to the power switch, lets you bypass the foot pedal to control sewing and can be a boon to people with limited foot mobility.

How to choose

PERFORMANCE DIFFERENCES. Most electronic machines sew very well and offer a great variety of features, stitches, and presser feet. In CONSUMER REPORTS tests, most excelled in ease of use. Sewing/embroidery machines had the best sewing ability. Their plethora of convenience features make them, as a group, extremely easy to use. It's possible to find very good performance from some mechanical models. Most of them are easy to use, but they offer fewer convenience features and stitches than do the other types of machine.

RECOMMENDATIONS. Before buying a sewing machine, assess your skills and needs. Consider, too, how you might use the machine later, when your skills improve. Typically, people keep a sewing machine at least 10 years.

If you know you'll never embroider, buy an electronic or mechanical model with as many features as you can afford. A mechanical model will do for basic hemming, clothing repairs, and one or two yearly projects. If your current projects or your ambitions include more numerous and complicated projects, you'll probably be more satisfied in the long run with an electronic model.

If there's a chance you might want to try embroidery, such a machine may be a wise investment. You'll also benefit from superior sewing capabilities.

You'd do well to wait for sales. Sears and Wal-Mart have larger selections of lower-priced models than other retailers. Specialty and fabric stores tend to sell more expensive brands but may offer training classes and an in-house repair shop—both a plus. Some independent dealers will accept a trade-in of your old model. Internet-based dealers offer good prices, but the warranties may be invalid if the dealer isn't manufacturer-authorized, and service may be very difficult to arrange.

When shopping, try out the machine with an experienced salesperson; ideally, take lessons after you buy. If you buy a used or reconditioned machine, ask the retailer for a warranty; manufacturers' warranties are usually not transferable.

TOASTING APPLIANCES

Some people like the straightforwardness of a toaster. Others prefer an appliance that toasts, bakes, and more. Either way, you can get good performance without spending a lot.

Piggybacking on the popularity of bagels, toaster pastries, and frozen, ready-to-heat omelets, manufacturers are redesigning the basic toaster for improved counter appeal and cachet.

New developments in toaster design include rounded sides; seamless housing; non-stick slots; a dedicated setting for bagels, in which only a single side of the bread is browned; and a cancel mode to interrupt the toast cycle. Black & Decker is introducing a model with clear glass sides that lets you watch the toasting operation. Extrawide and long-slot models are becoming increasingly popular, too.

A big change in the product is the move toward "smart" toasters with microchips and heat sensors that promise perfect doneness and supposedly adjust heat output so the first batch is identical to the last (they don't always deliver). Some models incorporate an LED indicator to show the darkness selection and to count down the time remaining in a particular cycle.

But you needn't buy a $100 or $200 toaster to do a masterful job browning bread. For $20 or less, you can buy a competent product that will make decent toast, two slices at a time, with all the basics: a darkness control to adjust doneness, a push-down lever to raise or lower the bread, and cool-touch housing to keep you from burning your fingers.

With increased demand for multifunction appliances—and the space savings that result from having one machine that can do the work of two—many people opt for a hybrid appliance that not only can toast four or more slices of bread but also can bake muffins, heat frozen entrées, or broil a small batch of burgers or a small chicken.

What's available

Toastmaster invented the pop-up toaster back in the 1920s and now shares shelf space with other venerable brands of toasters and toaster ovens such as Black & Decker, Hamilton Beach and Sunbeam, plus players such as Cuisinart, DeLonghi, Kenmore (Sears), KitchenAid, Krups, Rival, T-Fal, and West Bend. Dualit makes old-fashioned, commercial-style, heavy-gauge stainless-steel toasters. Toasters come in a variety of exterior finishes such as chrome and brushed metal.

Of the 12 million toasters sold annually, two-slice models outsell four-slicers 4 to 1. Nearly three-quarters of toaster ovens sold are equipped with a broiler function. Most toaster ovens are countertop models, though a few under-the-cabinet models are sold. Price range: toasters, $20 to $380; toaster ovens, $40 and up.

Key features

For all the bells and whistles, a simple **dial** or **lever** to set for darkness is sufficient. **Electronic controls** regulate shadings and settings with a touchpad instead. A **pop-up control** lets you eject a slice early if you think it's done. A **toast boost,** or manual lift, lets you raise smaller items such as bagel halves above the slots so there's no need to fish around with a fork, a potentially dangerous exercise if you don't pull out the plug. Another safety note: Underwriters Laboratory now requires that toasters shut off at the end of the toasting cycle even if a piece of bread jams in the carriage.

There are models that offer an astounding (and unnecessary) 63 time and temperature toasting options. One of the more curious entries comes from West Bend, with its unorthodox Slide Thru toaster. You insert the bread in the slot and remove it through a door at the base. The door doubles as a "dressing table" for spreading butter or jam.

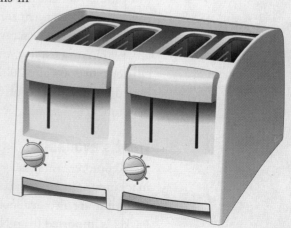

Recent toaster-oven innovations include a **liner** that can be removed for cleaning, and various ways to speed up the cooking process, including use of a **convection fan** or **infrared heat.**

A **removable crumb tray** facilitates cleaning. **Nonstick**

slots also make it easy to remove baked-on goop left by toaster pastries. More and more models incorporate a control that automatically defrosts and then toasts in a single step, nice if you regularly prepare items such as frozen hash-brown patties. With toaster ovens, **a removable cooking cavity** eases cleaning.

How to choose

PERFORMANCE DIFFERENCES. Most toasters make respectable toast. But few models, including those with microchips and heat sensors, toast to perfection. In CONSUMER REPORTS tests, problems included toast that came out darker on one side than the other and successive batches that were inconsistently browned.

As in the past, toaster ovens as a group were not as good as their plainer cousins at making toast, although their ability to bake and broil makes them more versatile. Elegant styling and a sleek design can carry a high price tag, but may offer little else.

RECOMMENDATIONS. If all you want is toast, a $20 toaster will do the job fine. Toaster ovens offer versatility so you needn't, for example, heat up your big oven to warm leftovers or use the stove to melt a grilled-cheese sandwich.

TOASTING APPLIANCES ◆ **Ratings:** Page 270

WASHING MACHINES

Almost all machines do a fine job washing. Top-loaders are usually less expensive, but front-loaders cost less to operate because they use less water and energy.

Until recently, about the only place you were likely to see a front-loading washing machine was in a coin laundry. But in the past few years this type of washer, which you load the same way you would a clothes dryer, has gained in popularity. Today about 10 percent of newly purchased washing machines are front-loaders, up from less than 5 percent several years ago.

Virtually any washing machine will get your clothing clean. Front-loaders do the job using less water, including hot water, and thus less energy than most top-loaders. Two top-loading designs—one from Kenmore and Whirlpool, the other from Fisher & Paykel—work somewhat like front-loaders. They fill partially with water and spray clothes with a concentrated detergent solution. In CONSUMER REPORTS tests, they outscored other top-loaders in water and energy efficiency.

Within the next few years, top-loading washing machines should become more energy efficient. In 2004 and 2007, the Department of Energy will phase in stricter standards regarding energy and hot-water use and water extraction. Front-loaders already meet the new, tougher standards.

What's available

GE, Kenmore (Sears), Maytag, and Whirlpool account for about 80 percent of the washing machines sold in the U.S. Smaller brands such as Amana, Frigidaire, Roper, and Hotpoint are also available. Asko, Bosch, and Miele are key European brands. Fisher-Paykel is imported from New Zealand.

TOP-LOADERS. Most top-loaders fill the tub with enough water to cover the clothing, then agitate it. Because they need room to move the laundry around to ensure thorough cleaning, these machines have a smaller load capacity than front-loaders—generally about 12 to 16 pounds. The Calypso models from Kenmore and Whirlpool are unusual in that they have a "wash plate," rather than an agitator to move clothes around. That enables them to hold 18-pound loads and makes them gentler on clothing.

It's easier to load laundry and to add items midcycle to a top-loader. But they're also noisier than front-loaders. Top-loaders are generally 27 to 29 inches wide. Price range: $250 to $1,300.

FRONT-LOADERS. Front-loaders get clothes clean by tumbling them in the water. Clothes are lifted to the top of the tub, then dropped into the water below. The design makes front-loaders gentler on clothing and more adept at handling unbalanced loads. They can typically handle 12 to 20 pounds of laundry. Front-loading washing machines require front-loader detergent, which produces less suds than detergent for top-loaders. Like top-loaders, they're typically 27 to 29 inches wide. Price range: $600 to $1,500.

SPACE-SAVING OPTIONS. Compact models are typically 24 inches wide or less and wash 8 to 12 pounds of laundry. A compact front-loader can be stacked with a compact dryer. (Many full-sized front-loaders can also be stacked with a matching dryer.) Some compact models can be stored in a closet and rolled out to be hooked up to the kitchen sink. Price range: $450 to $2,000.

Washer-dryer laundry centers combine a washer and dryer in one unit, with the dryer located above the washer. These can be full-sized (27 inches wide) or compact (24 inches wide). Capacity is about 12 to 14 pounds. Performance is generally comparable to that of full-sized machines. Price range: $700 to $1,900.

Key features

A porcelain-coated steel **inner tub** can rust if the porcelain is chipped. Stainless-steel or plastic tubs won't rust. A porcelain top/lid resists scratching better than a painted one.

High-end models often have **touchpad controls;** others have traditional **dials.** Controls should be legible, easy to push or turn, and logically arranged. A plus: **lights** or **signals** that indicate cycle. On some top-loaders, an **automatic lock** during the spin cycle keeps children from opening the lid. Front-loaders lock at the beginning of a cycle but usually can be opened by interrupting the cycle, although some doors remain shut briefly after the machine stops.

Front-loaders automatically set wash speed according to the **fabric cycle** selected, and some also automatically set the spin speed. Top-loaders typically provide **wash/spin speed combinations,** such as Regular, Permanent Press, and Delicate (or Gentle). A few models also allow an **extra rinse** or **extended spin.**

Front-loaders and some top-loaders set water levels automatically, ensuring efficient use of water. Some top-loaders can be set for four or more levels; three or four are probably as many as you'd need.

Most machines establish wash and rinse temperatures by mixing hot and

GUIDE GUIDANCE
Until recently, there were two scales for the DOE's Yellow EnergyGuide Stickers: one for top-loaders, and one for the generally more efficient front-loaders. Now both types are presented on the same scale.

cold water in preset proportions. For incoming cold water that is especially cold, an **automatic temperature control** adjusts the flow for the correct temperature. A **time-delay feature** lets you program the washer to start at a later time, such as at night, when your utility rates are low, for example. **Detergent** and **fabric-softener dispensers** automatically release powder or liquid. **Bleach dispensers** can prevent spattering. Some machines offer a **hand-washing cycle.**

How to choose

PERFORMANCE DIFFERENCES. All washing machines get clothes clean. In CONSUMER REPORTS tests, differences in washing ability tended to be slight. Differences in water and energy efficiency and in noisiness were greater. Front-loaders have the edge on all counts.

The water efficiency of any washing machine rises with larger loads, but, overall, front-loaders use far less water per pound of laundry and excel in energy efficiency. Washing six loads of laundry per week, the most water-efficient front-loaders can save almost 6,000 gallons of water a year. Using electricity to heat the water, and using an electric dryer, the most energy-efficient front-loaders can save you about $60 worth of electrical energy a year compared with the least efficient top-loader. (Costs are based on 2002 national average utility prices; differences would narrow with a gas water heater, gas dryer, full loads, or carefully set water levels.) Front-loaders are generally quieter than top-loaders except when draining or spinning, and they are usually gentler on your laundry.

RECOMMENDATIONS. Top-loaders generally cost less than front-loaders and do a fine job. Best values: midpriced top-loaders with few features, which you can usually find for less than $500. Features such as extra wash/spin options or an automatic detergent dispenser may add to convenience but don't necessarily improve performance.

While front-loaders are usually more expensive to buy, they can cost significantly less to operate, especially in areas where water or energy rates are very high. In general, though, the savings are not likely to make up the price difference over a washer's typical life span.

Buying one of the more expensive top-loading or front-loading models can get you larger capacity and features that give you more flexibility, such as programming frequently used settings.

WASHING MACHINES ◆ **Ratings:** Page 289 ◆ **Reliability:** Page 302

2

Home Entertainment

A look inside a consumer-electronics store reveals a transformation that can be described in one word: digital. In recent years, digital-entertainment products such as DVD players, digital video recorders (DVRs), and satellite-TV receivers have made their mark on the marketplace. Other products, such as camcorders, cameras, receivers, and some TV sets, have moved from analog to digital and in the process have made leaps in what they promise and often can deliver.

CONSUMER REPORTS tests of this new equipment show that digital capability often results in giant leaps in performance. Audio CD players consistently reproduce sound better than turntables did. The typical digital camcorder provides much clearer video than the best of their older, analog cousins. Receivers supporting digital audio can provide more realism when you're watching movies at home than those with earlier, analog-audio standards. High-definition TV (HDTV) shows not just the football game but the sweat glistening on the arms of the players.

But despite digital's superiority over the analog ways of cassette tape, videotape, and traditional NTSC-standard TV, analog products will still be sold for some time to come. If industry infighting and consumer reluctance are any indication, it may be a long time coming. Here's what you can see in today's home-entertainment products:

MOVIES GO DIGITAL, BUT NOT THE SET. DVDs, with their capacity for extra features and director commentary tracks, are well on the way to replacing videotapes as the home movie choice. Meanwhile, DVD players have quickly become almost a commodity, with excellent performance the norm and prices dipping below $100.

Despite the record pace of DVD adoption, analog TVs and VCRs are still by far the most-sold home-entertainment products, and the best of them are fine performers despite their "nondigitized" nature. VCRs still are a mainstay, though digital recorders, sold under TiVo, Replay, and other names, can record with greater speed and commercial-erasing finesse. Recordable DVD is growing more slowly than predicted because of high cost, technical difficulties, and wrangles over copy-protection concerns. TiVo, Replay, and others still require you to transfer material to videotape for permanent storage.

THE DIGITAL REVOLUTION IN AUDIO KEEPS ROLLING. It turns out that the introduction of CD players in 1982 was just part one of the digital revolution in consumer audio—the playback part. Part two: the current boom in digital recording options. Audio CD player/recorders, which allow you to create your own CDs for a dollar or two each, have been dropping in price; you can now buy one for a few hundred dollars. New MP3 players offer huge capacity—5 to 20 gigabytes—in very small packages. Digital-music options make music "liquid"—you can pour out what you want to hear, in the order you want, in the format you choose, at home, in the car, or while jetting to Bermuda.

Improvements in digital audio technology, such as DVD-Audio and Super Audio CD (SACD), take full advantage of the surround-sound speaker systems developed for movies.

HOME ELECTRONICS: SHOPPING OPTIONS

When shopping for home electronics, you can visit a huge variety of stores, surf web sites, or leaf through catalogs. Here is a headstart on figuring out how to shop efficiently:

Electronics chains. The national chains Best Buy and Circuit City dominate. Stores are vast enough to display a broad selection of types and brands. Another strength is low prices on select items. A considerable amount of store space is devoted to computers, peripherals, music, and movies. Listening rooms and home-theater salons let you try before buying. A pitch for extended warranties from sales is more likely than at other shopping venues. Returns may include a restocking fee. RadioShack stores take a somewhat different approach, emphasizing accessories and repairs as well as selling equipment.

Big retailers. The chains JCPenney and Sears and the mass merchandisers Kmart, Target, and Wal-Mart have a selection of home electronics. Mass merchandisers used to emphasize lower-priced brands, but it's now easier to find high-end products such as projection TV sets or digital camcorders at these outlets.

Warehouse clubs. More and more space in these huge selling barns—chiefly Costco and Sam's Club (Wal-Mart's warehouse sibling)—is being devoted to electronics. These stores emphasize value over convenience, ambience, selection, or almost any other nicety. An annual member-ship fee of $35 to $40 is required, though a free temporary membership may be available. Widely used credit cards may not be accepted. There's usually no pressure to buy extended warranties since they're rarely even offered.

Catalog sellers and web sites. Nearly all the major electronics chains, mass merchandisers, and warehouse clubs sell home electronics via their web sites, but selection is typically more limited than in their stores. By contrast, just about anything you can buy at a well-stocked electronics store can also be ordered through the catalogs or web sites of vendors such as Buy.com, Crutchfield (*www.crutchfield.com*) and J&R Music World (*www.jandr.com*).

Their web sites usually provide interactive menus to help you tailor the choice of model to your needs. Prices are generally low but shipping can add up to 5 percent and can cost $100 or more for large TV sets or speakers. Returns can be expensive. You may have to pay for returns of items bought from the web sites of bricks-and-mortar chains, but many allow you to return items to chain outlets.

Audio boutiques. These exceptions to the general gigantism dominating home-electronics retail can often boast a courteous and knowledgeable staff that the chains can't quite match. Selection includes high-end products that the chains seldom sell, but some well-known brands may be left out.

Such capability has worked its way into some high-end DVD players.

SURROUND SOUND MARCHES ON. To get the most out of a DVD, you need surround sound. Dolby Digital is the surround sound most common on DVD movies. To take full advantage of it, you need a home-theater speaker system and a Dolby Digital receiver to manage them, in addition to your TV and DVD player.

You can buy those components separately or you can buy a system, speakers only, or a "home theater in a box," which often includes a receiver sometimes with a built-in DVD player as well. See "Setting Up a Home Theater" on the following page for more information.

PRODUCTS GROW SMALLER ... YET AGAIN. Manufacturers continue to shrink hard drives, batteries, and other parts of audio and video components. The MP3 player can be as small as an ink pen. Portable CD and DVD players can be as thin as 1 inch. "Executive sound systems" have shrunk minisystems into microsystems that fit readily on a desk or into flat systems that hang on a wall.

MORE OPTIONS BUT FEWER PROVIDERS. Even as consumers' ability to control how they see and hear content continues to expand, corporate mergers are further shrinking the number of companies that control the flow of content. Content providers now own media organizations and vice versa, with Internet service in the mix as well. GE owns NBC; Viacom owns CBS, MTV, VH1, and Blockbuster; Walt Disney owns ABC; Sony owns Columbia and Tristar; AOL Time Warner includes Warner Brothers and Turner/TNT. BMG owns Napster, and Vivendi Universal Net owns MP3.com and rollingstone.com, among others. These deals mean that, more than ever, forces other than viewer preference can affect what's available.

COPYRIGHTS AND WRONGS. At the same time, copyright issues are limiting control of content—and possibly increasing prices. The creators and publishers of content such as movies and music have legitimate claims to legal protection of what belongs to them. But copyright concerns have led to hardware that blocks you from copying a DVD title you've purchased onto a VHS tape for your personal use. (Expect similar roadblocks when DVD recorders go mainstream.) Blank CDs for recording music include a surcharge to cover royalties the music industry believes would otherwise be denied to musicians.

LESS PRIVACY. Every company with which you contract for your home entertainment seems to have gone full-throttle into data mining. Rent a videotape or DVD from Blockbuster or order pay-per-view on cable, and the transaction is recorded in some way. Ditto when you buy a CD off the web, choose a channel on your cable or satellite setup, or fill out a warranty card. You'd expect the original company to use that information to offer related products and services to you. But it's another thing to be bombarded with phone calls, letters, e-mail, and other offers from companies you've never heard of, simply because they have purchased data on you.

MORE COMPLEX CHOICES ALL AROUND. One more effect of the so-called digital revolution is that it's even harder to be an informed consumer. Products are more complicated, requiring you to study to make a smart choice.

More products involve a service provider—not just computers and cell phones but now some video equipment. Not only do you have to choose between competing services, but also once you've chosen and bought the hardware, you're committed to that provider—switching can involve paying hundreds of dollars more to buy new, provider-specific gear, as with satellite-TV equipment or DVRs.

More and more electronics components need to connect with one another, requiring compatible video and audio connections for best results. And competing formats mean that early adopters are betting that the format they choose will be the one that prevails, as manufacturers invent new media formats, music-encoding schemes, and connection specifications.

All this, of course, means a greater challenge for consumers shopping for home-entertainment products. That's where CONSUMER REPORTS can help.

SETTING UP A HOME THEATER

Adding surround sound to a TV can transform the viewing and listening experience even more than buying a bigger set.

Most TV sound can be improved by adding external speakers; a pair of self-powered speakers is a simple, easy way to do that. But for a real home-theater experience, you need a big TV, a video source (hi-fi stereo VCR or DVD player), a surround-decoding receiver/amplifier, and five speakers plus a subwoofer. For details on the components that make up a home-theater system, including home theater in a box and minisystems, see the articles later in this chapter. Here's an overview of the whole system:

Surround sound explained

Surround sound adds additional channels to familiar two-channel stereophonic sound for stronger movie-theater realism, allowing additional speakers to carry the multichannel sound found on movies.

What you'll hear depends on three things: the format used for the source (a TV show or DVD, for instance), the software decoder (on the receiver or DVD player) used to decipher the format, and the number of speakers you have. If your gear lacks the latest, most sophisticated decoder, it can still handle the TV broadcast or DVD, but it will do so with fewer audio channels and less dramatic effect. Conversely, state-of-the-art hardware can play older material only because new decoders are generally backward-compatible with early formats. Again, you'll hear fewer channels.

Here's a rundown on the major formats:

Dolby Surround, an early version of surround sound, is an analog encoding scheme used mostly for VHS movies and TV shows. It combines four channels into stereo soundtracks. With no decoder—say, on a TV—you'll hear stereo.

With a **Dolby Pro Logic** decoder, you'll hear four channels: left, right, center, and one limited-range surround channel. A newer version, **Pro Logic II,** has the same left, right, and center channels, but also has two discrete, full-range surround channels for a total of five channels. Most new receivers have Pro Logic II; older models may have only Pro Logic. You'll need four or five speakers for optimal sound.

The next step up is **Dolby Digital,** a digital encoding scheme that's also called Dolby Digital 5.1. Like Pro Logic II, it has full-range left and right channels in front and rear plus a center channel; it adds a subwoofer channel for deep bass (called ".1" because it's limited to low-frequency effects). Dolby Digital is used on digital media such as DVDs, digital cable, digital broadcast TV, and satellite transmissions. It can also decode material that uses Dolby Surround. Virtually all new receivers and some DVD players have Dolby Digital decoders. You'll need five full-range speakers and a subwoofer for optimal sound.

DTS (Digital Theater System) is a rival to Dolby Digital, also with six channels. It's offered on most new receivers and on some DVD players. It calls for the same speaker setup as Dolby Digital.

Dolby Digital EX and **DTS-ES** are "extended surround" formats that add either a center-rear surround channel or an extra pair of rear-surround speakers that go behind the listener. With Dolby Digital EX, the two flavors are referred to, respectively, as Dolby Digital 6.1 (with three surround speakers) and 7.1 (with four surround speakers). Both formats are still relatively new and not widely used on either equipment or programming. At this stage, they are mostly for video enthusiasts. You'll need seven or eight speakers for the full effect.

THX is a certification by Lucasfilm (owner of the standard). It indicates that a multi-channel audio product has passed certain performance and ergonomic tests and can process sound to stimulate movie-theater acoustics.

Connecting the components

VIDEO CONNECTIONS. The way you connect your audio and video equipment can affect the quality of the sound and images you receive. Here's a primer on the various kinds of connections you'll find on your equipment and what you can expect from each:

Even the best TV set won't live up to its potential without a high-quality video source and a high-quality connection. TV sets can have four different types of inputs, each of which accepts a specific kind of signal. Most TVs 25 inches and larger have an RF antenna/cable, composite-video, and S-video input; a component-video input is found mostly on higher-end models.

The **antenna/cable input,** sometimes called a UHF input, is the most common connection. It's the easiest to use because it's the only one that carries both sound and picture on one cable—in this case, the familiar coaxial cable. (The other video inputs carry only the picture, requiring the use of a separate pair of audio inputs to carry the sound.) The antenna/cable input is used with video sources such as antennas, cable boxes, and VCRs.

The **composite-video input** offers a small step up in quality. It uses a single standard RCA-style jack—a round jack (frequently yellow) with a single pin—to pass video signals. Two separate RCA jacks are used to pass the stereo audio signals. Most video sources have a composite video connection, including cable boxes and VCRs, as well as DVD players.

The **S-video input,** a round jack with four pins,

VIDEO CONNECTIONS

TVs can be connected to a host of other devices. All TV sets have RF antenna/cable inputs. Full-featured sets also have up to three additional types of video inputs. They are, in order of quality, composite-video, S-video, and component-video.

RF antenna/cable

Composite video

S-video

Component video

accepts even better-quality signals. This input separates the signal into two signals—color and luminance (black and white)—which improves the image quality. This can be used to connect your TV to DVD players, satellite receivers, and digital-cable boxes, along with digital, S-VHS, or Hi8 camcorders.

The **component-video input,** a three-cable connection found on some higher-end TVs, carries potentially the best-quality signals. It separates the video signal into three signals, two color and one luminance. This input is used primarily with DVD players. On HD-ready sets, this input is specially designed to handle signals from HDTV tuners and progressive-scan DVD players.

Some TVs have more than one S-video, composite-video, or component-video input so that you can connect several devices. On many sets, a composite-video or S-video input is on the front of the set for easy access.

AUDIO CONNECTIONS. The picture is only half the story. You also need to hook up your sound equipment. To obtain the audio from devices such as a VCR, DVD player, cable or satellite receiver, or camcorder, you generally connect one or a pair of audio inputs to your

SETTING UP A HOME THEATER: THE BASICS

Setting up a home theater can be complicated. The trick is arranging components in a way that maximizes their capabilities. The room you choose has a fundamental bearing on sound quality. Strike a balance between acoustically "live" (bare floor and walls) and "dead" (carpeted floor and curtained walls) for best sound.

Upholstered furniture, wall hangings, and stocked bookshelves can help deaden the front of a room. The back of the room should be live. The size and shape of room also matter. A 15'x12' room with an 8-foot ceiling is ideal. A square room can make bass sound boomy or uneven. The charts at right show "sweet spots" for various shapes of rooms.

If you want to be able to watch one cable TV channel while taping another, you'll probably need to attach an RF splitter and A/B switch. Otherwise, you'll probably be satisfied with a home-theater setup a little less elaborate than the one illustrated on the opposite page.

When hooking up components, go left to right across the back of the receiver. Here are steps to follow:

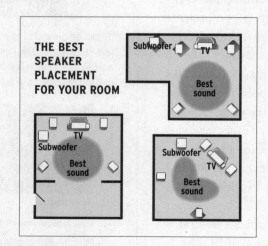

THE BEST SPEAKER PLACEMENT FOR YOUR ROOM

1. Connect the receiver to the audio devices with stereo patch cords.

2. Connect the video devices, using the best video signal that your TV set, receiver, and DVD player have: component video, if you have that; S-video, if you have that; or composite, in all video equipment.

3. With speakers, start with as close to the ideal as you can. The main speakers should form an equilateral triangle with you, the listener, and should be at the same height as your ears. The center speaker should be atop or below the TV and aligned with, or only slightly behind, the main speakers.

The surround speakers can be placed alongside the seating position, facing each other or facing the back wall. The subwoofer can go anywhere convenient, for starters.

4. Connect the speakers, observing polarity; connect the power cords.

5. Experiment with the speaker location and tweak the tone controls.

receiver, which routes sound to the speakers. Stereo analog audio inputs are labeled L and R for left and right. Newer multichannel receivers will also have coaxial or optical digital-audio inputs for providing surround sound; some have both. These are used for connecting a DVD player and some digital-cable and satellite receivers. Make sure the receiver's input matches the output of any device you want to connect—in other words, to use an optical output on the DVD player, you need to have an optical input on the receiver.

To output the sound, every multichannel receiver will have at least six speaker terminals so it can accommodate a surround-sound system with six speakers. You don't have to use all six terminals; you can use only two of these for a stereo setup, for instance. Some receivers also have a **subwoofer pre-amp out,** an output that carries unamplified low-frequency signals to an active (powered) subwoofer.

Some receivers have 5.1 **inputs,** six connectors that accept multichannel analog audio signals that another device, such as a DVD player that has a built-in Dolby Digital or DTS decoder or that plays DVD-Audio or SACD discs, has already decoded through a process that splits a signal into six or more audio channels. The inputs are typically marked Front

ONE EXAMPLE OF HOW TO SET UP A HOME THEATER

This receiver-based system uses an audio/video receiver as the nexus for TV signals from a cable box (it could also be from a satellite box or an antenna), along with video and audio signals coming from the DVD player, VCR (or DVR), and CD player. Sound is handled by the receiver, not the TV set. You use five speakers plus a subwoofer in a typical surround-sound setup.

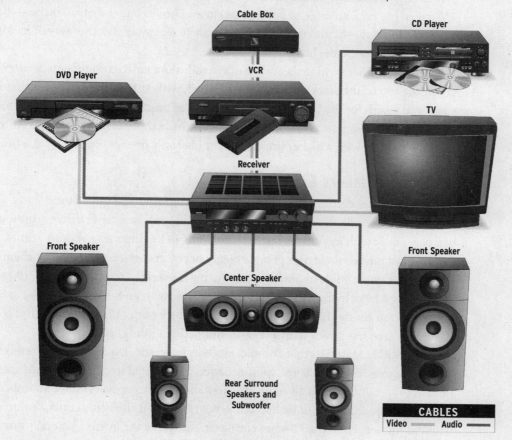

Cable Box

CD Player

DVD Player

VCR

TV

Receiver

Front Speaker

Center Speaker

Front Speaker

Rear Surround Speakers and Subwoofer

CABLES
Video ▬▬▬ Audio ▬▬▬

L and R, Rear (or Surround) L and R, Center, and Subwoofer (which also may be labeled LFE, for low-frequency effects).

User manuals should take you through much of the setup process. Hang on to them. Give yourself easy access to the back of the receiver and other components. You'll need good lighting to read the labeling on the back panels, so have a flashlight ready. Connect audio devices first, using the cables that came with each component.

To connect speakers, you typically strip off enough insulation from the ends of the wires to connect them, without shorting, to adjacent wires. Observe proper polarity; like a battery, a speaker has "+" and "−" terminals. (The insulation of one wire in each pair should have a distinguishing feature, such as color or striping.) Reversing polarity will cause a loss of bass.

You can plug almost all of your components into a two-prong AC power strip—preferably a unit with surge suppression. The exceptions are the three high-powered devices—the TV, receiver, and powered subwoofer. Plug those into the wall or into a three-prong AC power strip. Or you can plug all of your components into a power control center, which controls the entire system and can include surge suppression.

Arranging the equipment

Make sure your room has enough distance between you and the TV for comfortable viewing. The ideal for viewing a conventional, 30- to 40-inch set: 8 to 12 feet. That gives your eyes enough distance to visually knit the scan lines into a unified picture. A high-definition TV screen has no scan lines, so you can sit closer. For sets larger than 40 inches—flat panel or projection sets—figure on sitting more than 10 feet away. Another way of looking at it: The bigger the room, the bigger the TV can be.

Receivers generate more heat than other audio and video components, so they need to go on the top of the stack or on their own shelf, with at least a couple of inches of head space and a path for the heat to escape. If a receiver's surface becomes hot to the touch, try one of the following: turn down the volume; provide more cooling, perhaps with a small fan; use speakers with a higher impedance; or play only one set of speakers at a time.

Matching speakers & receiver

Speakers and the receiver must match in two ways: power and impedance.

POWER. Generally, the more power (measured in watts) a receiver delivers, the louder you can play music with less distortion. Each doubling of loudness uses about 10 times as much power. Most models these days provide plenty of power—at least 60 watts per channel.

Here's a quick guide to power requirements for various room sizes: 80 to 100 watts per channel for a large living room (15x25 feet or more with an 8-foot ceiling); 40 to 80 for an average living room (12x20 feet); 20 to 40 for a bedroom (12x14 feet). A "live" (echoey) room will need less power than a "dead" (muffled-sounding) room.

IMPEDANCE. Materials that conduct electrical current also resist the current's travel to varying degrees. This resistance, or impedance, is measured in ohms. Standard speaker impedance is 8 ohms, which all receivers can handle. Many speakers have an impedance as low as 4 ohms, according to CONSUMER REPORTS tests. All else being equal, 4-ohm speakers demand more current than 8-ohm speakers. The use of the former generally doesn't pose a problem at normal listening levels but may eventually cause a receiver to overheat or trip its internal overload switch when music is played very loud. Before buying 4-ohm speakers to regularly play loud music, check the manual or back panel of your receiver to confirm that the unit is compatible.

Some speakers overemphasize various frequencies when placed against the wall or tucked in a bookshelf. Manufacturers' recommendations can help you decide on the optimal placement in your particular room.

The best position for the main front speakers is an equilateral triangle whose points are the left speaker, the right speaker, and you, the listener (see the diagram on page 52). Try to place them at about the same height as your ears. The center speaker should be atop or below the TV and aligned with, or only slightly behind, the main speakers. The left and right surround speakers can be placed alongside the seating, facing each other or the back wall. The subwoofer can go anywhere convenient—under a table, behind the sofa. Watch out for corners, though. They accentuate the bass, often making it unacceptably boomy.

The fine-tuning

You can optimize the system by properly setting audio levels and taking advantage of some of your components' features.

DVD AUDIO SETTINGS. A DVD player can output each disc's audio signal in a number of ways. The raw "bitstream" signal is undecoded; use this setting if your receiver decodes Dolby Digital and DTS audio. If you have only a digital-ready (or DVD-ready) receiver and your DVD player has a built-in Dolby Digital or DTS decoder, use the "analog 6-channel output" setting, which outputs decoded audio to the receiver. And if you have only a stereo receiver or TV (or just stereo speakers), set the DVD player for "analog 2-channel;" this downmixes the multiple channels into two.

SUBWOOFER ADJUSTMENTS. Most powered subwoofers have two controls: cut-off frequency and volume level. The former is the frequency above which the subwoofer won't reproduce sound. If your main speakers are regular, full-range types (not satellites), set the subwoofer to the lowest setting, typically 80 hertz. If they're satellites with no woofers, see the manual regarding how to set up the satellite and subwoofer combination. Adjust the subwoofer's volume so its contribution is noticeable but subtle.

RECEIVER SETTINGS. Using your receiver's user manual as a guide, adjust the receiver, speaker by speaker, according to each speaker's size, distance from the listener, and sound level relative to the other speakers. With most audio systems, you should be able to sit where you will be listening and make the proper adjustments by using the receiver's remote control.

CAMCORDERS

Fine picture quality and easy editing have improved the functionality of these movie makers. That's especially true for digital models, which are replacing analog.

Home movies—those grainy, jumpy productions of yesteryear—have been replaced by home movies shot on digital or analog camcorders that you can edit and embellish with music using your PC and play back on your VCR, or even turn into video shorts to e-mail.

Digital camcorders generally offer very good to excellent picture quality, along with very good sound capability, compactness, and ease of handling. Making copies of a digital recording won't result in a loss of picture or sound quality.

Analog camcorders generally have good picture and sound quality and are less expensive. Some analog units are about as compact and easy to handle as digital models, while others are a bit bigger and bulkier.

What's available

Sony dominates the camcorder market, with multiple models in a number of formats. Other top brands include Canon, JVC, Panasonic, and Sharp.

Most digital models come in one of two formats: MiniDV or Digital 8. New formats such as the disc-based DVD-RAM and DVD-R and tape-based MicroMV have also appeared. Some digital models weigh as little as one pound.

MINIDV. Don't let the size deceive you. Although some models can be slipped into a large pocket, MiniDV camcorders can record very high-quality images. They use a unique tape cassette, and the typical recording time is 60 minutes at SP (standard play) speed. Expect to pay $9 for a 60-minute tape. You'll need to use the camcorder for playback—it converts its recording to an analog signal, so it can be played directly into a TV or VCR. If the TV or VCR has an S-video input jack, you can use it to get the best possible picture. Price range: $600 to more than $2,000.

DIGITAL 8. Also known as D8, this format gives you digital quality on Hi8 or 8mm cassettes, which cost $6.50 or $3.50 respectively, less than MiniDV cassettes. The Digital 8 format records with a faster tape speed, so a "120-minute" cassette lasts only 60 minutes at SP. Most models can also play your old analog Hi8 or 8mm tapes. Price range: $500 to $900.

DISC-BASED. Capitalizing on the explosive growth and capabilities of DVD movie disks, these formats offer benefits tape can't offer: long-term durability, a compact medium, and random access to scenes as with a DVD.

The 3¼-inch discs record standard MPEG-2 video, the same format used in commercial DVD videos. The amount of recording time varies according to the quality level you select: from 20 minutes per side at the highest-quality setting for DVD-RAM up to about 60 minutes per side at the lowest setting. DVD-RAM disks are not compatible with many DVD players, but the discs can be reused. DVD-R is supposed to be compatible with most DVD players and computer DVD drives, but the discs are write-once. Expect to pay $25 to $30 for a blank disc.

Most analog camcorders come in one of three formats: VHS-C, Super VHS-C, and Hi8. They usually weigh around 2 pounds. Picture quality is generally good, though a notch below that of digital.

VHS-C. This format uses an adapter to play in any VHS VCR. Cassettes most commonly hold 30 minutes on SP and cost $3.50. Price range: $300 to $500.

SUPER VHS-C. S-VHS-C is the high-band variation of VHS-C and uses special S-VHS-C tapes. (A slightly different format, S-VHS/ET-C, can use standard VHS-C tapes.) The typical S-VHS-C tape yields 30 minutes at SP and costs $6.50. JVC is the only brand that offers models in this format. Price range: $350 to $500.

HI8. This premium, "high-band" variant of 8mm (an analog format that is virtually extinct) promises a sharper picture. For full benefits, you need to use Hi8 tape and watch on a TV set that has an S-video input. A 120-minute cassette tape costs about $6.50. Price range: $200 to $400.

Key features

A flip-out **LCD viewer** is becoming commonplace on all but the lowest-priced camcorders. You'll find it useful for reviewing footage you've shot and easier to use than the eyepiece viewfinder for certain shooting poses. Some LCD viewers are hard to use in sunlight, a drawback on models that have only a viewer and no eyepiece.

Screens vary from 2½ to 4 inches measured diagonally, with a larger screen offered as a step-up feature on higher-priced models. Because an LCD viewer drains the battery pack faster than an eyepiece manifold does, you don't have as much recording time with an LCD viewer.

An **image stabilizer** automatically reduces most of the shakes from a scene you're capturing. Most stabilizers are electronic; a few are optical. Either type can be effective, though mounting the camcorder on a tripod is the surest way to get steady images. If you're not using a tripod, you can try holding the camcorder with both hands and propping both elbows against your chest.

Designing a camcorder means trying to strike the proper balance between picture quality, low-light performance, and image stabilization; we've seldom seen a camcorder that excels in all three areas. If you need a camcorder with very good low-light capability, check the specs.

Full auto switch essentially lets you point and shoot. The camcorder automatically adjusts the color balance, shutter speed, focus, and aperture (also called the iris or f-stop with camcorders).

Autofocus adjusts for maximum sharpness; manual focus override may be needed for problem situations, such as low light. (With some camcorders, you may have to tap buttons repeatedly to get the focus just right.) With many camcorders, you can also control exposure, shutter speed, and white balance.

The **zoom** is typically a finger control—press one way to zoom in, the other way to widen the view. (The rate at which the zoom changes will depend on how hard you press the switch.) Typical optical zoom ratios range from 10:1 to 26:1. The zoom relies on optical lenses, just like a film camera (hence the term "optical zoom"). Many camcorders offer a digital zoom to extend the range to 400:1 or more, but at a lower picture quality.

Regardless of format, analog or digital, every camcorder displays **tape speeds** the same way as a VCR. Every model, for example, includes an SP (standard play) speed. MiniDV and Digital 8 types have a slower, LP (long play) speed, which adds 50 percent to the recording time. A few 8mm and Hi8 models have an LP speed that doubles the recording time. All VHS-C and S-VHS-C camcorders have an even slower, EP (extended play) speed that triples the recording time.

With analog camcorders, slower speeds can worsen the picture quality. Slow-speed picture quality doesn't suffer on digital camcorders. Using slow speed, however, does mean sacrificing some seldom-used editing options and may restrict playback on other camcorders.

Quick review lets you view the last few seconds of a scene without having to press a lot of buttons. For special lighting situations, preset **auto-exposure settings** can be helpful. A "snow & sand" setting, for example, adjusts shutter speed or aperture to accommodate the high reflectivity of snow and sand.

A **light** provides some illumination for close-ups when the image would otherwise be too dark. **Backlight** compensation increases the exposure slightly when your subject is lit from behind and silhouetted. **An infrared-sensitive recording mode** (also known as "night vision," "zero lux," or "MagicVu") allows shooting in very dim or dark situations, using infrared emitters. You may use it for nighttime shots, although colors won't register at all in this mode.

Audio/video inputs let you record material from another camcorder or from a VCR, useful for copying part of another video onto your own. (A digital camcorder must have such an input jack if you want to record analog material digitally.) Unlike a built-in microphone, an external microphone that is plugged into a **microphone jack** won't pick up noises from the camcorder itself, and it typically improves audio performance.

Features that may aid editing include a **built-in title generator,** a **time and date stamp,** and a **time code,** which is a frame reference of exactly where you are on a tape—the hour, second, and frame. A **remote control** helps when you're using the camcorder as a playback device or when using a tripod. **Programmed recording** ("self-timer") starts the camcorder recording at a preset time.

Some camcorders can double as a **digital still camera** at the flip of a switch. Digital cameras, however, are far better for still photos.

How to choose

PERFORMANCE DIFFERENCES. Digital camcorders get high marks in CONSUMER REPORTS picture-quality tests. The top-performing models yield pictures that are sharp and free of streaks and other visual "noise" and have accurate color. Audio quality is not quite as impressive, at least using the built-in microphone. Still, digitals record pleasing sound that's devoid of audio flutter (a wavering in pitch that can make sounds seem thin and watery), if not exactly CD-like, as some models claim.

Typically, the best analog models we've tested are good—on a par with the lowest-scoring digitals. The lowest-scoring analog models delivered soft images that contained noticeable video noise and jitter, and they reproduced colors less accurately than any digital model. And while sound for 8mm and Hi8 analog camcorders is practically free of audio flutter, all the VHS-C analog camcorders suffered from some degree of that audio-signal problem.

RECOMMENDATIONS. If you don't want to spend a lot, an analog camcorder is a good value—many are now priced at about $300. Analog models may also appeal to you if you have little interest in video editing. If you want to upgrade, however, consider a digital model. Prices are as low as $500 and are continuing to fall.

Try before you buy. Make sure a camcorder fits comfortably in your hand and has controls that are easy to reach.

CAMCORDERS   ♦ **Ratings:** Page 202   ♦ **Reliability:** Page 296

CD PLAYERS

The familiar console CD player is rapidly being replaced by more capable devices.
Delivering superb performance at an affordable price, the CD is the music medium of the moment, having turned vinyl LPs into niche products for audiophiles and music collectors. But regular console CD players are losing ground to DVD players, which can play CDs along with DVDs, and to units that can record as well as play CDs.

Niche models are still thriving. Jukebox models can hold hundreds of discs. Portable players are now incorporating MP3 capabilities.

What's available

Sony dominates the CD-player category, making nearly one in three CD players sold. Other big sellers are Pioneer and Technics.

CONSOLE MODELS. Single-disc models have virtually disappeared. Multiple-disc changers, typically holding five or six discs, can play hours of music nonstop. A magazine changer uses a slide-in cartridge the size of a small, thick book. Cartridges double as convenient disc storage boxes. Carousel changers are easier to load and unload than the magazine type. (Most let you change waiting discs without interrupting the music.) They've taken over the market. Price range: $100 to $250.

MEGACHANGERS. Also known as CD jukeboxes, these typically store 100 to 400 discs. Marketed as a way to manage and store an entire music collection, most models let you segment a collection by music genre, composer, artist, and so forth. The unit flashes album titles as you hunt through the discs. Inputting all the necessary data can be a tedious task (made easier on models that connect to a computer keyboard). But it's worth the effort, because you can then set a jukebox to shuffle and play random selections all night or play discs only from your genre choice. To fit all those CDs, megachangers can be quite large. In fact, some may not fit the typical stereo rack. And all models aren't equally efficient: Some are inconvenient to load, or noisy and slow in selecting CDs. Price range: $170 to $450.

PORTABLE PLAYERS. Small, sporty, and single-disc, these have simple controls. A growing number of models also play CDs you record yourself, using both the CD-R and CD-RW formats (see CD player/recorders for more on these formats) and digital file formats such as MP3. Early portables often skipped or had poor-quality headphones. Today's players skip less, and many have good headphones that will convey decent sound. But some still have mediocre headphones; you'll enjoy better listening if you replace them.

Battery life is improving, but it varies considerably from model to model: In

CONSUMER REPORTS latest tests, batteries typically lasted 16 to 30 hours but went as long as 40 hours. Some models come with an AC adapter, and some have a built-in battery charger. Most portable players can be connected to other audio gear, and in that case many will play music as well as any home unit. Price range: $30 to $200.

Key features

Console models come with more features than portables. Their controls should be easy to see in dim light. A **calendar display** shows a block of numbers indicating the tracks on the active disc and highlighting the current track. As play continues, previous track numbers disappear—you can quickly see how many selections are left. A **numeric keypad** on the remote gets you to a particular track more quickly than pressing Up or Down buttons.

A **remote control** is convenient and now nearly standard equipment. Buttons should be grouped by function or color-coded and should be visible in dim light. Most CD remotes operate the player only.

Some changers and jukeboxes have a handy **single-play drawer** or slot so you can play a single disc without disturbing any already loaded. **Cataloging** capability offers various ways to keep track of the many CDs stored inside a jukebox, such as categorizing by genre.

Memory features that make track selection easy include **delete track,** which allows you to skip specified tracks but otherwise play a disc from start to finish, and **favorite track** program memory, which lets you mark your preferences. **Music sampling** (also called track scan) plays a few seconds of each selection. Most models can be programmed to play tracks in sequence, to shuffle play (look for nonrepeat shuffle), or to repeat a track. A **volume-limiter switch** lets you hear softer passages without having other sounds at ear-splitting levels.

People who do a lot of taping will appreciate **auto edit** (also called time fit for recording): You enter the cassette's recording time, and the CD player lays out the disc's tracks, usually in sequence, to fill both sides of your tape. With **comprehensive time display,** you

DVD-AUDIO AND SACD: TWO ALTERNATIVES

DVD-Audio and Super Audio CD (SACD) are formats that encode music into up to six channels, promising fuller, richer sound than from stereo CDs. Relatively few players can handle these formats. You should have six full-range speakers for optimal sound.

Both formats include interesting extras. SACD discs include song/artist identification that shows up on some players, and have the potential for graphics or video. Some SACD discs have a CD layer that allows them to deliver stereo sound on a plain CD player or a DVD player.

DVD-A music discs can include video, such as still pictures, slide shows, and short full-motion clips. DVD-A players have a video output that connects to a TV set.

Releases often include a Dolby Digital 5.1 or DTS version of the program for playback on conventional DVD players—backward compatibility for users who intend to, but haven't yet, invested in a DVD-A player.

In recent CONSUMER REPORTS tests, sound quality was subtly better than what you'd hear on a standard CD or DVD player, but you'd need a superb audio system to appreciate the difference.

DVD players with DVD-A support start at about $300. SACD-compatible DVD players also start at about $300. A few models can play both formats. Few discs currently come in these formats, and it's not clear how widespread they will be.

check time elapsed and time remaining for the current track and for the entire disc. **Running-time total** lets you total the time of tracks to be recorded to fit the maximum on a tape. **Music-peak finder** scans for the loudest passage in a track you're going to record, allowing you to adjust the tape deck's recording level correctly and quickly. **Fade out/fade in** performs the audio equivalent of a movie fade for less abrupt starts and endings. **Auto spacing** inserts a few seconds of silence between tracks.

With a **synchronizing jack,** you can connect a cable to a tape deck of the same brand so you can run both machines simultaneously. Those recording digitally to a MiniDisc recorder or a digital tape deck need a **digital output jack** to attach a fiber-optic or coaxial cable.

Portable features focus on sound-quality enhancement and power management. Most portables have a **bass-boost control** to compensate for the thin bass of poorer headphones. Some have a **digital signal processor** (DSP), which electronically simulates the ambience of concert-hall music.

Most portables have a **liquid crystal display** (LCD) showing which track is playing and a **battery-level indicator** that warns of low batteries. (The best indicators show a shrinking scale to reflect power remaining.) An **AC adapter** runs the player on house current and enables some players to charge rechargeable cells. Rechargeable batteries may cost extra.

Colorful "sports" models tend to be pricier than the rest of the pack and differ in a few other respects: Their lid is secured with a **latch** and sealed with a **rubber gasket,** and they have **rubberized plugs** covering jacks for an AC adapter and headphones. The latch keeps the lid closed so successfully that some sports models are a bit hard to open. The gasket and plugs help resist sand, dirt, and moisture, though you'll need to wipe off a player that's dusty or wet before you open it. Keep in mind that these players are **water-resistant,** not waterproof—the difference between a splash and total immersion.

A car kit, standard with some portables, consists of an adapter that powers the unit through a car's cigarette lighter and a cassette adapter that pipes the player's sound through the car's tape player and speakers. (You can also buy aftermarket kits at electronics or auto-supply stores.) Some adapters, CONSUMER REPORTS tests showed, add noise to the sound or otherwise compromised performance. A line-out jack is a better choice than the head-phone jack for connecting a portable to a component receiver or other gear.

How to choose

PERFORMANCE DIFFERENCES. Many CD players can produce excellent sound—accurate tonal balance and free of coloration or distortion. However, not all CD players are equally convenient to use.

Better home units have an uncluttered front-panel display with clearly labeled main buttons grouped together by function. They also include features that make it easy to produce tapes from CDs. For portable players, skip-free performance depends on a good buffer, a memory feature that scans the disc, continuously storing upcoming music (typically from 10 to 45 seconds, sometimes more) so the player won't cause audio dropouts. CONSUMER REPORTS tests also found that good shock absorption of the lower assembly that records the disc is also important. Some models skipped with just a mild jouncing, others only when

BUY THE RIGHT DISCS

Blank discs for use in computers can't be used in CD player/recorders. Look for the words "for digital audio recorders" on the package. Discs for music cost more than ones for computers. The price includes a surcharge to cover royalties that the music industry believes should be paid to musicians.

jolted hard. Battery life in recent tests varied from 5 to 40 hours of continuous play.

Headphones differ in comfort and performance. Comfort is very subjective, depending on the individual. Headphones tested by CONSUMER REPORTS ranged from decent to mediocre. For some models, at least, you can improve sound by buying replacement headphones. A decent set costs about $10 to $30.

RECOMMENDATIONS. If you're looking to play CDs in a home-theater setup, consider getting a DVD player instead of a CD player. Some are nearly as cheap as CD players. The price of CD player/recorders has also dropped enough to make them a reasonable alternative, with the premium for the extra functionality perhaps $100.

If you want to play only CDs, a multidisc changer will save you from having to swap discs in and out. Shoppers for portable players should weigh battery life heavily if they're frequent listeners. They should also pay particular attention to antiskip performance if they're active users.

CD PLAYER/RECORDERS

These devices make it easy to burn the music you want onto CDs. Because it's all digital, copies show no loss of quality.

Audio CD player/recorders let you make your own recordings and play back prerecorded material. They still cost more than CD players without recording capability, but prices are dropping. They sell as stand-alone units and as components of some minisystems.

There's another way to make your own music CDs: Record them using a computer. CD drives that burn CDs are now standard on many computers and can be as adept as component CD player/recorders, often doing it faster.

Both CD player/recorders and computer CD burners let you copy entire discs or dub selected tracks to create your own CD compilations. There's no quality lost in high-speed CD-to-CD dubbing. Recording speeds usually are real-time or 4x, which records in one-quarter of that time. (Computer CD burners can be as fast as 16x.)

With either approach, you can record to CD-Rs (discs you can record on only once) or to CD-RWs (rewritable discs that can be erased and rerecorded). CD-Rs play on almost any CD player, whereas CD-RWs generally play only on new disc players that are configured to accept them. Be aware that some older DVD players will have problems reading CD-R and CD-RW discs.

What's available

Audio CD player/recorders come from audio-component companies such as Denon, Harmon-Kardon, JVC, Philips, and Pioneer.

DUAL-TRAY MODELS. One tray is for play/record, another for play. Price range: $350 to $600.

CASSETTE DECKS: A FADING ALTERNATIVE

Cassette decks will someday give way to digital devices such as CD player/recorders. But for now, they're still the least expensive means of recording. Tape's inherent limitations—slow access to individual tracks, background hiss, and a limited ability to capture the whole audio spectrum—are not as problematic as they once were. Even inexpensive cassette decks usually include music search to find a particular track and Dolby B and C Noise Reduction (NR) to make playback clearer. (Dolby S, a step up, further enhances dynamic range—the ability to reproduce noiseless loud and soft passages.)

JVC, Pioneer, and Sony are the leading brands in this fading market. Dual-deck cassette players, priced from $100 to $350, are the most commonly sold type and are useful for copying tapes and playing cassettes in sequence for long stretches of uninterrupted music. Single-record dual-decks allow playback from both cassette wells but can record from only one; dual-record dual-decks allow playback and recording from both wells.

Single-deck cassette players, once the cheaper type, are now mostly expensive audiophile models, with a tape drive that's a cut above what's available in dual-deck mod-els. Single-deck models are worth considering if you do a lot of serious recording. The three-head design of many single-deck players lets you monitor music as you record it. Microphone inputs found on higher-end models allow live taping. Expect to pay $200 and up for two-head single-decks, with three-head single-decks starting at $300.

When shopping for a cassette deck, look for logically laid-out, clearly labeled controls, informative displays, and well-lighted cassette wells. You'll want separate adjustments for the recording level and left and right balance. Recording-level meters (typically, lighted displays that work like animated bar graphs) should clearly present sound levels. Playback controls should let you skip easily from one selection to the next, repeat a selection, play both sides of the cassette automatically (or even play the cassette endlessly), and rewind rapidly.

Which tape to use depends on how good it needs to sound. Type I (normal bias) has the narrowest dynamic range; Type IV (metal tape) the highest; Type II (high bias) is in between. Avoid bargain tapes with nonbrand names, but don't overbuy. Using expensive tape for making party tapes for a boom box is a waste of money.

CHANGER MODELS. These hold multiple discs, usually three for play and the fourth for play/record. Price range for changer models: $400 to $600.

Key features

The computer approach makes compiling "mix" discs pretty easy. Once a blank CD is inserted into a computer CD drive, the accompanying software displays a track list and allows you to "drag" the desired tracks into the lower panel. As you insert successive CDs, you can see the **playlist** for your CD-to-be and even change the order of the tracks, combine two or more tracks or files into one, or split a track or file into two or more. With CD recorders, you program your selections from up to three discs installed in the changer; the steps will be familiar to anyone who has programmed a CD changer. Most units give you a **running total** of the accumulated time of the tracks as you are programming them.

With both the computer option and a CD player/recorder, you must program selections from each disc in succession. **Defining tracks** on the CD onto which you're recording is accomplished with varying degrees of flexibility. How many track numbers a given player/recorder can add per disc, for example, differs from one model to another; additionally, assigning track numbers when you're recording from cassettes may be automatic or manual. (Such tracks are inserted automatically when recording from CDs.)

Text labeling lets you type in short text passages such as artist and song names, a much easier procedure with a computer keyboard than with a console's remote control.

The number of **delete-track modes** grants you flexibility, whether you need to delete one track or the entire disc. One-track, Multitrack, and All-disc are three common modes. An audio CD player/recorder typically has three playback modes: **Program** (used to play tracks in a specific order); **Repeat**; and **Random Play** (or Shuffle) plays tracks randomly.

Connection types can affect what external sources you're able to use to make a CD. A digital input jack may be optical or coaxial. An analog input jack lets you record your tapes and LPs. A **microphone input** offers a low-cost way for home musicians to make digital recordings of their performances. A **record-level control** helps you control loudness while recording digitally from analog sources—a problem you don't face when recording from digital sources. An **input selector,** included on some models, makes for faster connections than going through a menu process.

How to choose

PERFORMANCE DIFFERENCES. Either method of burning a CD—using an audio CD player/recorder or a computer—makes a recording that's audibly (even electronically) indistinguishable from the original CD.

Audio CD player/recorders excel in versatility; you can record from CDs, LPs, cassettes, and even TV or radio sound (anything, in fact, that you can connect to a sound system's receiver). This method is the clear standout for recording LPs, since connecting a turntable to a computer requires additional equipment.

The computer method has its own strengths. Because it affords a connection to the Internet, the computer option lets you burn downloaded MP3-encoded files onto CDs. A computer offers more setup choices when you're assembling your own CD from several prerecorded discs. And when you're recording from analog sources, the computer's burning software often includes sound processing that will reduce the snap and crackle of a vinyl LP or the tape hiss of a cassette tape.

RECOMMENDATIONS. The relatively low cost of making high-quality CDs makes CD recording a good alternative to making cassette tapes. If you're buying a CD player/recorder, first consider a changer model; its multidisc magazine or carousel will make it easy to record compilation CDs or to play uninterrupted music.

The computer-based CD-recording option allows you to record music from both CDs and the Internet. If you don't already have a CD-burning drive in your computer, you can buy it and the necessary software for about $160 to $250. If you're buying a new computer, you'll find that a CD-RW drive is standard equipment on many models. We'd expect any CD-burner drive to perform competently.

DVD PLAYERS
These play high-quality videos and also play CDs. Prices are surprisingly low.

As the fastest-growing consumer-electronics product in history—more than 13 million units were sold in 2001 alone—DVD players offer picture and sound quality that clearly surpasses what you'll get with a VCR. DVDs are CD-sized discs that can contain a complete two-hour-plus movie with a six-channel Dolby Digital or DTS soundtrack, plus extra material such as multiple languages, interviews, additional camera angles for chosen scenes, behind-the-scenes documentaries, and even entire replays of the movie with commentary by the director or some of the actors.

DVD players also play standard audio CDs. Prices on multidisc models are low enough for a DVD player to serve as a practical stand-in for a CD player. There is a catch if you record your own CDs: Some models may still have problems reading the CD-R and CD-RW discs that you record yourself.

The DVD player is still a product in transition. New capabilities include being able to play DVD-Audio or SACD (See "DVD-audio and SACD: Two alternatives," on page 60), two competing high-resolution audio formats designed to offer two- to six-channel sound. Coming are reasonably priced DVD recorders. For recording your favorite TV programs, VCRs or digital video recorders are the way to go for now.

What's available

Apex, Panasonic, Sony, and Toshiba are among the biggest-selling brands. DVD players are rapidly changing as manufacturers seek to differentiate their products and come up with a winning combination of features. You can choose from a console or portable model. Some consoles offer built-in karaoke features, MP3 and Windows Media playback, or the ability to play video games.

SINGLE-DISC CONSOLES. Console models can be connected directly to your TV for viewing movies or routed through your receiver to play movies and audio CDs on your home-entertainment system. More low-end models include all the video-output jacks you might want. Price range: less than $100 to more than $800.

MULTIDISC CONSOLES. Like CD changers, these players accommodate two to five discs. DVD jukeboxes that hold up to 300 discs are also available. Price range: $200 to $1,000.

PROGRESSIVE SCAN. Some DVD players are so-called progressive scan models. This provides HD-ready TVs with a sharper, more stable image by letting the set draw 480 consecutive lines of the image 60 times per second. (On a conventional TV, typically every other line is redrawn at that rate.)

You can use progressive-scan DVD players with a conventional TV, but you'll see the added benefit only with a set that supports 480p, such as a high-definition or HD-ready set. Price range: $200 to $300.

PORTABLES. These DVD players generally come with small but crisp wide-screen-format LCD screens and batteries that claim to provide three hours or more of playback. Some low-priced models don't come with screens; they're intended for users who plan connections only to TVs. You pay extra for the portability either way. Price range: $200 to $1,000.

WITH OLDER TVS

If you're connecting a DVD player to an older TV with only an antenna input, you'll need to add a special converter to convert the DVD player's composite video and audio output signal to an RF output signal.

Key features

DVD-based movies often come in various formats. **Aspect-ratio control** sometimes lets you choose between the 4:3 viewing format of conventional TVs (4 inches wide for every 3 inches high) and the 16:9 of newer, wide-screen sets. Portable DVD players with screens are generally in wide-screen format. (See "Digital screen shapes," on page 52.)

A DVD player gives you all sorts of control over the picture—control you may never have known you needed. **Picture zoom** lets you zoom in on a specific frame. **Reverse frame-by-frame** gives you backward incremental movement in addition to the **forward frame-by-frame** and **slow motion** that most players provide.

Black-level adjustment brings out the detail in dark parts of the screen image. If you've ever wanted to see certain action scenes from different angles, **multiangle capability** gives you that opportunity. Note that this feature and some others work only with certain discs.

Navigation around a DVD is easy. Unlike a VHS tape, DVDs are sectioned for easy navigation. **Chapter preview** lets you scan the opening seconds of each section or chapter until you find what you want. **Go-to by time** lets you enter how many hours and minutes into the disc you'd like to skip to. **Marker functions** allow easy indexing of specific sections.

A **composite connection** can produce a very good picture, but there will be some loss of detail and some color artifacts such as adjacent colors bleeding into each other. An **S-video output** can improve picture quality. It keeps the black-and-white and the color signals separated, producing more picture detail and fewer color defects than standard composite video.

Component video, the best connection you can get on a DVD player (but possibly lacking on the lowest-end models), improves on S-video by splitting the color signal, resulting in a wider range of color. If you use a DVD player attached with an S-video or component connection, don't be surprised if you have to adjust the TV-picture setup when you

---

DVD/VCR COMBOS: TWO VIDEO DEVICES IN ONE

DVD players are *the* hot electronics product, gaining favor for playing movies, though VCRs are still the device of choice for recording TV programming. Some consumers are trying to hedge their bets—and save space—by buying combination VCR/DVD players.

Combo players have many pluses. They measure only slightly larger than a VCR alone. Like separate units, they let you play a DVD or CD while recording something on videotape. Most allow you to copy DVD content onto tape, but only if the DVD has not been copy-protected (so forget about most movies). With combo units, there's only one device to connect to your TV. Some will work with the cable/antenna input that may be the only choice on older sets, but if you have a newer TV and don't mind making multiple connections, you can get better video by connecting the VCR and DVD to the TV's S-video, composite

video, or component-video inputs.

There are downsides to a hybrid device, however. Combination units may be less likely to have various features, such as VCR Plus, a feature that can simplify programmed recording, or the ability to see a gallery of still shots from a DVD's chapters. The combo units we recently tested didn't match stand-alone VCRs for picture quality, although the DVD picture quality was fine. If either component breaks you may lose both, because they share some common circuitry.

If CONSUMER REPORTS' experience is any indication, you get more for your money buying separate devices. A $70 VCR and a $100 DVD player could give you more features than a combo unit costing $200 to $300. Still, if compact size and easy connections are your top priorities, a VCR/DVD player combo may be just the ticket.

switch to a picture coming from a VCR or a cable box that uses a radio-frequency connection or composite connection.

One selling point of DVD is the ability to enjoy movies with **multichannel surround sound.** To reap the full benefits of the audio that's encoded into DVD titles, you'll need a Dolby Digital receiver and six speakers, counting a subwoofer. **Dolby Digital decoding built-in** refers to circuitry that lets a DVD player decode the six-channel audio encoded into DVD discs; without the built-in circuitry, you'd need to have the decoder built into the receiver or use a separate decoder box to take advantage of six-channel audio. (A Dolby Digital receiver will decode an older format, Dolby Pro Logic, as well.) Players also may support **Digital Theater System (DTS) decoding** for titles using that six-channel encoding format. When you're watching DVD-based movies, **dynamic audio-range control** helps keep explosions and other noisy sound effects from seeming too loud.

DVD players also provide features such as **multilingual support,** which lets you choose dialog or subtitles in different languages for a given movie. **Parental control** lets parents "lock out" films by their rating code.

How to choose

PERFORMANCE DIFFERENCES. In CONSUMER REPORTS tests, most DVD players delivered excellent picture quality, all but eliminating noise, jitter, and other aberrations typical of pictures from a VCR. They also offered CD-quality sound and, depending on the program material, multichannel capability. Some models may be more convenient to use than others. Remote controls vary considerably, so it's worth checking them out before making a purchase.

RECOMMENDATIONS. A DVD player offers better picture quality for movies than a VCR. Provided you have the receiver and speakers to back it up, the sound is also superior to that of a VCR. You'll need a VCR or a DVR to record, however.

Even a low-end DVD player will provide excellent video and audio. A single-disc model is cheaper, and it should do the job if you watch mostly movies. A multidisc console makes more sense if you also plan to play music CDs.

If your audio/video setup includes a receiver with built-in Dolby Digital and DTS decoding, you don't need to pay the premium to get these decoders on your DVD player. Such models tend to be among the more expensive. Even a low-end player will allow you to enjoy six-channel surround sound, assuming you have the required speakers.

If you plan to buy a digital TV, it may be worthwhile paying a little bit extra to get a progressive-scan DVD player. It will work with your conventional TV now and allow you to take advantage of the superior video quality when you get your digital set.

DVD PLAYERS ◆ Ratings: Page 226

DIGITAL VIDEO RECORDERS

DVRs outperform VCRs in many ways, but you'll still need a VCR to archive recordings.

Digital video recorders (DVRs) combine the easy navigation of a DVD player with the recording capability of a VCR and the convenience of a program guide. These set-top receivers have hard drives much like those in computers, generally with space for 20 to 60

hours of programming, although capacities can go as long as 320 hours. Some DVRs are integrated into devices such as satellite-TV receivers or digital TV decoders. Depending on which provider and plan you choose, you usually pay for the service as well as the equipment—either a one-time activation charge or a monthly fee on top of your current cable or satellite-TV bill.

Because they can record and play at the same time, DVRs allow you to pause (and rewind or fast-forward) the current show you're watching, picking up where you left off. Should you pause a one-hour show for 10 or 15 minutes at the beginning, you can resume watching it, skip past all the commercials, and catch up to the actual live broadcast by the end of the show. Dual-tuner models can record two programs at once, even as you're watching a third recorded program.

A DVR does not replace your usual programming source. You must still get broadcasts via cable, satellite service, or antenna. Program guides are downloaded via your phone line, generally late at night to avoid tying up the line. These guides are customized according to which broadcast channels are available in your area and which cable or satellite service you subscribe to.

What's available

Most DVRs resemble VCRs in size and shape but don't have a slot for a tape or disc. (The internal hard drive is not removable.) They connect to your television like a cable or satellite receiver, using composite, S-video, or RF antenna outputs to match the input of your set.

There are only two service providers, TiVo and ReplayTV. Hardware prices depend mostly on how many hours of programming you can store; service charges vary. The DVRs intended for use with one provider will not work with the other.

TiVo, the older of the two companies, has offered service since late 1999. You can buy the equipment directly from TiVo, from AT&T Broadband, or from Hughes or Sony under their brand names. Price range: $300 to $400.

Service requires a paid subscription of $13 per month or $250 for the life of the DVR (transferable if you sell it). You can also get a DirecTV satellite receiver that incorporates TiVo capability. Price range: about $400, but often discounted; TiVo service charges (with the purchase of a satellite receiver, $10 a month or a one-time fee of $250) still apply.

Recently acquired by SonicBlue, ReplayTV offers some models bundled with lifetime service included in the equipment price. Newer models don't include service in the purchase price but carry a one-time activation fee of $250. In either case, you must buy equipment directly from the company. Price range: $450 to $1,800.

Some ReplayTV models let you distribute programs to other ReplayTV owners via the Internet. ABC, CBS, and NBC and their parent companies have filed suit against SonicBlue, citing copyright concerns.

Key features

A recorder's **hard-drive capacity** varies in actual usage. Like digital cameras, DVRs record at **different compression settings** and thus different quality levels. For the best image quality, you have to record programming at the DVR's lowest level of compression. To get the maximum capacity advertised, you have to use the highest level of compression, which gives the lowest quality. For example, a model that advertises a 30-hour maximum capacity will fit only about nine hours at its best-quality setting.

The **program guide** is an interactive list of the programs that can be recorded by the DVR for the next 7 to 10 days. You can use it to select the show currently being broadcast to watch or record—or you can search it by title, artist, or show type for programs you want to record automatically in the future.

Custom channels, available with some models, are individualized groupings of programs according to your preferences; the feature allows you to set up your own "channel" for something like crime dramas or appearances by William Shatner, whether on "Star Trek," a talk show, or any other programming. A DVR can also record a specified show every time it runs.

A **remote control** is standard. Common features include **instant replay, fast-forward, rewind,** and **pause** of a live program. The newest ReplayTV models allow users to **stream video** to other ReplayTV units in the home using an Ethernet port.

How to choose

PERFORMANCE DIFFERENCES. At the highest-quality settings, the picture quality of DVRs in recent CONSUMER REPORTS tests fell below that of most DVD players and was on a par with that of high-quality VCRs. At the lowest-quality setting, picture quality matched run-of-the-mill VHS VCRs standard play (SP), at their best recording speed. Audio quality is a notch below CD quality.

Ultimately, the DVR's picture quality, like the VCR's, depends on the quality of the signal coming in via your cable or satellite provider. A noisy or mediocre signal will produce mediocre digital recordings.

RECOMMENDATIONS. TiVo and ReplayTV represent an intriguing technology, but the market is still developing. No one can say for sure whether the technology will prove compelling enough for these products and services to build the broad customer base they need to succeed in the marketplace. That said, your own viewing habits can provide the best indication of whether a DVR is worth your consideration. Avid TV watchers are prime candidates, as are those who seldom watch TV at prime time but want to see prime-time programming. DVRs are also a good bet for those people who hate sitting through commercials.

If satellite dishes are an option, consider a dish receiver that includes a DVR. Keep in mind that you'll have to pay a separate fee for the DVR service. Satellite DVRs work only with satellite programming and won't record from cable or an antenna.

Today's DVR can't replace a VCR, which you'll need if you want to make a permanent copy of what you record. Consider a DVR as a companion product, not a replacement, for your VCR.

HOME THEATER IN A BOX

No time to mix and match speakers and receiver? All-in-one systems can minimize the hassle, although some make it tough to hook up other components.

Good speakers and the other components of a home theater cost less than ever. But selecting all those components can be time-consuming, and connecting them is a challenge even for audiophiles.

You can save some hassle by buying an all-in-one product that combines a receiver with a six-speaker set. And unless your needs are very demanding, you will compromise little on quality.

A "home theater in a box" combines, in a single package, all you need for the guts of a home theater: a receiver that can decode digital-audio soundtracks and a set of six compact, matched speakers—three front, two surround, and a subwoofer. You'll also get all the cables and wiring you need, labeled and color-coded for easy setup. Usually the presumption is that you already own a TV and a VCR or DVD player, although some systems come with a separate DVD player or have one built in to the receiver.

What's available

Sony, Kenwood, Pioneer, and Yamaha account for more than half of sales, with Sony commanding almost a third of the market. The cheapest models probably don't include a DVD player. Expect to pay about $300 for a basic system, $500 to $750 for a system capable of handling digital signals and a powered subwoofer. Systems aimed at audiophiles can cost $2,000 or more.

Key features

The receivers in home-theater-in-a-box systems tend to be on the simple side. They usually include both Dolby Digital and DTS decoders. Controls should be easy to use. Look for a front panel with displays and **controls** grouped by function and labeled clearly. **Onscreen display** lets you control the receiver via a TV screen.

Switched AC outlets let you plug in other components and turn on the whole system with one button. Some receivers offer **sleep,** which turn the receiver on or off at a preset time. The included receivers also offer about 20 or more presets you can use for AM and FM stations.

Remote controls are most useful when they have clear labels and different-shaped and color-coded buttons grouped by function. A universal remote can control devices made by the same manufacturer or by others.

To get the best picture quality, look for **component video outputs** on the receiver that can connect to relatively high-end TVs; not many receivers have these outputs. Instead, most have the next-best output, **S-video,** which is better than composite-video or RF (antenna) connections.

Look also for **S-video inputs,** which let you connect an external DVD player, digital camcorder, or certain cable or satellite boxes. Any player you might want to connect will need the same digital-audio connections, either optical or coaxial, as those of the included receiver. And if you want to make occasional connections at the front—perhaps for a camcorder or an MP3 player—you'll need **front-panel inputs.**

Home-theater-in-a-box receivers that do not decode digital audio may have **5.1 inputs;** these accept input from the decoder in a DVD player or other components with multichannel audio signals.

DSP (for **digital signal processor**) modes use a computer chip to duplicate the sound measurements of, say, a concert hall. Each mode represents a different listening environment. A **bass-boost** switch amplifies the deepest sounds. You are less likely to find stand-alone receiver controls such as a graphic equalizer.

A **subwoofer** may be powered or unpowered. Either type will do the job, but a powered subwoofer requires fewer wires, provides more control over bass, and lets a powered receiver drive the other speakers.

Models with an **integrated DVD player** typically have fewer features than do stand-alone DVD players. Features to expect are **track programmability** (more useful for playing CDs than DVDs), **track repeat,** and **disc repeat.** If you want a more fully featured player, a stand-alone DVD player may be the wiser choice.

How to choose

PERFORMANCE DIFFERENCES. In recent tests, CONSUMER REPORTS found that performance doesn't always depend on price. The receivers of these systems generally had very good FM tuners and adequate power, plus they did a fine job of switching signals. But performance fell short of component systems, and in terms of features, the boxed systems were a notch below component receivers, particularly in how easy their remote controls and onscreen menus were to use.

RECOMMENDATIONS. Home theaters in a box offer convenience and decent sound, better than you'd get from a typical minisystem with home-theater capability. The trade-off for that convenience is that you'll generally have to settle for less than the best in receiver and speaker technology.

HOME THEATER IN A BOX ◆ Ratings: Page 230

MINISYSTEMS

These all-in-one sound systems offer decent sound in an economical, convenient package.

A minisystem can be just the ticket if you're cramped for space or don't have the time or inclination to search out individual components and set them up. Minisystems typically include a receiver, an AM/FM tuner, a CD changer, and a dual-cassette tape deck in a bookshelf-sized box with two separate speakers. The sound on the better models is quite good, but even the best won't match the sound quality you can get from a component-based system. Still, a minisystem costs considerably less than the $1,000 or so you'd pay for a full complement of decent components, so it can be a good value for many listeners.

BOOM BOXES: MUSIC TO GO

Slim down a minisystem, ruggedize it for the outdoors, give it a handle, an antenna, and a battery, and it's a boom box. Basically a minisystem you can take with you (though they weigh roughly 10 to 20 pounds), boom boxes come as one-piece units (relatively full-featured, with a single CD player and sometimes just one speaker) or as larger, heavier, two- or three-piece units with detachable speakers (and possibly a subwoofer), more powerful amplification, and a CD changer. There are also hybrids.

The nondetachable speakers of small boxes usually can't reproduce sound faithfully. Bigger models offer respectable sound quality, though still not on par with a decent minisystem or component system. Nor do such models play bass as loudly or deeply as a good minisystem does.

Boom boxes have some of the same features as min-isystems, along with others that are relevant to portability. AC/DC power lets you plug in the system to conserve battery power. Built-in battery charging uses nickel-cadmium batteries (sometimes included) that recharge when your unit is connected to AC power. Auto power-off can cut the power, which conserves the battery.

Antishock circuitry minimizes the effect of any blows or vibrations; the newer standard, called Generation 2, is intended to help compensate for excessive movement both horizontally and vertically. Antishock memory provides buffering to aid in CD playback amid vibrations–the more seconds of memory, the better. Certain models are also water-resistant.

Look for sufficient audio power and a good remote control. Prices range from $25 to $150, with multipiece models starting at about $50.

What's available

Aiwa is the dominant brand. Other top-selling brands include Panasonic, Philips, RCA, Sharp, and Sony. Three-quarters of the models sold are two-channel stereo systems. You'll also find surround-sound systems that come with multichannel decoders like Dolby Digital on the receiver. Such systems complement the usual two speakers with additional speakers for center- and surround-channel sound.

Models with a CD player/recorder instead of a playback-only CD changer are becoming more common. Some systems eliminate the tape deck for maximum compactness.

Most minisystems integrate everything but the speakers into a console that's more or less a 12-inch cube with a black or silver chassis and blinking displays. More compact minisystems, or microsystems, are as narrow as 6½ inches—considerably smaller than a 17-inch standard-sized component. Price range: $100 to $500. Lower-priced minisystems may have limited power and anemic bass. Buying one of the more expensive models may get you more amplifier power, CD recording capability, Dolby B noise reduction, or more speakers.

Key features

Minisystems have some of the same features of full-sized components. But controls are more integrated, and displays are often more vivid, even hyperactive.

Minisystems vary in how much power their **amplifiers** deliver to the speakers—from 15 to 70 watts per channel. In recent tests, CONSUMER REPORTS found that all the systems tested, regardless of claimed wattage, produced enough sound to fill the typical office, dorm room, or bedroom, but would probably strain in a large room or noisy party. Also, power ratings in minisystem ads are calculated in so many different ways that the claims are of little use when you're comparing brands.

Among worthwhile CD-player features, **play exchange** lets you change the CDs that are not being played without interrupting the one being played. **Direct-track access** lets you go straight to a specific track. A display of the **time remaining** on either the track or the disc is useful when you're taping off a CD.

Music peak finder sets the recording level for the highest sound level on the disc, and **digital output** lets you record onto a CD or MiniDisc using a separate recorder. Some models can play CD-R or CD-RW discs you've recorded yourself.

Some models have **dual-cassette tape decks;** such players are becoming less important and somewhat less common, given the predominance of CDs. If you are a tape listener, though, one feature CONSUMER REPORTS considers important for basic tape use is **auto reverse,** so you don't have to flip the tape over to play the second side. An **auto tape counter** helps find a particular location on a tape.

High-speed dubbing doubles the speed when you're copying from one tape onto another, though with some loss of quality. If you're likely to play the tapes on a good car stereo or component system, look for the ability to record and play **Type II tapes** and for **Dolby B Noise Reduction,** which reduces background hiss.

Full-logic controls are soft-touch electronic buttons on the body of the device. The remote control may group two or more functions on one button, sometimes confusingly, although remotes for the latest models have improved. A few models have a **microphone input jack,** along with **karaoke capability.**

A **subwoofer output** lets you connect a separately powered subwoofer, helpful for maximizing the lowest tones from a movie's surround-sound encoding. (This is not the same thing as a "built-in powered subwoofer," which is a speaker component.) Instead of bass and treble tone controls, some models provide a three- or five-band **equalizer,** which gives you slightly more control over the full audio spectrum and is a bit easier to use. Some models have only **tone settings** such as Pop, Jazz, and Classical, which automatically determine the bass/treble mix, often overboosting the bass in the process.

A **clock** lets you program the system to turn on at a predetermined time; an accompanying **timer** lets you make timed recordings. Some systems permit you to set the cassette deck to record from the radio, just as you time-shift with a VCR.

How to choose

PERFORMANCE DIFFERENCES. Overall sound quality varies, largely depending on the quality of the speakers. Models in the last round of testing by CONSUMER REPORTS were judged anywhere from fair to very good for sound quality. Most systems had adequate power for their speakers, although a few distorted the sound when played at very high volumes.

The FM tuners on most minisystems are fine, CONSUMER REPORTS has found. The AM tuners are mediocre, but that's true of component receivers, too. The CD players' sound quality is typically excellent across the board. Tape deck performance was adequate for playing and recording cassettes, according to the most recent CONSUMER REPORTS tests.

RECOMMENDATIONS. By bundling all the major audio functions in one package, a minisystem can save you the trouble of choosing separate components—and several hundred dollars in the bargain. While these units would disappoint a demanding listener, the qual-

MEMORY FOR MUSIC
Figure on roughly one minute of music per megabyte of memory to save MP3 files at the CD-quality level.

ity of the better minisystems is surprisingly good considering the price. Don't expect top sound quality much below $150, however.

Take along a few familiar CD recordings to play when you go to the store. If you expect to play tapes much, consider trying out a few cassettes as well. Adjust the tone controls to see if you like the sound. Check out the controls and the appearance, which can be anything from sedate to high-tech. Ask about return or exchange policies in case the sound of the minisystem isn't to your liking when you get it home.

MINISYSTEMS ♦ **Ratings:** Page 248

MP3 PLAYERS

They usually store at least a CD's worth of music files. You'll have to take the time to load them, and legal controversy still surrounds some usage.

MP3 encoding is currently the predominant means of compressing music files for digitizing music. Many of those files are transferred from computers to handheld MP3 players. Despite copyright-infringement lawsuits by the music and movie industries, free music-sharing web sites carry on. The sites let users download music files for transfer to MP3 players or burning onto CDs. The music industry has responded with subscription-based services that allow you to stream or download music and play it on your computer. (One service, Pressplay, allows a few songs to be burned each month.)You can also load these small devices with music "ripped" from CDs, creating your own custom playlists and giving you new ways to manage your music library. Many MP3 players look like portable radios, headphones and all. Others resemble large pens or watches. MP3 playback has been incorporated into some digital cameras and even cell phones, as well as some CD players and Sony's MiniDisc player. Music can be encoded digitally in a number of formats; MP3 is the best known. The abbreviation stands for Moving Pictures Expert Group Layer 3, a file format that can compress music from one-tenth to one-twelfth the space it would ordinarily take.

Other encoding schemes include Windows Media Audio (WMA) and Adaptive Transform Acoustic Coding (ATRAC), a proprietary format used by Sony products.

What's available

More than 30 brands of MP3 players are on the market. Sony and SonicBlue, which makes the Rio line, are the biggest brands, followed by RCA, Samsung, Creative Labs, and other, smaller brands. Some hybrid models incorporate CD-player functionality and PDA-like features.

Players come in all sizes and shapes. Many are quite small. A player with 64 megabytes (MB) of memory holds about an hour of music recorded at CD-quality setting. A player with 128 MB holds twice that. The MP3 standard also lets you save music at lower sampling rates; this may diminish quality but increases the amount of music you can store.

High-capacity versions (sometimes called "jukeboxes") are larger, similar in size to a portable CD player, and store the music on a hard drive. These currently store as much as 20 gigabytes (GB), equivalent to more than 300 hours of music.

Many devices offer the option to add more memory via card slots, or "backpacks" on the unit. Players typically come with some combination of internal and/or external memory such as CompactFlash, MultiMedia Card, or Smart Media. Some models use MagicGate (an encrypted-audio version of Sony's existing MemoryStick media), or SecureDigital. Additional memory can cost anywhere from $10 to more than $150, depending on what's compatible with your player.

All players are battery-powered and have headphone outputs, along with a means of connecting to a computer for file transfer. Price range: $90 to $300 for regular players; $300 and up for high-capacity players.

Key features

MP3 players come with **software** for interfacing with a computer, using a Universal Serial Bus (USB) or less often, the faster FireWire connection. Most support Windows and many support Macs; more manufacturers are working toward Mac compatibility. (Apple's iPod is now compatible with Windows.) The computer-to-player interface consists of software drivers that let the computer and player communicate, along with a software application for transferring files to the player's memory. Some players are represented as hard-drive icons on your computer's desktop for easy drag-and-drop transfer of files. Many players are bundled with a more fully featured software application, such as MusicMatch or Real Jukebox, that helps you keep track of your MP3 files, manage playlists, and record songs from audio CDs.

On many players, the **firmware**—the player's built-in operating instructions—can be upgraded so the player does not become obsolete. Upgrades can add or enhance features, fix bugs, and add support for other formats and operating systems. (Check the manufacturer's web site for such upgrades.) Most upgrades these days are to eliminate bugs.

LCD screens on most players show such information as track number, song title, and memory used. **Volume, track forward/reverse,** and **pause-play** controls are standard. Most have play modes such as Repeat All and Random. A **customizable equalizer (EQ) setting** gives you the most control over the sound, but some units have just a simple bass boost control. Many also have presets for various music types (rock, classical, and so forth), along with viewable song lists.

Standard players generally use one or two AA or AAA batteries, either alkaline or rechargeable. Most high-capacity models use four AA rechargeable batteries. Either alkaline or rechargeable batteries are preferable to nonremovable batteries; when these no longer hold a charge, the player must be professionally serviced. A **battery-life indicator** on most models helps keep track of how much power is left.

A number of players incorporate an **FM radio tuner.** Some MP3 players have features more commonly found on a personal digital assistant (PDA), such as **voice recording** and **data file storage capability.** (PDAs that run the newest version of the Pocket PC operating system from Microsoft, and some Sony PDA models, can play MP3-encoded files. Handspring's Visor clones of Palm PDAs have an expansion slot to which you can attach an MP3 player.) Certain models can be used to transfer data files between computers, sometimes via the external memory card.

How to choose

PERFORMANCE DIFFERENCES. In recent CONSUMER REPORTS tests, the processing necessary to turn music into an MP3 file led to very slight degradation of the audio signal on most models, evidenced by noise or a muffling in some frequency ranges. Poor sound quality was more likely to be caused by mediocre or poor headphones bundled with the player. These can be replaced, so the problem can be remedied easily and cheaply.

CONSUMER REPORTS tests found that the players will run between 5 and 24 hours before their batteries give out—a wide range. Most play eight hours or more. Manufacturers' specifications are useful guides to battery life. Getting started can be tricky with some devices. When CONSUMER REPORTS connected some tested models to a computer, the PC often didn't recognize the player, and we had to resort to trial and error.

Upgrading firmware also proved time-consuming. MP3 players use one of two methods for upgrading; one method, which executes the upgrade file on the PC while the player is still attached, can cause permanent damage to the player if there's even a slight interruption during execution.

RECOMMENDATIONS. Memory size counts. For people who like to have lots of music in a small package, we recommend a standard MP3 player that has some memory built in (often 64 MB, but ranging from 32 to 128 MB) yet allows expansion via external memory cards. A 64-MB card usually costs $35 to $70. If capacity is more important than the smaller size, a high-capacity model would be a better choice. The 20 GB of storage on the most capacious models provides enough space to archive and organize a sizable library of music. Some let you record from an audio system onto the player without a computer.

If you want to minimize the odds that your player will fall behind the technology curve, look for a player with upgradable firmware that can accommodate newer encoding schemes or variations of MP3 compression. The more additional formats a model can play—such as WMA or ATRAC—the more flexibility you have in downloading and transferring music files now and in the future.

Before you buy, make sure the player is compatible with your Windows or Mac computer (including the version of the operating system your computer uses) and that your computer has the USB or FireWire connection the player requires. (Apple's iPod supports FireWire.) Also, look for LCD displays and controls that are easy to read and controls that can be worked with one hand, as you would with other handheld devices.

RECEIVERS

For a home-theater surround-sound system, look for a receiver that can decode Dolby Digital and DTS soundtracks.

The receiver is the brain of an audio/video system, providing AM and FM tuners, amplifiers, surround sound, and switching capabilities. Receivers have connections for various audio components (CD player, cassette deck, turntable, multiple speakers), and most also

HOW MUCH POWER DO YOU NEED?

These days even inexpensive receivers have plenty of power. But if you want to figure out how much power your sound system actually needs, here's one way to do it:

First, assess the sound "liveness" of your listening room. A space with hard floors, scatter rugs, and plain wood furniture will be acoustically "live"; one with thick carpeting, heavy curtains, and upholstered furniture is considered relatively "dead."

Locate the room size (in cubic feet) and liveness type in the chart and note the multiplier. Look up the speakers' minimum power requirement, as determined by the manufacturer, in the speakers' owner's manual. To determine the watts per channel needed, multiply that figure by the multiplier.

For a 4,000-cubic-foot room with average acoustics, the multiplier is 1.5. With speakers that require 12 watts of power, the minimum amplification you would need to drive the speakers at moderately high volume is 18 watts of power per channel (1.5 times 12). To do justice to bass-heavy music, double or triple that figure.

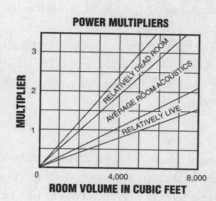

POWER MULTIPLIERS

MULTIPLIER

RELATIVELY DEAD ROOM
AVERAGE ROOM ACOUSTICS
RELATIVELY LIVE

ROOM VOLUME IN CUBIC FEET

handle video sources (TV, DVD player, VCR, satellite system). Even as receivers accumulate new audio-switching capabilities, features that were common when receivers were the center of audio systems—tape monitors and phono inputs—are disappearing. Manufacturers say they must eliminate those less-used features to add others.

What's available

Sony is by far the biggest-selling brand. Other top-selling brands include Denon, JVC, Kenwood, Onkyo, Panasonic, Pioneer, RCA, and Yamaha. Most models now are "digital," designed for the six-channel surround sound formats encoded in most DVDs and some TV fare. Here are the types you'll see, from least to most expensive:

STEREO. Basic receivers accept the analog stereo signals from a tape deck, CD player, or turntable. These receivers provide two channels that power a pair of stereo speakers. For a simple music setup, add a cassette deck or a CD player. For rudimentary home theater, add a TV and VCR. Power typically runs 50 to 100 watts per channel. Price range: $125 to $250.

DOLBY PRO LOGIC. Dolby Pro Logic is the fading analog home-theater surround-sound standard. Receivers that support it can take three front channels and one surround channel from your TV or hi-fi VCR and output them to five speakers: three in front, and one or two in back. Most receivers supporting the Dolby Pro Logic standard are "digital-ready," which means they have the capability to send six channels of predecoded sound to the speakers. "Ready" means you must use a DVD player with a built-in digital decoder. (You won't be able to decode other digital audio sources such as satellite TV.) Power for Dolby Pro Logic models is typically 60 to 100 watts per channel. Price range: $150 to $250.

DOLBY DIGITAL. Now representing the prevailing digital surround-sound standard, Dolby Digital receivers have a built-in decoder for true six-channel audio capability: front left and right, front center, two rear with discrete wide-band signals, and a powered subwoofer for bass effects. Dolby Digital is also the sound format for most DVD, high-definition TV (HDTV), digital cable TV, and some satellite TV broadcast systems. To take advantage of this capability, also called Dolby AC-3, you'll need speakers that can reproduce full-spectrum sound well. Receivers with digital decoding capability can also accept a signal that has been "digitized," or sampled, at a given rate per second and converted to digital form. Price range: $200 to $500 or more.

DTS. Receivers that add Digital Theater Systems capability support an additional, less common form of digital surround sound that is used in some movie tracks. Price range: $250 to $1,000 and up.

THX-CERTIFIED. The high-end receivers that meet this quality standard include full support for Dolby Pro Logic, Dolby Digital, and DTS. THX Select is the standard for components designed for small and average-size rooms; THX Ultra is for larger rooms. Price range: $800 to $2,500 and up.

Key features

Controls should be easy to use. Look for a front panel with displays and controls clearly labeled and grouped by function. **Onscreen display** lets you control the receiver via a TV screen, a squint-free alternative to the receiver's tiny LED or LCD. **Switched AC outlets** (expect one or two) let you plug in other components and turn the whole system on and off with one button.

Remote controls are most useful when they have clear labels and buttons that light up, come in different shapes, and are color-coded, easy to access, and grouped by function—a goal that is seldom achieved in receiver remotes. A **learning remote** can receive programming data for other devices via their remote's infrared signal; on some remotes, the necessary codes on other manufacturers' devices are built-in.

Input/output jacks matter more on a receiver than on perhaps any other component of your home theater. Clear labeling, color coding, and logical groupings of the many jacks on the rear panel can help avert setup glitches such as reversed speaker polarities and mixed-up inputs and outputs. Input jacks situated on the front panel make for easy connections to camcorders, video games, MP3 players, digital cameras, MiniDisc players, and PDAs.

A stereo receiver will give you a few audio inputs and no video jacks. Digital-ready receivers with Dolby Pro Logic will have 5.1 inputs; these accept input from a DVD player with its own built-in Dolby Digital decoder, an outboard decoder, or other components with multichannel analog signals.

S-video and **component video jacks** allow you to route signals from DVD players and other high-quality video sources through the receiver to the TV. **Tone controls** adjust bass and treble. A **graphic equalizer** breaks the sound spectrum into three or more sections, giving you slightly more control over the full audio spectrum. Instead of tone controls, some receivers come with tone styles such as Jazz, Classical, or Rock, each accentuating a different frequency pattern; often you can craft your own styles. But tone controls work best for correcting room acoustics and satisfying listening preferences, not enhancing a musical genre.

DSP (digital signal processor) modes use a computer chip to duplicate the sound characteristics of a concert hall and other listening environments. A **bass-boost** switch amplifies the deepest sounds, and **midnight mode** reduces loud sounds and amplifies quiet ones in music or soundtracks.

Sometimes called "one touch," a **settings memory** lets you store settings for each source to minimize differences in volume, tone, and other settings when switching between sources. A similar feature, **loudness memory,** is limited to volume settings alone.

Tape monitor lets you either listen to one source as you record a second on a tape deck or listen to the recording as it's being made. **Automatic radio tuning** includes such features as seek (automatic searching for the next listenable station) and 20 to 40 presets to call up your favorite stations.

To catch stations too weak for the seek mode, most receivers also have a **manual stepping** knob or buttons, best in one-channel increments. But most models creep in half- or quarter-steps, meaning unnecessary button tapping to find the frequency you want. **Direct tuning** of frequencies lets you tune a radio station by entering its frequency on a keypad.

How to choose

PERFORMANCE DIFFERENCES. The most recent CONSUMER REPORTS tests of receivers show that you needn't spend more than $250 to $300 to get a fine performer. (The exception: THX models, which begin at $800.) Most models we have tested have been very good at amplifying and in tuning FM stations, but only fair or good for AM stations. Ease of use was often somewhat disappointing.

RECOMMENDATIONS. Don't buy more receiver than you need. The size of the room you're using, how loudly you play music, and the impedance of the speakers you'll use all determine how much power is appropriate. Generally, 50 watts or more per channel should be fine for a typical system in a typical 12x20 foot room. Then it's a question of features and usability.

Look for clear labeling, color coding, and logical groupings of the jacks on the receiver's rear panel. Make sure the model you're considering has all the connection types you need. Check for how well the receiver impedance matches your speakers.

To compare receivers at the store, have the salesperson feed the same CD or DVD soundtrack to the receivers, adjust each receiver's volume to be equally loud, and select between each receiver's speaker output using the same set of speakers. Compare two receivers at a time. Stop the CD and listen for background hiss. Explore the layout of the front panel and remote control to see how easy they will be to use.

RECEIVERS ◆ Ratings: Page 257

SATELLITE TV

Before you opt for satellite TV, make sure a dish be mounted on your property with a clear view of the satellite. Then choose the system and the hardware.

Frustration with cable companies has fueled the growth of satellite-TV broadcast systems. Some 18 million homes sport a saucer-shaped dish antenna. In a recent survey of satellite- and cable-TV subscribers, CONSUMER REPORTS found that satellite-TV subscribers were more satisfied overall than their cable-TV counterparts.

Once renowned for offering hundreds of channels with the notable excep-

**A GUIDE TO
PROGRAM GUIDES**

Digital-cable and satellite services typically provide an interactive guide system that, among other features, allows you to select a program by clicking on its listing and watch a program as you interact with the guide. On recording models, the guide also shows programs that the unit is set to record. Analog-cable program guides are rolling listings that allow no interaction and force you to wait for particular channel listings to appear.

tion of local stations, the two satellite providers—DirecTV (also called DSS) and EchoStar's Dish Network—now provide local service in more than 40 cities and outlying areas, with more programming imminent. That's the result of a 1999 federal law that allowed satellite companies to offer so-called local-into-local service. In January 2002, the FCC ruled that if a satellite company offered one local channel, then it had to carry all local channels in the markets where local service was offered.

People in an "unserved" household—those living in rural areas where an acceptable signal cannot be received via a rooftop antenna—can pick up local stations (regional affiliates of major networks) from a satellite provider. According to the FCC, you should be able to confirm your status through the satellite provider from which you're getting your setup.

For much of the country, however, cable remains the only way to receive all local programming. Since satellite providers have a limited spectrum for broadcasting additional channels, the number of markets where they can offer local service is limited. This is a major reason these companies are requesting a merger.

What's available

DirecTV and EchoStar's Dish Network offer comparable programming fare, including a choice of up to 400 to 500 channels. DirecTV is stronger in sports, while Dish Network holds the advantage in foreign-language programming. In addition to television, both providers carry 30 to 40 commercial-free music services in many genres.

Basic service, with a 100-channel package, is about $32 per month. Local-channel service adds about $5 per month. Expanded programming, with 100 to 150 channels, will run you about $45 and adds music and some specialty channels. Premium channels such as HBO and Showtime are $6 to $10 each, sometimes less if you take two or more. Pay-per-view is usually $7 per movie. Sports packages available on DirecTV run $139 to $169 per season. Limited high-definition programming is available from both providers.

The dish and receiver will work with only one of the providers' signals. These components come with various extras, including receivers that double as digital VCRs or DVRs. Typically, the dish and receiver are sold together. Hughes, RCA, and Sony are among the companies that offer DirecTV equipment; JVC and EchoStar offer Dish Network equipment.

Satellite dishes are typically 18 or 24 inches. The larger dishes offer increased programming options, such as more channels, pay-per-view movies, HDTV reception, and international programming. Sometimes a second 18-inch dish may be required to receive some of those services.

Receivers accept the signal from the dish, decode it, and transmit it to your TV. If you want to be able to watch different programs on different TVs at once, you'll need one receiver for each TV. To facilitate this, you need a dish with multiple low-noise block converters. Alternatively, the receiver's RF-output jack or an inexpensive splitter may be used to send the same channel to multiple TVs. Extra receivers cost about $100 each and add about $5 apiece to the monthly bill.

For pay-per-view ordering and other provider contact, satellite-TV receivers must be connected to a telephone line. Typically, you can use your existing line.

Price range for a dish-receiver package: $150 to more than $800. Price range for dishes: $30 to $50 for single-room, $40 to $60 for two-room, and $150 to $250 for multiroom. Frequent promotions offer lower prices.

Key features

On the receiver, the number and type of **audio and video output jacks** make a difference in the quality of your picture and in what equipment you can connect. The lowest-quality connection is radio-frequency, which is the typical antenna-type connector. Better is a **composite video output;** better still are **S-video outputs,** provided your TV is appropriately equipped, which can take advantage of the higher visual resolution of the digital video source.

An **onscreen signal-strength meter** lets you monitor how well the satellite signal is coming in. Satellite receivers with **Dolby Digital audio** capability may have optical or coaxial output for a direct digital connection to a Dolby Digital audio receiver.

Some remote controls accompanying the receiver are infrared, like TV or VCR remotes, and may also control a VCR. Others use a radio-frequency signal, which can pass through walls, allowing the receiver to be placed in an unobtrusive, central location and controlled from anywhere in the house.

Remotes typically include a **program-description button,** which activates an onscreen program-description banner. The program guide helps you sort through the hundreds of channels.

Program guide with picture lets you continue to watch one program while you scan the onscreen channel guide for another. Some receivers have a **keyword search:** You can enter the full or partial name of a program or performer and search automatically through the listings.

How to choose

PERFORMANCE DIFFERENCES. The differences between the two satellite providers are subtle. The best DirecTV setups are a little easier to use, with slightly better remotes, than EchoStar equipment. But the EchoStar/Dish Network system did offer a slightly better overall picture for New York network affiliates in the most recent CONSUMER REPORTS tests. When test engineers viewed pictures from both satellite providers, we saw some subtle picture defects.

You may notice minor visual impairments, mostly in fast-moving scenes (the most bandwidth-hungry screen content), which may be caused by expanded channel offerings at the expense of bandwidth.

RECOMMENDATIONS. Find out what the program offerings are in your area, including whether digital cable is available (or when it will be) and if local channels are available. Choose the service, then the hardware. You need a clear view of the southern horizon and a place to mount the dish. Satellite dealers and installers will come out to assess your location. Be aware that if you decide to switch providers, you'll need to pay for everything all over again.

SPEAKERS

Speakers can make or break your audio or video setup. Try to listen to them in a store before buying. If you can splurge on only part of your system, splurge here.

The best array of audio or video components will let you down if matched with poor-quality speakers. Good speakers need not bust your budget, though it's easy to spend a lot. For a home-theater system, you can start with two or three speakers and add others as your budget allows. Size is no indication of quality.

What's available

Among the hundreds of speaker brands available, the major names include Bose, Infinity, JBL, Pioneer, Polk, RCA, Sony, and Yamaha. Speakers are sold through mass merchandisers, audio/video stores, "boutique" retailers, and online—where shipping can add up to $100 to the bill, since speakers can be fairly heavy.

Speakers are sold as pairs or sets for traditional stereo setups, and singly or in sets of three to six for equipping a home theater. The front (or main) speakers supply stereo effect and carry most of the sound to the listener's ears. The center (or center channel) speaker chiefly delivers dialog and is usually placed on top of or beneath the TV in a home-theater setup.

Dialog demands a full-range, high-quality speaker. A subwoofer carries the lowest tones. Price range: $400 to over $1,000.

BOOKSHELF SPEAKERS. These are among the smallest, but at 12 to 18 inches tall, many are still too large to fit on a shelf, their name notwithstanding. A pair of bookshelf speakers can serve as the sole speakers in a stereo system or as the front or rear duo in a home-theater setup. One can serve as the center-channel unit, provided it's magnetically shielded so it won't interfere with the TV. Small speakers like these have made strides in their ability to handle deep bass without buzzing or distortion. Any bass-handling limitations would be less of a concern in a multispeaker system that uses a subwoofer for the deep bass. Price range: $200 to more than $600.

FLOOR-STANDING SPEAKERS. Typically about 3 to 4 feet tall, these large speakers can also serve as the sole speakers in a stereo system or as the front pair in a home-theater system. Their big cabinets have the potential to do more justice to deep bass than smaller speakers, but we believe many listeners would be satisfied with smaller speakers that scored well for bass handling. Even if floor models do a bit better, their size and cost may steer buyers toward smaller, cheaper bookshelf models. Price range: $400 to more than $1,000.

CENTER-CHANNEL SPEAKER. In a multichannel setup, the center-channel speaker sits on or below the TV and primarily handles dialog. Its range doesn't have to be as full as the front pair's, but its sound should be similar so all three blend well. Dedicated center-channel speakers are short and wide (6 inches high by 20 inches wide, for instance) so they perch neatly atop a TV. Price range: $100 to $300.

REAR-SURROUND SPEAKERS. Rear speakers in a multichannel setup carry mostly background sound such as crowd noise. Newer multichannel formats such as Dolby Digital,

DTS, DVD-Audio, and SACD make fuller use of these speakers than earlier formats. You'll get the best blend if the rear pair sounds similar to the front pair. Rear speakers tend to be small and light (often 5 to 10 inches high and 3 to 6 pounds), so they can be wall mounted or placed on a shelf. They're often called satellites. Price range: $100 to $350.

THREE-PIECE SETS. Designed to be used as stand-alone systems or integrated with other speakers, they have two satellites for midrange and higher tones and a subwoofer for bass. Price range: $300 to $800.

SIX-PIECE SETS. These systems have four satellites (used for the front and rear pairs), one center-channel speaker, and a subwoofer. Six-piece sets save you the trouble of matching the distinctive sounds of six speakers. That can be a daunting task at home, and even more of a challenge amidst the din of a store that doesn't have a decent listening room. Price range: $400 to more than $1,000.

OTHER SHAPES AND SIZES. A "powertower" is a tower speaker, usually priced above $1,000, with a side-firing, powered subwoofer in its base. Flat-panel speakers save space and are priced at $500 and up per pair.

Key features

Lovers of loud sound should pay attention to a speaker's **measured impedance,** which affects how well the speaker and receiver get along. **Power range** refers to the familiar advertised watts per channel. The **wattage** within a matched pair, say front or rear, should be identical. Also, the power range should exceed the watts per channel supplied by your receiver or amplifier. Speakers sold to be near a TV set typically have magnetic shielding so they won't distort the picture with their core magnets.

How to choose

PERFORMANCE DIFFERENCES. What distinguishes the best from the rest is the accuracy with which they reproduce the original signals fed to them. Most models we've tested have been capable of reasonable accuracy. Some models, however, require adjustments to a receiver's tone controls to compensate for the speaker's shortcomings. Making those adjustments is usually a minor, one-time inconvenience.

No speaker is perfect. Every speaker that CONSUMER REPORTS has tested alters music to some degree, overemphasizing some sounds and underemphasizing others. Some speakers "roll off" entirely at extremes of bass and treble, meaning they can't reproduce some low or high sounds at all. Some speakers buzz, distort, or otherwise complain when playing low notes at window-rattling volume.

RECOMMENDATIONS. Look for the size and configuration that fit your listening space. Models of equal accuracy will sound different, so try to audition before you buy, using a familiar piece of music. Especially demanding: music with wide dynamics and frequencies, such as classical symphonies, and simple music, such as a solo piano performance.

Listen to the music soft and loud, for clarity and lack of harshness in the high range and a lack of boominess in the low. Start in the best position, in an equilateral triangle with the speakers, and move off-center until you find the angle at which the high frequencies become muffled. The farther you can go, the better. Sharpen your judging skills by first comparing each store's top performer with its low-priced entry-level model.

To keep a balanced system, buy left and right speakers in pairs. The center-channel speaker should be matched to the front speakers; if it's very close to the TV, it should be magnetically shielded.

SPEAKERS ♦ **Ratings:** Page 264

TV SETS

Conventional TVs, projection sets, digital TVs, flat screens—you have more (and better) viewing choices than before, at ever-lower prices.

Because the transition to digital broadcasts is proceeding slowly, any analog TV you buy now will serve you well for many years. Even when digital programming becomes widespread, the TV you buy now can do the job with the addition of a converter. CONSUMER REPORTS tests show that there are plenty of fine TVs to choose from, including some real bargains. You can find a very good 27-inch model for around $450, a 32-inch for about $600, and a 36-inch set for $750.

Sets capable of carrying HDTV cost considerably more—$1,100 or more. If your antenna or cable connection provides a good, strong signal, an HD-ready set has a noticeably improved picture compared with an analog set. An HD-ready set will show an even better picture when connected to a progressive-scan DVD player. These sets can display the much higher-resolution HD image, but only with the addition of a digital-TV receiver set-top box.

True HDTVs come with a built-in digital-TV receiver, for $1,500 and up. The availability of high-definition programming is still limited. Like an HD-ready set, an HDTV will let you enjoy superior video when hooked up to a progressive-scan DVD player or when watching standard TV fare.

What's available

Panasonic, RCA, Sony, and Toshiba are among the biggest-selling brands of TVs measuring 27 inches and larger. Other brands include JVC, Philips, Samsung, Sanyo, Sharp, and Zenith.

SMALL SETS. Sets with a 13-inch screen are usually equipped with monophonic sound and few features. Higher-end models may offer a few more features, such as extra inputs. Price range: $90 to $300.

Sets with a 19- or 20-inch screen are also pretty basic. Most lack high-end picture refinements such as a comb filter (which can increase visual detail). Models with stereo sound usually have extra inputs for a VCR or a DVD player. Price range: $140 to $450.

MIDSIZED SETS. A 27-inch screen, once thought large, is now the norm. Sets with a 25-inch screen (difficult to tell in size from a 27-incher) are their economy-minded cousins; together the two are the biggest-selling sizes. Sets with a 27-inch screen frequently offer many features, including picture-in-picture (PIP), an S-video input jack, simulated surround-sound effects, a universal remote control, and, usually, a comb filter. These 27-inch models are among the best values for TVs, and the respectable sound quality found on some 27-inch sets can make them all many people need. What's more, they fit in most entertainment-center cabinets. Price range: $300 to $1,000. Sets with the new "flat" TV screens are at the high end of the price range.

LARGE SETS. A 32-inch screen represents the entry level for big-screen TV; these sets often offer two-tuner PIP, universal remotes, simulated surround sound, and plenty of input jacks. The largest direct-view sets (with 36-inch screens) are feature-rich but can weigh more than 200 pounds; they might be too wide and too high for conventional component shelving, including entertainment-center cabinets. Price doesn't predict quality, CONSUMER REPORTS tests have found. Price range: $400 to $2,700.

PROJECTION ANALOG SETS. Measuring 42 to 73 inches diagonally, these sets typically don't match the picture quality of a conventional picture tube. The image appears dimmer as your viewing position angles away from the center of the screen. Projection sets have plenty of features, such as two-tuner PIP and custom settings. But readers have reported that parts can be hard to get and repairers hard to find. Price range: $1,000 to more than $4,000.

HD-READY SETS. These digital sets can display higher-resolution images, even from analog signals such as a good cable connection or a DVD player. They display superior images when paired with an HD source. They're available both as projection sets and direct-view sets. Picture size comes in one of two shapes, expressed as the width-to-height ratio: the conventional squarish 4:3 and the wider 16:9, which is shaped more like a movie-theater screen. An HD-ready set requires a separate digital-TV receiver ($650 and up) to display high-definition material. One advantage to a separate tuner is that it's possible to upgrade the receiver alone should technology advance in the future. Price range: $1,100 to more than $10,000.

HDTV SETS. Also referred to as true high-definition sets, they come with a built-in digital-TV receiver. Most of them are projection sets with the 16:9 picture size. Price range: $1,500 to more than $10,000.

Key features

Flat tubes, a departure from the decades-old curved TV tubes, reduce off-angle reflections and glare, but they do not necessarily improve picture quality. A **comb filter,** found on most sets, minimizes minor color flaws at edges within the image and increases picture clarity. An **auto-color control** can be set to automatically adjust color balance to make flesh tones look natural. **Color "warmth" adjustment,** or **adjustable color temperature,** lets you shade the picture toward the blue ("cooler," better for images with outdoor light) or red ("warmer," preferred for flesh tones and interiors) range.

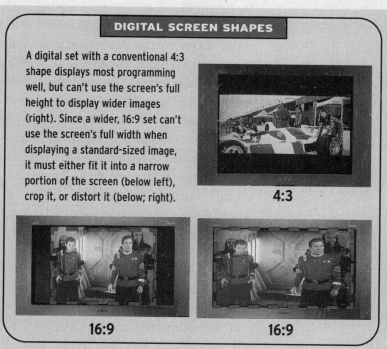

DIGITAL SCREEN SHAPES

A digital set with a conventional 4:3 shape displays most programming well, but can't use the screen's full height to display wider images (right). Since a wider, 16:9 set can't use the screen's full width when displaying a standard-sized image, it must either fit it into a narrow portion of the screen (below left), crop it, or distort it (below; right).

4:3

16:9

16:9

HOW BIG A SCREEN DO YOU NEED?

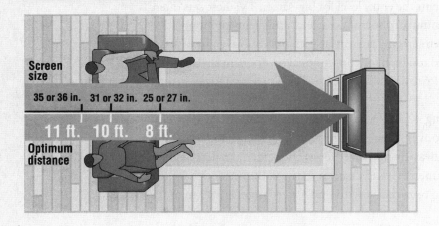

Bigger screens mean you need to sit further away from the TV set. Shown are distances that offer the ideal compromise between image size and picture quality for conventional analog TVs. You can comfortably view HD-ready sets of those sizes from half those distances.

Picture-in-picture (PIP) shows two channels at once, one on a small picture inserted in the full-screen image. Unless the set has two-tuner PIP, watching two channels typically requires extra connections using the tuner in a VCR or cable box. This can be complicated to set up and use.

All sets over 13 inches have **closed captioning,** but some also have closed captioning when muted, which automatically displays the dialog on screen while the sound is muted. **Video-noise reduction** lowers the picture-degrading "noise" from poor reception but at the expense of detail.

Stereo sound is virtually universal on sets 27 inches or larger, but you'll generally discern little stereo separation from a set's built-in speakers. For a better stereo effect, route the signals to a sound system. A few larger TV sets have an **audio amplifier** that can power regular (unpowered) speakers connected to the set's audio output jacks, eliminating the need for a receiver. **Ambience sound** is often termed "surround sound" or the like, but this is not true surround like that from a multispeaker Dolby Digital or Pro Logic home-theater system; rather, it's accomplished through special audio processing. Some people find the wider "soundstage" pleasing; others find it distracting. Side-firing speakers can enhance the stereo effect, but not as much as external speakers, and their sound can be muffled in some TV cabinets. **Automatic volume control** compensates for the jarring volume jumps that often accompany commercials or changes in channel.

Virtually all TV sets come with a **remote control** to change channels and adjust sound volume and picture. A **universal remote** will control all or most of your video (and some audio) devices once you program it by entering codes. Some sets have a **"smart" remote,** so you don't have to enter a code for each device. (Aftermarket universal remotes typically cost $10 to $40.) Active-channel scan automatically detects and memorizes active channels, eliminating the need to scan manually.

Last-channel recall lets you jump to the previously viewed channel. With **channel labeling,** you enter channels' names (ESPN, CNN, AMC) so you'll know where you are as you change channels. Some models offer an **Extended Data Services (XDS) decoder,** which briefly displays channel and programming information on the show that you're watching (if the station transmits that information). **Guide Plus,** which several manufacturers offer on their sets, displays program listings. The set receives program information when it's off but still in "standby."

Some features are important to specific users: **Separate audio program** (SAP) lets you receive a second soundtrack, typically in another language. Multilingual menus are also common. **Parental controls** include the V-chip, which blocks specific shows based on their content rating; for access, you must enter a code. A TV with **channel block-out** will block specific channels and may also prevent use of the audio/video input jacks to which video games are connected.

Cable/antenna, or **radio frequency** inputs are the most basic; the next step up is **composite video.** An **S-video input jack** lets you take advantage of the superior picture quality from a satellite-dish system, a DVD player, or a digital camcorder. **Component video input** offers even better quality but is useful only with equipment that comes with component outputs, such as some DVD players.

Two or more **audio/video input jacks** are useful if you need to connect more than a single video source; for a camcorder or video game, **front-mounted jacks** are easiest. Most sets of 27 inches or larger have at least two video jacks and one audio input jack, which together allow one external signal source (a VCR, for example) to be connected in a way that generally provides better picture and sound than you would get using the set's antenna jack. Audio output jacks, essential for a home-theater setup, let you direct a stereo TV's audio signal to a receiver or self-powered speakers. A headphone jack lets you watch (and listen) without disturbing others.

Sets that are **1080i/720p capable** refer to those that can display digital signals in the two high-definition specifications, termed 1080i and 720p. True HDTV sets have a built-in HDTV tuner, although the technical details remain subject to change. High-definition programming is not yet widely available, but you can watch regular TV programming on these sets. **VGA/SVGA input** lets your TV accept signals from a computer's graphics card.

How to choose

PERFORMANCE DIFFERENCES. Most of the TV sets CONSUMER REPORTS has tested do at least a good job. Some of the biggest differences show up in the sound quality, which won't matter if you're outputting the audio to the external speakers of a sound system. Price doesn't track with performance.

RECOMMENDATIONS. Before you start shopping, decide whether you want to stick with a direct-view set or go with a big-screen projection set, and whether you want a conventional analog TV or one that can handle high-definition signals—either an HD-ready

HDTV PROGRAMMING

Four years after digital broadcasting began in the U.S., it's still not as widely available as had been hoped. Consequently, it's likely that the FCC will extend its 2006 deadline for phasing out analog broadcasts. As of late 2002, digital broadcasts were available via antenna from only 210 of the country's 2,800 TV stations. To receive such signals, you must live in one of the dozens of cities that have the broadcasts and in a location where the signals will be strong enough.

For viewers whose homes have an unobstructed view of the southern sky, high-definition versions of movie channels such as HBO and Showtime are available via satellite.

And although equipment to connect digital TVs to home cable outlets is starting to become available, cable companies have so far chosen to use their bandwidth to add more conventional stations instead of high-definition ones, so they provide very little high-definition programming to their tens of millions of subscribers. High-definition digital programming shouldn't be confused with the widely available "digital cable" service, which allows broadcasters to offer more conventional channels.

model or an HDTV set with an integrated tuner.

Size is another key consideration. For a fine picture plus many useful features, a 27-inch model may be the best deal. Prices continue to drop for 32-inch sets; some may go for as little as $400. Spend more and you get PIP, flat tubes, and better sound-enhancing features. A 35- or 36-inch set has about 20 percent more screen—at a price roughly 50 percent higher than a 32-incher.

Also consider how your TV will fit in with the other components of your home theater. If you plan to output sound to external speakers, you'll want audio output jacks. Similarly, plan for the future. DVD players, digital camcorders, and other devices require one or more S-video jacks; for DVD players, a component video input is better. Check with your cable-service provider regarding availability of digital cable service.

Be sure to measure a set before buying it, and make sure you have appropriate furniture—some 36-inch TVs may not fit in an entertainment center's cubbyhole. Given the size and weight of these sets, you may want to look into delivery and setup.

TV SETS ◆ **Ratings:** Page 274 ◆ **Reliability:** Page 300, 301

VCRS

They don't match the picture and sound quality of DVD players, but VCRs are still the most versatile and inexpensive way to play, record, and keep videos.

Today's VCRs are more of a bargain than ever. Hi-fi models, which cost $155 to $290 when we tested them in November 1998, now have list prices as low as $80 and may sell for as little as $50.

What's available

Panasonic, RCA, Emerson, and Sony are among the biggest-selling brands. Most low-end VCRs are standard VHS models, but models starting at about $200 typically can record higher-resolution S-VHS format tapes as well.

Monophonic models, starting at about $50, record sound adequately for playback through a small TV speaker, but hi-fi VCRs cost little more and offer sound of near-CD quality. They are much better for larger TVs with stereo sound or for connection to a receiver.

Hi-fi models can also play surround-sound movies if used with an audio receiver that decodes surround-sound information. Dual-deck models let you copy tapes easily. There are also a few digital VCRs recording digital satellite–TV content. Price range: hi-fi, $80 to $250; dual-deck, $200 to $350; digital, $800 and up.

Key features

Hi-fi models record **high-fidelity sound,** a desirable feature for a home-theater setup. **S-VHS** (for Super VHS) records more information onto a tape for better picture detail. S-VHS requires special tapes, but a relatively new variation, **S-VHS ET,** uses standard VHS tape.

Cable/satellite-box control, also referred to as C3 (for "cable-channel changer"), lets the VCR change the channel anytime you tape a program. **VCR Plus,** now quite common, lets you set up the VCR to tape a program simply by punching in a code number from your local TV listings. Two variations, **VCR Plus Gold** and **VCR Plus Silver,** allow you to bypass the hassle of channel mapping by entering your ZIP code when prompted; the Gold version goes one better by including C3.

Memory backup saves programming information should the VCR temporarily lose power; depending on the VCR, you may have a few minutes or less before the program settings are gone.

Editing features include **shuttle and jog controls,** which let you scan large segments or move forward or backward one frame at a time to find the exact spot you want. **Audio dub,** a higher-end feature, lets you add music or narration to existing recordings. A **flying erase head** lets you insert segments without noticeable video glitches.

Many features aim to save you time. There are various "skip" features. **Automatic commercial advance** lets the VCR bypass all commercials during playback by fast-forwarding past such cues as fade-to-black and changes in sound level. **Movie advance** lets you fly over previews at the beginning of a rented tape.

One-button skip lets you fast-forward 30 seconds or a minute with each button press. And there are different kinds of search: A **go-to search** skips to a section according to the time on the counter, a **zero search** finds the place on the tape where the counter was set to zero. An **index search** forwards the tape to a specific index point set by the machine each time you begin a recording.

An **onscreen menu** uses the TV to display your setup and programming choices. **Front-mounted audio/video input jacks** let you easily connect a camcorder, a video game, or another VCR.

Plug and play eases setup; you connect the VCR to the cable system or an antenna, then plug it in. It reads signals from broadcasters to automatically program the channels and the clock. The latter feature is also known as **auto clock set.**

Some VCRs can automatically switch from SP to EP speed, a feature called **auto speed-switching,** to extend recording time and help ensure you don't miss a climactic scene because you ran out of tape.

A **universal remote** lets you control other devices along with your VCR; if the kids misplace it, a **remote locator** will page the remote, causing it to beep from its hiding place. **Child lock** disables the VCR's controls to keep programming from being changed.

How to choose

PERFORMANCE DIFFERENCES. Because DVD players have redefined excellence in picture quality for inexpensive video gear, none of the VCRs that CONSUMER REPORTS has tested could produce what we now consider an excellent picture. Still, most models have performed very well; the best VCRs in CONSUMER REPORTS' last tests were as good as any we'd tested in the past. And the best picture you can get from a VCR is almost as good as what you'd get from a typical DVD player.

RECOMMENDATIONS. For basic recording of movies and TV shows, VCRs offer great value, with even inexpensive models now offering hi-fi sound and some level of VCR Plus programming. If you have an S-VHS-C, a Hi8, or a digital camcorder, you'll want a VCR that supports S-VHS to view the improved video quality. If you're hooking a VCR into a home-theater system that includes a DVD player, note that built-in encryption contained in many DVD discs typically won't let you copy DVD movies onto videotape. Such copying is a copyright violation in most cases.

While most VCRs come with four or more heads, more heads do not necessarily translate into better performance. For the best assurance of quality before you buy, try to get a side-by-side demonstration of the models you're considering.

VCRs ♦ **Ratings:** Page 284

3

Yard & Garden

Innovations are making home and yard gear easier and safer to use, as well as friendlier to the environment. Some of the changes have been prompted by tougher state and federal environmental regulations. That means buying a new piece of equipment, rather than nursing along an old one, may be a good move. Here are trends you'll see this year:

"GREENER" PRODUCTS. New government rules for emissions by lawn mowers and other gasoline-powered yard tools are designed to reduce emissions from gasoline-powered lawn and garden equipment by hundreds of thousands of tons per year. Emissions aren't the only type of pollutant: Towns and cities have also been enacting laws designed to quiet gasoline-powered leaf blowers.

FRIENDLIER, SAFER CONTROLS. Clutchless hydrostatic transmissions on a growing number of ride-on mowers and tractors make mowing go more smoothly. All of these machines stop the engine and wheels when the operator leaves the seat. Even the least expensive push and self-propelled power mowers stop the blade when you release the safety handle. Some higher-priced models stop the blade but not the engine, eliminating the need to restart the mower. Almost all chain saws are now equipped with kickback shields and lockout switches to prevent injuries.

MORE CAPABILITY–AND MORE LUXURY. Some lawn and garden tractors can power extra-cost accessories that allow you plow and tow, as well as throw snow. Many models have become the backyard equivalent of sport-utility vehicles with their large engines and ever-wider cutting swaths. You'll also find a growing number of "zero-turn-radius" mowers and tractors that can turn 360 degrees in one spot to better maneuver around obstacles.

Built-in gas barbecue grills with stainless-steel finishes now rival multithousand-dollar, pro-style ranges in size and price. You'll also find stainless-steel stand-alone grills priced at $1,000 and beyond, though you can get grills with a thousand-dollar look for about $500.

MORE SHOPPING OPTIONS. Yard and garden products are sold over the Internet through sites such as Amazon.com, HomeDepot.com, Lowes.com, and Sears.com. Such online sites can be useful, especially as research tools, but there's still a lot to be said for the local hardware store or home center. Large chains such as Sears and Wal-Mart usually have the best selection of lower-priced brands. Home centers such as Home Depot and Lowe's offer a mix of low-priced, midpriced, and upscale brands. Local hardware stores and other independent dealers tend to carry midpriced and upscale brands. Such stores often offer service that mass merchandisers and home centers don't provide.

BARBECUE GRILLS

Many people are choosing models that do more than just grill. Go high-end, and you can pay as much as you would for a pro-style kitchen range.

A $15 charcoal hibachi is all it takes to give burgers that outdoorsy barbecue taste. But a gas or an electric grill offers more flexible controls and spares you the hassle of starting the fire and getting rid of the ashes when you're done. Many have extras such as a warming rack for rolls or an accessory burner for, say, boiling corn on the cob. Those looking for a backyard status symbol will find models that cost thousands of dollars and include stainless-steel exteriors and grates, porcelain-coated steel and aluminum lids, several separately controlled burners, utensil holders, and other perks. You'll also find more modest grills that can serve up flavor and convenience for $200 or so.

What's available

Char-Broil, Kenmore (Sears), Sunbeam, and Weber account for more than 80 percent of gas-grill sales. Char-Broil and Sunbeam are mass-market brands, with Char-Broil selling both gas and electric models. Weber is a high-end brand that also markets its classic dome-top charcoal grills. Sears covers the entire spectrum, with Kenmore and its upscale Kenmore Elite line.

GAS. These grills are easy to start, warm up quickly, and usually cook predictably, giving meat a full, browned flavor. Step-up features include shelves and side burners. Better models offer added sturdiness and more even cooking. Price range: $100 to more than $2,000.

ELECTRIC. You can start them easily, and they offer precise temperature control and allow you to grill with nonstick cookware. On the downside, electrics generally take a bit longer than gas models to warm up and be ready to grill. Price range: about $100 to $300.

CHARCOAL. These provide an intense, smoky flavor prized by many. But they don't always light easily (using a chimney-style starter can help remedy that). They also burn less cleanly than gas, their heat is harder to regulate, and cleanup can be messy—major reasons why charcoal models are no longer the top-selling type. Price range: usually $100 or less.

Key features

Most cooking **grates** are made of porcelain-coated steel or the somewhat sturdier porcelain-coated cast iron, bare cast iron, or stainless steel. A porcelain-coated grate is rustproof and easy to clean, but it can eventually chip. Bare cast iron is sturdy and sears beautifully, but you have to season it with cooking oil to fend off rust. The best of both worlds: stainless steel, which is sturdy, heats quickly, and resists rust without a porcelain coating. CONSUMER REPORTS has also found that cooking grates with wide, closely spaced bars tend to provide better searing than grates with thin, round rods, which may allow more food to fall to the bottom of the grill.

Both gas and electric grills are mounted on a **cart,** usually of painted steel tubing assembled with nuts and bolts. Higher-priced grills have welded joints, and a few have carts made of stainless steel. Carts with two wheels and two feet must be lifted at one end to move; better are two large wheels and two casters or four casters, which make moving easier. Wheels with a full axle are better than those bolted to the frame, which over time can bend.

Gas and electric grills generally have one or more **shelves,** which flip up from the front or side or are fixed on the side.

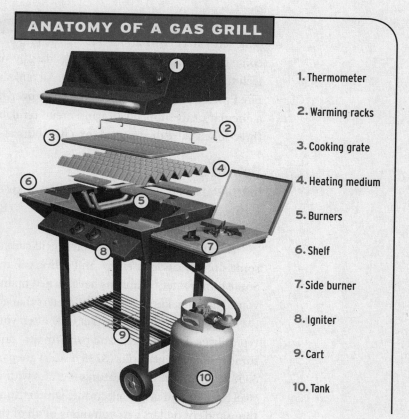

ANATOMY OF A GAS GRILL

1. Thermometer
2. Warming racks
3. Cooking grate
4. Heating medium
5. Burners
6. Shelf
7. Side burner
8. Igniter
9. Cart
10. Tank

Shelves are usually made of plastic, though some are made of wood or stainless steel, which are more durable. Some grills also have **interior racks** for keeping food warm without further cooking. Another plus for gas or electric grills is a **lid** and **firebox** made of stainless steel or porcelain-coated steel, both of which are more durable than painted aluminum.

Still other features help a gas grill start more easily, cook more evenly, and last longer. An example is the **igniter,** which works via a knob or a push button. Knobs emit two or three sparks per turn, while push buttons emit a single spark per push. Better are **battery-powered electronic igniters,** which produce continuous sparks as long as the button is held down. Also look for **lighting holes** on the side of or beneath the grill, which are handy if the igniter fails and you need to use a wooden match to start the fire.

Most gas grills have steel **burners**, though some are stainless steel, cast iron or cast brass. Those premium burners typically last longer and carry warranties of 10 years or more. Most grills have two burners, or one with two independent halves. A few have three or four, which can add cooking flexibility. A side **burner,** which resembles a gas-stove burner and has its own heat control, is handy for cooking vegetables or sauce without leaving the grill. Other step-up features include an **electric rotisserie**, a **smoker drawer,** a **wok,** a **griddle pan,** a **steamer pan,** and a **nonstick grill basket.**

Most gas grills also use a **cooking medium**—a metal plate or metal bars, ceramic or charcoal-like briquettes, or lava rocks—between the burner and grates to distribute heat and vaporize juices, flavoring the food. CONSUMER REPORTS tests have shown that no one type is better at ensuring even heating. But grills with nothing between the burner and cooking surface typically cook less evenly.

Gas grills typically include a **propane tank,** sometimes with a **fuel gauge;** buying a tank separately costs about $25. Some tanks can be converted to run on natural gas or come in a natural-gas version. Tanks usually sit next to or on the base of the grill and attach to its gas line with a handwheel. All tanks must now comply with upgraded National Fire Protection Association standards for **overfilling protection.** Noncompliant tanks have a circular or five-lobed valve and aren't refillable, although they can be retrofitted with a three-lobed valve or swapped for a new tank at a hardware store or other refilling facility.

How to choose

PERFORMANCE DIFFERENCES. Most grills, gas or electric, do a good job at grilling hotly and evenly. Salespeople might say that more Btus (British thermal units) mean faster warm-up, but that's not always true.

Assembling a gas or an electric grill can take anywhere from 30 minutes to 3 hours; some stores include assembly and delivery in the price, while others charge for that service. Some minor safety problems have turned up in CONSUMER REPORTS tests. Typically they involved handles, knobs, or thermometers that got too hot to handle without pot holders.

RECOMMENDATIONS. Consider how often you cook outdoors and how many people you typically feed. While price and performance don't track precisely, our tests have shown that some midpriced gas grills ($275 or less) are particularly good values. Gas models priced at $350 to $575 have more features—grates with wide bars, ample warming shelves, stainless-steel burners and grates, electronic igniters, longer warranties, and sturdier carts. Spending thousands of dollars gets you many or all of those features plus more burners and mostly stainless-steel construction, but few consumers spend that much on a grill.

An electric grill is a good option for places where gas grills aren't allowed. Charcoal grills cost the least overall, but they require the most preparation and cleanup work.

BARBECUE GRILLS ♦ **Ratings:** Page 200

CHAIN SAWS

They're still noisy, but many of the latest are safer and cleaner. Gasoline-powered saws still out-power electrics, although plug-in models can be fine for light-duty use.

Chain saws are inherently dangerous and noisy, though modern designs attempt to improve usability on both counts. Nearly all chain saws now have multiple features aimed at minimizing "kickback," which occurs when the saw snaps up and back toward the operator.

Electric models are quieter than gasoline-powered ones. Gasoline-powered saws are cleaning up their act as tougher federal standards reduce allowable emissions for these two-stroke, handheld machines.

What's available

You'll find gasoline- and electric-powered chain saws at home centers, discount stores, and lawn and garden dealers. Major brands include Craftsman (Sears), Homelite, Husqvarna, Poulan, Remington, and Stihl. Gas-powered saws use a small two-stroke engine that requires a mixture of gasoline and oil. Nearly all electric saws plug into an outlet and run off an electric motor. A few rechargeable, battery-powered chain saws are available, but they tend to be underpowered for most jobs.

As with most outdoor tools, gas-powered chain saws tend to offer the most power and mobility. But plug-in electrics compensate somewhat with lighter weight, less noise, and trigger starting. They also emit no exhaust, don't need engine tuneups, and typically cost less. Price range: gas, $100 to $300; electrics, less than $100 for most.

Key features

Chain saws are typically marketed by the size of the bar (the metal extension that supports the chain—usually between 14 and 20 inches long) as well as the engine or motor (measured in cubic centimeters for gas saws, amps for electrics). Usually, the larger the saw, the more you'll pay, though smaller models with high-end names such as Husqvarna and Stihl can cost more than larger ones from Craftsman, Homelite, and other lower-priced brands.

Other features are aimed mainly at safety and convenience. Major kickback-reducing devices include a **reduced-kickback chain** with added guard links to keep the cutters from taking too large a bite, along with a narrow-tipped, **reduced-kickback bar** that limits the contact area where kickback occurs. All saws also have a **chain catcher**—an extension under the guide bar that keeps a broken chain from flying rearward. Some saws have a **chain brake,** which stops the chain almost instantly when activated, or a **bar-tip guard,** which prevents kickback by covering the bar's tip, or "nose."

Other safety features for most chain saws include a **trigger lockout switch** that must be pressed for the throttle trigger to operate and, for gas saws, a **shielded muffler** designed to prevent burns from accidental contact.

Common labor-saving features include an **automatic chain oiler,** which eliminates the need to periodically push a plunger to lubricate the chain and bar, and metal **bucking spikes,** which act as a pivot point when cutting larger logs. Some saws have a **chain-adjuster screw** mounted accessibly on the side of the bar, and a few Stihl models feature a **tools-free adjuster** that lets you loosen or tighten the chain by turning a wheel. Visible bar oil and fuel levels are also convenient, as is a wide rear handle that eases gas-saw starts by allowing room for the toe of a boot to secure the saw on the ground. Also look for **anti-vibration bushings** or **springs** between the handles and the engine, bar, and chain, along with a combined **choke/on-off switch** that activates a gas saw's ignition while closing off air to its carburetor for easier starting.

How to choose

PERFORMANCE DIFFERENCES. Tests by CONSUMER REPORTS have confirmed that gas saws cut faster than electrics and more

FOR SAFETY AND CONVENIENCE

1. Reduced-kickback chain
2. Reduced-kickback bar
3. Chain brake
4. Bar-tip guard
5. Trigger lockout
6. Shielded muffler
7. Chain adjuster
8. Bucking spikes
9. Font handle
10. Visible bar-oil level
11. Visible fuel level
12. Rear handle

saws now have important safety features. But they still must be used with care. What's more, even quieter electric saws remain noisy enough for CONSUMER REPORTS to recommend ear protection.

RECOMMENDATIONS. Buy a gasoline-powered saw if you need go-anywhere mobility. The best electrics, which cost less than $100, are fine for small branches and other light-duty cutting. In either case, you'll find a light saw (less than 14 pounds for gas models, less than 10 pounds for electrics) easier to use for longer periods. Unless you're felling large trees, a 14- or 16-inch bar should be more than adequate.

CHAIN SAWS ♦ **Ratings:** Page 205

10 ESSENTIAL GARDEN TOOLS

Tools for digging in the earth and harvesting its bounty are as old as civilization, with classic shapes honed through the centuries. But if you haven't looked at the tool section of your local hardware store in a while, you might be surprised at the new designs aimed at making digging, raking, pruning, and harvesting easier.

Here are 10 garden tools that every homeowner should have, with tips on how to choose them. You'll find them at home centers, mass merchandisers, hardware stores, and through online retailers such as Toolsforless.com and Amazon.com, and catalogs such as A.M. Leonard and Smith & Hawken.

1 TROWEL

Look for a trowel with a forged-steel head, which is thicker and sturdier than stamped steel, or one made of aluminum. Stainless steel and aluminum resist corrosion. The connection between head and handle is a trowel's weak spot. Look for a model with a strong "throat." Models with one-piece construction eliminate weak connections between the head and handle.

2 CULTIVATOR

A cultivator breaks up compacted surface soil and loosens weeds with the sharp tines of its three- or four-pronged metal claw. The handle is often hardwood or fiberglass, although some short-handled cultivators are made entirely of aluminum. Wood provides shock absorption that may be welcome when working hard soil. Aluminum and fiberglass are lighter weight and may be less tiring to use. The claw is typically made of steel. You'll want a sturdy shank connecting the handle to the claw.

3 & 4 SPADE AND SHOVEL

A sharp-edged spade is a versatile digging tool for planting, edging, digging perennials, and lots of other chores short of moving soil. That's where a scoop-shaped shovel comes in. Spade and shovel handles may be hard wood or fiberglass. Both are sturdy, so choose what's comfortable. Shovels usually have a long, straight handle. Choose one that reaches to about shoulder level. Spade handles are shorter to give you good control in tight spaces.

For best durability, look for features such as a long, fully welded shank joining the head to the handle. Forged steel will hold up better against rocks and other obstacles. Stainless steel is relatively easy to maintain, but you pay a premium for it. Forged carbon steel is sturdy, but beware of rust. Don't skimp on a cheap stamped-steel spade or shovel. It may not be up to the work required.

5 SCUFFLE HOE

A hoe with a flat steel head is good at cultivating soil and mixing fertilizer, but it's not the best at weeding. A scuffle hoe, also known as a stirrup hoe or an oscillating hoe, does all three jobs as you push and pull, eliminating wasted motion. Made with a hollowed-out trapezoidal steel head, it's especially good at weeding in open spaces. Look for a long, fully welded shank or a stirrup-style attachment secured with sturdy bolts joining the head to the handle.

6 PRUNER

There are two basic types of this indispensible garden tool. Bypass pruners are better for shaping shrubs, removing spent blooms, and taming overgrown vines. Their

HEDGE TRIMMERS

A good electric trimmer is all most people need to keep greenery shapely. Gasoline- or battery-powered models free you from a cord, but you pay for that convenience.

A gas or electric hedge trimmer can be a useful addition to your tool shed if your property includes lots of shrubs. Both types of trimmers can save you some of the physical effort hand clippers require, since an engine or motor—rather than elbow grease—powers their oscillating blades. But using any powered hedge trimmer can still be hard work, since you're holding these devices in midair, often with arms out, for extended periods. That can make a trimmer's weight, balance, and vibration as important as its cutting power.

blades pass each other like scissors and provide close, clean cuts in live wood. Anvil pruners crush branches between a sharp blade and a flat "anvil," a design that allows the pruner to cut through larger objects. They're better for dead wood.

Handles are typically an integral part of the tool, and range in length from 6 to 9 inches. When shopping, hold the tool to make sure it's comfortable in your hand. Try the blade-locking mechanism to make sure it operates easily, reliably, and conveniently.

With pruners, you get what you pay for. Pricier models have rotating handles that reduce the pressure on hands and fingers, along with removable blades that can be sharpened or replaced.

7 LOPPER

Loppers are essentially long-handled pruners used to trim tall shrubs or to tidy short trees while you stand firmly on the ground. As with pruners, the blade design is either bypass or anvil. Handles are often made of wood. Longer handles give you more leverage as you cut thick branches. Pricier models may sport lighter fiberglass handles, telescoping aluminum handles that can extend your reach by 2 to 3 feet, or a rotating or swiveling head that allows you to angle the blades for a precise cut without having to be a contortionist.

8 HEDGE CLIPPERS

Manual hedge clippers are the tool of choice for precisely shaping an ornamental shrub or trimming a few foundation shrubs. Basic models typically have a wooden handle and 9½-inch blades, which is fine for most needs. Check for weight and balance. Clippers that are blade

heavy or heavy overall will tire extended arms quickly. So will clippers that are hard to open and close; be sure there is a tension-adjustment knob. Also look for a limb notch located close to the handles on one of the blades. It's designed to snag thicker branches that may elude an unnotched blade's grip.

9 LEAF RAKE

Rake tines are made of bamboo, steel, or plastic. Bamboo tines can dry out and snap off over time. (An occasional soaking can reduce brittleness.) Steel tines are sturdy; plastic tines can snap in cold weather. Look for closely spaced tines, which will better contain leaves and other yard debris. Some rakes have an adjustable fan that can be widened for raking large areas and narrowed for getting between closely spaced plants or shrubs. Handles may be wood or fiberglass, some with rubber cushioning.

10 WHEELBARROW

Gardening requires hauling sacks, mulch, garden debris, and more. A wheelbarrow cuts down on the number of trips and the wear and tear on your back. Because a wheelbarrow's single tire makes it tippy, the wider the tire, the better the balance. Models with two closely spaced wheels have better balance still, but are less maneuverable.

The body, or "tray," of the wheelbarrow is commonly made of galvanized metal, painted metal, or polyethylene plastic. A polyethylene tray offers the advantage of lighter weight and resists corrosion. A galvanized tray is a good, tough choice. With painted metal, wear and tear will erode the paint, leaving the metal vulnerable to rust.

What's available

Black & Decker makes electric-powered models and sells more than half of all hedge trimmers. Craftsman (Sears) is Black & Decker's largest competitor, and sells electric plug-in and battery-powered trimmers as well as gas-powered models. Other brands include Echo, Homelite, Husqvarna, Little Wonder, Stihl, Ryobi, Toro, and Weed Eater.

ELECTRIC CORDED HEDGE TRIMMERS. Most homeowners prefer plug-in electric trimmers for several reasons. They are relatively light and quiet, start with the push of a button, produce no exhaust emissions, and require little maintenance. The best can also perform comparably to gasoline-powered models—provided you're within 100 feet of a power outlet. Price range: about $30 to $100.

GASOLINE-POWERED HEDGE TRIMMERS. Commercial landscapers favor gas-powered models for their power and mobility. Indeed, a gas-powered, long-reach trimmer can provide access to remote spots a corded electric trimmer can't reach. But their two-stroke engines entail the fuel-mixing, pull-starting, maintenance, and exhaust emissions of other gas-powered, hand-held yard tools. Gas trimmers can also be expensive. Price range: about $120 to $450.

ELECTRIC BATTERY-POWERED HEDGE TRIMMERS. Cordless trimmers combine the mobility of gas models with the convenience, clean running, and easy maintenance of plug-in electrics, courtesy of an onboard battery. On the downside, battery-powered trimmers offer relatively little cutting power, along with little running time before their battery must be recharged. They can also cost as much as some gas-powered models. Price range: about $80 to $120.

Key features

A hedge trimmer's **blades** comprise two flat metal plates with tooth-lined edges. Blade length typically ranges from 13 to 30 inches, although most are between 16 and 24 inches long. **Blade gap**—the distance between teeth—is also important, since it helps determine how large a branch the trimmer can cut. In general, the wider the gap, the larger the branch a trimmer can handle and the easier it is to push through a hedge.

Gasoline-powered, professional-grade trimmers have blade gaps of 1 inch or more, while homeowner-grade models typically have ⅜- to ¾-inch gaps—narrow enough to help keep fingers safely out.

Still other factors make some blades more effective than others. **Double-sided blades** allow cutting in both directions, letting you stand in one position longer than you can with **single-sided blades,** which cut in one direction only. Pricier trimmers also tend to use **dual-action blades,** where both the top and bottom blade plates move back and forth, reducing vibration compared with **single-action blades,** where only the top blade moves.

Handle designs also vary. Trimmers with a **wrap-around front handle** let you keep your hands in a comfortable position as you pivot the trimmer to cut vertically or at odd angles. Safety features include **tooth extensions,** which are designed to prevent thighs and other body parts from contacting the blade teeth. Some tooth extensions are part of the blades and move with them; CONSUMER REPORTS thinks separate, **stationary tooth extensions** provide better protection. Trimmers also have a **front-handle shield** designed to prevent your forward hand from touching the blade.

How to choose

PERFORMANCE DIFFERENCES. Any powered hedge trimmer should be up to light-duty tidying. The best can cut branches just shy of ⅝ inches in diameter, while dense ¼-inch-thick branches were enough to stop battery-powered trimmers CONSUMER REPORTS tested.

RECOMMENDATIONS. Begin by deciding which type of trimmer matches the trimming chores you do. Electric corded models are relatively quiet and inexpensive. They also deliver the best combination of cutting power, maneuverability, and ease—provided you stay within range of a power outlet. Battery-powered trimmers offer cord-free convenience, but their lack of cutting power and limited run time between charges make them best suited to touch ups and other light-duty work. In either case, look for an Underwriters Laboratories (UL) seal, which requires trimmers to have crucial safety features. Gasoline-powered models are for heavier-duty trimming beyond the range of a cord. Wear hearing protection when using gas-powered trimmers. And make sure you wear protective work gloves, safety glasses or goggles, and nonskid shoes when using any powered trimmer. Also be sure to work with care and do your trimming on firm footing or on a steady ladder. Don't try to work beyond your reach. And if you're using an electric trimmer, make sure the cord trails away from the blades.

LAWN MOWERS & TRACTORS

Practically any mower will cut your grass. But you can get better results with less effort by choosing a machine based on lawn size, your mowing preferences—and your budget.

Mowing options range anywhere from $100 manual-reel mowers to tractors that can cost $4,000 and beyond. Manual-reel and electric walk-behind mowers are appropriate for people with small yards, while gasoline-powered walk-behind mowers are fine for most lawns up to about half an acre. Those with lawns larger than that will appreciate the ease and speed of a riding mower or a lawn tractor.

Gasoline-powered mowers produce a disproportionate amount of air pollution compared with cars. Federal regulations aimed at reducing smog-producing lawn-mower emissions by 390,000 tons annually are being phased in over the next several years.

What's available

Manual-reel mowers are still made by a few companies, while major electric-mower brands include Black & Decker and Craftsman (Sears). Craftsman is also the largest-selling brand of gasoline-powered walk-behind mowers, riding mowers, and lawn tractors. Other less-expensive, mass-market brands for gas-powered mowers and tractors include Murray, Scotts, Stanley, Yard Machines, and Yard-Man. Pricier brands traditionally sold at outdoor power-equipment dealers include Ariens, Cub Cadet, Honda, Husqvarna, John Deere, Lawn Boy, Snapper, and Toro, although models from several of these brands are now available at large retailers.

Which type is best for your lawn? Here's what to think about for each:

MANUAL-REEL MOWERS. Pushing these simple mowers turns a series of curved blades that spin with the wheels. Reel mowers are quiet, inexpensive, and nonpolluting. They're also relatively safe to operate and require little maintenance other than periodic blade adjustment and sharpening. On the downside, our tests have shown that most can't cut grass higher than 1½ inches or trim closer than 3 inches around obstacles. Cutting swaths just 14 to 18 inches wide are also a drawback. Consider them for small, flat lawns a quarter acre or less. Price range: $100 to about $250.

ELECTRIC MOWERS. These push-type walk-behind mowers use an electric motor to drive a rotating blade. Both corded and cordless versions start with the push of a button, produce no exhaust emissions, and, like reel mowers, require little maintenance aside from sharpening. Most offer a side or rear grass catcher, and many can mulch—a process where clippings are recut until they're small enough to hide unobtrusively within the lawn. But electrics tend to be less powerful than gas mowers and less adept at tackling tall or thick grass and weeds. What's more, their narrow, 18- to 19-inch swaths take a smaller bite than most gas-powered mowers.

Both corded and cordless electrics have other significant drawbacks. Corded mowers limit your mowing to within 100 feet of a power outlet—the typical maximum length for extension cords. Cordless versions, while more versatile, weigh up to 30 pounds more than corded models and typically mow just one-quarter to one-third acre before their sealed lead-acid batteries need recharging. That makes both types of electrics suitable mainly for small, flat lawns a quarter acre or less. Price range: corded, $125 to $250; cordless, $300 to $400.

GASOLINE-POWERED WALK-BEHIND MOWERS. These include push as well as self-propelled models with driven wheels. Most have a 3.5- to 6.5-hp four-stroke engine and a cutting swath 20 to 22 inches wide, allowing them to do more work with each pass and handle long or thick grass and weeds. And all can mow as long as there's fuel in the tank. But gas mowers are relatively noisy and require regular maintenance.

Most gas mowers provide three cutting modes: bagging, which gathers clippings in a removable catcher; side-discharging, which dispenses clippings onto the lawn; and mulching, which cuts and recuts clippings until they're small enough to nestle and decompose in the lawn. Consider a push-type model for lawns of about a quarter acre that are relatively flat or for trimming larger lawns; a self-propelled model for lawns of a half acre or more or

---

BASIC MOWER MAINTENANCE

How to make your mower run better and last longer:

GAS-POWERED MOWERS

Clean the deck. According to manufacturers, built-up clippings interfere with airflow and hurt performance. Especially in damp conditions and at the end of the mowing season, disconnect the spark-plug wire and remove the clippings with a plastic trowel.

Sharpen the blade. A dull blade tears grass rather than cutting it, promoting disease. Remove the blade and sharpen it with a file, about $10, or pay a mower shop to do it. Sharpen the blade at least once each mowing season.

Change the oil. Once each mowing season, drain a four-stroke engine's crankcase and refill it with the oil recommended in the owner's manual. Check the level before each mowing and add more if needed. Two-stroke engines require no oil changes.

Clean or replace the air filter. Some mowers have a sponge filter you can clean and reoil, though most now use a disposable paper filter. Service when dirty—as often as once per mowing season.

Replace the spark plug. Do it when the inner tip has heavy deposits—sometimes as often as once per mowing season. A new plug makes for easier starts and cleaner running.

Store the mower properly. At the end of the mowing season, drain the gasoline and replace it with fresh fuel. Manufacturers suggest adding a stabilizer to prevent deposits that can clog the fuel passages, then briefly running the engine to circulate the mixture.

ELECTRIC MOWERS

Clean beneath the deck. First disconnect the mower's cord or, on cordless models, remove the safety key.

Keep the blade sharp. Follow the procedure for gas mowers.

Save the cell. With cordless models, stop mowing and plug in the charger when the battery starts running down. Draining a battery completely shortens its life. New ones cost about $100. Manufacturers also suggest leaving the battery on "charge" whenever you're not using the mower.

those that are hilly. Price range: push-type, $100 to more than $400; self-propelled, $250 to $900.

RIDING MOWERS AND TRACTORS. These are suitable for lawns one-half acre or larger. Riding mowers have their engines in back and tend to be smaller, simpler, and easier to maneuver than tractors. While their 28- to 33-inch mowing swath is larger than a walk-behind mower's, it's far smaller than the 38 to 48 inches offered by lawn tractors and the 60 inches available with some larger garden tractors. Lawn and garden tractors have larger engines mounted in front for better weight distribution. Both can also accept attachments that allow them to plow and tow a cart as well as clear snow, while garden tractors accept soil-tilling equipment. Lawn tractors have become far more popular than garden tractors, although even these usually can't mulch or bag without accessories; figure on another $25 to $150 for a mulching kit and $200 to $450 for a bagging system.

Zero-turn-radius riders and tractors are also gaining ground in the marketplace. With most, you steer by pushing or pulling control levers, each controlling a driven rear wheel, although John Deere manufactures a zero-turn lawn tractor that uses a conventional steering wheel. The payoff for these tight-turning machines is added maneuverability in tight spots and around obstacles. But you pay a premium for that agility. Price range: riding mowers, $700 to $2,000; lawn tractors, $800 to $3,500; garden tractors, $2,000 to $6,000; zero-turning-radius mowers, $3,000 to $7,000.

Key features

FOR ELECTRIC MOWERS. A **sliding clip** helps ease turns with corded mowers by allowing the cord to move from side to side. Some have a **flip-over handle** you move from one end of the mower to the other as you reverse direction, say, at the end of a row.

FOR GAS-POWERED MOWERS. Some more expensive models have a **blade-brake clutch system** that stops the blade but allows the engine to keep running when you release the handlebar safety bail. This is more convenient than the usual **engine-kill system,** which stops the engine and blade and requires you to restart the engine. A **four-stroke engine,** which burns gasoline alone, runs more cleanly than a **two-stroke engine,** which runs on a mixture of oil and gasoline. An **overhead-valve** four-stroke engine tends to pollute less than traditional **side-valve** four-stroke engines.

With most gas mowers, you press a small rubber bulb called a **primer** to supply extra fuel for cold starting. Those with a **choke** ease the cold-start process. **Electric starters** are easier to use than a **recoil starter,** though they typically add $50 to $100 to the price. Most mowers with recoil starters are easier to start than they once were, however. Some models from MTD-made Cub Cadet, White, and Yard-Man now have a spring-powered **self-starter,** which uses energy generated as the engine is shut off to provide push-button starts without a battery or outlet. CONSUMER REPORTS tests have found the device effective, provided you don't attempt starts in thick grass.

Some self-propelled mowers have just **one speed,** usually about 2½ mph; others have **several speeds** or a **continuous range,** typically from 1 to 3½ mph. Driven mowers also include **front-drive** and **rear-drive** models. Front-drive mowers tend to be easier to maneuver and turn, although rear-wheel-drive models tend to have better traction on hills and better steering control. Mowers with **swivel front wheels** offer the most maneuverability by allowing easy 180-degree turns. But on many, each front casterlike wheel must be removed to adjust cutting height.

You'll also find several different deck choices. Most are steel, although some mowers offer **aluminum** or **plastic** decks, which are rust-proof; plastic also resists dents and cracks. Even many lower-priced mowers now have **tools-free cutting-height adjusters,** which raise and lower the deck with one or two levers. Most models also allow you to change mowing modes without tools, although a few still require wrenches and, sometimes, a blade change. Some models use a **side-bagging deck design,** where a side-exit chute routes clippings into a side-mounted bag or out onto the lawn—or is blocked with a plate or plug for mulching.

Mowers with a **rear-bagging deck** tend to cost more, but their rear-mounted bag holds more than side bags and eases maneuvering by hanging beneath the handlebar, rather than out to the side. The rearward opening is fitted with a chute for side-discharging or a plug for mulching. Some **"hybrid" rear-baggers** have a discharge port for clippings on the side of the deck as well as one for the bag in back.

FOR RIDING MOWERS AND TRACTORS. Most are gear-driven and require a lever and combination brake/clutch to change speed. Some gear-drive models use foot pedals with a pulley that allows continuously variable speed changes without the usual shifting. Spending more will buy you a model with a clutchless **hydrostatic drive,** which allows even more convenient continuously variable speed changes. Most models have a **translucent fuel tank,** making it easy to check fuel level. Some have a **fuel gauge.** Still others allow you to remove the collection bags without flipping the seat forward.

How to choose

PERFORMANCE DIFFERENCES. Nearly all push and self-propelled gas mowers now handle mulching, bagging, and side-discharging. In tests, CONSUMER REPORTS found that most did at least a good job at mulching, the fastest and easiest way to dispose of clippings. All but the best mulchers in CONSUMER REPORTS tests left a few visible clippings on the lawn, while the worst left enough clippings to require raking. Even the best mulchers won't work well if the grass is too tall or wet, however.

Tests also found that a mower's horsepower rating tends to have little bearing on mowing performance. Rear-bagging mowers, whether gas or electric, tended to perform better than side-baggers. Electric models did a decent job at mulching, bagging, and side-discharging. But they struggled with tall grass or weeds, and they take a relatively narrow bite with each pass.

Virtually all riding mowers and tractors can also handle all three mowing modes. In tests, most did a thorough job of vacuuming up clippings when bagging, although some clogged before their bags were full. The best held more than twice as many clippings as the best push mowers.

RECOMMENDATIONS. Balance the size of your yard with how much you want to spend. Gas-powered push and self-propelled mowers are appropriate for many lawns. Electric mowers offer cleaner, quieter running and easy maintenance—but they're limited by a cord or, for cordless models, relatively little mowing time between charges. Homeowners with small lawns can also consider a manual-reel mower. Just be sure that your lawn isn't too thick and that you don't skip a week. If you decide to ride, you'll probably want a lawn tractor unless your lawn has lots of tight areas and obstacles. Then the smaller size of a riding mower is an advantage. You can also opt for a zero-turn mower or tractor, which combines a wide deck with 360-degree turning; but at $3,000 and beyond, it remains an expensive option.

LAWN MOWERS AND TRACTORS ♦ **Ratings:** Page 236, 238, 241 ♦ **Reliability:** Page 298

POWER BLOWERS

Gasoline-powered models are cleaner and less noisy; electric models are quieter still, and more powerful than before.

These miniature wind machines take some of the effort out of sweeping and gathering fallen leaves and other small yard and driveway debris. Many can also vacuum and shred what they pick up. But practically all still make enough noise to be obtrusive. Indeed, some localities have ordinances restricting or forbidding their use.

What's available

Mainstream brands include Black & Decker, Homelite, Craftsman (Sears), Toro, and Weed Eater. Pricier brands of gas-powered blowers include Echo, Husqvarna, John Deere, and Stihl. As with other outdoor power tools, gas and electric blowers each have their pros and cons. You'll also find variations among gas-powered models. Here are your choices:

ELECTRIC HANDHELD BLOWERS. Designed for one-handed maneuvering, these are light (about 7 pounds or less). They are also relatively quiet, produce no exhaust emissions, and many can vacuum and shred. Some perform as well as handheld gas-powered models, although their mobility is limited by their power cord. Price range: $30 to $100.

GASOLINE HANDHELD BLOWERS. These perform similarly to the best electrics, but can venture as far as their fuel tank takes them. Tougher regulations have reduced allowable emissions for gas blowers as they have for other equipment, while manufacturers have quieted these machines in response to new noise ordinances. Most models are still loud enough to warrant hearing protection, however. Other drawbacks include added weight (most weigh 7 to 12 pounds) and the fuel-and-oil mixing that is required by the two-stroke engines most models use. A few models, notably from Ryobi, have four-stroke engines that burn gasoline only. Price range: $75 to $225.

GASOLINE BACKPACK BLOWERS. At 15 to 28 pounds, these are heavier than handheld blowers. But the payoff with most is added power and ease of use for extended periods, since your shoulders support their weight. Backpack blowers don't vacuum, however, and hearing protection is recommended. They can also be expensive. Price range: $200 to $500.

GASOLINE ROLLING BLOWERS. These offer enough oomph to sweep sizable areas quickly. All use four-stroke engines that require no fuel mixing. But these machines are large, heavy, and require pushing. They also cost the most and tend to be hard to maneuver, which can make it difficult to precisely direct leaves and other yard waste. And because they're noisier than gas lawn mowers, count on using hearing protection. Price range: $500 to $700.

Key features

Look for an **easy-to-use on-off switch** on electric blowers, a **variable throttle** you can preset on electric and gasoline-powered models, and a **convenient choke** on gas-powered units. Blowers that excel at cleaning usually have **round-nozzle blower tubes; oblong** and **rectangular nozzles** are better for moving leaves. A **control stalk** attached to the blower tube of a backpack model improves handling, while an **auxiliary handle** on the engine or motor housing of a handheld unit eases use—provided the handle is comfortable. Other useful features in gas-powered models include a **wide fuel fill** and a **translucent fuel tank,** which shows the level inside.

How to choose

PERFORMANCE DIFFERENCES. In CONSUMER REPORTS tests, the strongest blowers could push leaves into piles 20 inches high, while the weakest had trouble building 12-inch piles. The best electric blowers are on a par with most gasoline-powered models and tend to be lighter and easier to handle. Backpack blowers, while heavy, tend to be easiest to use for extended periods, since the blower tube is all you hold in your hands.

RECOMMENDATIONS. Begin by matching the blower to your property. The smaller the leaf-clearing job, the less blowing power you'll need. You can also get by with less power if you'll be clearing mostly hard surfaces such as a driveway—jobs for which relatively quiet, light, and inexpensive handheld electric machines may suffice. Models that vacuum can be handy for sucking leaves out from corners and beneath shrubs. Whichever power blower you're considering, find out about any local noise restrictions before buying.

STRING TRIMMERS

An electric model can do a good job for many trimming tasks. But for strong all-around performance, you'll need a gasoline-powered trimmer.

A string trimmer can pick up where a lawn mower leaves off. It provides the finishing touches, slicing through tufts of grass around trees and flower beds, straightening uneven edges along a driveway, and trimming stretches of lawn your mower or tractor can't reach. Gasoline-powered models can also whisk away tall grass and weeds. A

All string trimmers can venture into rock-strewn areas that would destroy a mower's metal blades, thanks to their flexible plastic lines. Some, however, are less capable and convenient at those tasks.

What's available

Black & Decker, Craftsman (Sears), Homelite, Ryobi, Toro, and Weed Eater are the major mainstream brands, with Weed Eater selling the most. Leading high-end brands include Echo, Husqvarna, and Stihl. You'll also find several kinds of trimmers. Here's how to determine which will work best for your needs.

GASOLINE-POWERED TRIMMERS. These are better than electrics at cutting heavy weeds and brush, and are often better at edging, where you turn them so that their spinning lines cut vertically along a walk or garden border. They also go anywhere and cut relatively large swaths up to 18 inches wide. Some accept a metal blade (usually an option) that can cut branches up to about 3⁄4-inch thick. On the downside, gas trimmers can be heavy, weighing from about 10 to 16 pounds. Most have a two-stroke engine that requires a mixture of gas and oil, tends to pollute more than the four-stroke engines, and entails pull-starting and regular maintenance. Price range: less than $100 to more than $300. Most models, however, cost from $100 to $200.

ELECTRIC CORDED TRIMMERS. These are least expensive and lightest; many weigh only about 5 pounds. Some work nearly as well as gas trimmers for most trimming, and all are quieter and easier to start and stop than gas trimmers; you simply pull a trigger, rather than a rope. But their power cord limits their range to about 100 feet from an outlet. Many models have the motor at the bottom of the shaft, rather than at the top, making them harder to handle. And even the most powerful models are unlikely to tackle the tall grass and weeds that the best gas-powered trimmers can tackle. Price range: $25 to $75.

ELECTRIC BATTERY-POWERED TRIMMERS. Cordless trimmers combine the free range of gas trimmers with the convenience of corded electrics: less noise, easy starting and stopping, no fueling, and no exhaust emissions. But they're weak at cutting and run only about 15 to 30 minutes before their onboard battery needs recharging, which can take a day. They also tend to be pricey and heavy for their size (about 10 pounds), and models with the motor at the bottom of the shaft can be even harder to handle than lighter corded versions. Price range: $70 to $100.

Key features

All trimmers have a **shaft** that connects the engine or motor and controls to the **trimmer head** where the plastic lines revolve. **Curved-shaft trimmers** are the most common, and can be easier to handle when trimming up close. **Straight-shaft trimmers** tend to be better for reaching beneath bushes and other shrubs. On models without a clutch, the string is always spinning while the engine is running—an inconvenience. Some models have a **split shaft** that comes apart so that you can replace the trimmer head with a leaf blower, edging blade, or other yard tool, though CONSUMER REPORTS has found that some of these attachments aren't very effective.

Most gas-powered trimmers have **two cutting lines,** while many electrics use just one, which provides less cutting with each revolution. Most gas and electric trimmers have a **bump-feed line advance** that feeds out more line when you bump the trimmer head on the ground; a blade on the safety shield cuts it to the right length.

Auto-feed systems add convenience by automatically feeding out new line as they

TRIMMING SAFELY

A trimmer's string can give you a painful sting even through clothing, draw blood on bare skin, and also fling dirt and debris. When you're trimming, wear gloves, long pants, sturdy shoes, safety glasses, and, with a gas trimmer, ear protection.

sense a change in the centrifugal force exerted by a shortened line. But some auto-feed systems don't work very well and may compromise cutting performance. In either case, replacing the line usually involves removing and rethreading the empty spool. With some trimmers, you simply pull off the old spool and push on a new one.

Most gasoline models use **two-stroke engines,** which burn lubricating oil with the gasoline. Federal law requires manufacturers to slash exhaust emissions for new gas-powered trimmers by 70 percent by 2005, while California has required that emissions reduction since 2000. Some trimmers use inherently cleaner **four-stroke engines,** but these tend to weigh and cost more. Corded and battery models typically use a 1.8- to 5-amp motor.

To start most gas trimmers, you set a **choke** and push a **primer bulb,** then pull a rope. On most, a **centrifugal clutch** allows the engine to idle without spinning the line—safer and more convenient than models where the line continues to turn. Electric-trimmer lines don't spin until you press the switch. Some models make edging more convenient with a **rotating head, shaft,** or **handle** that makes the trimmer head easier to move to the vertical position. Heavier-duty models often offer a **shoulder harness** that can ease handling and reduce fatigue. Other convenient features include **easy-to-reach** and **easy-to-adjust switches, comfortable handles,** and—on gas models—a **translucent fuel tank.**

How to choose

PERFORMANCE DIFFERENCES. While almost any machine can trim a small, well-maintained lawn, some corded electric trimmers and all the battery-powered models in the most recent CONSUMER REPORTS tests proved weak. As a rule with electric trimmers, the higher the amperage, the better they cut. Slicing through tall grass and weeds generally requires a gasoline-powered trimmer, although our tests have shown no correlation between engine size and performance with these units.

RECOMMENDATIONS. Look for a trimmer that fits your physique, allowing you to work without stooping and to maintain good balance so that your arms don't tire before the work is done. For competent performance on a range of trimming and edging tasks, you'll probably prefer a gas-powered model. For smaller spaces and lighter-duty trimming, consider a corded electric trimmer. Look for one with the motor on top of the shaft for better balance and easier handling. Consider a cordless electric model only for the lightest of trimming chores.

STRING TRIMMERS ◆ Ratings: Page 267

Home 'Software'

Shoppers looking for things such as mattress sets, sheets and towels, or Oriental rugs and carpeting—home "software" as we call it—can face hard choices. Comparison shopping can be difficult in these categories. Price ranges for similar-looking items can be quite broad, model numbers can be obscure, often purposefully so, and product specifications spotty. The names of essentially identical mattress sets can vary from store to store. Manufacturers often make little tweaks at the behest of retailers, which benefit by having a product under their own brand name. Buying sheets can be tricky because labeling isn't clear. Not all sheet manufacturers have caught up with changes in mattresses, so sheets labeled "deep-pocketed" don't necessarily fit a 12-inch-deep pillowtop mattress. Prices of Oriental rugs are lower than they were in the late '80s and early '90s, but it's still possible to pay more than you should for what you get. Shopping for wall-to-wall carpeting also poses pitfalls. Many stores provide little in the way of important information such as pile height or tufts per square inch. Buying even the humble towel requires plumbing the mysteries of pima, Supima, and other fibers.

MATTRESS SETS

Once you've settled on the firmness and size you want, compare quality details and price from brand to brand and store to store.

If you think shopping for a car is an ordeal, try shopping for a mattress. Sure, you can lie down on a mattress, maybe even take it home for a 30-day "test drive." But try to peek at its innards and you'll be thrown out of the showroom. Worse still, while a Ford Taurus is a Ford Taurus nationwide, the names of essentially identical mattresses—called "comparables" by the industry—often differ from store to store. Independent bedding shops typically offer mattress sets from manufacturers' national lines. Major chains such as Macy's and Sears and telephone-order sources such as Dial-A-Mattress sell mattresses from the same manufacturers' lines but with names unique to the chain. Comparables are supposed to share basic components, construction, and firmness but may differ in color, fabric pattern, or quilting stitch. Consumers are the losers, since they can't comparison shop. This name game allows retailers to vary the price of similar mattresses by hundreds of dollars.

What's available

Sealy, Serta, and Simmons account for nearly three out of every four mattresses sold, but there are more than 35 other brands. The big makers offer no-frills models, but most people are more familiar with their flagship lines: Sealy Posturepedic, Serta Perfect Sleeper, and Simmons Beautyrest.

You can buy a mattress filled with water, foam, or air, but innerspring mattresses—named for their coiled steel springs sandwiched between layers of padding—remain the most widely purchased type. The padding, usually identical on top and bottom so you can flip the mattress, is generally made of several materials, including polyurethane foam, puffed-up polyester, or cotton batting. Mattresses used to be about 7 inches deep. Now they can range from 9 to 18 inches. If you buy a thicker mattress than what you have now, you may have to buy sheets with deeper pockets or corners.

Key features

Most stores have a cutaway or cross-section of at least some of the mattress sets on display. Here's what you should look for and ask about:

Ticking is a mattress's outermost layer. On most models, the ticking is polyester or a cotton-polyester blend. Low-end mattresses may have vinyl ticking, which can eventually stretch and sag. Fancier mattresses have damask ticking with the design woven into the fabric, not printed on it. Some also contain a bit of silk, which is more a marketing gimmick than any substantial benefit.

In most cases, **quilting** attaches a few layers of padding to the ticking. Stitch design varies and is largely an aesthetic consideration. Make sure stitches are uniform and unbroken; broken threads can allow the fabric to loosen and pucker. Top padding is generally polyurethane foam, with or without polyester batting. Batting provides a uniform, soft feel but tends to lose its loft faster than does a soft foam.

Middle padding lies below the quilted layer and often starts with foam. Convoluted foam, shaped like an egg carton, feels softer than a straight slab of the same type of foam, and it spreads your weight over a wider surface area, which should make you more comfortable. Soft, resilient foams feel almost moist to the touch. Foams that feel dry or crunchy won't spring back as readily. Other padding often consists of garnetted cotton (thick wads of rough batting that provide loft but compress quickly) and more foam of varied thickness and density. In some mattresses, firmness differs from area to area. One side may be firmer than the other, or a middle section may be firmer than the head or foot. A "test nap" is the only way to tell if a mattress is right for you.

Insulation padding lies directly on the springs and prevents you from feeling them.

ANATOMY OF A SLEEPSET

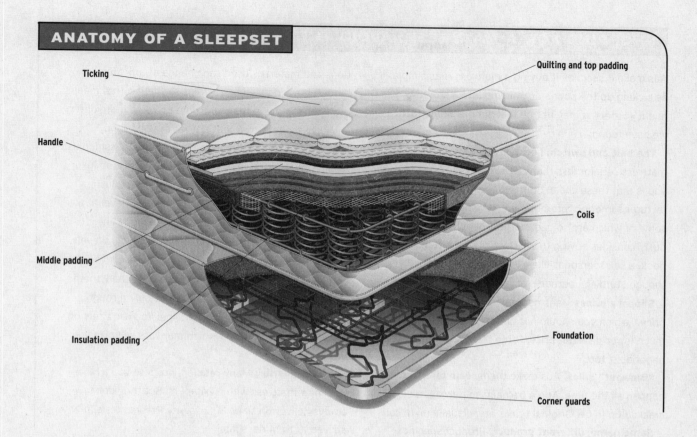

Ticking

Handle

Middle padding

Insulation padding

Quilting and top padding

Coils

Foundation

Corner guards

Commonly used bedding insulators include "coco pad," the fibrous matter from a coconut husk, and "shoddy pad," pieces of fabric that are matted and often glued together. Coco pad, especially in more than one layer, makes a mattress stiffer. Plastic webbing, nonwoven fabric, or a metal grid directly atop the springs can help keep them from chewing up the pad.

Extra support is added to certain areas—at the edge, say, so you have a solid place to sit when you tie your shoes. If you want extra support at the head, foot, sides, or center, ask whether the mattress beefs up those areas by means of more closely spaced coils, slabs of stiff foam inserted between the coils, thicker wire, or extra springs.

Coils are the springs that support you. While coil design doesn't affect a mattress's ability to withstand use and abuse, it does shape the bed's overall "feel." The wire in springs comes in a range of thicknesses, or gauges. As a rule, the lower the gauge number, the thicker and stiffer the wire and the firmer the mattress. The higher the gauge number, the thinner the wire and the softer the mattress.

Handles let you reposition the mattress on the box spring. They're not meant to support its full weight, which is why most warranties don't cover broken handles. Best are handles that go through the sides of the mattress and are anchored to the springs. Next best are fabric handles sewn vertically to the tape edging of the mattress. Most common is the weakest design: handles inserted through the fabric and clipped to a plastic or metal strip.

The foundation, or box spring, can be a plain fiberboard-covered wooden frame, a wooden frame containing heavy-gauge springs, or even a metal frame with springs. A plain wooden frame, usually found with cheaper sleep sets, is adequate only if the wood is

SHOPPING FOR A MATTRESS: AVOID THE PITFALLS

Ads make it seem as if buying a mattress is as simple as picking up the phone or waltzing into a store. As you might suspect, it may not be that simple. Some tactics we have found:

The bait and switch. Low-ball ads tout name-brand mattress sets for less than $40. What they don't tell you is that these cheap mattresses are from the manufacturer's inferior "promotional" or "subpremium" lines, some of which are so bad that few people would seriously consider buying them. Once you've bitten the hook, a salesperson is likely to steer you to a costlier, though sturdier, upgrade.

Slippery prices. Tags generally note a fictitious "list price," which you should not dream of paying, and a much lower discount price. Often the discount price is negotiable, too.

"Blowout" sales. Ads make them seem rare, but they happen all the time. And a bargain isn't always all it's cracked up to be. Original prices are virtually mythical.

Same name, different product. Product specifications and materials used can change at any time, though the model name remains the same. That means the floor sample in the showroom could be quite different from the mattress that arrives at your door.

Confusing jargon. You'll see mattresses classified as, say, premium, superpremium, ultrapremium, and luxury, and firmness levels described as pillow soft, plush, cushion firm, and superfirm or no firmness level at all. There can be dozens of variations within any line. Sealy, for instance, offers several quality and firmness levels. The descriptions of quality and firmness levels vary by brand—one company's firm may be harder than another's extra firm—and should be used as only a rough guide within brands. The bottom line: You can't rely on product labels to tell you which mattress will give you the desired feel.

Late deliveries. Many retailers promise you'll have your new mattress within 24 hours. But they don't always deliver on time. In CONSUMER REPORTS tests, many arrived 10 to 14 days late.

straight and free of cracks. Placing a mattress atop a plain wooden frame can make the mattress seem harder than it actually is. Corner guards help keep the foundation's fabric from chafing against the metal corners of the bed frame.

How to choose

PERFORMANCE DIFFERENCES. A firmer mattress won't resist permanent sagging better than a softer mattress. A thicker mattress sags more than a thinner mattress. And because all the permanent compression is within the padding layers, not the springs, more padding equals more potential for sagging.

RECOMMENDATIONS. The only way to judge mattress comfort is to try out a variety of brands and models in the store. (If you buy by phone, of course, you'll have to do your testing at home—after having made sure you can exchange an unsatisfactory mattress.) A good mattress will gently support your body at all points. Although we could find no published scientific data on which type of mattress is best, orthopedic experts generally recommend the firmest mattress that you find comfortable.

Never pay list price for a mattress. Sales are common, and deeper savings are often possible if you bargain. If you spend at least $450 for a twin-size mattress set, $600 for a full-size, $800 for a queen-size, and $1,000 for a king-size, you can get a high-quality, durable product. Spending more for a mattress gets you thicker padding, damask ticking, and perhaps a pillowtop—a cushion on both sides of the mattress that's filled with foam, wool, silk, or a down blend. Mattress-by-phone businesses usually offer rock-bottom prices, especially if you persist in seeking low quotes, but you buy the bedding unseen and untried. Be sure you can exchange it. When you buy a mattress, buy a box spring, too; they perform as a unit. Putting a new mattress on an old box spring could void your warranty.

ORIENTAL RUGS

Intricate patterns, lustrous yarns, and artfully blended colors help explain the timeless allure of Oriental rugs. But some aren't where from the label says they're from—and some are overpriced.

Handmade rugs are less expensive than they were in the late 1980s and early 1990s and there's a wider selection of patterns and colors. Machine-made rugs are improving in quality and come in increasingly varied designs. Synthetic yarns are also better able to mimic natural materials, while new looms permit 20 or more colors in a machine-made rug. Credit some of that windfall to computer-aided design and computerized weaving, which have led to faster production—and faster response to buyers' desires and to changes in fashion. The bad news: Many Oriental rugs are still overpriced for what they are. You can wind up with one that curls up, bleeds, or lies about its origins—or is less "antique" than it appears.

What's available

Technically, an Oriental rug is knotted by hand of wool, silk, cotton, or rayon, and has a raised pile, not a flat surface. Common parlance broadens that definition to include rugs made in an Oriental style. Such a rug can be made by hand or by machine; made of natural or synthetic fibers; and qualify as antique (made before 1915, as a rule), semiantique (made between 1915 and 1950), or contemporary. And it can be made in the traditional places—China, India, Iran (formerly Persia), Pakistan, Turkey—or elsewhere.

Historically, patterns and colors were specific to a city, village, or tribe. Today, designs are not restricted to their countries of origin. India, China, and Pakistan, the countries where the majority of handmade rugs are produced, turn out rugs in most of the traditional patterns and colors. As a result, you'll often see patterns preceded by the prefixes Indo-, Sino-, or Pak-. (The Federal Trade Commission requires labels to list the country of origin and the business name of the distributor.) Whatever its pattern, a rug is called "tribal" if it has been woven by members of a nomadic group. Such rugs tend to be small rather than room-sized.

Several other factors affect an Oriental rug's desirability beyond its price. While traditional Oriental rugs are made of wool, you'll also find them in silk, silk blends, and—these days—artificial fibers such as olefin. The typical price range for wool is between $12 and $75 per square foot compared with as little as $2 per square foot for olefin. All wools and weaves aren't created equal, however. Nor does the word "handmade" guarantee better quality.

You'll find new Oriental rugs of one kind or another at department stores, specialty shops, home centers, mass marketers, auction houses, and mail-order companies. You'll also find semiantique and antique rugs sold by big-city rug dealers. Avoid shopping for rugs at "hotel auctions." You can't return goods if you're not satisfied, and you may not get what you think you're getting.

ORIENTAL RUGS: A PRIMER ON PATTERNS

Oriental rugs come in many different patterns. Four common ones—Heriz, Kirman, Sarouk, and Tabriz—are named for rug-making centers in Iran (formerly Persia). Heriz is usually a geometric pattern with a central medallion on a brick-colored field with a navy border. Kirman, Sarouk, and Tabriz are floral patterns. Kirmans can feature pastels or bright jewel tones. Sarouks often have a red background and sprays of flowers. An "American" Sarouk was woven in Persia in the 1920s or 1930s and was meant for the U.S. market; weavers used salmon-colored yarn that was hand-painted maroon in the United States. Tabriz can come in various designs.

Heriz

Kirman

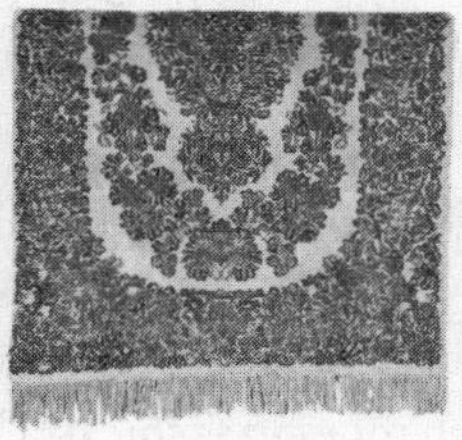

Sarouk

Tabriz

Aubusson designs, originally found in flat-woven tapestry rugs from France, are typically made in China or India, where the thick wool pile is "carved," creating an embossed look.

Aubsson

Bokhara, named for a city in Uzbekistan where tribal rugs were sold, is generally a geometric design in which a smallish round mark called a "gul" or "elephant's foot" is repeated.

Bokhara

Key considerations

Made by hand or machine? Handmade should mean hand-knotted; each strand of yarn has been tied to the rug's foundation by hand. Although the term conveys a certain cachet, the quality of those rugs depends on the skill of the maker. A good machine-made rug can be a better value than a poor-quality handmade one. Moreover, the overall quality of machine-made rugs is more consistent than that of handmade rugs. And if the wool and construction are good, a machine-made rug should last as long as a handmade one—and those can last more than 100 years.

Still, machine-made rugs lack the subtleties of design or the unique character of hand-knotted rugs, and the best machine-made rug can't compare with the best handmade, which can take more than a year to make. Because labels need not identify whether the rug was made by hand or by machine, it pays to check for yourself. Here's how to recognize a handmade rug:

◆ With the rug facing up, bend the pile back across the width of the rug—a process that is known as grinning. A handmade rug will have a small knot at each yarn's base, near the backing.

◆ Look also at the fringe. In a handmade rug, it's usually an extension of the warp yarns—the foundation threads that run the length of the rug (as opposed to weft threads, running the width of the rug). In a machine-made rug, there are no knots, and the fringe is generally sewn on separately.

HOW GOOD IS THE WEAVE? An enthusiastic salesperson (and occasionally a tag) may boast that a rug has 200 knots per square inch, implying that knot count is an indicator of quality. It is—but only one of many. Rugs with an identical knot count can differ greatly in overall quality.

Other factors being equal, a higher count renders a more detailed design and will usually make for a longer-lasting rug. But the count will vary based on design (floral or curved designs generally require more knots than geometric designs) and the yarn's thickness (thin yarn allows for more knots). Expect a higher knot count to mean a higher price per square foot, too.

Clouding matters further, the method of counting varies with the type of rug. Chinese rugs have a line **count**—220, for example—representing the number of knots in a horizontal foot (across the rug's width). Contemporary Tabriz rugs are often graded by **"raj,"** the number of knots in 2¾ horizontal inches, rounded to the nearest 10 (you'll see numbers such as 70 raj). Rugs from Pakistan often carry two numbers, such as 16/18. The first represents the number of knots in a horizontal inch; the second, the number of knots in a vertical inch.

Machine-made rugs have their own system for counting the density of yarns—points per square meter or tufts per square inch—but you'll see it less often. While actually counting the knots in a handmade rug may not be practical, you can tell a lot about a rug's weave by looking at its back. The weave should be fairly consistent, though the knots won't be perfectly uniform. And each color should be fairly consistent, though slight horizontal variations, called abrash, caused by yarns of different dye lots, are OK.

WHAT'S IT MADE OF? In general, wool is generally considered the best pile fiber for a rug: It wears extremely well, takes dyes well, doesn't mat, and is generally easy to clean. But wool quality is critical.

You can assess the quality of the wool in a new rug by running your hand back and forth a few times over the surface. If the rug sheds lots of fuzzy fibers on your hand or on the rug's surface, it is probably made of low-quality wool and will not hold up well. Very soft "sweater" or "garment" wool bends back and forth when vacuumed and is inappropriate in any rug, though you may see it in Chinese rugs with an Aubusson design. "Dead wool"—chemically separated from the hide of a dead sheep rather than shorn from a live one—feels dry and brittle or wiry, sheds easily, and won't hold up over time. It's found most often in very cheap rugs from India.

Some rugs have a "Wools of New Zealand" label, certifying that the rug is made of at least 80 percent New Zealand wool, which is of high quality. On a handmade rug, the certification also claims to mean that the rug was produced without child labor.

Olefin, also called polypropylene or a brand name such as Exellan, is a plastic fiber. It wears well but is hard to clean if stained with something oily. Labels generally warn against dry cleaning. Olefin can be a good choice in a basement or in any moist climate because it tolerates humidity and resists mold and mildew. Although the patterns and colors are the same as those used in wool Orientals, it's fairly easy to identify low-priced olefin. It has a somewhat artificial-looking shine, and colors tend to be flat or monochromatic. More-expensive olefin looks a lot like wool.

Silk rugs are fragile and hard to clean, and can be expensive. If the price of a silk rug seems too good to be true, the rug is probably rayon or mercerized cotton. If you're considering a silk rug, ask the seller to pull a small bit of yarn and burn it. When burned, silk smells like burned hair and leaves a small bead; rayon or cotton smells like burned paper. Cotton leaves ash, and rayon leaves no residue.

Also, beware of labels that say "art. silk." "Art." does not refer to the skills of a talented rug designer; it means artificial. Art. silk is rayon, and a poor fiber for rugs. "A. silk" and "faux soie" mean rayon, too. Many such rugs are made in China or India.

How to choose

PERFORMANCE DIFFERENCES. How well an Oriental rug holds up to cleaning depends on more than just its pile fiber. While the Federal Trade Commission requires that pile-fiber information be on the label, information about the backing fiber needn't be—and wasn't in the rugs CONSUMER REPORTS tested. That means "100 percent wool" refers only to the pile yarn, not the fringe or foundation, which is usually made of cotton or wool in handmade rugs and synthetic fiber or wool in machine-made rugs. That difference can become significant during cleaning, so it's important that the cleaner be a professional who can identify the fibers. Rugs with wool pile should generally be wet-cleaned; those with silk pile should generally be dry-cleaned. Rugs with rayon pile should always be dry-cleaned.

Colorfastness is another variable among Oriental rugs. Historically, Oriental rugs were colored with vegetable dyes, and some still are. Most new rugs are dyed with synthetic chemicals. Either way, rub a damp white cloth over dark portions of the pile. If color comes off on the cloth, the rug will bleed during cleaning.

White knots occur when warp yarns break during weaving and the weaver splices the pieces together. These knots eventually work their way to the surface of the pile and become more visible as the rug wears. A few white knots are inevitable, even in the hands of the best weavers, but avoid rugs liberally sprinkled with white knots. If you're tempted to cut them out, don't. You'll break the rug's backing and create a hole.

As for symmetry, no handmade rug will measure precisely, say, 4½ feet on each side, but the measurements should at least be close.

RECOMMENDATIONS. Your budget and your family life are the best guides to narrowing down your choices. For less expensive rugs, a good-quality machine-made wool rug combines good looks and practicality. We found well-made Couristan and Karastan rugs in attractive designs and colors and with a moth-resistant finish.

Consider a low-priced olefin rug if you want something to cover the floor until you can afford something better. Olefin rugs that cost about $7 to $9 per square foot tend to be more attractive than the $2-per-square-foot rugs we bought.

Another option is a dhurrie or kilim, which can provide a lot of decoration for as little as $4 per square foot. Unlike traditional Oriental rugs, dhurries and kilims are flat-woven—they have no pile. Dhurries are made in India of cotton or wool. Kilims are made in Turkey, China, and Egypt, among other countries, and are usually made of wool. Although both are somewhat less durable than pile rugs, they should hold up for years, even in high-traffic areas. Wool will be somewhat more durable than cotton. One drawback: Kilims and dhurries don't mask stains as well as pile rugs, since there's nowhere for dirt to hide.

When buying pricier handmade rugs—or for that matter, any handmade rug—try to get a detailed receipt listing the country of origin, the fiber content of pile and foundation, the age, and (for new rugs only) the grade, as indicated by knot count. Sellers will often write "fine-quality Indo-Persian" or some such. That isn't good enough.

The Oriental Rug Retailers Association's code of ethics says rugs must be marked with a price, but many retailers ignore that guideline. Even when prices are shown, they're often a figment of the dealer's imagination. We found one Indo-Heriz with an original price of

SPOTTING A PROBLEM ORIENTAL RUG

Several common flaws and deceptions mean there's less to some Oriental rugs than meets the eye. Watch for:

Chemical wash. This common technique adds luster to wool and mutes colors so a new rug looks antique. How to tell: Fold back the pile to expose the base of the fibers. The original colors are more garish.

Surrogate silk. Rayon pile on cotton backing is typical of the phony silk rugs sold at sales in hotels or at itinerant auctions. Its dyes generally won't be colorfast. How to tell: Ask the dealer to burn a bit of yarn. Silk will smell like burning hair.

Curling. One salesman told us the curled, Heriz-design rug we bought would flatten out after a few days on the floor. It didn't. How to tell: Just look. This problem has a solution: Two-inch strips of vinyl can be sewn underneath the sides.

Dry rot. Another common problem, particularly on some antique rugs. How to tell: Bend sections of the rug with your hands. If you feel and hear something like breaking matchsticks, don't buy the rug.

A paint job. Paint on the back may hide areas where bleach used on the fringe wicked into the foundation.

During cleaning, the paint will blacken the fringe. How to tell: Wipe a damp white cloth over the foundation and see if color comes off.

Tea wash. A wash of tea or dye can also make a new rug look antique. Tea washes aren't a problem unless they're done badly. How to tell: Look for splotches on the rug's back. Rub the pile with a wet white towel and see if the stain comes off.

Bleeding. Sometimes dye bleeds from the field onto the fringe, often during a chemical wash. How to tell: Peer at the area between a dark color and a lighter one, and at both ends of the fringe.

Handmade vs. hand-knotted. Some rugs are made with a tufting gun—operated by hand but a far cry from hand-knotting. How to tell: Check for hand-knotting. And be suspicious when cotton monk's cloth hides the latex backing that holds in the tufts.

Applied fringe. Fringe on a handmade rug should be a continuation of the warp yarns; otherwise the rug may have been repaired. Although a separate fringe can be applied expertly, it can affect value. How to tell: Look for stitching or discontinuous warp yarns.

$1,259 marked down to $440. In fact, $440 is the price the rug should have been from the start. Be wary of discounts exceeding 20 percent; they're usually an indication that the original price has been inflated somewhere along the line.

Beware of auctions other than those by such well-known houses as San Francisco's Butterfield & Butterfield and Boston's Skinner Galleries. In any case, you'll need to be expert in judging rugs, and you can't return what you've bought. And wherever you buy, determine up front whether you can return the rug or take it home on approval. If you buy from a catalog, you'll have to pay shipping charges if you return the rug.

Also remember that, true to the old stereotype, getting the best price on an Oriental rug usually involves some bargaining. You won't be able to do that via mail order, of course, and it may be hard in department stores, though you can always ask the salesperson to "do a little better." The best way to compare value is to calculate each rug's price per square foot. Finally, don't expect to reap a profit. Few Oriental rugs made after 1950 increase in value. The bottom line: Buy a rug you like at a price you like.

If you're considering an antique or silk rug, ask to take the rug home (some dealers require a deposit), get a due-back date in writing, and set up an appointment with a qualified independent appraiser. Most appraisers charge at least $100 per hour, so discuss your expectations beforehand. Avoid appraisers who charge a percentage of the rug's value as a fee and those who offer free appraisals.

MAINTAINING YOUR RUG. Good rugs deserve good care. In the past, rugs were hung over a sturdy pole and beaten. Today, you'll need a vacuum cleaner with a beater bar. Vacuum the rug's surface at least twice a month. Because gritty dirt abrades the rug's backing, vacuum the back of the rug occasionally, too.

When it's time for a real cleaning—every one to three years, depending on household traffic—take the rug to a professional cleaner experienced with Oriental rugs. When the rug comes home, place it in a position 180 degrees from where it was before cleaning to equalize wear.

SHEETS

In addition to deciding on a color or pattern, you'll have to choose from an array of materials and sizes. Finding sheets that fit extra-thick mattresses can be tricky.

It's easy to become obsessed with style when you're selecting sheets. You can spend hours deciding whether to coordinate with the bedroom wallpaper, cozy up with a Laura Ashley vintage floral, or go minimalist with Calvin Klein. But even the most stylish bedding can lose its charm if the hems unravel after washing or you need The Rock to wrestle the fitted sheet over the mattress.

Sheets and pillowcases are often individually packaged and priced as "open stock," or sold as sets, with coordinating flat and fitted sheets plus two pillowcases (one for a twin). Accessories such as curtains, dust ruffles, and sham pillowcases may also be available.

The price of sheets can be affected by a stylish brand, but it also tracks with material type and thread count. Cotton-polyester sheets, still the most popular type, are generally less expensive, but a growing number of shoppers are choosing all-cotton. High-end sheets use premium cotton varieties including Egyptian, pima, and Supima. At the very expensive end of the price spectrum are a few linen or silk sheets.

What's available

Three manufacturers—Fieldcrest Cannon (owned by Pillowtex), Springs Industries, and WestPoint Stevens—account for about 70 percent of sales and make many different brands including designer names.

Sizes include twin, full, queen, and king. You'll see claims about fitting today's thick, pillow-top mattresses, some as deep as 15 or 18 inches. View those claims somewhat skeptically. Keep the receipt.

Sheets made of cotton-polyester blends are renowned for easy care—less shrinkage, fading, and wrinkling. Some all-cotton sheets claim to be wrinkle-free, but we've found that they typically emerge from the dryer somewhat wrinkled, no better than a number of regular cottons and not as good as any of the blends. Regular cotton becomes combed cotton when it is carded (that is, combed) to removed short fibers and leave only the longest to be spun into yarn. In theory, the long fibers found in premium cottons should make a sturdier yarn that feels smooth and is less likely to pill. CONSUMER REPORTS tests, however, found that this doesn't necessarily hold true. Price range of a typical queen set: cotton/polyester, $20 to $150; all-cotton, $40 to $250 and up.

Key features

Thread count indicates the number of warp (lengthwise) and weft (crosswise) yarns, or threads, in a square inch of woven fabric. This is often regarded as the benchmark for quality in sheets. Sheets that have a thread count of 130 have thicker yarns. Sheets with a higher thread count have a tighter weave, finer yarns, a softer "hand," or feel, and a higher price. But CONSUMER REPORTS has found that above 180 or 200 threads per square inch, it's hard to detect any difference in softness.

Sheets made of woven fabric with plain weaves (muslin, percale, and variants) make up the majority of all sheet sales. Don't be surprised if you can't discern the differences in the various weaves—the detail is difficult to see without a magnifying glass.

Muslin, a plain weave (using a one-over, one-under pattern), has the lowest thread count—typically around 130—and the lowest price. It has a reputation for being coarse and scratchy and isn't widely sold. **Percale,** a fine, closely woven type of plain weave, is the most-prevalent fabric for sheets. The thread count usually ranges from 180 to 200. Percale sheets with a thread count of 220 to 250 are sometimes labeled **pinpoint.** A step up in price

LINEN LINGO

LINEN is a fabric woven from the fibers of the flax plant. It was once more widely used for sheets, napkins, and tablecloths, thus the terms "bed linen" and "table linen." Today, real linen's a luxury and the word generically. But linen sheets are still an option, if you can afford the price and don't mind a lot of ironing.

COTTON is the most popular material for sheets. Many prefer the feel of 100 percent cotton, though cotton/poly blends are popular because they're cheaper and more wrinkle-resistant.

SANFORIZED means preshrunk.

MERCERIZED cotton has a bit of a sheen to it.

MATTRESS TOPPERS can include electric pads for warmth and sheepskin for coziness. The recommended minimum is a simple pad or cover to protect the mattress.

DUVET OR COMFORTER COVER are one and the same. The cover is like a giant pillowcase or sham and covers just the top of the bed.

THERMAL LAYERING There's more than one way to make a bed, but technique does matter. A thermal blanket has little holes to trap air. If you use that over the sheet and

use a regular blanket next, you will be warmer than if you do it the other way around. Similarly, electric blankets work best with another layer on top, with the top layer trapping the heat.

DUST RUFFLES, also known as bed skirts, are designed to dress up the box spring and hide any dust bunnies–or boxes, shoes, skis, etc.–that may be lurking under your bed.

SHAMS are decorative pillowcases that are usually ruffled or flanged and tie or button closed, instead of being open at the end, like a pillowcase.

FLANGED refers to a dec-

orative band of fabric, as on a pillowcase, that is flat instead of ruffled.

BEDSPREADS cover the whole bed, including the pillows and the box spring.

COVERLETS generally do not cover the pillows or the box spring. They often come with matching shams.

BLANKET COVERS go over wool blankets on the bed to keep them clean. They are thin and decorative, often with satin or lace trim.

DROP refers to the length a bedspread or dust ruffle will extend as it "drops" toward the floor.

BASIC MATTRESS DIMENSIONS
Sizes can vary.
For best results, use a
measuring tape

Twin:
39x75 inches

Extra-long twin:
39x80 inches

Full (double):
54x75 inches

Queen:
60x80 inches

King:
76x80 inches

Western (California) king:
72x84 inches

from regular percales, these use what's called a basket, or rib weave, in which two or more threads are grouped in a one-over, one-under weave pattern.

Widely perceived as luxury-class linens, **sateen** sheets have a slight sheen and a soft, smooth feel. This weave has one crosswise thread floated over four or more lengthwise threads. The thread count starts at about 230 and can climb to more than 300. (Sateens, which are typically all-cotton, are not related to the synthetic satin sheets of yesteryear, which were often slippery and uncomfortable.)

Flannel sheets, typically all-cotton, have a napped surface that produces a fuzzy appearance and a soft feel. **Knit** sheets are supposed to be as comfortable as a favorite T-shirt; indeed, they're very soft when new, less so after laundering (probably because of a finish that's removed in the wash).

How to choose

PERFORMANCE DIFFERENCES. In tests, CONSUMER REPORTS found differences in softness, strength, and appearance, generally related to fiber content and weave. Fit varied as well. Cotton-polyester blends generally had a pleasant feel, unlike the stiff blends of decades past. Sateens were very soft, but our tests showed they might not stand up as well as other types of sheets to everyday wear. Percale sheets, especially those made of cotton-polyester blends, are good in terms of strength.

The way corners are sewn—angled seam or straight seam—doesn't affect the fit or how easy it is to put a fitted sheet on a mattress. And neither type is stronger. When sheets failed our strength tests, the fabric tore before the seams broke.

Dark colors such as hunter green and navy blue sometimes faded considerably after 20 washings. But if you wash all the bedding together, the set should remain a consistent color.

RECOMMENDATIONS. Fit comes first. Measure your mattress and choose sheets sized appropriately. When shopping for yourself, you may wish to buy on sale—with frequent one-day events and scheduled "white sales," you won't have to wait long. Consider shopping outlets and off-price stores for discounts, but inspect items carefully for flaws in fabric or construction that could affect long-term durability, usability, or comfort.

Hold on to packaging and receipts until you've laundered the linens several times. It's a good idea to wash sheets before the first use to remove any finishes and get a better idea of the fit. If the sheets shrink, fade, or otherwise fail to live up to expectations, return them to the place of purchase. Be wary of "final sale" sheets (especially irregulars) that can't be returned.

TOWELS

Even the best can change color, shrink, and distort significantly, so it's a good idea to check the retailer's return policy before buying.

All towels are not created equal. In addition to differences in size, color, softness, and absorbency, you may encounter unwelcome surprises. If a component of a towel's dye mixture isn't fixed properly, that component may disappear, altering the overall color of the towel. The metamorphosis can be so gradual that you don't realize it. Towels that shrink in length don't usually shrink much in width, and vice versa—it's all a function of how the towel is woven. Some towels shrink in the borders of each end, leaving them fat in the middle and flared at the ends.

What's available

Large retailers get their towels mainly from three manufacturers—Fieldcrest Cannon (owned by Pillowtex), Springs Industries, and WestPoint Stevens. Cotton bath towels typically cost between $2 and $25 and are sold at discounters such as Kmart, Target, and Wal-Mart, chains such as JCPenney and Sears, specialty stores such as Bed Bath & Beyond, Linens 'n Things, department stores, and mail-order catalogs. Sizes range widely from around 39x25 inches for the cheapest bath towels to a more generous 55x30 inches for pricier versions.

Key features

Aside from size, several other attributes explain the wide differences you will find in the price of towels.

THICKNESS. As a rule, expect towels that are thick and densely woven to absorb more water than those that are thin and loosely woven. Thick towels may dry you better, but they also take longer in the dryer.

FIBER. You'll see simply "cotton" as well as "premium" cottons: combed, Egyptian, pima, or Supima (a trademark for some pima cotton). With combed cotton, fibers are put through a process to eliminate short fibers and leave just the longer ones. Removing short fibers can help reduce shedding and pilling.

Egyptian cotton, grown along the Nile River, consists of long, strong fibers that are particularly lustrous. Pima cotton is the American version of Egyptian, grown in Arizona, California, New Mexico, and Texas. Towels made of premium cotton generally ranked higher in our tests than those made of ordinary cotton.

FEEL. Softness sells, but don't buy a towel based solely on how it feels in the store. A finish is used to achieve that new-towel feel, and after a laundering or two once you get the towel home, the finish washes away. One way to keep towels soft through multiple washings is to use liquid fabric softeners or dryer sheets. There's a down side, though: fabric softeners leave a waxy film on towels that reduces absorbency.

How to choose

PERFORMANCE DIFFERENCES. In CONSUMER REPORTS tests simulating about a year's worth of washing, many blue and green towels changed color. But only two of the bright red towels we tested bled in the wash—and just a little bit at that. Towel makers generally advise washing all dark colors separately, which is sensible. Practically all cotton towels shrink, even if you wash them in cold water and dry them on Low, as we did. Some of the worst shrinkers in our tests lost more than 9 percent in length—a loss of 4½ inches on a 50-inch towel. Another problem with some towels was pilling.

RECOMMENDATIONS. A bath towel that costs only a few dollars is likely to be less absorbent, less soft, and smaller than a more expensive towel. But you don't have to spend top dollar for quality. When shopping, look for a thicker towel, which is usually more absorbent.

PLAN AHEAD
When you purchase new towels, buy an extra washcloth in the same color and put it aside with the sales receipt. If you then have a serious problem with your towels fading after just a few times through the wash, you can return the faded towels to the store—and bring the unwashed washcloth with you as a point of comparison.

Discounters are a good source for inexpensive towels. Consider off-price stores, too. Their towels may be irregular or come in limited colors, but prices can be half those charged by department and specialty stores. When buying colored towels in sets, compare them carefully under good lighting. Even towels of the same basic color will vary somewhat from one dye lot to another.

WALL-TO-WALL CARPETING

Different types of fiber wear in different ways. Choose on the basis of where the carpet will go and how it will be used.

When you shop for carpeting you have to shop first for the fiber type, then the carpet brand. Highly advertised brands such as Anso from Honeywell, Stainmaster from DuPont, and Wear-Dated from Solutia are brands of nylon fiber, not brands of carpet. Because different retailers may sell the same carpet under different carpet brand names, comparison shopping is difficult. You'll probably have to take copious notes on carpets you like and look for samples with similar specifications in other stores. But basic information on things such as pile height and tufts per square inch is often lacking. You also need to consider installation.

What's available

Carpet is sold at stores such as CarpetMax, Carpet One, and Sears, which sell name brands as well as their own store brands; at home centers such as Home Depot and Lowe's; and at independent flooring stores, where you'll see carpet brands such as Aladdin and Philadelphia. Carpet is also available by mail, from companies such as S&S Mills.

The price of a carpet depends largely on its fiber content, pile weight, and style. Wool is very expensive compared with synthetics. Nylon, the best-selling carpet fiber, typically costs more than polyester or olefin. Branded fiber tends to cost more than unbranded.

Wool, the standard against which synthetic carpets are measured, has outstanding resilience, comparable to that of nylon, so its crushing and matting resistance is very good. The best wool carpets are also known for their soft feel underfoot, though nylon can feel just as soft. But unlike nylon, wool may abrade. It also stains easily and tends to yellow in bright sunlight. Nylon is mildew resistant and offers good resilience and resistance to abrasion. Olefin, also known as polypropylene, generally resists staining, fading, abrasion, and moisture, making it a good choice for a basement playroom. Polyester resists staining, but its resilience is only fair. Some polyester carpet is made from recycled plastic soda bottles.

Price range: nylon, $10 to more than $30 per square yard; olefin, $7.50 to $22 per square yard; polyester, $8 to $15 per square yard; wool, $24 to $60 per square yard.

Key considerations

Generally, a heavier **pile weight**—the ounces of yarn per square yard—is considered better and is more expensive. A longer **pile height** is better if you want a luxurious look and feel. Pile whose height variations give it a textured look minimizes footprints or vacuum-cleaner tracks. A carpet with a high **tuft density** wears better. You can figure it by multiply-

CARPET FACTS

The Carpet and Rug Institute can confirm that carpet and padding qualify for a "green label," which means the product meets industry standards regarding volatile organic compounds (VOCs). It also offers installation tips. Call 800-882-8846 or visit the organization's web site at *www.carpet-rug.com*.

ing the number of tufts per inch, left to right, by tufts per inch, up and down. You can check tuft density by folding back a carpet sample. With a denser carpet, you won't see much backing peeking through. Like high tuft density, **highly twisted yarn** provides better resistance to wear. Labels may note that the yarn is heat set to help retain its shape.

Cut-pile styles, including saxony and plush, are made of yarn that's attached to the backing and cut at the top. The deeper and thicker the pile, the more luxurious the carpet may feel, but the more likely it is to retain dirt. Cut pile generally crushes under foot traffic more than other styles, so it's best reserved for low-traffic areas such as a formal living room or a master bedroom. Textured saxonies are better at hiding footprints.

In a **level loop**, yarn is looped over so both ends are attached to the backing. Short, densely spaced loops may not feel very soft, but they provide a smooth surface that wears well and is fairly easy to vacuum because there aren't crevices for dirt to sink into. High-density level loop is good for stairs, family rooms, and other high-traffic areas. Low-density level loop doesn't perform as well.

Berber is a variation of level loop, but with thicker yarn. Genuine Berber is handmade from wool. Less expensive Berber-style carpeting can be made of wool, nylon, olefin, or a nylon blend. The thicker yarn can snag, making this not the best choice for a foyer or hall.

Multilevel loop has long and short loops that give a textured appearance. The short loops create pockets that can make vacuuming difficult.

Retailers may include **padding** in the price of a carpet, but often it's a cheap grade. Low-density padding that you can easily compress between your fingers feels spongy underfoot and won't provide much support for the carpet. Better is medium-density padding made of prime urethane, a type of foam; rubber; rebond, made of leftover bits bonded with adhesive, hence its multicolored appearance; or pressed fiber, which is felt-like.

All new carpets emit volatile organic compounds (VOCs)—air pollutants associated with carpet manufacture—for a few days after installation. Though emissions are generally at a very low level, not everyone agrees what's safe. Current scientific evidence indicates that the level of VOCs emitted is probably not harmful to most people. The Carpet and Rug Institute has made reduction of "4-PC," the most-odorous carpet VOC, a goal of its Indoor Air Quality Carpet Testing Program. Carpets, padding, and adhesives that pass may carry a "green label."

How to choose

PERFORMANCE DIFFERENCES. Branded nylons generally resist stains, while many unbranded nylons may not. In CONSUMER REPORTS tests, branded nylon, which is usually treated with stain and soil repellent before the backing is put on the carpet, generally performed better than unbranded. We analyzed the yarn in one unbranded model and saw why: More than twice as much stain repellent was on the top quarter-inch of the carpet as at the base of the yarn, indicating that repellent was sprayed only on the surface. Dense level loop and short cut-pile retained the least dirt after vacuuming. Multilevel loop and longer cut-pile models retained the most. With our worst performer, a multilevel-loop carpet, 70 percent of the dirt couldn't be vacuumed out. As for carpet wear, Home Depot's performance appearance rating (PAR) and Sears' carpet assurance program (CAP) scores are useful guides. They correlated closely with the CONSUMER REPORTS wear-test score. A carpet with a PAR of 4 to

A WARNING ABOUT WARRANTIES

Manufacturers and salespeople like to emphasize warranties. Some warranties promise to replace a carpet, others state they'll replace just the damaged area. But beware of the fine print: Coverage for "wear" or "staining" of a carpet, for example, may not mean what you probably think.

Warrantied "wear" refers to abrasion that leads to a loss of 10 percent of the fiber. While wool abrades, most modern synthetics don't, so for them the warranty is essentially meaningless. Stain warranties can also be misleading. To the consumer, a stain is a stain, whether it's from tea or an accident by a pet. But to manufacturers, the stains covered by warranties are generally caused by food dyes such as the ones in fruit drinks. (A good carpet cleaner can handle those.) Other stains–say, from mustard or acne cream (which can bleach dark fibers)–don't count. You may be offered an extended warranty that defines "stains" more broadly. Our advice: Save your money.

To maintain a warranty, you must prove that you cared for the carpeting as specified, so save receipts showing that it has been professionally cleaned.

5 or a CAP of 8 to 10 is appropriate for moderate- to high-traffic areas.

RECOMMENDATIONS. Choose the most appropriate fiber, style, and construction for the room where the carpeting will go and shop for color and price. For example, for a formal room, you might opt for the lustrous appearance and feel of cut-pile or wool. For a child's room or basement playroom, you'd be better off with olefin fiber for its stain and wear resistance—and a level-loop construction for easy vacuuming.

INSTALLATION. Most people arrange this through the retailer, who sends employees or a subcontractor to do the job. Work out the details beforehand, and get them in writing. Decide, for example, who will be responsible for trimming doors, if that's necessary. Make sure installers double-glue seams—even seams under furniture. If you rearrange your furniture and expose a seam to foot traffic, fibers around an improperly glued seam can become fuzzy, and stitches may unravel.

When the installer arrives, ask to keep the identifying label from the plastic that the carpet comes wrapped in. That will probably be your only official record showing that you received what you ordered. Ask also for a scrap of the carpet, at least 12x24 inches, and file that along with the label, the sales receipt, and the warranty. This documentation can be important if you have a problem later. Have the installer inspect the carpet surface and backing for flaws before it's installed. Anything less than perfect warrants a call to the retailer.

You can minimize problems with VOCs by asking the installer to air out a new carpet for a day or so before installation. After it's installed, keep windows open and a fan going for two or three days. Make sure the installer seals seams with adhesives that have a CRI green label.

Keeping It Shipshape

Equipment to keep your house clean, safe, and in working order continues to be refined, notably in the area of battery technology. Manufacturers of cordless tools have begun to use nickel-metal hydride batteries, which are safer for the environment and claim to provide more power than a comparable nickel-cadmium battery. More sophisticated designs have made garage-door openers safer, and constantly changing "rolling codes" have made these remote-controlled systems more secure from thieves. And some operate more quickly and with less disruption. Upright vacuum cleaners, which historically have been more appropriate for carpeting, now also do well with bare floors. Canister vacs, which were always the way to go for bare floors, now likewise do a very good job with carpeting as well.

Fatal fires and litigation have underscored the need for two complementary types of smoke detection: ionization, the most common type, and photoelectric. A carbon-monoxide alarm is another indispensable safety device.

CORDLESS DRILLS

Many of the latest models are powerful enough to handle construction and repair chores formerly reserved for corded models.

Better battery packs allow today's cordless drills to run longer and more powerfully per charge. The best can outperform corded drills and handle decks and other big jobs before their batteries need to be recharged. Much of the credit goes to nickel-cadmium (NiCad) batteries, which can be charged hundreds of times. NiCads must be recycled, however, since the cadmium is toxic and can leach out of landfills to contaminate groundwater if disposed of improperly. Incineration can release the substance into the air and pose an even greater hazard. Some cordless drills have nickel-metal-hydride (NiMH) batteries, which don't contain cadmium and are safer for the environment. In a recent test, CONSUMER REPORTS found that a 15.6-volt NiMH-powered drill ran longer than many 18-volt NiCad-powered models, yet weighed much less.

What's available

Black & Decker and Craftsman (Sears) are the major brands. Along with Ryobi and Skil, both brands are aimed primarily at do-it-yourselfers. Bosch, Craftsman Professional, DeWalt, Hitachi, Makita, Milwaukee, and Porter-Cable offer pricier drills with professional-style features.

Cordless drills come in several sizes, based on battery voltage. In general, the higher the voltage, the greater the drilling power. The most potent models pack 18 to 24 volts, while the smallest, 6- to 9.6-volt models, are usually limited to light-duty use. In between lie the 12- and 14.4 volt drills. Prices tend to track with voltage and features. Price range: 6- to 9.6-volt, $30 to $130; 12-volt, $50 to $190; 14.4- and 18-volt, $60 to $270. There are still some 24-volt models, going for $300 to $370. Sometimes, you'll also find a flashlight or a cordless saw bundled with a drill and sold as a kit.

Key features

Most cordless drills 12 volts and higher have **two speed ranges**: low for driving screws and high for drilling. Low speed provides much more torque, or turning power, than the high-speed setting, which is useful for driving long screws and boring holes. Most drills have a **variable speed trigger**, which can make starting a hole easier, and an **adjustable clutch** used to lower maximum torque; that can help you avoid driving a screw too far into soft wallboard or mangling the heads or threads once the screw is in.

Most drills have a ⅜-**inch chuck** (the attachment that holds the drill bit), though high-voltage, professional-grade models have a ½-**inch chuck**. In either case, most drills have replaced the little key needed to loosen and tighten the chuck with a **keyless chuck.** Most of today's models are also **reversible**, letting you easily remove a screw or back a drill bit out of a hole.

Still other features make some drills easier to use than others. Some models have a **T-handle** in the center of the motor housing, which provides better balance than a **pistol grip** on the back, although a pistol grip lets you slide your hand up in line with the bit to better apply pressure. Models with **two batteries** allow you to use one while the other is charging, while a **smart charger**—found with many models—charges the battery in an hour or less, rather than three hours or more for a conventional charger. Some smart chargers also extend battery life by adjusting the charge as needed. And many chargers switch into a **maintenance** or "**trickle-charge" mode** after the battery is fully charged.

An **electric brake** stops some drills instantly when you release the trigger—a handy

DISPOSING OF NICADS

The makers of rechargeable batteries have established a nationwide program for recycling batteries. In response to a 1996 federal law, all rechargeables must now be easy to remove—if not always easy to replace—with simple household tools. That allows consumers to toss spent batteries in one of tens of thousands of battery-recycling bins at participating retailers such as RadioShack and Wal-Mart. To find a bin near you, call the Rechargeable Battery Recycling Corp. at 800-8-BATTERY (800-822-88370 or go to *www.rbrc.com.*

feature that helps you avoid damaging the work piece and allows you to resume drilling or driving without waiting. Some models also include a **built-in bubble level;** others feature a **one-handed chuck** that eases bit changes.

How to choose

PERFORMANCE DIFFERENCES. New cordless drills are more capable than those sold a few years ago. The most powerful cordless drill CONSUMER REPORTS tested outperformed several powerful corded models. While higher voltage equals greater power, it also tends to mean added weight. That can make a drill tiring to hold for any length of time, especially overhead. What's more, some 18-volt models can nearly equal a 24-volt drill's performance with less weight and a lower price tag.

RECOMMENDATIONS. A 24-volt cordless drill delivers power and endurance, but it can weigh up to 8 pounds and cost about $300. If you're a contractor or serious do-it-yourselfer, you'll find plenty of power and endurance in a 14.4- or 18-volt model. The best selection is available in those sizes. CONSUMER REPORTS also considers those to be the best value. Drills with 12 volts or less are a dubious choice; although they are lightweight, many are suitable only for light-duty chores. What's more, recharging many of the least expensive models can take anywhere from 3 to 16 hours to charge.

Whichever size you choose, make sure you're comfortable with its weight and ergonomics. And, if possible, try before buying.

CORDLESS DRILLS ♦ Ratings: Page 220

> ### OTHER CORDLESS TOOLS
>
> **Hammer drills.** These operate like a regular cordless drill but have a hammer mode that combines bit rotation with percussion (rated in blows per minute, or bmp) to quickly blast holes through concrete, brick, block, and stone. The models we've tested match the performance of a corded hammer drill. Price range: $150 to $300.
>
> **Jigsaws.** Also called saber saws, these can make curved cuts through wood or metal. None of the ones we've seen is a match for a corded model. Cutting curves without a cord is a significant advantage, though. If the jobs you do are typically light-duty or you're patient, a cordless jigsaw may be worth considering. Price range: $250 to $275.
>
> **Reciprocating saws.** These are used for cutting holes through a wall or roof where the blade might encounter nails and other tough impediments. In CONSUMER REPORTS tests, some models worked almost as well as corded saws. Price range: $250 to $350.
>
> **Screwdrivers.** These in-line tools are limited to light-duty screw tightening and loosening and are much slower and less powerful than even the least potent drill. But cordless screwdrivers are inexpensive, and you may want one if you aren't strong enough to turn screws by hand, have many screws to drive, or have to work in quarters too cramped for a drill. Price range: $15 to $35.

CIRCULAR SAWS

Circular saws are a mainstay for cutting two-by-fours, plywood, and the like.

A circular saw is an essential tool for any but the most rudimentary workshop. Most models run on an electric motor. A few models are battery powered.

What's available

Black & Decker, Craftsman (Sears), DeWalt, Makita, Milwaukee, Porter-Cable, and Skil brands account for most of the circular saws sold.

CORDED MODELS. These models run on an electric motor that can range from 10 to 15 amps. The higher the amps, the more power you can expect. Most models are oriented so the motor is perpendicular to the blade. Another type uses a "worm drive" design in which the

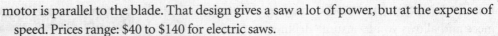

motor is parallel to the blade. That design gives a saw a lot of power, but at the expense of speed. Prices range: $40 to $140 for electric saws.

BATTERY-POWERED MODELS. These use 18- or 24-volt motors. They're more expensive than corded models. Price range: $200 to $480.

Key features

Every saw has a big main **handle,** which incorporates the **on/off switch,** and a stubby auxiliary handle. Some saws include an interlock you have to press before the on/off switch will work. This adds a level of safety, but can make the saw awkward to use.

Inexpensive saws have a stamped-steel **base** and thin housing; pricier models use thick, rugged material that stands up to hard use. A **blade** with two dozen large teeth cuts fast but can splinter the wood; a blade with 40 or more teeth gives a cleaner cut. The thinner the blade, the faster the cut and the less wasted wood.

Bevel adjustment is used to change the angle of the cut from 0 to 45 degrees. The **depth adjustment** changes the blade's cutting depth. A circular saw works best when the teeth just clear the bottom of the wood. The notch in the base plate that is in line with the saw blade is the **cutting guide,** which helps you follow the cutting line you've drawn on the wood.

A **blade-lock button** keeps the blade from turning when you change blades. The **dust chute** directs the sawdust away so you can see what you're doing.

How to choose

PERFORMANCE DIFFERENCES. Seconds count if you have a lot of wood to cut. Speed also affects safety; you're more likely to push a slow saw, dulling the blade quickly and overheating the motor, or making the saw jam or kick back. Typically, slower saws come with a steel blade while carbide blades are on the fastest models. Most corded saws have adequate torque for any typical home-workshop job. Battery-powered saws are much weaker. A weak saw could strain when used on thick hardwood or for other tough work.

Design points that can make a saw easy to use include a visible cutting guide, a blade that's simple to change and to adjust for depth and angle, good balance, a comfortable handle, and a handy on/off switch. How well the saw is constructed impacts its potential for a long, trouble-free life. It should have durable bearings, motor brushes that are accessible for servicing or replacement, a heavy-duty base, and rugged blade-depth and cutting-angle adjustments.

RECOMMENDATIONS. Judging from CONSUMER REPORTS tests, you can get a fine saw for as little as $60. For $120 to $160, you can get an excellent model. A battery-powered saw lacks the might for tough jobs but might do for occasional light work.

Whichever you buy, if it comes with a steel blade, replace it with a carbide one. Be sure to match the number of teeth with the material you want to cut; a blade for plywood, say, has more teeth than one for rough cutting.

All the saws are loud enough when cutting to warrant hearing protection. All kick up a lot of chips and dust, so safety glasses or goggles are a must. You may also want to wear a dust mask, especially when cutting pressure-treated lumber.

CIRCULAR SAWS ♦ Ratings: *Page 207*

GARAGE-DOOR OPENERS

Garage-door openers are safer and more secure than ever. Some are also quieter and quicker. Because installation can be tricky, you may want to hire a professional.

Whether you're replacing a garage-door opener or buying one for the first time, technology is on your side. The latest ones require less force to automatically stop and reverse the door if it touches a person, a pet, or another obstructing object. Remote controls with constantly changing "rolling codes" thwart thieves. And unlike older models, which entailed lengthy code setting, the latest do most of that setup for you.

What's available

Most garage-door openers are made by one of two manufacturers. Chamberlain makes LiftMaster and Craftsman models, as well as its own brand. Overhead Door makes Genie and Genie Pro models as well as its own brand. Craftsman is by far the biggest-selling brand.

"Install-it-yourself" garage-door openers are sold at large retailers, such as Sears or Home Depot, while "professional" models are sold by installers and can have a higher price, though not always. Other differences can be found in details. A professional model, for example, has a one-piece rail. Don't assume, however, that professional openers are necessarily sturdier or better. Price range: $150 to $350, plus about $125 or so if you hire an installer.

Key features

Among components housed in the **power head** are the **motor,** the **drive pulley,** the **lights** that come on when the opener is operated, and, on most models, **travel-limit switches** that control when the door stops opening or closing. The motor of a garage-door opener is one-half or one-third horsepower and either alternating current (AC) or the quieter direct current (DC). The **drive system** connects the motor to the **trolley,** which slides along a rail and raises and lowers the door. There are several types of drive system: **cogged-belt, chain-and-cable, screw,** and **straight-chain.**

The trolley can be disconnected so you can operate the door manually from inside the garage. With some screw-drive models, you must climb a ladder or use a broom handle to reconnect the trolley—an annoyance. An **electric eye** on most openers immediately stops and reverses the closing door if a light beam near the ground is broken—an important safety feature. An **added reverse feature** is designed to act as a backup if, say, you don't break the light beam and the door makes contact with you.

Most openers come with two remote controls and a **wall console** that includes a **door control, light switch,** and **vacation setting** to let you disable all or part of the system. A few models include an outdoor keypad.

How to choose

PERFORMANCE DIFFERENCES. All of the garage-door openers that CONSUMER REPORTS recently tested had ½-horsepower motors and lifted a 16-foot-wide test door with ease. Several models are especially quiet—a plus for light sleepers if there is a living space over the garage. Models with a cogged belt emitted 48 to 53 decibels (dBA), compared with 57 to 63 dBA for others tested. Most openers made a penetrating hum, though two screw-drive

HOW GARAGE-DOOR OPENERS WORK

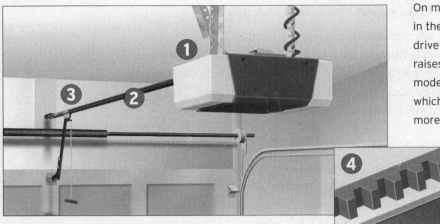

On most garage-door openers, the motor in the powerhead **1** is connected by the drive system **2** to the trolley **3**, which raises and lowers the door. Several new models use a cogged-belt drive system **4** which helps move the trolley and door more quietly. An electric eye stops and reverses the closing door if its light beam is broken. A backup does the same thing if the closing door touches a person, pet, or object.

models made a less intrusive clatter. A DC motor helped several units operate quietly. In tests, most models took 12 to 13 seconds to open or close the door; the fastest opened the door in just 8 seconds, though it took as long to close the door as the others.

RECOMMENDATIONS. Because solid performance and a high degree of safety are pretty much givens, you can choose a garage-door opener on the basis of how quietly and quickly you want it to work—and cost. Choose a cogged-belt-drive model or one with a DC motor if quietness tops your wish list. Warranties can vary. The motor usually has a separate one. Ask the dealer to spell out terms before buying.

Because the job of installing a garage-door opener requires respectable mechanical skills and several hours, you may want to hire a professional. With most models, you usually have to assemble the rail pieces, hang the power head and rail from the ceiling, and attach the trolley to the door, along with wiring the electric eye, power head, and control console. Travel-limit switches can be hard to adjust. A professional model's one-piece rail makes assembly easier, although its length—11 feet—may make it hard to bring home.

If you decide to install a garage-door opener yourself, set aside a day and get someone to help you. Before you begin, check the door's balance. When a properly balanced door is operated manually, it will stay in place wherever it is positioned and shouldn't take a lot of effort to open. If it isn't balanced, or if you want the springs checked for soundness, consider calling in a professional.

SMOKE & CO ALARMS

Smoke alarms can cut by half your chances of dying in a house fire.
Carbon monoxide detectors sniff out an invisible threat your senses can't.

A fire can start from a greasy pan on the stove or even from faulty wiring in your walls. Carbon monoxide (CO), another potentially deadly risk, may be generated by a malfunctioning furnace with a leaky heat exchanger, a fireplace with a blocked chimney, or a poorly vented water heater. Simply warming up a barbecue, car, mower, or snow thrower inside an attached garage creates CO, which can seep into living areas. To protect yourself and your family, you need two kinds of smoke detection—ionization and photoelectric—as well as CO detection.

Ionization smoke alarms use a harmless amount of radioactive material to sniff out fire. They tend to react quickly to fast-flaming fires, such as paper fires and those fed by flammable fluids. But they can be slow to detect the smoky, slow-starting bedding and upholstery fires that often kill sleepers. By contrast, the light beams and sensors of photoelectric alarms react much more quickly to smoke than they do to flames.

CO alarms are also essential. CO kills some 500 Americans and puts an estimated 10,000 in hospital emergency rooms each year. It displaces oxygen in the bloodstream, so it works slowly and is deadly above a certain level. The concentration of CO is measured in parts per million (ppm). While exposure to CO levels of 150 ppm for 1½ hours isn't likely to cause more than a headache for healthy adults, levels of 400 ppm for that duration can cause loss of consciousness and lead to brain damage or death. Pregnant women, children, the elderly, and those who are chronically ill are especially sensitive to CO and may experience problems at lower levels. A CO alarm can reveal the presence of this deadly gas before it becomes dangerous.

Many new homes have smoke alarms built in to comply with building codes. With interconnected built-in alarms, one alarm can trigger others. Additionally, many hardwired home-security systems incorporate smoke and CO sensors. If your home doesn't have a hardwired system, you'll have to install separate smoke and CO alarms.

What's available

First Alert accounts for more than half of the smoke-alarm market and, with Kidde-owned Nighthawk, sell the lion's share of CO alarms. Other major brands are Family Guard, Firex, and Lifesaver for smoke alarms, and American Sensors, Fyrnetics, and Senco for CO alarms.

Install-it-yourself smoke alarms run on batteries and typically go on ceilings or high on walls. Ionization alarms are still more common than photoelectric units, although a home needs both types of protection. Battery-powered dual-detection alarms combine ionization and photoelectric technologies, and provide the most complete coverage. Hardwired, interconnected smoke alarms are found in newer homes. You can also get models with built-in or separate strobe lights to alert the hearing impaired. Price range: $10 and up for ionization smoke alarms, $20 and up for photoelectric and dual-detection smoke alarms.

DISPOSING OF IONIZATION ALARMS

The Nuclear Regulatory Commission doesn't require discarded ionization alarms to be recycled or sent to hazardous landfills. But it and the Environmental Protection Agency are reconsidering how to dispose of old units, given the long life of radioactive material and the growing number of ionization alarms being thrown away. For now, ask your local fire or waste authorities how to dispose of an old smoke alarm, or return the unit to the manufacturer (at your expense).

CO detectors can be battery-powered, plug-in, or hardwired. Battery-powered CO alarms are usually mounted on a wall. Plug-in models go where there's an outlet. Some alarms combine an ionization smoke alarm and a CO alarm, although they lack the protection of a photoelectric smoke alarm. Price range: $30 to $110.

Key features

Both smoke and CO alarms have a **horn** of at least 85 decibels, which sounds when an alarm detects smoke, flames, or carbon monoxide. A **test button** lets you ensure that the alarm is working. CO alarms and a few smoke alarms have a **hush button,** which silences the horn for several minutes. If there is still a threat, the alarm will sound again minutes later.

Most battery-powered alarms use a 9-volt cell that should be replaced annually; a **chirp warning** sounds when batteries are weak. You may also find alarms with a **long-life lithium battery.** Hardwired smoke alarms and plug-in CO alarms with **battery backup** can remain active during a power outage, while plug-in CO alarms with a **power cord** allow you to mount them on a wall or place them on a table.

CO alarms with a **digital display** tell you the concentration of CO. While alarms with this feature tend to cost more, we think the added premium is worth it. Most such alarms use a **liquid-crystal display** (LCD); models with **light-emitting diodes** (LEDs) may be easier to read in poor lighting, however.

How to choose

PERFORMANCE DIFFERENCES. Most smoke and CO alarms are UL- or CSA-listed, which means they comply with safety and other standards. In Consumer Reports tests, all of the ionization alarms reacted to smokeless, 3-foot-high flames within 30 seconds, while none of the photoelectric alarms responded to that kind of fire even after 3 minutes. But the photoelectric models reacted to our smoky fire within about 5 minutes, when visibility was still unimpeded, while the ionization models took as long as 21 minutes to respond. By then, smoke had cut visibility significantly. The dual-detection alarms did well in both tests.

Most performance and safety standards require CO alarms to sound when levels reach 70 ppm and remain at that level for as little as one hour. In Consumer Reports tests of CO alarms, nearly all sounded within 15 minutes at a concentration of 400 ppm and within 50 minutes at 150 ppm. Most of the alarms silenced themselves within minutes of the air being cleared of CO. The most accurate digital displays came within 20 percent of actual levels. Other displays, however, were still accurate enough to be useful.

RECOMMENDATIONS. For basic protection, be sure there's a dual-sensor smoke alarm or both a photoelectric and ionization alarm on each floor of your home. Your home should also have at least one CO alarm.

When shopping for a smoke or CO alarm, try to make sure the unit was manufactured recently. Roughly one out of every six CO alarms we bought for our tests were at least two years old and did not meet current standards. All smoke and CO alarms should have a manufacture date stamped on the back, but you won't be able to see it without opening the package in the store. Ask a clerk for assistance.

Then test all smoke and CO alarms in your home at least monthly by pressing the test button. Replace batteries once a year—on an easy-to-remember date such as the Sunday in October when clocks return to Standard Time. Vacuum alarms regularly, since dust, insects, and cobwebs may clog vents and reduce an alarm's effectiveness or lead to false alarms. Replace smoke alarms every 10 years and CO alarms every five years, using the date stamp to help you keep track.

SMOKE ALARMS ♦ **Ratings:** Page 262

WHERE TO INSTALL SMOKE AND CO ALARMS

Every home should have smoke and CO detection. A good approach is to place a smoke alarm or a pair of smoke alarms in each bedroom or in an area adjacent to the bedrooms, such as a hallway. A CO alarm should be placed so it can be heard throughout the home. If the bedrooms are upstairs or there is a basement, you'll need additional smoke detection and maybe additional CO detection as well.

Install smoke alarms on the ceiling at least four inches from the nearest wall–or high on the wall but at least four inches down from the ceiling–to keep them out of the "dead" space that smoke may miss. Since CO tends to mix with the room's air, a CO alarm, unlike a smoke alarm, needn't be on or near the ceiling. If the CO alarm has a digital readout, you'll want to put it where you can read it.

Avoid placing smoke alarms in corners and areas near windows, outside doors, or vents, where air currents can sweep smoke away from the alarm and delay or prevent its response. Cooking smoke, vehicle-exhaust gases, and bathroom humidity tend to trigger false alarms in kitchens and bathrooms.

Don't put a CO alarm in the garage–high CO concentrations will set it off. Avoid mounting near doors or windows because fresh air can cause misleadingly low CO readings.

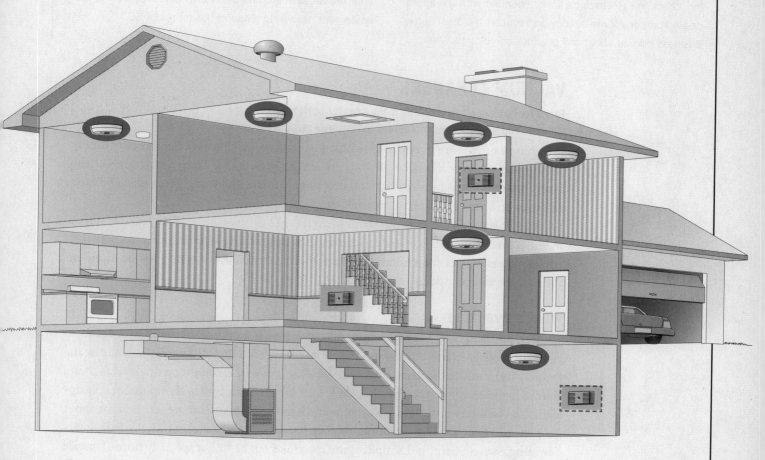

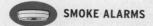 **SMOKE ALARMS**   **CO ALARMS**   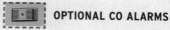 **OPTIONAL CO ALARMS**

AVOIDING FIRE AND CO DANGERS

The Consumer Product Safety Commission recommends inspections of your home's electrical wiring every 20 years. That's 20 years from the time the home was last inspected, not 20 years after you moved in. If you've added high-wattage appliances or renovated, you should consider an inspection sooner.

If you are experiencing flickering lights, hot outlets, or other warning signs of electrical fire, disconnect appliances on overworked circuits. Then hire a qualified, licensed electrician to inspect your home and make repairs. To find an electrician, start by asking your neighbors for recommendations. If your state requires licensing, check the electrician's license number with the appropriate state or county agency and contact the local Better Business Bureau about any previous complaints. When you hire the electrician, obtain an estimate in advance, and ask the electrician to list priorities and specify costs.

Remember that a safe home includes fire extinguishers and rope ladders. You should also plan escape routes and conduct fire drills.

To avoid problems with carbon monoxide, regularly inspect and maintain heating and other fossil-fuel-burning equipment and their venting systems. If an alarm sounds, throw open windows to ventilate the area and move everyone to fresh air immediately. Watch for symptoms of CO poisoning—including nausea, headache, dizziness, or drowsiness—and get immediate medical attention. Notify your fire department and utility provider. They'll bring the equipment needed to pinpoint the source of CO.

VACUUM CLEANERS

Fancy features don't necessarily make a better upright or canister vacuum. You'll find lots of competent models at a reasonable price.

Which type of vacuum to buy used to be a no-brainer. Uprights were clearly better for carpets, while canisters were the obvious choice for bare floors. That distinction is being blurred somewhat as more upright models clean floors without scattering dust and more canisters do a very good job with carpeting.

You'll also see a growing number of features like dirt sensors and bagless dirt bins as manufacturers attempt to boost performance. Some of those features, however, may contribute more to price than function. Other, more essential features may not be found on the least-expensive models.

What's available

Hoover, the oldest and largest vacuum manufacturer, is a midpriced brand with about 70 different models. Many of those models are similar, with minor differences in features; the "variety" is mostly in the marketing. And some are made exclusively for a single retail chain. Eureka has been a low-priced brand, while Dirt Devil (made by Royal Appliance) sells uprights and canisters as well as stick brooms and hand vacuums. Kenmore accounts for about 25 percent of all canister vacuums sold in the U.S. Brands such as Miele, Panasonic, Samsung, Sanyo, Sharp, and Simplicity are more likely to be sold at specialty stores. Upscale Electrolux and Oreck vacs are sold in their own stores and by direct mail, while Kirby models are sold door-to-door.

Better uprights and canisters clean carpet very well. Uprights can also do an excellent job on bare floors, thanks in part to an on-off switch for the brush. When cleaning with tools, the brush switch can help protect the user from injury, the power cord from damage, and furnishings from undue wear. Uprights also tend to be less expensive and easier to store than canister models. A top-of-the-line upright might have a wider cleaning path, be self-propelled, and have a HEPA filter, dirt sensor, and full-bag indicator. Price range: $50 to $1,300.

Canister vacuums tend to do well on floors because they allow you to turn off the brush or use a specialized tool to avoid scattering dirt. Most are quieter than uprights and more adept at cleaning on stairs and in hard-to-reach areas. Price range: $100 to $900.

Stick vacs and hand vacs—corded or cordless—lack the power of a full-sized vacuum cleaner, but they can be handy for small, quick jobs. Price range: $20 to $75.

Key features

Typical attachments include **crevice** and **upholstery tools**. You'll also appreciate **extension wands** for reaching high places. The canisters CONSUMER REPORTS has tested have a **power nozzle** that cleans carpet more thoroughly than a simple suction nozzle, and most machines have a cord of 20 to 30 feet long. While most upright vacuums require you to manually wrap the cord for storage, canisters typically have a **retractable cord** that rewinds with a tug or push of a button.

A **full-bag alert** can be handy, since an overstuffed bag impairs a vacuum's ability to clean. Lately, many uprights have adopted a **bagless** configuration with a see-through dirt bin that replaces the usual bag. But as we've found, emptying these bins can raise enough dust to concern even those without allergies. Another worthwhile feature is **manual pile-height adjustment**, which can improve cleaning by letting you match the vacuum's height to the carpet pile more effectively than you can with machines that adjust automatically.

Also look for **suction control**. Found on most canisters and some uprights, it allows you to reduce airflow for drapes and other delicate fabrics. You'll also find more uprights with a **self-propelled feature** to make pushing easy, though that can also make them heavier and harder to carry up or down the stairs.

Some models have a **dirt sensor** that triggers a light indicator according to the concentration of dirt particles in the machine's air stream. But the sensor signals only that the vacuum is no longer picking up dirt—not whether there's dirt left in your rug. Result: You keep vacuuming longer, working harder and gaining little in cleanliness.

Fine particles may pass through a vacuum's bag or filter and escape into the air through the exhaust. Many models claim **microfiltration** capabilities, using a bag with smaller pores or a second, electrostatic filter in addition to the standard motor filter. Some have a **HEPA filter**, which may benefit someone with asthma. But many models without a HEPA filter performed as well in CONSUMER REPORTS emissions tests, since the amount of dust emitted depends as much on the design of the entire machine as on its filter.

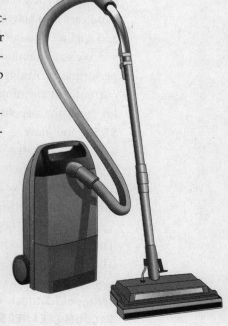

A vacuum's design can also affect how long it lasts. With some uprights, for example, dirt sucked into the vac passes through the blower fan before entering the bag–a potential problem, since most fans are plastic and vulnerable to damage from hard objects. Better

CARE AND FEEDING OF YOUR VACUUM

A vacuum cleaner requires periodic maintenance. Often it's simply a matter of replacing the bag or belt, which is outlined in the owner's manual. A replacement belt generally costs about $1 to $2; bags are even less. Some vacuums may require more serious work, including replacement of the brush assembly or repair or replacement of the motor.

You may be able to avoid some repairs if you watch what your vacuum inhales. Objects such as coins and paper clips can damage the motor fan.

A regular vacuum has no tolerance for wetness and should never be used outdoors. Even moisture from a recently shampooed carpet may be enough to damage the motor. String can snarl up the works as it winds itself around the rotating brush. If your vacuum swallows something hard or stringy, turn off the power and disconnect the electric plug before trying to dislodge the foreign object. Machines with a motor-overload protection feature turn themselves off; others use an air bypass to help protect the motor from damage.

Given the chance, a vacuum may gnaw on its own cord. If you can, turn off the rotating brush while you use an upright's attachments. If you can't, try to keep the cord out of the power nozzle's path.

systems filter dirt through the bag before it reaches the fan; while hard objects can lodge in the motorized brush, they're unlikely to break the fan.

Like bagless uprights, stick vacs and hand vacs typically have messy dirt-collection bins. Some have a **revolving brush**, which may help remove surface debris from a carpet. Stick vacs can hang on a hook or, if they're cordless, a wall-mounted charger base.

How to choose

PERFORMANCE DIFFERENCES. Virtually all recently tested uprights and canisters did at least a good job overall. Bagless vacs filtered dust as well as bag-equipped models overall, but emptying their bins released enough dust to make wearing a mask a consideration. We have found stick vacs less impressive, with few excelling at all types of cleaning. Overall, hand vacs do a better job along wall edges than stick vacs by coming closer to the moldings and angling into nooks and crannies.

We've also found that high-end features such as dirt sensors don't necessarily improve performance. And ignore claims about amps and suction. Amps are a measure of running current, not cleaning power, while suction alone doesn't determine a vacuum's ability to lift dirt from carpeting. Some vacuums are extremely expensive—anywhere from $800 to $1,500 and more.

CONSUMER REPORTS tests have shown that high-priced brands such as Electrolux, Filter Queen, Kirby, Miele, and Rainbow often perform well, but so do many models that cost $200 to $300. We've also found that many of the least expensive uprights sacrifice key features as well as performance.

RECOMMENDATIONS. Begin by deciding whether you prefer an upright or a canister. Then choose a model that performs and has the right features for your kind of cleaning. Those with varied cleaning needs may want to consider a vacuum-cleaner arsenal—an upright for carpets, a compact canister when tool use is important, and a hand vac or stick vac for quick touch-ups around the kitchen and family room.

VACUUM CLEANERS ◆ **Ratings:** Page 279

WET/DRY VACUUMS

Aimed at sawdust, wood chips, and spills, these machines are to regular vacs what pickup trucks are to sedans.

Wet/dry vacuums are meant for life's meaner tasks. Their place is typically in the workshop or garage, where their multigallon capacities and appetite for rough stuff make them right at home. Lately, manufacturers have been plugging their smallest portable models for kitchen duty: draining a clogged sink, sucking up soda spills, or picking up broken glass. Other capabilities can include use as a handheld blower for outdoor debris or as a pump. Wet/dry vacs of any size make poor housemates, however. Even the quietest are as loud as the noisiest household versions. And while their high-pitched whine is more annoying than dangerous, some are loud enough to make ear protection advisable. Still another concern is the fine dust these machines tend to spew into the air—a potential problem if you have allergies. But a high-efficiency cartridge filter significantly reduces those emissions and is available for many models.

What's available

Craftsman (Sears) and Shop-Vac account for three out of every four wet/dry vacs sold. Ridgid—sold mostly at Home Depot—and Genie are a distant third and fourth among leading brands. Ridgid and Craftsman models are made by the same manufacturer, Emerson Electric.

Wet/dry vacuums have claimed canister capacities ranging from 6 to 20 gallons for full-sized units and 1 to 2 gallons for compacts. Most units can fill about three-quarters of their canister with water before the float, an internal part designed to prevent overfilling and spilling, seals off the flow. Claimed peak motor power ranges from 1 hp for the smallest portables to more than 6 hp for the largest. The numbers denote peak horsepower, rather than actual output while in use, however. Larger models with more powerful motors tend to pick up debris or liquid faster, according to CONSUMER REPORTS tests. But some smaller units outperform larger ones. Use claims of canister capacity and peak motor power as a guide for comparing models within a brand or size group—not as an absolute. Price range: compact, $30 to $70; full-size, $40 to $250.

Key features

A wet/dry vacuum's **hose** usually comes in one of two diameters: 1¼ inches or 2½ inches. Models with a wider hose tend to pick up liquids and larger dry debris more quickly. A **hose lock**, found in some models, secures the hose to the canister better than a simple press-on fit, which can release as you pull the hose.

Most models come with accessories. A **squeegee nozzle**—essentially a wide floor nozzle with a rubber insert—helps slurp up liquid spills more quickly and thoroughly. Other nozzles include a **utility nozzle** for solid objects and a **dirt** and a **crevice nozzle** for corners. Some nozzles include a **brush insert** for improved dry pickup. A **built-in caddie** allows the vacuum to hold all of these accessories conveniently, though some models provide other onboard storage.

Filters are another key feature. The two basic types include **cartridge** and **two-piece paper/foam**. Cartridge filters tend to be easier to service and can stay in during wet vacuuming; with a two-piece filter, you must remove the paper element for wet cleanup. A **high-efficiency cartridge filter** (about $20 to $30) reduces the fine dust spewed into the air. While it also reduces suction slightly, allergy sufferers should find the sacrifice worthwhile.

Other notable features include **large carrying handles** molded into the sides of the canister, which help you move the vacuum securely over ledges and up stairs. An **assist handle** mounted at or near the top of the unit also makes jockeying these machine easier. Some models have **power cords** as short as 6 feet; look for one at least 15 feet long to avoid the safety risk of using an extension cord in standing water. A **drain spout** found in some models lets you simply open a drain, rather than lift and tilt the machine, while long **extension wands** reduce stooping.

How to choose

PERFORMANCE DIFFERENCES. A wet/dry vacuum's ability tends to track with its size. Compact models proved relatively wimpy in CONSUMER REPORTS tests, though they're fine for small areas and pint-sized spills. While all units we've seen pick up small wood shavings, chips, and sawdust, those with a wider hose suck up lighter dry and wet debris faster and often more thoroughly. Heavier dry waste tends to be a problem for all sizes, however.

RECOMMENDATIONS. Match the size of the vac with your needs. For example, models that hold 10 to 15 gallons can provide a good balance of size, power, and maneuverability. A large canister is handy for large spills. A large vac is harder to maneuver and store, however, while a small one must be emptied more often.

Maintenance includes cleaning the filter—typically about a five-minute job that involves removing it and brushing it clean (for paper elements) or washing it (for foam elements). An extra filter (about $15) you can quickly swap for a dirty one can come in handy, though changing filters is a messy task.

Hassle-Free Remodeling

Remodeling isn't redecorating. Redecorating means painting, buying new or recovering old furniture, hanging new draperies, and so on. Remodeling involves taking apart some portion of a home and building something different. It can be as straightforward as installing kitchen cabinets or modernizing a bathroom in the existing space. Or it can mean tearing out walls to make a larger space or adding a room or wing to a home. Redecorating is inconvenient. Remodeling is disruptive.

If you're married, a remodeling project should perhaps come with the equivalent of a manufacturer's warning label stating, "This project could be hazardous to your marriage." Just because you and your spouse have been living in your existing home, you may assume that both of you have similar tastes. Don't count on it. One of you may be dreaming of an all-white kitchen while the other sees bright colors on the walls and countertops. Added to all the complications that come with remodeling is a somewhat tight labor market. In parts of the country, some of the best contractors are booked solid. There is a bright side if you're a homeowner eager to get a remodeling project started, though. A delay gives you time for the most cost-saving activities a homeowner can engage in: complete planning and thorough research of products, materials, and people.

GETTING STARTED

Most remodeling projects are evolutionary rather than revolutionary. They begin with dissatisfaction over your house the way it is. You could be feeling a twinge of envy that comes after seeing a friend's recent renovation, or a twinge in your back as you lug the laundry up from the basement for the third time in a day. The more you know what you need, and the

DESIGN SOFTWARE

Special software lets you create contractor-ready plans for home remodeling. One example is 3D Home Architect Deluxe 5.0, a Windows program from Broderbund for $39.99 (*www.broderbund.com*).

surer you are about the styles and colors you like, the easier it will be to come up with a design. If you know you want something else but you're not sure what, clip pictures, plans, and suggestions out of magazines and newspapers. These will come in handy when you meet with an architect or a contractor. Instead of groping for words, you will be able to show pictures of what you want.

Assessing the status quo

Take a good look at what you already have. Analyze the room or rooms carefully, noting everything that's annoying, inconvenient, or just plain ugly. Ask questions such as these:

- ◆ Is the lighting functional and attractive?
- ◆ Do traffic patterns make sense?
- ◆ Do you need more storage space?
- ◆ Is there enough kitchen or bath counter space?
- ◆ Do the doors of kitchen appliances and cabinets open without bumping into anything?
- ◆ Can you get from refrigerator to range to sink with a minimum of walking back and forth? (Designers recommend a triangular arrangement.)
- ◆ Can more than one person cook (or get ready for work) at the same time?

This exercise in planning can go on for months, even years. (Of course, with some busy people, it can, by necessity, take place over a weekend.) Make lists of what you want and need, both for the immediate future and later years, when children leave the nest or aging parents move in.

If you start remodeling without a firm idea of what you intend to do, you're asking for higher costs, longer construction time, and an unhappy contractor.

Mapping out your dreams

To lend some reality to your plans, measure your house and draw the existing floor plan on quarter-inch graph paper. Obviously, if you're only remodeling one room or installing a bath, you don't have to measure the whole house, but at the very least you should be aware of what's beside, under, and over the area you're planning to work on. For instance, an added or relocated toilet will require a vent stack that has to go all the way up through the roof. Blending a 4-inch pipe into the decorative motif of the master bedroom can be a real challenge to a decorator.

Once you have all the dimensions, get a fresh piece of graph paper and translate your rough drawing to scale. Your goal is to draw a plan of the shell of the space you want to remodel. Use layers of tracing paper over the original drawing to make sketches of various layouts with a soft-lead pencil. Don't erase. Just flip over a new piece of tracing paper.

Anything you can do to visualize your project helps. You can also use kits (including paper cutouts shaped like furniture and walls) or software to experiment with layouts. Or use chalk or string to mark out a layout or the size of any components.

Drawing floor plans is the least expensive part of remodeling, so don't hold back. Play around with various changes. You can make one room out of two or three rooms, or two or three rooms out of one, or add baths and redesign kitchens with relative ease. It's best to leave the fireplace and chimney where they are and try to stay within the original walls. Once you start adding rooms and ells to the outside of the house, or dormers and a second

PUTTING IT ON PAPER

Sketches on graph paper can help you firm up your remodeling plans. Here's an approach you can follow.

1. Do a rough drawing of your existing floor plan. Measure and note all the distances.

2. Translate your drawing to scale.

3. Use tracing paper over the scale drawing to try out various ideas.

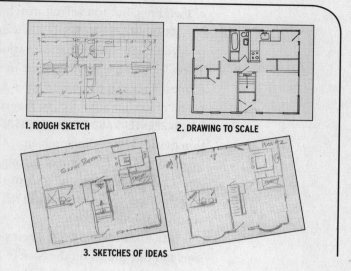

1. ROUGH SKETCH

2. DRAWING TO SCALE

3. SKETCHES OF IDEAS

story on top, you're getting into a whole new range of complications and costs. These floor plans are for information only. Leave the creation of the working drawings to your designer, architect, or builder. Then he or she, not you, will be responsible for their accuracy. As you work, remember that this isn't a high-school project in which you must do all the work yourself or lose credit. If you run into a creativity block, ask for help.

Consulting an expert

RENT-AN-ARCHITECT. You can hire an architect on an hourly basis to review your plans and suggest creative approaches to solving problems. This type of service has become more common. If you're planning a major structural change, you might want to keep the architect for the creation of the working drawings and material specifications for your remodeling project. That is one way to ensure that your contractors will bid on the same project. You can also retain the architect to handle the bidding process, interview contractors, analyze bids, possibly do some negotiating, and help you select the winner.

If you don't have the time or inclination to oversee your own project, you can also hire an architect as a "clerk of the works" to oversee the job, sign off at each stage on the quality of the work and changes, and generally act for you on the job. Be aware that some contractors may not like this arrangement.

BUILDING-SUPPLY STORES OR LUMBERYARDS. If your budget is tight and you're worried that your plans might be bigger than your wallet, you might check with a local building-supply store or lumberyard. Many keep an estimator on staff who can tell you what your materials cost is likely to be, even from your rough floor plans. The estimate will not include the cost of a general contractor or various subcontractors, but a good estimator should be able to give you a pretty good idea of where you stand. In return for this help, the estimator, of course, will expect the opportunity to bid on the building supplies you will need.

KITCHEN AND BATH SPECIALISTS. If a kitchen or bath remodeling is on your mind, you might explore your options with one or more of the many companies specializing in kitchen and bath projects. Remember that these suppliers are in business to sell materials, fixtures, and sometimes construction services and will be nudging you toward the high end of their lines. But you will ultimately make the final decisions.

SOLARIUM SPECIALISTS. If you want to add a single room to your house or even expand one, you might investigate the various solariums, or sunrooms, available on the market. These lean-to-like structures are usually made of insulated glass on aluminum or wood frames. They can be used to solve a design problem by extending a living room, dining room, or kitchen a few feet, or they can be built on an existing porch or deck.

CARPENTERS AND OTHER CRAFTSPEOPLE. Don't overlook the possibility of a simple solution to your remodeling problems. Adding a bow window to the kitchen, taking out a wall between two small rooms, or tearing out the bathroom floor and replacing the sink with a new vanity may create the look or the space you need. Call in a carpenter to discuss the project. An experienced one will tell you how the job can be done and may come up with creative ideas or solutions.

DESIGN/REMODELING FIRMS. These fill the gap between a full-blown architect-generated design and one drawn on the back of an envelope by a carpenter. They provide conceptual drawings and estimates and also build what they design if you hire them to go the whole way.

The typical design/remodeling firm has a draftsman on staff. Many firms have made the move to computer-aided design (CAD) systems to create with the push of a few keys everything from deck designs and kitchens to a complete house.

Larger design/remodeling firms tend to treat the design and remodeling functions as separate operations. The construction side of the business is free to bid on projects originated by other designers or architects, and the design arm is free to sell its services separately. Many of the firms have subcontractors and craftspeople on staff and will be able to schedule them into your job. You're generally free to get estimates on the firm's designs from other contractors as well.

SELECTING MATERIALS AND PRODUCTS

You will get more accurate bids from your contractors and will be better able to compare bids if you stipulate the appliances, cabinets, fixtures, and materials you want in your new space. Otherwise, one bid may be based on low-end products and another on high-end. Make a list of the items you want with model numbers and prices.

If you have trouble making decisions, you're in for a difficult time. There are hundreds of decisions to be made and you need to make them in a timely manner to prevent work from coming to a halt. The floor can't be laid if you're still debating the merits of tile over linoleum in the bathroom. All kitchen work will stop if you take too long to select the style and composition of your cabinets.

In Chapter 7, "Fresh Starts," you can compare various options regarding components, such as countertops, faucets, and interior lighting. Chapter 1, "Kitchen & Laundry," discusses the major kitchen appliances available. Those and other sections of this book will help you make informed choices, but you must make the decisions that balance your budget with your dreams. It may help to see and touch the products. Consider visiting distributors' showrooms, lumberyards, building-supply warehouses, plumbing-supply stores, carpet-supply houses, appliance vendors, and wallpaper and decorating stores. A caveat: You will be strongly tempted by beautiful and costly choices. If you simply must have, say, an $800 faucet set for your kitchen, try to balance it with a low-priced but adequate dishwasher.

CHOOSING A CONTRACTOR

Don't count on newspaper advertisements or the yellow pages. The best contractors don't have to advertise. They get work through satisfied customers' referrals. Consult friends and neighbors who have had work done. Another source is the National Association of Home Builders (*www.nahb.com*). After a little pointing and clicking, you can bring up the names and area of specialty of every member contractor within 20 miles of your ZIP code. Kitchen-and-bath shops or other suppliers may try to steer you to contractors they use regularly, but don't feel you must use one of them.

Call the Better Business Bureau or a local consumer-affairs agency for complaint histories of the ones you're considering. One or two gripes shouldn't necessarily induce you to look elsewhere. But be wary of a contractor with more problems than that. You'll also want to check with the appropriate agency to see if the contractor is properly licensed and insured. Some states or counties as well as many large cities or townships license contractors; other jurisdictions require them to be registered. As a rule, licensing entails passing a test to measure competency, while registering involves only payment of a fee. If a problem arises, a government agency may be able to pursue a licensed or registered contractor on your behalf.

Licensing won't guarantee success, but it indicates a degree of professionalism and suggests that the contractor is committed to his or her job. The same holds true for membership in or certification by an industry group such as the National Association of the Remodeling Industry, the National Kitchen & Bath Association, or the NAHB Remodeling Council—usually a sign of someone who is in business for the long run and not the quick buck. The National Association of the Remodeling Industry will even try to resolve disputes between member contractors and homeowners, if requested.

When checking references, ask whether the contractor is insured and, if applicable, licensed to do the work. If, for example, someone gets hurt or your neighbor's property is damaged by an unlicensed or uninsured contractor, you could wind up paying. It's wise to know what your homeowners' insurance covers before work starts.

No matter how you find potential contractors, be sure to ask for a list of previous customers; then call them or, better yet, visit their homes to look at the work. Ask some penetrating questions such as these:

- ◆ Would you hire this contractor again?
- ◆ Were you satisfied with the quality of the work?
- ◆ How did the contractor handle cleanup each day?
- ◆ Was the contractor easy to talk to?
- ◆ How did the contractor handle differences and changes?
- ◆ Was the job completed on time and at the bid? If not, why not?

You might also ask the contractor for a list of his or her building-material suppliers. Call them to see if the contractor has an account or pays for items upon delivery. Most suppliers are willing to extend credit to financially reliable contractors.

KEEPING TRACK

Get a spiral-bound notebook and keep it with you when you go fixture shopping and during your conversations with your contractor. Use a page for each of the major items and appliances you need to buy. Note model numbers, prices, and locations as you find them. Keep a log of all meetings with your contractor, noting changes and additions along with the contractor's estimates. Remember to date items.

Do you need a general contractor?

According to a general rule, if your job requires more than three subcontractors, a general contractor may be a good idea. A general contractor can free you from such burdens as maintaining a work schedule, obtaining necessary permits, and resolving disputes with suppliers. He or she will have more leverage than you do with subcontractors, since you're only a one-time job. In a tight labor market, that could be important. A general contractor may get discounts at lumberyards and supply houses. Whether or not these savings are passed on to you or retained as part of the contractor's fee is something that should be covered in the contract.

Evaluating bids

Industry groups recommend that you get a written estimate from at least three contractors. An estimate should detail the work to be done, the materials needed, the labor required, and the length of time the job will take. Obtaining multiple estimates is a good idea. An estimate can evolve into a bid—a more detailed figure based on plans with actual dimensions. Seeking more than one bid will increase your odds of paying less. Once agreed to and signed by you and the contractor, a bid becomes a contract.

The cheapest bid isn't always the best. Homeowners who accept a rock-bottom bid may wind up less satisfied overall than those willing to pay more. One bidder may be using smaller-diameter copper tubing or cheaper tile. He or she may also be bidding on exactly what you say you want, without making it clear that your pre-World War II house may also need new wiring and water lines, which will cost extra.

Make sure all bidders are bidding on the same specifications and job description. Take the time to choose materials and fixtures yourself, since you may not always like or agree with the contractor's selections. The term "comparing apples and oranges" may well have been invented during the bidding process.

Know your plans. It can be costly to change job specifications after the work has begun. Revising your plans can add substantially to cost overruns, with changes resulting in lengthy delays. A less-than-straightforward low bidder is counting on these changes to make the job profitable.

Negotiating a fair contract

A contract spells out all the terms of the work, helping you and the contractor minimize misunderstandings and wasted effort caused by poor instructions. It should include the contractor's name and address, license number, timetable for starting and finishing the job, payment schedule, names of subcontractors, and the scope of work to be done.

Other basic items include a specification of materials and equipment needed, demolition and cleanup provisions, approximate start and finish dates, terms of the agreement, and room for signatures and the date. Watch out for binding arbitration provisions that limit your right to sue in the event of a dispute.

MODEL CONTRACTS

For help in writing a contract, consider tapping into the expertise of industry associations:

◆ The American Homeowners Foundation offers a comprehensive model contract ($8) that can save you time and headaches when coming to terms with a contractor. To order, call 800-489-7776.

◆ The American Institute of Architects can supply excellent fill-in-the-blanks contract forms for virtually any type of building project. Prices vary. To order, call 800-365-2724 or visit www.aia.org.

SPOTTING A QUESTIONABLE CONTRACTOR

A warning signal should sound in your head if you encounter any of the following:

◆ A contractor who makes unsolicited phone calls or visits. Be especially wary of people who offer a bargain price, claiming that they're doing a job in the neighborhood and have leftover materials.

◆ A contractor whose address can't be verified, who uses only a post office box, or who has only an answering service and no separate listing in the telephone book.

◆ A contractor who isn't affiliated with any recognized trade association.

◆ License or insurance information you can't verify.

◆ A contractor who can't (or won't) provide references for similar jobs in your area.

◆ The promise of a hefty discount—but no mention of the total cost of the job.

◆ The promise of a deep discount if the contractor uses your home as a "demo."

◆ High-pressure sales tactics or threats to rescind a special price if you don't sign on the spot.

◆ A contractor who tries to scare you into signing a contract by claiming that your house puts you at peril (i.e., "Your electrical wiring could start a fire if it isn't replaced.")

An excellent addendum to a contract is the contractor's statement of what isn't included. This will include the assumptions the contractor has made about your job, such as that the existing wiring and plumbing lines are adequate, that the homeowner will pay for all trash removal, that the subflooring is sound, that the existing baseboards and window trim will be usable, and so on.

Do your homework and specify the materials and brand names of products, appliances, and fixtures to be used. The contract should also give the contractor the burden of obtaining building permits. Most municipalities have a building code; the person who obtains the permit is usually liable if the work doesn't come up to code.

It's common to pay for a project in stages over the course of the work, especially as key materials and supplies are delivered. Try to limit the down payment to 10 percent or less. Contractors who ask for a substantial amount up front may use your money to hire help to finish their previous job, leaving you to fume at delays. In some states, it's illegal to require large deposits. Some projects, however, require deposits on components that have to be made to order—kitchen cabinets, for instance. In such a case, a higher down payment may be required and justified.

Your contractor should agree to resolve problems that arise during the course of work rather than afterward. They might readily fix sloppy plastering or a leaky roof as soon as it's pointed out but be less willing to fix it later on. That's a good reason to hold back part of the final payment until after a job is completed. You can negotiate such terms and include them in the contract. Withholding the last 5 to 10 percent of the money for 30 days isn't an unreasonable stipulation.

Never make the final payment until you have obtained signed mechanic's-lien waivers or releases from all subcontractors and suppliers. These are basically receipts acknowledging payment for goods and services; they free you from third-party claims on your property in the event that you pay the contractor but he or she doesn't pay subcontractors or suppliers.

Doing it yourself

If you have a fairly uncomplicated remodeling project in mind and think you can handle it yourself, you will need three things:

TIME. Unless you're experienced, chances are you'll take longer to do a job than a professional carpenter or plumber would. And, unless you're retired, you probably have something else to do eight hours a day or more during the week. This could dim some of your enthusiasm for a lengthy stint of after-work and weekend labor. If your project is in the basement, attic, or some closet out of the main traffic area, the extra time may not matter. But if you have put the kitchen or a bathroom out of commission, you could quickly find yourself working in a pretty anxious family environment.

TALENT. Remember, you'll be doing something for the first time that a contractor has done many times. You'll take longer and probably make more mistakes than the professional. Most people underestimate the scope of a building task and overestimate their skills; try to be realistic in your appraisals of both.

TOOLS. Figure in the cost of new tools and mileage for trips to the hardware store in your project estimates. Most projects require specialized tools. Hanging a door, for example, needs a router, special bits, and setup jigs for both the hinges and lock sets.

If you have some doubts about your ability to handle a remodeling task by yourself but still want to be involved and save some money, consider hiring a contractor who will let you work with him or her as an unpaid assistant. That way you can take over some of the simple yet time-consuming tasks such as sanding, puttying, painting, cleaning up each day, or just holding up one end of a plank. Be sure to work out this arrangement with your contractors before they bid on the job. Some will welcome your help; others may not.

There are hundreds of good books dedicated to the do-it-yourselfer, offering step-by-step descriptions, drawings, and photos covering virtually any home project you may have. Check your local bookstore or library. There are also web sites that can offer you help. Search the NAHB web site (*www.nahb.com*) for the project you have in mind for step-by-step help.

OBTAINING FINANCING

Because you may be living with the financial consequences of a costly project for years to come, start by answering two questions: What will the improvement you want to make add to the resale value of your home? And what's the best way to pay for the job?

Projects that add value

If you're planning to stay in your home for a while, the most important reason for remodeling is your own comfort and convenience. The project may also add to the value of your home. You won't recoup your entire investment; some projects yield better returns than others. (See "Remodeling: What pays most and least," at right.) If you do decide to remodel, use the newer homes in your neighborhood as a benchmark.

Most upgrades are appealing to potential purchasers. Adding a second bathroom to a one-bathroom house, for example, is a big plus. But adding a swimming pool or hot tub

REMODELING: WHAT PAYS OFF?

Many consumers believe that money poured into their houses will always net them a big return on their investment. CONSUMER REPORTS decided to test the proposition. We first turned to Remodeling magazine's annual survey, which polls hundreds of real-estate professionals, mostly brokers and sales agents supplied by the National Association of Realtors, to find out the amount various projects are likely to return. (More information is available at *www.remodeling.hw.net*. Once there, go to "Cost vs. Value 2001.") The survey assesses how much a homeowner can expect to recover if the house is sold a year after the project is completed. We submitted Remodeling's projects to real-estate appraisers provided by the Appraisal Institute, a professional association; they estimated how much homeowners were likely to recover from improvements over the same period. After three years, return is impossible to estimate, say our appraisers. They added other observations. On colors: stick with neutrals because they don't date themselves. On swimming pools: in some areas, a pool can subtract from a house's value because the homeowner is on the hook for liability insurance and maintenance. On all projects: Those that add square footage to bring a house up to–but not beyond–community norms pay off the most. Projects are presented showing highest to lowest returns, as calculated by our appraisers.

PROJECT	DESCRIPTION	COST*	VALUE RECOVERED*	APPRAISERS' ESTIMATE OF VALUE RECOVERED	APPRAISERS' COMMENTS
Major kitchen remodeling	Add 30 feet of new semicustom wood cabinets, laminate countertops, resilient floor, center island, midpriced sink and faucet. Include built-in appliances.	$38,800	81%	50% to 75%	The more expensive the house, the more you will earn from the remodeling. It doesn't pay, however, to install an ultra-expensive kitchen in a modestly priced house.
Bathroom remodeling	Update a 25-year-old 45-sq.-ft. bathroom with new fixtures, ceramic-tile walls in tub, and vinyl wallpaper.	9,500	85	50 to 75	Same as above. Adding a new bathroom to bring number of baths in line with community standards brings greater returns than restyling an existing one.
Attic bedroom addition	Build 225-sq.-ft. room; install 35-sq.-ft. shower/bath, heat, central air conditioning, insulation, and carpet.	31,400	74	50 to 75	Your new space is expensive relative to the potential resale recovery, unless finished attics are the norm for your area.
Master suite addition	Build new 384-sq.-ft. master bedroom over crawl space, with walk-in closet, ceramic-tile shower and whirlpool tub.	63,300	75	60 to 74	Most new houses have master-bedroom suites; the addition is an amenity that people will pay for, particularly in upscale neighborhoods. Brings an older home more in line with new housing.
Basement refinishing	Add a 600-sq.-ft. entertainment area with a wet bar, 40- sq.-ft. full bath, and 144-sq.-ft. auxiliary room.	39,700	69	60 to 70	If of the same quality as the rest of the house, a finished basement will be a plus. Amateur, do-it-yourself jobs won't yield maximum return.
Deck addition	Build 320-sq.-ft., treated-pine deck.	5,900	77	50	A very large deck like this won't add significantly to the value of a modest home. A deck also may not add much if a patio is standard for the neighborhood.
Two-story addition	Add a 384-sq.-ft. wing, over crawl space, with a first-floor family room and a second-floor bedroom with full bath. Include prefabricated fireplace, 11 windows, an atrium-style exterior door, heating, and cooling.	67,700	84	40 to 50	Added square footage itself is what an appraiser would value.
Family-room addition	Add a 400-sq.-ft. room on new crawl-space foundation with wood-joist floor framing, wood siding on exterior walls, fiberglass shingle roof. Add 180 sq. ft. of glazing, including windows, atrium exterior door, and two skylights. Tie into existing heating and cooling systems.	46,700	80	40 to 50	Because a family room is an amenity, it could bring a lower return than an extra bedroom or bath, unless every house in the neighborhood has one. It costs more to retrofit a family room on a house than to have it in new construction.
Sunroom addition	Add a 200-sq.-ft. sunroom to two-story post-World War II house including footings and foundation, walls of extruded aluminum with windows of double-paned glass. Insulate roof and ceiling. Add ceiling fan.	27,100	60	40 to 50	Adds square footage but as an amenity, not a necessity.
Reroofing	Remove existing roofing to bare wood; install 3,000 sq. ft. of fiberglass shingles with felt underlay.	10,000	60	10	Buyers expect houses not to have leaky roofs. They don't want to pay extra for a new roof.
Home office	Refurbish spare room.	10,500	55	10	Adds little to resale value. So-called smart houses, automated by computer, also add little.
Exterior repainting	Add coat of wood primer and coat of satin acrylic latex paint for two-story wood-sided house built post-1980.	8,300	75	10	Buyers expect a home with a decent paint job. Painting is maintenance, not an improvement. Further, we recommend 2 topcoats.

* According to *Remodeling* magazine survey.

may make your house less desirable to safety-conscious potential buyers who have small children. Other cost-effective upgrades include remodeling an aging kitchen and converting a master bedroom into a suite by linking it to a dressing area and private bath.

Keep good records and hold on to contractors' receipts. Money spent on home improvements adds to the "cost basis" of your home and reduces the capital-gains tax that may be due when you sell. You'll need complete records of your outlays to do your income-tax return the year you sell. Don't wait until you get organized. Get a box, or select a drawer and throw all the receipts, contracts, change orders, bills, and memos into it. You can sort it out later.

Paying cash

Because even a relatively modest home improvement such as replacing siding or adding a deck can cost well over $5,000, paying for remodeling projects out of current income or readily available savings can place a huge strain on a household's budget. With sufficient planning and saving, you may be able to finance modest home improvements—siding, kitchen cabinets, windows—without resorting to borrowing.

Another way to self-finance a project is by tapping your other investment accounts—selling some mutual-fund holdings, for example. But think this option through carefully. You should determine that the combination of additional comfort and home-value appreciation will be worth more to you than the return you could expect by leaving your money where it is.

One option you should consider only as a last resort is using a credit card to pay for a significant home improvement. Unless you're prepared to pay off the full amount when you receive your monthly statement, you'll begin to incur stiff interest charges, sometimes at an annual rate of 18 percent or higher.

Smart ways to borrow

Using loans that can be paid off in installments may be the only way to make remodeling affordable. Borrowing can have distinctive advantages—if you shop for loan terms and choose a reputable lender. Avoid unsecured personal loans; at today's average interest rate of about 15 percent, they can be almost as costly as using a credit card.

The best source of collateral you have for a remodeling loan is the equity you've already accumulated in your home. Your lender might also offer you a larger loan based on the increased value of your home after the remodeling. Interest rates on loans based on home equity are usually the lowest a homeowner can find anywhere. On top of that, interest you pay on a home-equity loan is apt to be tax-deductible, further reducing your cost of borrowing.

There are several ways to borrow against your home equity. Here's a look at the pros and cons of each:

HOME-EQUITY LOANS. Also known as second mortgages, these provide a lump sum of money at a fixed rate of interest. They're available through credit unions, banks, home-finance companies, and even some big brokerage houses that cater to retail customers. Borrowing limits usually range from 70 to 80 percent of the value of your house, minus any amount outstanding on your first mortgage. Some banks are now offering far more—up to 125 percent of home value in some instances—but CONSUMER REPORTS strongly advises against such a loan. The reason: You owe more than your house is worth.

Home-equity loans are most often repaid over 10 to 20 years, although terms range from 5 to 30 years. In late 2001, the average interest rate on home-equity loans nationwide was just over 6 percent, but rates can vary widely, so shop carefully. Financing companies, such as Household Finance, typically market their loans to borrowers with spotty credit histories and charge interest rates up to 5 percentage points higher than commercial banks.

A home-equity loan can be a good way to pay for a relatively costly renovation, such as a new bathroom, a home-office addition, or some other large project that you can expect to complete within a period of several weeks. These are jobs for which you want to lock in a favorable fixed-interest rate so you can budget your payments, knowing that rising rates won't cause them to rise.

HOME-EQUITY LINES OF CREDIT. These differ from closed-end home-equity loans in that they generally allow a homeowner to draw upon his or her available equity when needed. Most credit lines allow the borrower simply to write a check; the interest charges vary with the rates prevailing when the credit is tapped. As a homeowner pays off past borrowings, the credit line is replenished. Some financial institutions charge a nominal annual fee to keep the credit line open, though most do not.

Home-equity lines of credit are the most flexible way to borrow money for home improvements. You may want to consider a credit line if you plan to do a series of remodeling projects, working with several different contractors over an extended period of time. For example, you may plan to re-side your home this spring, build a deck next summer, and replace windows the following fall. With an open credit line, you needn't apply for a separate loan for each of these projects, and you can take advantage of favorable interest-rate trends. In late 2002, the average interest rate on home-equity lines of credit nationwide was about 5½ percent.

CASH-OUT REFINANCING. With the average rate on a conventional 30-year fixed-rate mortgage at just over 6 percent (in late 2002), you may want to consider cash-out refinancing. This allows you to replace your current mortgage with a larger new one. For example, if you currently owe $80,000 on the mortgage you took out when you originally bought your home, you may be able to refinance that loan and expand the amount you borrow to, say, $100,000. That $20,000 difference is cash you can use to pay for a major home renovation.

A cash-out refinancing may be especially worth considering if interest rates are at least a percentage point below the rate of your original mortgage. If that's the case, you may discover you can have access to funds you need for remodeling while keeping your monthly mortgage payment only a little above—or even no more than—what it had been before you refinanced. Don't forget that you may face substantial closing costs based on the full amount you borrow, but these costs have been coming down.

A FIRST MORTGAGE. This can help if you're buying a home that's in immediate need of refurbishing. You'll be able to amortize the remodeling costs over the full 30-year life of your new home loan. The advantage, of course, is that you can begin renovations that will make your home more livable soon after you move in. The lender may increase the appraised value of your home considering the proposed renovations.

But there are some downsides. If borrowing more results in your down payment's falling below 20 percent of the total amount of the loan, you may be required by your lender to pay private mortgage insurance (PMI). The premiums for PMI, which protects

LIVING WITH WORK-IN-PROGRESS

You may think of it as your home, but to your contractors, it is their workplace. They will arrive each morning on their schedule—usually between 7 and 8 a.m. If those hours don't fit your family's usual schedule, change it.

On the first day, show the crew which bathroom they can use, put out some towels, give them room in your fridge to store their lunches and sodas, give them permission to use your water, and set out some glasses. Let your contractor use your phone to line up the next day's subcontractors or check on deliveries.

Set aside room in the garage for the crew's tools. If workers keep their tools at your place, they save time packing and unpacking; what's more, they have to show up each day. Also consider letting the crew use the garage as a workshop and place to store cabinetry or other materials as they're delivered.

Children and construction projects don't mix. Your children will not agree with this, but it is dangerous and your workers should not have to act as babysitters or unplug their saws and drills after every use. Arrange for summer camp or recruit your family or neighbors for day-care help.

As work progresses, particularly if it involves some of the basic operations in your life such as the kitchen or bathrooms, your life is going to become difficult. You will be living with dust and noise. If your contractor is kind, he or she will leave you the use of your kitchen sink, refrigerator, and stove as long as possible or move your appliances into another room. When the water in the kitchen is turned off, you may have to wash dishes in the bathtub.

If you are adding a room to an outside wall, the contractor shouldn't break through the wall into your home until the very last step. This will isolate all the dust and noise for most of the project.

There may come a time when it would be best to move out for a few days to a motel or a relative's or friend's home. It's not advisable to go on an extended vacation because you really should check in each day to preview and review the work being done.

your lender against the risk that you will default on your loan, can add significantly to your monthly mortgage payment for years.

SPECIAL BANK LOANS. These can help when rehabilitating a home. Some programs are limited to borrowers who live in disadvantaged neighborhoods or whose annual income does not exceed the median of their communities; others are available to anyone. Ask your bank or other financial institution whether it offers home-improvement mortgage loans, rehabilitation mortgage loans, home-improvement loans, or second mortgages from the government-sponsored agencies Fannie Mae or Freddie Mac. Or call Fannie Mae at 800-732-6643 for a referral to lenders near you.

ENERGY-EFFICIENCY LOANS. Some utility companies work with local lenders to make it less costly for homeowners to undertake energy-efficient renovations, such as installing new windows or insulating an attic. Families with incomes of up to $30,000 per year can qualify for interest-free loans ranging from $500 to $4,000. Those with higher incomes are eligible for loans with an annual interest rate of just 5 percent. Some companies promote their rebate and loan offerings through bill inserts or billboards. Fannie Mae, the government-sponsored agency that buys home loans from lenders to resell on the secondary market, buys and resells energy loans. A caveat: Some utilities are abandoning these programs to cut costs and to be more competitive as the industry becomes deregulated. To find out whether there are any special programs in your area, call your local utility and ask if it sponsors home-energy audits, rebate programs, and low-cost loans.

CORRECTING MISTAKES

If you have ever rearranged furniture, you'll have some idea of how slim the chances are that your remodeling will come off without any hitches or changes. Things look different in real life than on paper. If some aspect of the remodeling bothers you and you don't change it, it will go on bothering you. There are several kinds of mistakes:

◆ Things that are done correctly but look wrong.

◆ Things that are done wrong but look OK. The flooring is laid east to west rather than north to south. You catch it but not before it has all been laid. Talk it over with your contractor. Is it really worth holding his or her feet to the fire to change it or could you adjust?

◆ Things that are done wrong and look wrong. There are only two electrical outlets over the kitchen counter, and the plans call for six. You are entitled to have your contractor correct the mistake at his expense. It will ease the atmosphere, however, if you have caught such a mistake before the wallboard is up. Visit the job regularly, and set up meetings with your contractor to go over what has just been done and what is coming up next.

When there is a problem, talk it over with the contractor. He or she may have some ideas for correcting the problem. If not, it is time for a change order. If you caught the problem early, it's possible that a lot of work will not have to be torn out. That is why you should check how the job is progressing every day.

A change order should be regarded as a new contract. Your contractor should furnish you with an estimate of the costs involved in time and materials, and you should sign off on those revisions and calculate the additional expenses into your budget. It is for this reason that you should budget 20 percent for unanticipated problems.

FIRST THINGS FIRST
Don't let your contractor tear out the old kitchen cabinets or bathroom fixtures until the replacements you ordered from the factory are sitting in your garage. Deliveries can be weeks or even months late. And make sure everything is correct in terms of style and color and is free of damage.

WRAPPING UP THE PROJECT

Don't be discouraged if the work seems to slow to a crawl as the project nears its end. You and the family are sick and tired of the daily mess, the noise, and having to share your house with a bunch of people with power tools and dirty boots. The hammering will be slower, the sounds of the cutoff saw shorter and farther apart. You are at the finish-carpentry phase of the project.

Finish carpenters are the elite of the business. No more than one or two will be on your project. Their job is to install the kitchen cabinets, baseboards, moldings, and window surrounds. They may spend all day in your new master bedroom closet hanging rails and building shelving. They are probably working as fast as they should.

After the skilled carpenters come the painters. Their work, too, seems to go slower than you will think it should. It might be two or three days before they even open a can of paint. This, too, is how it should be done. All those nail holes and corner gaps have to be puttied and sanded.

Finally it's time for the final tour of the spaces with your contractor and the creation of the infamous "punch list"—a list of problems that need to be addressed before final payment is tendered. The tour can become like a victory lap after a race won. You get a chance to offer congratulations for the work done. Or you may have been harboring long-suppressed gripes about doors that stick, corners that gap, and missing window locks and light fixtures. But save it. Your contractor also has a list, and he or she can see these things as well as you can. Fixtures may be on back-order, or the people who can correct some of the problems are already on the next job and will be back.

Remember that the contractor wants you to be happy with the work because you may be the source of a future job, and you should still have 5 to 10 percent of his or her last payment in the bank. If all is in order or soon will be, release the check. If there is an $80 light fixture still to come, withhold that amount and pay the rest. Be sure to ask for the owner's manuals and warranties for the newly installed appliances. Most warranties start from the moment of installation, not from the date of purchase.

Making the final payment doesn't mean you are without recourse if things crop up later. Your contract probably calls for at least a year's guarantee on workmanship and materials. You should recognize that projects made of wood will move as they gain and lose moisture, that foundations will shift, that cracks will appear. This is all normal, as your contractor knows. If you have a door that sticks, he may put off calling on you until all the doors have had a chance to move and he can send someone in to adjust them all at once.

You are now free to move about in your new space. Enjoy it. You have earned some quiet time.

Fresh Starts

A new coat of paint can give your home's interior or exterior a fresh look. Wallpaper can transform the personality of a room and hide minor flaws. A wood floor can bring an elegant, classic look to a living room. A kitchen can be made more attractive and organized with new cabinetry, countertops, and flooring. Roofing and siding products are essential to a home's integrity. Improvements such as these make a home nicer to live in. And such work can also add to its value.

Warehouse-sized home centers such as Home Depot and Lowe's put an extensive selection of home-improvement products in one place, often at very low prices. Local hardware stores, specialty shops, and lumberyards sometimes deliver superior service. While relatively few people actually buy home-improvement products through web sites, many take advantage of the unparalleled access to product information that the Internet delivers. Studying the results of a web search on, say, "kitchen faucets" is a great way to prepare for a trip to the plumbing-fixtures store.

CABINETRY

If you're remodeling a kitchen or bathroom, you'll almost surely devote planning and money to cabinets. Be sure they're well made, since they're subject to heavy use.

Essentially, a kitchen cabinet is nothing more than a box with a door or drawer in the front. But many details distinguish those boxes: the materials they're made of, whether they're stock, semicustom-made, or custom-made, and how they're put together. The type of wood used affects the cabinet's price. Some store displays may boast that the cabinets are "all wood." That can mean they're made of plywood or particleboard. But few stock or semicustom-made cabinets are made entirely of solid-wood boards. The best you can hope for in stock cabinets is solid wood for the door and drawer fronts and the area that surrounds them.

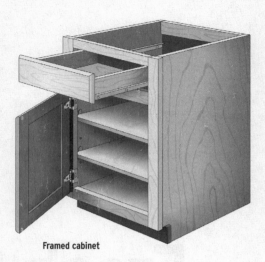

Framed cabinet

What's available

Before you delve into the details, you should understand the basic varieties of cabinet.

STOCK. The most affordable type, these come in standard styles off-the-shelf from kitchen-remodeling stores and home centers. Most are built to a manufacturer's standard selection of styles in standard dimensions. Stock cabinets range in width from about 9 to 48 inches in 3-inch increments. Since kitchens don't come in standard dimensions, installers use filler strips—boards matching the cabinet finish—to take up the odd few inches between cabinet and wall. Stock cabinets and filler pieces usually can be delivered in a week or so.

SEMICUSTOM. These come in more sizes, materials, finishes, exterior-trim choices, and with more storage accessories than stock cabinets. They are sold at home centers, cabinet dealerships, and in kitchen showrooms, These use the manufacturer's stock styles and finishes. Though they are available in standard widths, you can have base cabinets built taller than the standard 36-inch height or shallower than the standard 24-inch depth for a custom look. You can also add or subtract height or width. Delivery time is longer—a month or more isn't unusual—and the price is generally 20 to 30 percent higher than for standard stock cabinets.

CUSTOM. These are made to order, and, as such, are the most costly option. You or your kitchen designer can specify the style, materials, shapes, and sizes. You can hire a carpenter to build custom cabinets or order them from a factory, usually through a kitchen-and-bath dealer. Expect to pay dearly (anywhere from 30 to 100 percent more than for semicustom) and to wait six weeks or longer for delivery or construction on site.

Frameless cabinet

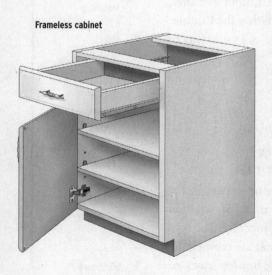

Key features

SURFACES. The modern answer to painted paneled doors, **Thermofoil**, consists of polyvinyl-chloride sheets heated and molded to a sculpted fiberboard substrate. Thermofoil-faced doors and drawers are easy to spot—they have a seamless finish. Salespeople like to point out that Thermofoil cabinets have few areas to trap dust and dirt. Indeed, the material is very easy to clean and resists scratches and staining, although it does occasionally yellow with age

Laminates come in an endless variety of colors and textures, including wood grain (although you probably won't mistake laminate for the real stuff). They're usually used on flat, contemporary-looking doors and drawer fronts. Laminated surfaces can be damaged by heat and dryness—from a range, for example. Sometimes referred to as low-pressure laminate, **melamine** is often used in the interior of mid- to high-priced cabinets. The material chips fairly easily and can bubble and lift from the underlying particleboard when exposed to high humidity. But it is not as fragile as low-end materials such as vinyl or paper. You can get the look of solid wood without the cost by choosing cabinets of **wood veneer,** a thin sheet of wood laminated to plywood or a composite such as particleboard. You can tell the difference between solid wood and veneer by comparing the grain on the outside and inside of the door. If the grain doesn't match, the panel is veneered. **Solid wood** may not necessarily be superior to a laminate veneer or Thermofoil and may actually be more prone to warping or cracking.

FRAMING. **Framed cabinets** have horizontal rails and vertical stiles that frame the door and drawers. **Decorative hinges** attach the door to the frame. Traditional styles with paneled doors and a wood finish usually distinguish framed cabinets. The **face frame** provides extra support, which helps keep the cabinet square during installation.

With **frameless cabinets,** the doors are attached directly to the cabinet sides with hinges that are hidden from view when the door is closed. Plain, contemporary styles are usually frameless. These cabinets provide slightly more interior room and easier access, but they're tricky and time-consuming to install. **Cross rails** add rigidity and stability, particularly important when installing frameless cabinets.

JOINING DETAILS. Look for **mortised corners** in better-quality framed cabinets, **doweled corners** in frameless models. By comparison, inexpensive cabinets often have simple **butt joints** in which the back and sides are glued and then nailed or screwed together. Corners are sometimes reinforced with braces. **Stainless-steel hinges** and **screws** help cabinets hold up over the long haul. In CONSUMER REPORTS high-humidity tests, plain-steel hinges began to rust. Good hinges should automatically close a cabinet door when it's left slightly ajar. Some types of hinge are **adjustable,** so doors can be realigned if they sag or shift over time. **Cup hinges** are designed to be totally concealed when the door of a cabinet is closed. Ask if they are adjustable (most are). Cup hinges generally limit the door opening to about 115 degrees. **Knife hinges,** like cup hinges, can be concealed when the door is closed, but most aren't adjustable. Knife hinges allow the door to open almost 180 degrees. **Barrel hinges** are an inexpensive hinge generally used on framed cabinets. A narrow cylinder is visible when the door is closed. Most aren't adjustable. Barrel hinges allow doors to open about 160 degrees. Cabinets need a solid anchor to the wall (called a **hanger rail).** Base cabinets have a rail at the top; wall cabinets have one at top and one at bottom.

SHELVES. These should extend the full depth of the cabinet for maximum storage. **Nonadjustable shelves,** though sturdy, offer no flexibility. **Adjustable shelves** can be positioned to suit oversized stock pots or flat frying pans. Choose **metal** or **wood supports** for adjustable shelves when there's an option. And beware of plastic clips, which can be flimsy and can bend under weight.

DRAWERS. CONSUMER REPORTS tests have shown that the most durable drawers have a box made of solid wood and a separate front attached to the box. **Dovetailed** or **doweled joints** hold better than stapled ones. Press down on the drawer bottom to see if it's sturdy. Those made of thin hardboard sagged under weight in tests. In most cabinets, **drawer rollers** move on tracks mounted on the sides of the cabinet. Look for **full-extension slides** that allow access to the entire drawer.

END PANELS. Choose base cabinets with **plywood** end panels if you can. When exposed

CABINET CORNERS

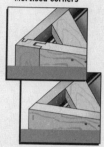

Mortised corners

Butt joints

HINGES

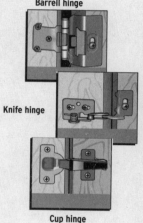

Barrell hinge

Knife hinge

Cup hinge

DRAWER JOINTS

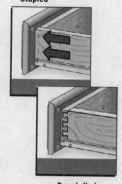

Stapled

Dovetailed

to high humidity (for example, next to a dishwasher), plywood held up better than particle board in CONSUMER REPORTS tests.

How to choose

PERFORMANCE DIFFERENCES. To a certain extent, you get what you pay for with kitchen cabinets. Less expensive ones might have stapled drawers, which don't hold up particularly well; a thin hardboard drawer bottom, which can separate from the rest of the drawer under a heavy load; and a vinyl or paper interior surface. You won't find a significant difference in quality between medium- and high-priced cabinets. With both, you can expect drawers and doors that can withstand severe impact. But you may also get an inferior finish.

For bathrooms, CONSUMER REPORTS testing found wood veneer or laminate cabinets to be more durable than ones faced with wood-grain paper or foil. Solid wood wouldn't be our first choice; humidity may warp the doors.

RECOMMENDATIONS. The choice of contractor is as important a decision as the choice of materials. Make sure the contractor will provide a warranty separate from the one provided with the cabinets. When your cabinets are delivered, examine them to make sure they are the same style and finish as those you saw in the store and that they have not been damaged. To check installation, look at the cabinet doors to be sure none are out of alignment; be sure doors and drawers move smoothly.

COUNTERTOPS

A countertop has to withstand considerable punishment over a long a period of time. And it needs to look good. Here's what you need to know about the leading types of countertop material:

What's available

BUTCHER BLOCK. Butcher-block countertops are made of hardwoods; maple is the most common, though red oak and teak are also used. A slab of butcher block near the sink is useful for chopping and slicing, but it can become marred with everyday use. Butcher block is relatively easy to install and repair. The wood will almost certainly become scratched, nicked, burned, or stained as it's used; fortunately, it can be sanded and resealed. Butcher block should either be treated regularly with mineral oil or beeswax, or sealed with a varnish suitable for food-preparation surfaces. Wood is vulnerable to fluctuations in humidity, so butcher block is a poor choice for over a dishwasher.

CERAMIC TILE. Ceramic tile comes in an almost limitless selection of colors, patterns, and styles. A professional or an adept do-it-yourselfer can install it easily. You can use tile to customize a countertop—on a backsplash or island top. Tile set into the counter near the range can serve as a built-in trivet. Glazed tiles are highly resistant to stains, scratches, and burns. And repairs are relatively easy and inexpensive. Grout can be tinted to match or contrast with the tiles, but the joints can trap crumbs and soak up unsightly stains. Cleaning it can be difficult unless the grout is sealed. Tile can be scratched by sharp objects and can chip or crack if hit hard enough.

ENGINEERED STONE. This artificial material is made primarily of small stone chips combined with resins and pigments. Engineered stone can look much like granite but has a more uniform appearance. It's resistant to stains, heat, and abrasion and never needs sealing. However, engineered stone doesn't withstand impact—especially a blow to the edge—as well as real granite.

GENUINE STONE. The most popular stones for kitchen countertops, granite and marble come in a spectrum of colors. They also stand up to almost any type of physical abuse, resisting scratches, nicks, and scorching from hot pans. Granite is the tougher material. Marble is slightly softer and more prone to staining and etching from the acids in foods and cleaners. The stone's cold surface also makes it ideal for keeping pastry dough cool and firm while it's being rolled or kneaded. Both granite and marble should be sealed with a protective, penetrating sealer that's applied periodically.

Because these are natural materials, the grain you see in a display may not be the same as in the stone delivered to your kitchen. But most suppliers will allow you to inspect and choose the stone slabs. Genuine stone is expensive, partly because it's heavy and difficult to install. Prices are coming down. And tiles are less expensive—and lighter weight—than thick slabs. Special equipment may be needed to move the slabs, which have to be arranged to match color and grain. Without sealing, polished granite stains easily, and the stains may be difficult to remove. Limestone, slate, soapstone, and sandstone are also used as counter-tops, though they are softer than either granite or marble.

LAMINATE. Laminates such as Formica and Wilsonart are lightweight and relatively easy to install, although edge treatments add to installation cost and complexity. Laminate is the most popular countertop material, probably because it comes in hundreds of colors and patterns and the price is right. Typically it consists of a colored top layer over a dark core; when laminate covers the top and edge of a countertop, part of that core shows as a dark line. Some manufacturers offer laminates colored all the way through. These cost a bit more, but they show no dark line and any surface scratches will be less visible.

Prefabricated seamless countertop-and-backsplash—known as postformed counter— is also available. Laminate is not as durable as other materials. Caustic substances, such as drain cleaner, can ruin the finish, and direct flame will scorch the surface. Solid colors and shiny finishes readily show scratches and nicks. Damaged areas can't be repaired. Water can seep through seams or between the countertop and backsplash, weakening the material underneath or causing the laminate to lift.

SOLID SURFACE. Solid-surface materials, which imitate marble and other types of stone, are sold under various brands: Avonite, DuPont Corian, Formica Surell, Nevamar Fountainhead, and Wilsonart Gibraltar. Solid-surface countertops are reasonably durable but expensive; they're best installed by a contractor that has been certified by the manufac-turer. Made of polyester or acrylic resins combined with mineral fillers, they come in various thicknesses and can be joined almost invisibly into one apparently seamless expanse. These materials can be sculpted so the sink and backsplash are integral and routed to accept contrasting inlays.

Scratches and nicks don't show readily on solid surfaces and can be buffed out with an abrasive pad; some gouges can be filled. Repair of a solid-color surface tends to be less discernible than repair of a surface that mimics a granite pattern. Prolonged heat may cause a solid-surface material to discolor.

How to choose

The overall kitchen design you've chosen and your budget will determine which material is most appropriate. Butcher block, laminate, and ceramic tile tend to be the least expensive, with some ceramic tiles costing as little as $4 a square foot, installed. Solid-surface materials range from $40 to $75 a square foot, and engineered stone starts at about $50 a square foot. Genuine stone can run as little as $50 per square foot up to as much as $300 a square foot.

PERFORMANCE DIFFERENCES. Our tests over the years have shown more differences between types of countertop than between brands of a type. Overall, engineered stone and granite are the toughest, closely followed by ceramic tile. Butcher block is the most vulnerable, mostly because the wood can be so easily scratched and gouged.

RECOMMENDATIONS. Comparison-shopping and research at home centers or kitchen-design outlets can go a long way toward helping you make the right choice. Listed above are the leading materials, but just about anything that's hard and flat—from plate glass to sheets of zinc—can make a countertop. Concrete and stainless steel are two options. The more exotic your choice, the more important it is to find a capable installer. You don't want to pay for sloppy work on material that's costing you hundreds of dollars for every square foot.

COUNTERTOPS ♦ **Ratings:** Page 216

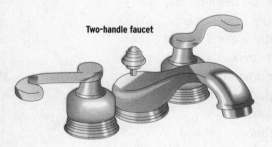

Two-handle faucet

Single-handle faucet

FAUCETS

Fixtures for kitchens and bathrooms range widely in price. Some of the newest models have improvements aimed at making them last longer.

According to manufacturers, most homeowners put style first, durability second, and function last in their search for a new kitchen or bathroom faucet. The style issue isn't surprising, considering kitchens and bathrooms are some of the most remodeled spaces in a home. But there's more to think about when choosing a faucet.

What's available

The most familiar names in kitchen and bath faucets include American-Standard, Delta, Eljer, Kohler, Moen, Peerless, Price Pfister, and Sterling. Kitchen and bath faucets fall into two basic styles: Single-handle faucets that regulate flow and temperature with one lever or knob and two-handle faucets that let you control hot and cold water independently. With the latter, the handles are 4 or 8 inches apart and require sinks with suitably spaced plumbing holes. Price range for faucets: $35 to $2,400 or more.

Key features

Deep inside the faucet is the key working component—the valve that shuts off the flow of water. There are many designs.

A traditional **washer-and-seat** faucet—a compression-valve design—relies on rubber or neoprene washers attached at the bottom of each handle stem to stop the flow of water as the handle is screwed down against a metal valve seat. While simple and easy to service, this system requires a lot of maintenance. The washers eventually become brittle, compressed, or worn; the small screws that attach them corrode; and the valve seats wear down under repeated friction and pressure. Annoying leaks and drips are the result. Most U.S. manufacturers have replaced this system with valve and flow-control options that are more durable. In some cases, though, the newer designs require more involved repairs than the older ones do.

Ball valves are what you'll find on some single-handle faucets. Introduced in the early 1950s, this design includes a metal ball housed in a brass or plastic sleeve. Turning the faucet handle in any direction moves the ball, which regulates both water temperature and flow. Ball valves are available on both kitchen and bathroom faucets.

Ceramic or **stainless-steel disks** use perforated disk-shaped regulators to control water flow. The disks rotate in pairs or against a fixed plate, often within a cartridge assembly. Repairs typically can involve replacing the entire cartridge.

Another cartridge design encompasses a single bored cylinder valve with **O-rings** that seal it within the faucet body. While the O-rings can be replaced individually, typically the whole cartridge is replaced. Manufacturers are so confident about the durability of these new valves that most faucets now come with a lifetime warranty against leaks and drips. The warranty covers only the faucet, however, and not the labor to replace it.

Spouts can be fixed or can swivel side to side. They can be standard, pull-out, or gooseneck-shaped. With the **pull-out** type, the single spout doubles as a sprayer that can be pulled out to rinse dishes and pots and pans. Gooseneck spouts are useful for washing large objects or filling buckets. Some kitchen faucets have **integrated water filters,** which you should change quarterly. You can also buy filters that attach to the outlet of the faucet.

Traditional **finishes** include chrome and epoxy-coated metal. The finish you'll see on many new faucets is known as **physical vapor deposition,** or PVD. Sold by various manufacturers under the trade names Brilliance, LifeShine, Vibrant, Pforever Pfinish, and others, these brass-, silver-, copper-, nickel- and titanium-hued finishes are said to be bonded to the faucet body. CONSUMER REPORTS has tested the durability of these and the more traditional finishes, and found them all to be fairly durable. Most faucet manufacturers offer a lifetime warranty against corrosion, tarnishing, and discoloration on all finishes. The warranty covers only parts, not labor.

How to choose

PERFORMANCE DIFFERENCES. You don't have to buy a manufacturer's priciest line to get a good faucet. Most faucets share many of the same basic parts and finishes. Even a relatively inexpensive faucet often has many of the functional qualities of a pricier model.

The simpler the mechanism, the fewer parts that can break or wear out. A single-lever model has only one flow regulator, while faucets with separate handles have two. Pull-out spouts with hoses protected by a flexible metal sleeve will be less easily damaged than those with unprotected hoses. And any long gooseneck faucet is more vulnerable to accidental bumps simply because there's more surface area in harm's way. Remember, too, that faucets with ornate spouts and other intricate styling details tend to have surface contours and crevices that invite soap-scum and mineral-scale deposits.

RECOMMENDATIONS. Match the faucet to the hole configuration in your sink. Choose

SCRATCH RESISTANCE

Recent tests of faucet durability showed that even nylon scouring pads could leave scratches on chrome, epoxy-coated metal, or PVD-finished faucets if scrubbing was vigorous enough. Consider choosing a faucet with a brushed or satin finish in chrome or PVD to help hide scratches.

based on style and utility. Don't forget to check the warranty. You can get a lifetime warranty on even low-priced faucets. Several manufacturers have also made do-it-yourself installation easier with top-mount fittings and tools-free connectors.

FLOOR VARNISH

Refinishing a wood floor requires a combination of art and craft. Which varnish you choose rests largely on the look you want, your time constraints, and how durable it must be.

You know it's time to refinish a wood floor when its finish is worn through or the surface is badly nicked. Deep gouges, split or warped boards, and other widespread damage, however, are signs that a wood floor needs more than just a facelift—it needs to be repaired or replaced.

Whether you refinish the floor yourself or hire a pro, expect days of disruption, dust, and fumes. You also face significant cost and convenience differences between water-based and solvent-based varnish—key reasons why choosing the right one for your needs is critical no matter who applies it.

What's available

The major brands of floor varnish are Flecto Varathane, Minwax, and Pro Finisher (available only at Home Depot). Water-based varnishes dry faster and allow easier cleanup, making the application process a bit less onerous. Solvent-based varnishes tend to go farther and cost less per square foot. The catch: Their longer drying time means more days to finish the job—and possibly more money you'll pay a pro if you hire the job out. Solvent-based varnishes leave an amber finish. Water-based products dry pale and practically clear; if you prefer the amber hue, you'll have to stain the wood first. Price range per gallon: water-based, $30 to $50; solvent-based, $15 to $40.

Key features

Sheen levels range from satin to high gloss. Varnishes with a satin finish showed the least appearance change in a CONSUMER REPORTS abrasion test—a plus for busy rooms. We found that low-gloss finishes went on smoothest with the fewest imperfections. They were also less likely to raise the wood grain—a condition in which the wood fibers "stand up" and create a rough surface.

Varnishes typically contain polyurethane—a resin designed to resist surface wear and provide a tough, no-wax finish that's easy to clean using a damp mop. Solvent-based "moisture-cure" varnishes promise an even tougher finish, though they aren't recommended for the average do-it-yourselfer. Their vapors are more pungent and hazardous than those of other solvent-based products.

Solvent-based, or oil-based, products use a solvent such as mineral spirits to deliver the resins that eventually form the finish. Water-based products hold their resins within an emulsion. Solvent-based varnishes tend to contain more solids than water-based products, which is why manufacturers estimate greater coverage and recommend fewer coats for solvent-based types.

Water-based varnishes tend to have lower levels of volatile organic compounds

(VOCs). Along with their distinctive odor, VOCs pose the possibility of headaches and nausea for those particularly sensitive to chemical odors. If you're applying varnish yourself, consider wearing a respirator with an organic filter cartridge (about $20 to $40). With water-based varnishes, brushes and varnish spills can be cleaned with water. Solvent-based products require mineral spirits and generate more VOCs, which are combustible.

How to choose

PERFORMANCE DIFFERENCES. Solvent-based varnishes have long enjoyed a reputation for greater resistance to wear and scratches—a reason why most varnish manufacturers recommend them for high-traffic areas. In CONSUMER REPORTS' real-life foot-traffic tests, this proved to be true. Dirt also became less imbedded in flooring finished with solvent-based varnishes than in those finished with water-based varnishes.

Bright, sunny rooms are one place where water-based varnishes have an edge. All of those we tested withstood intense exposure to lab ultraviolet (UV) light without changing color. By comparison, all of the solvent-based products we tested darkened. In spill tests, none of the varnished floors were damaged by vodka, beer, wine, cola, or water. But most were damaged by detergent, and a few were damaged by coffee, vinegar, or ammonia.

RECOMMENDATIONS. Start by deciding whether you'll hire a contractor or do the job yourself. Consider hiring a pro if the floor is especially uneven or needs repair. Then choose which type of varnish to use. Water-based varnish provides faster drying time, easier cleanup, and excellent ultraviolet resistance. Solvent-based varnish leaves an amber finish, and drying time between coats is longer and cleanup messier. It also tends to darken under ultraviolet light, but stands up better to traffic areas.

All varnishes require multiple coats, particularly in high-traffic areas. You'll wait only an hour or two for each coat of water-based varnish to dry, compared with anywhere from five hours to overnight for most solvent-based products. Water-based varnishes require more coats for heavy traffic—typically four, compared with three for most solvent-based products. You or a flooring contractor could get all of those coats down in one long day using a water-based varnish. You'll still have to wait anywhere from 12 hours to a day or two for any varnish to cure before it can handle heavy traffic, however.

FLOORING: VINYL TILES & SHEETS

Also called resilient flooring, vinyl may not be as elegant as wood or ceramic tile, but its durability and easy cleanup make it a smart choice for kitchens and other high-traffic areas.

A lack of variety will never be a problem if you're considering vinyl flooring, which comes in a vast array of patterns and colors. Prices are relatively low, and installation is easy; roughly half of those who buy sheet vinyl and some 90 percent of those who buy vinyl tiles lay down the flooring themselves.

What's available

The market leader in vinyl flooring is Armstrong. Other major brands include Congoleum and Mannington. Discount sources of flooring are home centers such as Home Depot and

Lowe's, but you'll probably get more attention at a specialty store. Stores that sell flooring can also arrange installation. Vinyl flooring comes two ways, in sheets and as tiles. Sheet vinyl generally costs $10 to $35 per square yard. Tiles typically measure a square foot and cost 50 cents to $2 each.

Key features

Peel-and self-stick tiles are clearly the easiest vinyl flooring to install and repair. But **sheet vinyl** offers a seamless look. You'll find two types of sheet vinyl. **Perimeter-bonded** floors are glued down only around the edge of the room and along any seams. **Fully adhered** flooring is laid in a coat of mastic that's spread over the entire subfloor. The two types are similar in cost and performance. Perimeter-bonded floors do a better job of hiding small surface imperfections in the subfloor below since they're not stuck down, but fully adhered vinyl lays flatter and is less likely to bubble up. Fully adhered sheet vinyl is installed almost exclusively by professional installers.

Vinyl flooring typically has a **protective coating,** or "wear layer," made of urethane or vinyl. Urethane proved more resistant than vinyl in CONSUMER REPORTS scuff and abrasion tests. The type of wear layer didn't seem to make a difference when CONSUMER REPORTS tested for puncturing. Sheets, however, performed better than tiles in the puncture test. Most sheets resisted puncture; most tiles didn't because they lacked the sheet vinyl's cushioned layer.

Textured surfaces hide dents best. We loaded various weights onto indentation tools of different diameters to simulate the effect of high-heeled shoes and furniture legs pressing into flooring. Most of the products bounced back from the depressions left by furniture, but few recovered completely from the heel test, which was more severe.

With the **rotogravure,** or roto, printing method, colors and patterns are printed on the surface of the base layer. In the more intricate **inlaid printing method,** the design is embedded in the vinyl. Models with inlaid printing tend to cost more, but they don't always prove to be the most durable.

How to choose

PERFORMANCE DIFFERENCES. With vinyl flooring, you usually get more by spending more. In CONSUMER REPORTS tests, the most expensive products weren't necessarily the best, but most performed very well. The cheapest products were consistently among the worst. Expect to spend at least $1.50 per square foot of floor space to get a sheet or tile that will hold up well.

In tests, several sheet-vinyl products were excellent overall, and most performed at least very well. Several of the vinyl tiles in our tests were very good, but as a group they fell somewhat short of the sheets. No matter how good the vinyl floor, it will not match ceramic tile's ease of cleaning and ability to maintain its appearance. The drawbacks of ceramic tile, however, are its propensity to crack if heavy objects are dropped on it and the high cost of installation.

Vinyl tends to be less slippery than other flooring types. When wet, only one vinyl tile in CONSUMER REPORTS tests proved to be as slippery as the wood, glazed-ceramic, and laminate flooring we tested.

RECOMMENDATIONS. If you plan to install the floor yourself, you're better off with vinyl tiles, as opposed to sheets. The no-wax variety is the easiest to maintain. Be sure to buy tiles in sealed boxes with the same lot number to avoid lot-to-lot color variations. Buy extras so you can redo mistakes and replace tiles that become damaged.

FLOORING: WOOD & WOOD ALTERNATIVES

Natural wood flooring has an attractive warmth and lasts, but easier-to-install copycats may sometimes be a better choice.

Solid wood remains many people's ideal for floors. Indeed, hardwood flooring can increase a home's resale value and speed its sale, according to the National Association of Realtors. Oak is the most popular and readily available choice. Others include maple, cherry, and hickory. Pine, a softwood, costs less. Solid wood flooring comes prefinished or unfinished.

Alternatives to solid wood include plastic laminate and engineered wood. Both are easier and cheaper to install. Laminate mimics wood (or tile or marble) by using a photograph of the real thing beneath its clear surface layer. Engineered-wood flooring incorporates a thin veneer of real wood over structural plywood. It costs about the same as solid wood. You'll also see bamboo flooring and parquet wood tiles.

What's available

You'll find wood and wood-look flooring at flooring suppliers and lumberyards as well as at mass merchandisers and home centers such as Home Depot, Lowe's, and Wal-Mart. Flooring suppliers tend to have the widest selection, particularly for exotic woods, while mass merchandisers and home centers usually offer the lowest prices.

The many brands of wood flooring include Anderson, Bruce, Harris-Tarkett, Hartco, and Permagrain. Brands of plastic-laminate flooring include Armstrong, Congoleum, Formica, Mannington, Pergo, Tarkett, and Wilsonart.

Price range, per square foot: prefinished solid wood, $4 to $7.25; engineered wood, $5 to $9; plastic-laminate, $3 to $4.50. Add $3 per square foot if you have the flooring installed professionally.

Key features

WITH PREFINISHED SOLID WOOD. Narrow boards are called strips; wide ones, planks. Most are ¾-inch thick or less. A finish layer protects the flooring from spills, stains, and wear. Thicker flooring is usually nailed to a plywood subfloor; thinner flooring is stapled or glued. Thinner flooring can also cover above-ground concrete using a vapor barrier. For nailing into wood, you'll need a manual or pneumatic nailer (about $20 per day to rent). You can usually refinish solid wood several times before it is sanded down to its tongue joints.

WITH ENGINEERED WOOD. A wear layer protects the wood veneer—usually ⅛-inch thick or less—on top of construction-grade plywood. Instead of the painstaking nailing needed to put down a solid-wood floor, engineered wood is usually stapled down (the most secure method) or glued to the subfloor, though sometimes it can be floated the way plastic-laminate flooring is. You may be able to refinish engineered wood—by lightly sanding and

TYPES OF WOOD FLOORING

Solid wood

Plastic laminate

Engineered wood

A QUICK GUIDE TO REFINISHING FLOORS

Varnishing a floor is rigorous work. These tips can help you survive the three to four days you may need to cover a moderate-sized area:

When to work. Do the job in warm weather, since you'll need to open doors and windows for maximum ventilation. Don't rush. Try to work when humidity is low and rain isn't in the forecast, since high humidity extends drying time.

What you'll need. Buy a broomstick applicator, lambs-wool pads, and brushes (natural bristle for solvent-based varnish, synthetic for water-based) for applying varnish to the floor's perimeter. You'll also need tack cloths; plenty of sandpaper in three grit levels, from coarse to fine; a sharp scraper for getting into corners; goggles; a dust mask; painters gloves; and mineral spirits for solvent-based cleanup (use plain water for water-based varnish). Also count on renting a drum sander, an edge sander, a wet/dry vac, and a buffer—about $110 per day for all four.

Total cost. Expect to pay about $180 to $200 for varnish and supplies for a moderate-sized, 200-square-foot area. Figure on paying from $300 to $600 to have a flooring contractor do the work.

Here are steps to follow if you decide do it yourself:

1. Setting up. Move the furniture out and then sweep the floor. Seal off the area you're working in with drop cloths or old bed sheets to keep dust contained.

2. Sanding. To remove old varnish and smooth the surface of the wood, pass the drum sander evenly over the old finishing, moving in smooth, straight lines parallel to the planks. Work in several passes, starting with coarse-grit sandpaper and progressing to fine-grit until the old finish is removed and the surface is smooth and even.

Preparing floor with a drum sander

Follow each pass of the drum sander with the edge sander along baseboards and other tight spots, using the same progression of sandpaper. Tips: Be sure the mechanism that holds each machine's sandpaper and dust collector is secure before leaving the rental shop. Keep all sanding machines moving while in use to prevent them from gouging

varnishing it—at least once, depending on the thickness of its veneer. (Most manufacturers recommend that a professional do this.)

WITH PLASTIC LAMINATE. Here, too, a wear layer protects against spills, stains, and wear and covers the pattern layer—essentially a photograph of wood, tile, marble, slate, or some other material. A fiberboard core supports the top layers. Plastic-laminate planks are interlocked with or without glue and held in place by their own weight in what is called a floating floor. A foam layer goes between the laminate and the subfloor. A vapor barrier is recommended between the subfloor and the foam layer if moisture is a concern. An alternative approach is gluing the flooring to the subfloor. Once the wear layer becomes worn or damaged, it can't be sanded and refinished. You may be able to do minor touch-ups with kits sold by flooring manufacturers. If not, you'll have to replace the offending section or—if problems are widespread—the entire floor.

How to choose

PERFORMANCE DIFFERENCES. Most of the solid-wood products resisted spills very well in CONSUMER REPORTS tests, and they should be able to stand up to close encounters with party drinks and other common household liquids. In a long-term foot-traffic test, the

Vacuuming with wet/dry vac

the surface. Maintain even pressure and a steady pace. When starting or stopping, tilt the sanding portion upward. Also be sure to sweep up after each sanding pass to prevent damage from grit.

3. Dusting. After sanding, sweep up every trace of sawdust and grit, then follow up with a wet/dry vac so debris isn't trapped in the varnish. You can also use a household vacuum. Wipe up the last bits of dust with tack cloths. Tips: Before you dust, remove the bed sheets that sealed off the area to keep them from adding dust to the floor. Be sure to dust walls, door frames, and other spots throughout the area before applying varnish.

4. Varnishing. Open all windows and doors to maximize ventilation. Begin by

Applying varnish

brushing varnish around the floor perimeter and other hard-to-reach areas. Then pour a thin line of varnish at the point farthest from the door, running parallel to the wood planks, and spread it in a continuous line with the lamb's wool. Tips: Overlap each pass, angling the pad away from the area you just covered to push excess varnish onto the new area to get smoother results. Using a watering can may make it easier to pour varnish onto the floor.

Buffing with floor buffer

5. Between coats. Prepare the fully dried surface for subsequent coats using a buffer or oscillating sander and fine-grit screen. Tips: Make sure the surface is dry by using your thumbnail to check that the film is hard. Then vacuum and dust the surface again with tack cloths before applying the next coat.

6. Wrap-up. When floors are dry, move furniture back in. Let varnish cure from 12 hours to a day or two before walking on it a lot.

laminates held up better than most solid wood flooring and all of the engineered wood flooring. Among the laminates, some brands were better than others in resisting denting, but all were much more dent-resistant than other types of flooring.

Plastic laminates proved impervious to stains from mustard, wine, and acidic liquids, although most of the solid-wood and engineered-wood flooring were close behind. All of the plastic-laminate products we tested came through hours of ultraviolet exposure in our lab with their original colors intact. Ultraviolet light from the sun and or from halogen lamps can change the color of real wood.

RECOMMENDATIONS. First determine whether you'll install the flooring yourself or hire a contractor. Your decision may affect which type of flooring you decide upon. Plastic-laminate flooring offers relatively easy installation and a tough surface for busy rooms. It mimics wood and other materials but is better at resisting abrasion, scratches, and dents than prefinished solid-wood flooring and engineered-wood flooring.

One noticeable drawback of plastic laminate is its faux-wood pattern, which can look unnaturally consistent over a large area. With real wood, each strip or plank has its own unique grain.

Prefinished solid wood is less damage-resistant and harder to install (you may want to hire a pro), but it offers authenticity and warmth. It can also be refinished several times; damaged or worn plastic-laminate flooring must be replaced.

Engineered-wood flooring offers a true wood surface without the painstaking nailing needed to put down a solid-wood floor. Unlike most solid-wood flooring, an engineered-wood floor can go in a basement or other damp area because of the added dimensional stability of its layered construction. But you won't save money by choosing an engineered floor; it costs about as much as solid wood and generally can't be refinished as often. Always purchase an extra box of flooring for future repairs.

FLOORING ◆ **Ratings:** Page 229

INTERIOR LIGHTING

Lighting adds to the ambience of a room in two ways: the look of the fixtures and the light they throw off. Styles range from unobtrusive to drop-dead dramatic.

Lighting choices have progressed far beyond soft-white, three-way bulbs in table lamps. Several different types of bulbs now deliver all the light you've grown accustomed to, and some can do it far more economically. You'll also find thousands of fixtures that can bathe a room in light, illuminate a small area, or focus light in a pinpoint beam. And prices range from a few dollars to a few thousand dollars.

What's available

Lighting stores, home centers, and even some well-stocked hardware stores carry a wide variety of lighting. There are three main categories.

AMBIENT. All rooms require ambient lighting for overall illumination. A collection of light sources is the traditional solution. How much ambient light you need depends largely on the activities in the room and the color of the walls. For example, a workshop needs bright, uniform lighting; a bedroom or foyer can be evenly but less brightly lit. Dark colors absorb light, so you need a lot more wattage with hunter green walls than with pale peach. Recessed ceiling fixtures are the usual choices for ambient light, although track lighting and wall-mounted sources are also good choices.

TASK. Rooms such as kitchens, family rooms, bedrooms, and bathrooms need task lighting to augment the ambient lighting. Kitchens may require a light fixture directly over the counter or the cooktop. Lights mounted under the front edge of cupboards provide shadow-free light for working.

In other rooms, a desk lamp helps with tasks such as paying bills, while a reading lamp lets you curl up with a good book. In the bathroom, good lighting around mirrors eliminates shadows so you can see what you're doing when shaving or applying makeup. Track lights and hanging ceiling fixtures are both excellent choices for task lighting.

ACCENT. This light plays up decorative elements—a painting, sculpture, or plant. It's a nice addition in a foyer, a formal living room, or a dining room. Accent lighting can show off china in a glass-front cabinet, or it can be installed above cabinets to soften their hard edges. Uplights, wall-washers, sconces, and track lighting can all provide effective accent lighting in a home.

Key features

Traditional **incandescent bulbs** are still the most commonly used in most homes—60 watt, three-way, soft white, and so on. They're inexpensive and typically last about 1,000 hours.

Halogen bulbs, unlike ordinary incandescent bulbs, are filled with a halogen gas. They're a bit pricier than regular incandescents, but they tend to last about 2,000 hours.

Introduced more than a decade ago, **compact flourescents** are gaining popularity. These bulbs can last 5,000 hours or more and now cost about $10. They're three to four times more energy efficient than incandescent bulbs, with some providing about the same light as a 100-watt incandescent while using only about 25 to 30 watts. You could put one in a fixture designed for, say, a 60-watt incandescent bulb to safely increase light output.

How to choose

PERFORMANCE DIFFERENCES. You get what you pay for. Halogen bulbs produce intense, very white light that can bring out the colors in a room. Compact fluorescent bulbs are the priciest type, but they last much longer than halogen or incandescent bulbs. The light of a compact fluorescent bulb is difficult to distinguish from that of an incandescent bulb. But a compact fluorescent bulb needs some time to warm up to full brightness. And it may need to be used for 100 hours or so before its brightness level stabilizes. Some bulbs get a little brighter after that; some slightly dimmer.

A compact fluorescent bulb may interfere with the remote control of your TV set, VCR, or hi-fi system. It may also cause static in an AM radio or cordless phone.

RECOMMENDATIONS. When shopping for fixtures, don't limit your choices to what is on display. Most lighting stores have catalogs from the manufacturers and will order the fixtures you want. A special order lets you select the finish you want—brass, chrome, and so on.

Some utilities offer rebates for compact fluorescent bulbs. You can shorten the lives of compact fluorescent bulbs if you use them improperly, however. Many are not meant to be used with dimmer switches or outdoors.

PAINT

A few hundred dollars worth of paint can improve the look of your home, protect it, and possibly boost its value.

Painting can be an arduous task, especially if there is a lot of preparation to do. And professional painters don't come cheap. High-quality paint can make a paint job last longer.

Interior paint should be washable and stain- and fade-resistant. Exterior paint (or stain) should hold its own against sun, rain, dirt, and mildew, and should resist cracking. Polymers in interior paint are relatively hard so they can hold up when scrubbed. In exterior paint, polymers are more flexible so the paint doesn't crack as the surface expands and contracts. Both interior and exterior paint should brush on easily and cover the surface thoroughly.

You'll also see kitchen and bath paints and garage-floor paints, as well as waterproofing coatings for use on basement walls. These latter coatings come in two forms: premixed liquids (water or oil based) and powders that must be mixed with water or a bonding agent.

Some people are sensitive to the fumes given off by wet latex paints. If you or a family member experiences headaches, nausea, or dizziness associated with the chemicals in paint, you can use a product labeled as having low levels of volatile organic compounds (VOCs) or none at all. Note that low-odor isn't the same as low-VOC or no-VOC. The fumes from relatively high levels of VOCs can be masked to make a low-odor paint. If you or someone in your family is bothered by paint fumes, a low-odor paint may not help. VOCs evaporate as the paint dries and can react with sunlight and pollutants in the air to produce ozone. Federal regulations limit the level of VOCs in indoor and outdoor paint. Some areas of the country, such as Southern California, require an even lower level.

What's available

Major brands include Behr (sold at Home Depot), Benjamin Moore, Dutch Boy, Glidden, Sherwin-Williams, and Valspar (sold at Lowe's). Ace, Sears, and True Value sell various brands including their own. You'll also see designer names such as Martha Stewart, Bob Vila, and Ralph Lauren, as well as many brands of paint sold regionally. Sico is sold in Canada.

Interior paints have several classifications. Wall paints can be used in just about any room. Glossier trim enamels are often used for windowsills, woodwork, and the like. Kitchen and bath paints are usually fairly glossy (sometimes very glossy) and are formulated to hold up to water and scrubbing and to release stains. Some paints contain mildewcide, useful in high-humidity areas. You can buy a mildewcide and add it to any paint, but we don't recommend its use because it may not be compatible with the paint you choose.

LATEX PAINT. This is relatively easy to use, and the popular choice for indoor and outdoor jobs. It dries fast with minimal odor, brushes on with few drips and sags, and cleans up with water. It also remains flexible and breathable, allowing pent-up humidity to escape. Because exterior latex paint can be applied to a damp surface, you can use it the day after it rains. But don't use latex paint outdoors when rain is forecast. A brisk shower can wash it off. Price range: $10 to $35 per gallon.

OIL-BASED (ALKYD) PAINT. This paint is useful as a stain-blocking primer, although latex and shellac-based stain-blocking primers are available. Oil-based paint has largely disappeared, partly because today's tighter solvent-emission laws rule against their relatively high levels of VOCs. Price range: $15 to $35 per gallon.

Key features

Paint typically comes in a variety of sheens—**flat, low luster,** and **semigloss.** The degree of glossiness can be different from one manufacturer to another. Flat paint keeps reflections to a minimum and hides surface imperfections. It is usually harder to clean and picks up more dirt than glossier formulas. Semigloss is easier to clean than flat, but it may be too shiny for larger surfaces. And some semigloss paints can remain sticky after the surface has dried, making them risky for trims and shelving. A low-luster finish—often called eggshell or satin—is the middle ground. It is easy to clean and reflects less light.

A **custom color** of paint is created by mixing a colorant with a tint base. Most brands come in several tint bases, including medium and pastel, to provide a full range of colors. The **tint base** largely determines toughness, resistance to dirt and stains, and ability to withstand scrubbing. The **colorant** determines how much the paint will fade, particularly with exterior paint and interior paint in a sunny room. Whites and browns tend not to fade (but whites can yellow); reds and blues fade somewhat; bright greens and yellows fade a lot. In a mixture of pigments, as the greens and yellows fade, other colors begin to stand out.

How to choose

PERFORMANCE DIFFERENCES. CONSUMER REPORTS tests have shown that few paints, especially whites, hide in one coat. All of the paints we tested did better with two coats. Most interior paints hold up well when scrubbed with a sponge and powdered cleanser. Nearly all low-luster paints do well when stains are cleaned away with a sponge and spray cleaner. Flat paints hold stains more tenaciously and are harder to clean. CONSUMER REPORTS has found that interior paint brands including Dutch Boy, Martha Stewart, Olympic, Pittsburgh, Sears, and Sherwin-Williams fade more than most.

The biggest difference we've found between regular paints and low-VOC paints is their drying time. Low-VOC paints dry very fast. You have to work quickly to avoid marks from overlapping roller strokes as well as brush marks around trim, and brushes and rollers may be harder to clean after applying a low-VOC paint.

Tests of exterior paint, lasting up to five years, have revealed significant differences in durability. Most paints still looked almost new after a year of exposure. But after two years, some started to show the effects of weathering. Testing conditions are somewhat accelerated. Each year of testing corresponds to between two and four years of real-life exposure.

Among waterproofing coatings, recent tests found the premixed formulations easier to use than the powdered varieties, some of which thickened to a nearly unspreadable consistency after a relatively short time. And water-based products make for an easier cleanup.

RECOMMENDATIONS. Most manufacturers offer three levels of quality—essentially, good, better, and best. Decades of CONSUMER REPORTS tests have clearly shown that it makes sense to look first at top-of-the-line paints.

Paint manufacturers estimate that a gallon of paint should cover 400 to 450 square feet. That's a good rule to follow when calculating how much paint you will need. Consider, too, the effect of the surface—the rougher, the more paint or stain it will take and the less square footage you'll get per gallon. Porous surfaces require a primer/sealer before painting. Some waterproofing coatings must be applied to a dry wall, hence it wouldn't be a good choice for a perpetually damp surface.

Whether you buy paint from an independent

CURES FOR THE COLOR BLUES

The right paint color can make the difference between a pleasing, inviting space and a room no one ever really enjoys.

If you can't change the room lighting, you'll have to change the paint, once you understand some basics about natural and artificial light.

♦ Fluorescent light enhances blues and greens but makes warm reds, oranges, and yellows appear dull. The yellow glow of incandescent light enhances warm colors.

♦ Sunlight changes throughout the day and throughout the year. A color that looks fine on a sunny day may be awful when the clouds roll in.

♦ Northern light seems cool; southern light, warm.

♦ Wall texture and paint gloss also affect color. A glossy finish reflects more light, so colors look brighter. Flat paints and textured walls absorb light, so colors appear darker.

When you're planning colors, collect the largest color swatches you can find and tape them to the wall. That way, you can study them at different times of day and under different lighting conditions. It's often smart to buy a quart of a color and paint a test square on the wall.

paint retailer, a company store such as Sherwin-Williams, a home center, or a mass merchandiser such as Wal-Mart, be sure to ask about discounts or deals on high-quantity purchases.

ROOFING

Materials such as slate and clay tile last a long time, but are costly. Asphalt shingles are the most common choice.

A secure roof is vital to the integrity of a house. In less than 10 years, extreme temperature and sunlight can crack, curl, and split shingles, rain and sleet can wear them down, and wind can tear them apart. But they can last much longer if you choose the right kind—and the right installation.

What's available

Named for the sticky, water-repellent substance that holds them together, asphalt shingles are essentially large rectangular mats made of cellulose (in organic shingles) or fiberglass impregnated or coated with asphalt. The usual size per mat is 12x36 inches, though 13x39-inch "metric" shingles are also available.

Asphalt shingles are coated on the bottom surface with sand, talc, and other mineral fillers for stiffness and to eliminate the stickiness of the asphalt material. The top surfaces are typically coated with granules colored with a hard ceramic glaze. These granules also protect the asphalt from the sun's ultraviolet rays and add weight to the shingle so it can better resist wind.

Major brands of asphalt shingles include Atlas, CertainTeed, GAF, Georgia-Pacific, and Owens Corning. Some of these manufacturers also make asphalt shingles that have zinc or copper particles mixed in with the surface granules. The metal oxides help prevent the formation of algae, the dark streaks on some roofs in hot humid regions.

Asphalt shingles are generally sold in "bundles," which contain about one-third "square" of three-tab shingles or one-fourth square of laminated shingles. (A square is enough to cover 100 square feet.) Most of the three-tab organic and fiberglass brands we tested cost $20 to $40 per square, weigh from 190 to 300 pounds per square, and have a 20- to 30-year warranty.

Since asphalt shingles first appeared more than 80 years ago, they've mostly used the same familiar three-tab format—a piece of shingle made of three 12-inch-wide tabs separated by slots. (This look has lost ground in recent years as the popularity of architectural shingles has grown.) Shingles with a fiberglass mat came out in the early 1970s. More than half the asphalt roofs installed in the U.S. use this type. A laminated shingle (architectural or dimensional) is a more expensive type of fiberglass shingle. It commonly consists of two or more layers laminated to create a three-dimensional effect that mimics wood or slate. It tends to weigh more than the other types and costs $40 to $170 per square. Warranties often run longer—sometimes the life of the house.

Organic shingles use a reinforcing mat made of cellulose. These shingles withstand freezing temperatures especially well. Some brands offer laminated organic shingles, a type CONSUMER REPORTS did not test.

How to choose

PERFORMANCE DIFFERENCES. While organic-based shingles cost less than fiberglass types and tend to fare better in cold weather, we recommend fiberglass shingles, plain or laminated, for most parts of the country. Fiberglass shingles fared much better than organic ones in CONSUMER REPORTS hot-weather tests—but only two fiberglass brands fared as well as the organics in cold-weather tests.

RECOMMENDATIONS. Asphalt shingles are a long-term investment, both from a quality and aesthetic standpoint. Before signing on the dotted line, consider how long you'll stay in your house. If it's only a few years—and the existing roof isn't that bad—you may want to let the next owner take on this expense. And even if you'll be staying there for a while, consider how the shingles you choose will affect your home's resale value down the road. That may mean balancing your personal taste with the need for your home to fit in with others.

New shingles can go over a single existing layer that doesn't show signs of damage. (Look for damage from the attic, or check topside for soft spots or undulations.) Don't add a third layer; the rafters may not support the weight. Shingles can be stapled, but the Asphalt Roofing Manufacturers Association recommends nailing. In windy areas, it recommends six nails per shingle instead of the usual four. A hammer is more precise than a nail gun.

Before you sign a contract, see that it spells out all details. Get the shingle maker's warranty from the roofer. And keep a wrapper from one of the bundles of shingles so you can identify what is on the roof should you need to use the warranty. There is a growing trend toward longer warranties. In addition, many brands are "certifying" installers who can offer a labor warranty at an additional cost.

Even the best asphalt shingles won't last if the plywood or solid-board sheathing beneath them is in poor shape. When installing new shingles, be sure any rotted, warped, or split sheathing is replaced. Also replace or reinforce any rafters that are badly cracked or bowed. Proper attic ventilation is also a key to long-lived roof shingles, since excess heat buildup can make them deteriorate faster. Have the installer make sure there are no obstructions blocking air flow from the soffit, ridge, and gable-end vents. Be sure all roof flashing is replaced when installing a new roof. Buy an extra bundle of shingles so you'll have matching shingles handy for spot repairs.

	ASPHALT	CEDAR	SLATE	CLAY TILE	STEEL
MATERIAL COST	$25 -$65	$100-$230	$300-$855	$300-$720	$80 -$340
INSTALLATION COST	$30-$70	$70-$130	$120-$160	$120-$180	$85-$105
WEIGHT	195-430 lbs.	300-400 lbs.	900 lbs.	900 lbs.	50-270 lbs.
LIFE SPAN	15-40 yrs.	20-50 yrs.	50 yrs.	50-100 yrs.	20-50 yrs.

Costs and weights are per "square"–enough to cover 100 square feet; underlayment not included; contractor markup can add 40% to the material cost.

SOURCE: R.S. MEANS CO.

SIDING

New siding, typically vinyl, ranks high on the payback scale. You may recoup more than 70 percent of your investment should you decide to sell your home later.

Sooner or later, most houses need new siding, either because the old siding has deteriorated or because you want something that is easier to care for. Choose a style that will be in line with the neighborhood and property values. Care should be taken when choosing a contractor. Installation mistakes can lead to warped, buckled siding and, if old asbestos material is being removed, health risks.

What's available

Houses can be sided with just about anything that can shed rainwater and block drafts. Siding materials are sold at lumberyards and home centers. Common materials include the following:

VINYL. A popular re-siding choice, it is easy to work with and requires little maintenance. It usually holds color well and is fairly resilient. And it comes in many colors, textures, profiles, and widths. But it can have a "plastic" look. Trim details don't mimic wood well. Vinyl may also be prone to crack in extreme cold if struck by a hard object. The biggest names in vinyl include Alcoa, Alside, CertainTeed (which also makes Wolverine and Ashland-Davis products), Georgia-Pacific, Jannock (maker of Armorbond, Bird, Heartland, and Mastershield), and Royal Building Products. Price per square foot: $1.50 to $2.50.

ALUMINUM. This siding is nearly extinct. Aluminum is low-maintenance at first. But since it is made of painted metal, fading and weathering eventually mean repainting or replacement. It dents easily, and it can corrode in saltwater regions. Major brands include Alcoa and Reynolds. Price per square foot: $2 to $2.50.

STEEL SIDING. This siding is similar to aluminum, but somewhat lower in price. Unlike aluminum, it has the potential to rust.

CEDAR CLAPBOARD. It has a traditional look that has been popular for hundreds of years. But clapboard requires time-consuming and costly upkeep, with painting or staining required to prevent deterioration. Clapboard is also available as primed redwood. Price per square foot: $1.70 to $3.

WOOD SHINGLES/SHAKES. The appeal of shingles lies in their texture and seasoned color. Shingles can be stained, painted, or left natural. But they require the same maintenance regimen as clapboard if painted. There's less upkeep required if they're allowed to weather. Price per square foot: $1.40 to $3.

FIBER CEMENT. This cement-based product with reinforcing fibers is supplanting wood clapboard because it provides a similar finished look but requires less upkeep. It's installed and painted like wood.

Key features

Vinyl and aluminum siding offer a variety of **colors** and **trim accessories.** The color should be chosen from the siding samples themselves; colors in catalogs may not be accurate. With vinyl siding, the color usually permeates the material, so it won't flake, chip, or rub off. With aluminum siding, the finish is baked onto the aluminum.

	VINYL	ALUMINUM	CEDAR CLAPBOARD	SHAKES
MATERIAL COST	$1.50-$2.30	$2.10-$2.60	$1.70-$3.10	$1.40-$3.10
Materials/installation cost ratio	45/55	45/55	55/45	45/55
Life span	50 yrs.	20-50 yrs.	10-100 yrs.	10-100

SOURCE: R.S. MEANS CO.

Surface texture options include wood-grain, smooth, and simulated brush strokes. The shapes of the siding have names such as "double-four beveled clapboard," which happens to be a single horizontal panel simulating two 4-inch-wide wood boards that appear to be thicker at the bottom than at the top.

Trim accessories such as crown moldings and fluted corner posts reproduce specific architectural styles.

How to choose

PERFORMANCE DIFFERENCES. CONSUMER REPORTS tests showed no connection between thickness and performance for vinyl siding—the best and worst were both 0.043 inch thick. (Aluminum siding proved more durable the thicker it was.) The tests also found that vinyl resists fading much better than aluminum.

RECOMMENDATIONS. Consider vinyl siding first if you want a moderately priced, low-maintenance exterior for your house. Vinyl comes in numerous colors and styles, it's relatively easy to install, and it should look presentable for years. Because it is flexible, it can look uneven, distorted, or wavy if the installer isn't careful—especially on long walls without windows or doors.

Cedar clapboard and wood shingles/shakes provide a traditional look that many people like, but a lot of maintenance can be involved.

The contractor's estimate will usually include both labor and materials. Be sure you specify brand, model, color, style, and shape. Have the contractor fix uneven or rotting sections of wall before putting up new siding.

If existing siding has covered over older asbestos siding, you may want to ask an asbestos-abatement contractor how best to deal with it.

SINKS

Unless unique shapes or exotic materials are must-haves, you can find high quality in low-priced enamel, stainless-steel, and acrylic models.

What's available

Choices include enamel finishes, stainless steel, and polyester or acrylic resins. In most home centers and plumbing-supply stores, you'll find brands such as American Standard, Eljer, Elkay, Kohler, and Moen.

Price does not relate to quality or durability, so this is one place in a kitchen makeover where you can save a few bucks. The more expensive sinks are usually made of enamel over cast iron, heavy-gauge stainless steel (the lower the gauge number, the thicker the steel), or solid-surface resins made to mimic granite, marble, and other natural materials. Less expensive models are typically enamel on steel, thin-gauge stainless, or an acrylic-resin film that looks like enamel over a molded fiberglass substrate.

Key features

Bowl depth typically ranges from about 6 to 10 inches. More depth means more room to wash and rinse big things like mixing bowls. A deep bowl also means less splashing.

Drains can be centered or positioned to the rear of the bowl. The latter provides more clearance and more flexible storage below.

Stainless-steel models with **sound-deadening pads** on the underside muffle the sounds of dish clatter best. Enamel surfaces are noisiest. All types deaden the sound of running water to some extent.

Sinks designed with a rim around the top simply drop into a hole cut into the countertop surface. Those without a rim install under the counter, which requires different mounting methods and more skill.

How to choose

Kitchen décor is an obvious influence. A stainless-steel sink is a good choice if you want to emulate the pro style. For a more traditional look, consider enameled or acrylic-resin sinks; they come in a wide range of colors. Solid-surface can be made to merge seamlessly with countertops and backsplashes.

PERFORMANCE DIFFERENCES. All surfaces resist staining well, even when stubborn stains, such as a tea bag or mustard, sit for hours. Stainless steel requires a bit more scrubbing than other types, but it will come clean. Drain cleaner can be difficult to remove from enamel finishes. Enamel-coated and stainless-steel surfaces resist scratches well and won't be burned by a hot pot. CONSUMER REPORTS engineers found that a $400 enamel-over-cast-iron sink can chip just as easily as a $300 enamel-on-steel one. And an expensive stainless-steel model can dent as readily as cheaper stuff.

The color of a solid-surface sink runs throughout the material, so you can also buff out scratches or burn. Dropping a very heavy object on some solid-surface sinks can cause them to shatter. If that happens, you'll have to replace the sink.

Acrylic-resin sinks don't chip and are least likely to dent or break under impact. Scratches show up, and they can't be buffed away. Hot pots can cause permanent damage to the surface.

RECOMMENDATIONS. You can probably find the look you want and the function you need for $100 to $200. Choices in this price range include enamel over steel, thin-gauge stainless steel, and acrylic.

High-priced models—such as heavy-gauge steel, enamel over iron, and solid-surface sinks—range from about $200 to $450. Beyond aesthetics, functionally there is no point in paying a premium for thick-gauge stainless or enamel over cast iron.

TOILETS

Low-flush toilets use 1.6 gallons of water per flush, and are the *only* toilets on the market today. They were mandated in federal water-conservation laws enacted in 1994.

The first low-flush toilets on the market earned a reputation for being problematic because they required two or more flushes to do their job—and often clogged in the process. Many of the newer models tested work quite well on a single flush. But there are large differences in performance—even within a given brand.

What's available

Most major manufacturers offer an extensive array of models in different designs and colors and in a range of prices.

GRAVITY-FLUSH TOILETS are the most common design. They work like old-fashioned toilets, using water pouring from the tank to clear the bowl and push waste down the drain. While some that we tested recently worked well, others didn't do a very good job of clearing solid waste.

PRESSURE-ASSIST TOILETS use a pressure tank to force water into the bowl. They work well but are noisy. Their loud whoosh can be disconcerting.

VACUUM-ASSIST models work well and quietly, but there aren't many on the market. This type uses a vacuum chamber inside the tank to help pull water and waste down the drain.

Prices for low-flush toilets range from as little as $100 to more than $600, in basic white porcelain. Colors cost more.

Gravity-flush models tend to be the least expensive. Vacuum-assist models cost just a bit more. Pressure-assist toilets are at the high end of the price range, generally $300 or more. Within types, more money does not buy better performance, just more upscale design.

Key features

Bathroom remodeling is the most common reason to buy a new toilet. Depending upon the configuration of the new bathroom, you may want a round-front or elongated **bowl.** A round-front style is generally a better choice for a small bathroom than an elongated one. Two-piece designs, with a tank that bolts onto the bowl, are less expensive than one-piece designs.

How to choose

PERFORMANCE DIFFERENCES. A gravity flush toilet is a good choice for bathrooms near bedrooms where quiet is important. Pressure assist might be best reserved for powder rooms some distance from the bedrooms, and if household water pressure is at least 25 pounds per square inch. Pressure-assist models will not work properly without at least that much pressure. Vacuum assist should work well in any bathroom in the house.

   RECOMMENDATIONS. Decide if you want gravity flush, vacuum assist, or pressure assist. A pressure-assist model should be the choice when clogging is a concern. You'll probably have to go to a plumbing-supply store to find one. They aren't likely to be offered in home-center chains.

TOILETS ◆ Ratings: Page 272

WALLPAPER

You'll find a broad array of colors, patterns, and textures. Vinyl-coated paper, which is relatively durable and easy to clean, is the popular choice of material.

Wallpaper, or wall covering, offers myriad decorating solutions. It can do things that paint can't. It can make a high-rise living room feel like a country cottage or give a small foyer the look of an art-deco stage set. Wallpaper can also hide some minor flaws in imperfect walls and add architectural interest to boring, boxy rooms.

What's available

Wallpaper is sold in home centers, paint-and-wallpaper stores, and decorator showrooms. You can also buy it on the Internet. A single manufacturer—Imperial Home Décor Group—makes about half the wallpaper brands. Another big chunk of the market, including the Village and Waverly brands, belongs to F. Schumacher. Other wallpaper makers include Blonder, Brewster Wallcovering, Eisenhart Wallcoverings, and York Wall Coverings.

   The price you see in a book, on a display, or on an Internet site isn't the price you pay. The stated price is for a single roll. But wallpaper doesn't come in single rolls. It comes in double and triple rolls that look like single rolls. You probably won't have to pay double or triple the stated price, though. Retailers commonly discount wallpaper by 30, 40, or 50 percent or more. Expect to cover about 60 to 70 square feet per double roll.

   Widths vary. So-called American rolls range from 18 to 36 inches wide; more often than not they are 27 inches wide. Euro, or metric, rolls are generally 20 to 21 inches wide.

   Wall covering comes in three basic types at a broad range of prices:

   PLAIN PAPER. This type of wall covering—often a reproduction of an antique pattern—is expensive, largely because it's usually made in limited quantities, printed in small mills, or even handcrafted. Plain paper has no protective coating, so it can't tolerate scrubbing.

   VINYL. Most wallpaper is paper or fabric coated with vinyl. It may be called paper-backed vinyl, vinyl-coated paper, expanded or textured vinyl, or even (incorrectly) solid vinyl. Vinyl by any of its names is the most widely sold wall covering because it's the easiest to hang and relatively simple to maintain. Many vinyl wallpapers are prepasted—the adhesive is activated when you wet the paper.

FABRIC AND GRASS CLOTH. If you have the money (and decorator connections, and a very tidy family), you can cover your walls in pure silk. But you're more likely to find grass cloth—heavily textured wall covering made of jute, linen, or grasses, woven and bonded to backing. Grass cloth is fairly expensive and difficult to install.

Key features

Many patterns have a **repeat,** which is the vertical distance between repetitions of an image on the roll. The repeat can be less than an inch to more than two feet. A large repeat may mean lots of wasted paper. Failing to properly match the pattern means amateurish results. When considering left-to-right alignment, a **random match** will be the most cost-effective. It matches no matter how adjoining strips of paper are aligned.

A **straight match** is easy to cut and align because the pattern follows a straight horizontal line. You do have to allow for the pattern repeat, though. A drop match means that the pattern on the left edge of the paper isn't the same as the pattern parallel to it on the right. So when you hang a new sheet, you have to position it, or "drop" it, to align the design.

Pretrimmed means there's no extra blank white paper on the edges of the roll. That's handy because it's a chore to trim that excess perfectly straight. **Strippable** products leave a minimum of adhesive behind, so it's easy to clean off the wall if you decide to switch to paint. With **peelable** wall coverings, a thin layer of the backing is left on the wall to serve as a liner for new wallpaper.

How to choose

PERFORMANCE DIFFERENCES. Wall coverings hold up to wear and tear in various ways. Resistance to staining depends on the construction. Plain-paper wall coverings are vulnerable. You have a better chance of removing stains from vinyls, but they aren't impervious. Resistance to fading depends largely on the color of the wallpaper, not the brand or type. CONSUMER REPORTS has found that wall coverings with a lot of bright-yellow pigment (including some greens, oranges, and beiges) fade the most.

Most of the vinyls we've tested held up impressively to scrubbing with a soft nylon brush. Plain paper, which can't tolerate scrubbing, may be labeled "spongeable" or "wipable." But watch out when using cleaning products. In CONSUMER REPORTS tests, a nonabrasive bleaching cleanser left faded areas on several brands. An ammonia-based spray cleaner left spots on several darker patterns.

RECOMMENDATIONS. The easiest type to hang is vinyl—it holds up well and is often easy to handle. The easiest patterns to hang are large florals, toiles, and random patterns. A pattern with a random match, a straight match, or a short drop match will give you the fewest headaches. Beware of stripes; if walls aren't perfectly straight where they meet in corners or at the ceiling, stripes will emphasize the problem. Grass cloth is easy to stain while hanging. The reflective surface of foils calls attention to every flaw. Dark colors may show the white backing if seams are less than perfect.

Ask for sizable samples to take home, even if you have to pay a small fee for them. Hang the swatches on a wall to see how the wallpaper will look in the room at different times of the day and at night. Some retailers substitute their own model numbers for the manufacturers' numbers to frustrate comparison shopping. You can often overcome this,

WELL MATCHED
A pattern with a drop match (top) takes careful alignment. A pattern with a straight match (bottom) aligns horizontally.

however, if you have the name of the sample book and the page number of the pattern.

If you plan to hire someone to hang wallpaper for you, get at least three estimates. The amount that contractors charge varies by region.

Some web sites (such as *usawallpaper.com, www.improvenet.com* and *doityourself.com*) offer free calculation pages to help you estimate the number of rolls you'll need for a job.

WINDOWS

Upgrading to energy-efficient windows will likely improve your comfort and your home's aesthetics, but it will take years to recoup the initial outlay from energy savings.

You'll probably want to install new windows when you're remodeling, when the old ones have deteriorated, or when you want windows that are easier to wash and maintain. Modern windows incorporate a frame made of all-vinyl or wood, the latter often covered in vinyl or aluminum, with two panes of glass. To cut energy use, those panes are separated with air or another gas and sometimes specially coated. Improved comfort in the summer and winter is the major benefit, and slightly reduced heating or cooling costs will be an added bonus.

What's available

Window styles include double hung, sliding, hopper, awning, casement, and bay. American

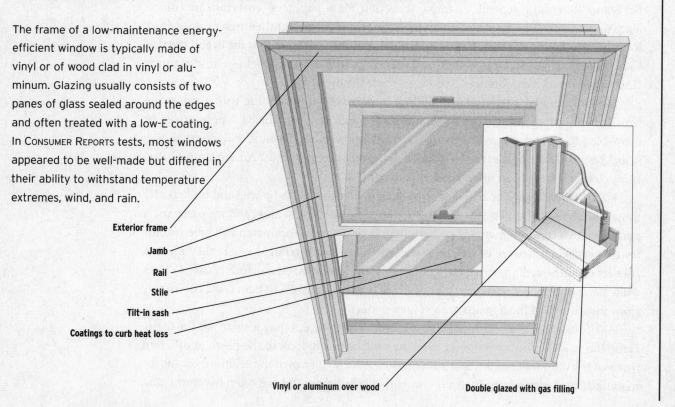

ANATOMY OF AN ENERGY-EFFICIENT WINDOW

The frame of a low-maintenance energy-efficient window is typically made of vinyl or of wood clad in vinyl or aluminum. Glazing usually consists of two panes of glass sealed around the edges and often treated with a low-E coating. In CONSUMER REPORTS tests, most windows appeared to be well-made but differed in their ability to withstand temperature extremes, wind, and rain.

Exterior frame
Jamb
Rail
Stile
Tilt-in sash
Coatings to curb heat loss

Vinyl or aluminum over wood

Double glazed with gas filling

Craftsman, Andersen, CertainTeed, Crestline, Marvin, Pella, Simonton (which also makes Sears models), and Weather Shield are the major brands. Some brands are sold at home centers such as Home Depot, Lowe's, and Menards. But most brands, including Sears, are typically purchased by contractors through distributors. Some windows come in custom sizes; others in stock sizes only. The materials that make a window frame can affect energy efficiency, maintenance, and price. Price range: $150 to more than $400 for 3x5-foot, double-hung, double glazed windows.

VINYL. These frames are easy to maintain, but they aren't usually available in many colors. And they are sometimes difficult to match with existing woodwork. Vinyl frame components tend to be less forgiving of deficiencies in design or construction.

ALUMINUM. As vinyl frames have become more popular, aluminum frames have become less so. The biggest drawback is that they allow heat to escape. That can make the area around the window chilly. In places with cold winters, a simple aluminum frame can become cold enough to condense moisture or frost on the inside, but where winters are mild, aluminum can be a good choice for its durability. If you are set on buying aluminum-framed windows, choose ones that have "thermally broken" frames, with insulating material between interior and exterior components.

WOOD. For elegance, wood is difficult to beat, although it usually costs more than vinyl and requires painting or staining and other maintenance. To minimize maintenance where it's usually needed most— the exterior side—many manufacturers cover, or clad, the wood in vinyl or aluminum. Wood composite frames—some made from a mixture of wood fibers and plastic resins—are supposed to combine the durability of wood with the low upkeep of plastics.

HOW TO DECODE LABELS

Standardized labels are supposed to make it easier to shop for windows, but use is not universal.

The NFRC Label. Alaska, California, Florida, Massachusetts, Minnesota, Oregon, Washington, and Wisconsin require windows to be certified by the National Fenestration Rating Council. In other states, many certified products bear the NFRC label even though it's not required. On the label are figures for U-factor, solar-heat-gain coefficient, and visible-light transmittance, each ranging from zero to 1. U-factor is a measure of thermal performance that describes a window's ability to conduct heat. The inverse of the U-factor—the R-factor—describes insulating ability. The higher the R-factor (or the lower the U-factor), the better a window will keep your home cool in summer and warm in winter.

Solar-heat-gain coefficient refers to the amount of sunlight that radiates through the windows from outdoors. A high number means the window allows the sunlight's heat to get indoors—a desirable trait in a northern Minnesota winter but thoroughly unwelcome in a Houston summer.

Visible-light transmittance refers to the amount of visible light entering a room. A window with a high number will allow in more light.

The Energy Star Label. So far, only a few manufacturers participate in the federally sponsored Energy Star label program. The label digests the data from the NFRC label and identifies a window as suitable for a specific region. You need only look at the map on the Energy Star label to see whether the window is appropriate for your area. But not all windows have the Energy Star label. Many unlabeled windows may actually be more energy efficient.

Key features

Three types of glazing are commonly available: single, double, and triple. A single pane of glass, or **single-glazed,** allows the highest transfer of energy and offers little insulation against frigid winters and searing summers. **Double-glazed** windows have two panes of glass. A few manufacturers offer **triple glazing.** The gas between the glass has a bearing on the quality of insulation. Plain old air works fine and is standard for some brand lines.

Argon gas, which provides better thermal performance, is standard in other brand lines; sometimes it is a step-up option. A few top-of-the-line windows incorporate **krypton gas,** which provides incrementally better insulation.

Double- and triple-glazed windows are sealed assemblies so they retain any special gas between the panes and also keep out moisture, which can condense between the panes. Should the seal fail, moisture, water droplets, and fogging between the glass panes can occur.

Clear glass lets a relatively large amount of radiant energy (heat in from the sun during the summer, heat out from your home during the winter) to pass through. **Low-E coatings** (the "E" stands for emissivity, or the ability of a surface to emit heat) enhance the insulation quality of a window by making it reflect heat. These coatings reduce some of the visible light that passes through the glass and may give a tinted appearance. The view out at night may be impeded somewhat. The coatings can be fine-tuned for different climates—a southern or a northern window, for example.

Most new double-hung windows have **tilting sashes,** a very handy feature that lets you pivot them inward for easier cleaning. With most, you simply flip a lever or two to tilt the sash inward. But with some, you must pull the sash out of the track. **Mullions** are decorative vertical elements that separate panes of glass. To help keep out water, some windows have a thin **lip**—a strip of wood or vinyl about an inch high—that rises from the sill. You'll need to work around it when installing a room air conditioner.

How to choose

PERFORMANCE DIFFERENCES. CONSUMER REPORTS has found most windows do a very good or excellent job at sealing out a fairly strong wind when the outside thermometer registers 70° F. Only a handful do well at sealing out a high wind when the outside temperature drops to zero. When it's that cold, weather stripping and other components can stiffen or shrink. Our tests have shown that frames made of aluminum are durable. But we have found windows with frames made of vinyl- or aluminum-clad wood can perform well, too.

RECOMMENDATIONS. If you're replacing windows, choose those that are designed for your region's climate. Cooling costs predominate in southern regions, so look for double glazing and a low-E coating. Give first consideration to windows with a low solar-heat-gain coefficient. The Department of Energy recommends that the number be 0.4 or lower.

Heating bills are of concern in northern regions. Give priority to well-insulated, double-glazed windows that are draft-free. A low-E coating isn't essential in places where summers aren't particularly hot. In central regions, both heating and cooling are concerns. As in southern regions, look for double glazing and a low-E coating. You'll also want high insulating performance and a solar-heat-gain coefficient of 0.55 or lower.

Heating, Cooling, and Filtering

The quality of the indoor air we breathe and the tap water we drink remains a concern for many. To address these concerns, there is an array of filtering products on the market, many of which do their job quite well. Before buying, however, consumers should make sure they truly need these products. If you're buying home-systems equipment for heating or cooling your home, you need to compare the premium you'll pay for the most energy-efficient model with the savings it will bring.

AIR CLEANERS

Whole-house and single-room air-cleaning products have limitations, but both can provide significant relief from some indoor pollutants when other measures don't work.

Indoor air is more polluted than the air on the other side of the window, estimates the U.S. Environmental Protection Agency (EPA). Indeed, the American Lung Association cites indoor pollution as a health hazard for millions of Americans with asthma or allergies. Indoor pollutants may include visible particles of dust, pollen, and smoke as well as invisible combustion byproducts such as carbon monoxide and nitrous oxide, along with other gaseous invaders such as fumes from carpet adhesives and upholstery.

Two commonsense solutions are proper ventilation and controlling the pollutant at the source. If dust is a problem, you might want to replace wall-to-wall carpeting with bare floors or area rugs. Frequent vacuuming may help, though some vacuum cleaners stir up dust. You can also lessen the effects of pet dander by designating pet-free rooms, particularly bedrooms. A ducted range hood can rid kitchen air of smoke and odor, while an exhaust fan in a bathroom can help squelch mold, mildew, and odor.

Air cleaners are the next step when those measures aren't enough. If your house has forced-air heating and cooling, choose an appropriate whole-house filter for your system; a room air cleaner's work would be quickly undone as the central system circulates unfiltered air from other rooms. For homes without forced-air heating and cooling, your only option is a room air cleaner.

What's available

WHOLE-HOUSE AIR CLEANERS. These range from ordinary fiberglass furnace filters, which begin at $1 or so, to electronic precipitators, which can cost more than $400 and must be installed professionally in a home's duct system. Major brands of whole-house systems include American Air Filter, Honeywell, Precisionaire, Purolator, Research Products, and 3M.

There are several types of filters:

Plain matted-fiberglass filters are the flat, 1-inch-thick filters used by many heating systems. They're meant to trap large particles of dust and lint and must be changed monthly. Price: about $1.

Pleated filters are made of fiberglass or another synthetic material; the pleats are designed to increase the surface area of the filter to hold more particles and do a better job. You change them quarterly. Price: about $5.

Electrostatically charged filters are designed to attract pollen, lint, pet dander, and dust. They come plain or pleated, disposable or washable, the latter reusable for up to 10 years for some models. Disposable versions should be changed quarterly, while washable models should be washed monthly. Price: disposable, $15 or less; washable, $20 to $25.

Extended-media filters are about the thickness of a box fan and contain inside a thick ruffle of accordion-pleated fiberglass or other material. These filters must be replaced annually. Price: about $200, plus $200 or more to install a holder into the ductwork.

Electronic-precipitator air cleaners are made by Honeywell and Trion, among others. They impart an electrical charge to particles flowing through them and then collect the particles on oppositely charged metal plates or filters. These more elaborate systems must be fitted into ductwork and then wired into house current. Most have a collector-plate assembly that must be removed and washed every one to two months. Price: about $400, plus installation, which can cost $200 or more.

ROOM AIR CLEANERS. These can work quite well, even on dust and cigarette smoke, whose particles are much smaller and harder to trap than pollen and mold spores. But they aren't good at trapping gases. And because most room units clean far better at their noisy, high-fan setting, balancing noise and performance typically involves lots of manual switching between speeds. Honeywell and Holmes account for nearly two-thirds of room units sold. Along with their own brands, Honeywell makes many Kenmore (Sears) products and Holmes makes Bionaire and Duracraft products.

The Association of Home Appliance Manufacturers (AHAM), a trade group, tests and rates room air cleaners using a measurement known as clean air delivery rate (CADR), which is determined by how well a filter traps particles and how much air the machine moves. Separate CADRs are listed for dust, tobacco smoke, and pollen. Most room air cleaners weigh between 10 and 20 pounds. They can be round or boxy, and can stand on the floor or on a table. Tabletop models are typically smaller, with correspondingly smaller CADRs. CONSUMER REPORTS conducts its own tests of air cleaners at both low and high speeds.

Two technologies predominate for room models. The most common is a filter system in which a high-efficiency particulate air (HEPA) filter mechanically strains the air of fine particles. The other technology uses an electronic precipitator that works like those in some whole-house models. Price range: low-end models, $40 to $90; high-end models, $125 to $475.

Key features

Whole-house air cleaners are generally available in widely used sizes or can be adapted to fit. Features are few. Some manufactures say their filters are treated with a special antimicrobial agent, presumably to prevent bacterial growth on the filter. CONSUMER REPORTS has not evaluated those claims.

Room air cleaners typically use a **fan** to pull air into the unit for filtration. Some models with an electronic precipitator or a HEPA filter incorporate ionizing circuitry that uses powered needles or wires to charge particles, which are then more easily trapped but may also stick to walls or furnishings, possibly soiling them. Indicators in most models let you know when to change filters.

HEPA filters are generally supposed to be replaced annually and can cost more than $100—sometimes equal to the price of the room air cleaner. Prefilters, which are designed to remove odors and/or larger particles, are generally changed quarterly, while washable prefilters should be cleaned monthly. An electronic precipitator's collector-plate assembly must be removed from the machine and washed every month or so; it slides out like a drawer and you can put it in a dishwasher or rinse it in a sink.

Most room air cleaners have a **handle**, while some heavier models have **wheels**. Fan speeds usually include low, medium, and high. A few units use a **dust sensor** and an **air-quality monitor** designed to raise or lower the fan speed automatically depending on conditions. Tests of one model with this feature found that it didn't respond well to very small particles in the air.

How to choose

PERFORMANCE DIFFERENCES. In tests of whole-house air cleaners, CONSUMER REPORTS tests found that the least expensive of these—plain fiberglass filters—did little to eliminate fine dust and smoke particles. Pleated filters and washable electrostatic filters were about as effective as plain fiberglass furnace filters, even though they cost more. Pleated filters with an electrostatic feature were 10 to 15 times as effective at cleaning the air as a plain fiberglass filter. The only extended media filter tested was about as effective as the best 1-inch plain fiberglass filters, although much more expensive (but it lasts for about a year). Most effective among whole-house models were those with an electronic precipitator. The four units tested worked about 30 times as well as a plain fiberglass filter at removing very small airborne particles. They're also far more expensive.

Room air cleaners provided varying levels of performance in CONSUMER REPORTS tests, with no one type—HEPA filter or electronic precipitator—clearly besting the others.

FILTER TYPES

Plain matted fiberglass

Electrostatically charged and pleated

CERTIFICATION

The Association of Home Appliance manufacturers' certification label gives the clean-air delivery rate (CADR), measured at the high fan setting in cubic feet per minute, for dust, tobacco smoke, and pollen. The higher the CADR, the faster a machine will clean the air. CONSUMER REPORTS conducts tests at the low and high settings.

When set at high, the best did a very good job of clearing a room of dust and smoke; other models were only good or fair. We found most room models easy to use. Electronic-precipitator models cost less to run because they don't require you to replace an expensive filter. All room air cleaners are noisy, especially at their high setting. While noise is reduced at lower speeds, so is performance. CONSUMER REPORTS has typically found the AHAM-certified CADRs to be accurate.

RECOMMENDATIONS. Choose an air cleaner based on how large an air-quality problem you have. Among whole-house units, one of the better pleated electrostatic filters may be all you need; consider an electronic precipitator if someone in your home smokes or has a chronic breathing problem. Also be sure a whole-house filter fits snugly in its mount, since leaks can make it less effective. (You can seal gaps with weather stripping.) Also remember that some whole-house units can make it harder for the heating and cooling system to work if airflow is already weak.

For room air cleaners, measure where you plan to operate the air cleaner. Then choose a model sized appropriately. CONSUMER REPORTS suggests choosing a room unit whose CADRs are at least two-thirds of the room's area, assuming an 8-foot ceiling. For example, a 12x15-foot room—180 square feet—needs a unit with a CADR of at least 120 for the contaminant you want to remove. The printed figure assumes you'll run the air cleaner at high speed. You may want to use medium or low speed to cut noise, however, so consider a unit with a CADR that is a bit higher than suggested for the room size. Also remember that a room with high ceilings requires a unit with a correspondingly higher CADR. Then follow instructions when placing any unit so it will work effectively. Some room air cleaners can sit against a wall; others belong in the middle of the room.

AIR CLEANERS ✦ **Ratings:** Page 197, 199

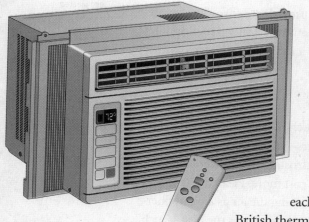

AIR CONDITIONERS

Individual room air conditioners are a relatively inexpensive alternative to central-air systems for cooling one or two rooms.

Refined features distinguish many of today's room air conditioners. Vague settings such as Warmer or Cooler are giving way to relatively precise electronic controls and digital temperature readouts.

New models are considerably more energy efficient than those made a decade ago. A yellow EnergyGuide tag now lists each new unit's energy-efficiency rating (EER)—its capacity in British thermal units per hour (Btu/hr.) divided by power consumption in watts. EERs for models now on the market range from about 9.7 to 12. A model with an EER of 10 should use about 20 percent less energy than one whose EER is 8, other factors being equal.

Window air conditioners that ate rated less than 8,000 Btu/hr. are required to have at least a 9.7 EER. Units rated between 8,000 and 13,999 Btu/hr. are required to have an EER of at least 9.8.

ESTIMATING YOUR COOLING NEEDS

Use the chart to determine roughly how much cooling you'll need for a space with an 8-ft. ceiling.

1. At the bottom of the chart, find the square footage of the room that you want to cool.

2. From there, move up the chart until you reach the shaded band that represents what's above your room: the thickest band represents an occupied area; the medium-width band, an insulated attic; the thinnest band, a noninsulated attic.

3. Within the band, move down for a room facing mostly north or

east; up for a room facing mostly south or west.

4. Read across the left to find the Btu/hr. figure.

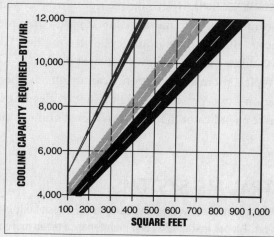

5. From that figure, subtract up to 15 percent for a northern climate, or add up to 10 percent for a southern climate. Subtract 30 percent if you'll use the unit only at night. If more than two people regularly occupy the area, add 600 Btu/hr. for each additional person. And add 4,000 Btu/hr. if the area includes the kitchen.

What's available

Fedders, GE, Kenmore (Sears), and Whirlpool are the leading brands of room air conditioners. Room air conditioners come in different sizes, with cooling capacities ranging from 5,000 Btu/hr. to as high as 33,000 Btu/hr. About half of room air conditioners found in stores range from 5,000 to 8,999 Btu/hr. The size you need depends on the size of the room to be cooled. Price range: $120 to more than $600, depending mostly on cooling capacity.

Key features

An air conditioner's exterior-facing portion contains a **compressor, fan,** and **condenser,** while the part that faces a home's interior contains a **fan** and an **evaporator.** But you'll find several different configurations depending on your needs. Most room models are designed to fit **double-hung windows,** though some are built for **casement** and **slider windows** and others for **in-wall installation.**

Most models now have **adjustable vertical and horizontal louvers** to direct airflow. Many offer a **fresh-air intake** or **exhaust setting** for ventilation, although this feature moves a relatively small amount of air. An **energy-saver setting** on some units stops the fan when the compressor cycles off. **Electronic controls** and **digital temperature readouts** are becoming common. A **timer** allows you to program the air conditioner to switch on (say, half an hour before you get home) or off at a given time. More and more models also include a **remote control.** Some models install with a **slide-out chassis**—an outer cabinet that anchors in the window, into which you slide the unit.

How to choose

PERFORMANCE DIFFERENCES. Most models CONSUMER REPORTS has tested do a very good job at cooling, with the better models keeping the temperature more even than the rest.

However, we found wide variations in quietness, along with significant differences in how well models direct airflow to the left or right with their louvers. Most units restart after a brownout. But some electronically controlled models must be restarted manually and reprogrammed after a power interruption.

RECOMMENDATIONS. Determine the right size air conditioner for the space you're cooling. An air conditioner with more cooling capacity than you need may not dehumidify properly because its compressor may cycle off too often. Check the unit's EER on the yellow EnergyGuide tag to find the most efficient model.

A typical room air conditioner can weigh anywhere from 40 to 100 pounds, making installation a two-person job. Maintain it by cleaning its air filter every few weeks; some units have an indicator that tells you when it's time to clean or change the filter.

CENTRAL-AIR SYSTEMS

You'll find a central air system in nearly every house built in the South and Southwest. Proper installation and maintenance mean more than the brand.

Room air conditioners are an economical alternative for cooling a room or two in regions with relatively short summers. But for many parts of the country, you'll need a central air-conditioning system that can cool the entire house. Unlike a room air conditioner, which is a self-contained unit, the most common central air-conditioning system comprises cooling equipment connected to ducts that distribute air throughout the home. A new minimum-efficiency standard is scheduled for 2006.

What's available

Major brands of central-air systems are American Standard, Bryant, Carrier, Coleman Evcon, Comfortmaker, Goodman, Heil, Janitrol, Lennox, Rheem, Ruud, Trane, and York. More important than brand, however, is how well the contractor sizes, fabricates, and installs the system, which efficiency level you choose, and how well you maintain the system once it's installed.

The most common central-air system is a split system, where refrigerant circulates between an indoor coil and a matching outdoor condenser with compressor. Refrigerant cools the air, dehumidifying it in the process, and a blower circulates it via ducts throughout the house. The heat-pump system functions like the central-air system but provides both heating and cooling. An air-source heat pump is most appropriate for areas with mild winters. When used as an air conditioner, a heat pump discharges heat from the house either into the air outside or deep into the ground. In cold months, a heat pump extracts heat from the ground or the outside air to warm the house. Price range: $3,000 for the equipment if you're replacing an old system; $6,000 or more if you need ductwork installed because you're starting from scratch or upgrading a forced-air heating system. Ground-source heat pumps cost even more.

Key features

The system's efficiency is expressed as the **Seasonal Energy Efficiency Rating (SEER)**, which describes how much cooling the unit delivers based on a partial load over the entire season. A SEER of 10 currently denotes a low-efficiency unit, a SEER of 11 to 12 medium-efficiency, and one of 13 or above high-efficiency. Size and cooling capacity are synonymous. Size is measured in **British thermal units per hour (Btu/hr.)** or in **"tons,"** with one ton of cooling equaling 12,000 Btu/hr.

Central-air systems also differ in their key components. While all use a **compressor** to pump refrigerant to the evaporator and condenser, some have **scroll-type compressors** that tend to be quieter and more efficient than **reciprocating** types be-

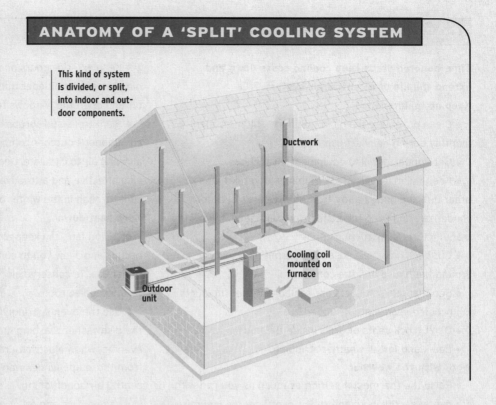

ANATOMY OF A 'SPLIT' COOLING SYSTEM

This kind of system is divided, or split, into indoor and outdoor components.

Ductwork

Cooling coil mounted on furnace

Outdoor unit

cause they have fewer moving parts. According to contractors CONSUMER REPORTS surveyed, reciprocating compressors are more repair-prone. Most manufacturers offer both types.

Pairing new equipment with old can cause problems. If you replace only one component, you have what is called a **field-matched system,** which may require more repairs than a totally new one. With **damper-zoned cooling,** a large or multistory house is often divided into several heating and cooling zones to improve temperature control. This type of system is complex and may have a relatively high repair rate. However, when designed correctly, it does improve the temperature uniformity in the home. An alternative is the installation of multiple independent heating and/or cooling systems. While more expensive, this can provide better temperature control in a large home where each floor of the home has its own system.

How to choose

PERFORMANCE DIFFERENCES. According to the contractors CONSUMER REPORTS surveyed, units with a SEER of 11 to 12 hold up best. Contractors told us that high-efficiency systems tend to be more complex, however, with more that can go wrong. Low-cost, low-efficiency builders' models also require more repairs, perhaps due to design shortcuts, the contractors said.

RECOMMENDATIONS. Improper installation can make even the best system work poorly. Systems with ductwork that's too small can result in poor cooling or excessive noise in one or more rooms. Also troublesome are ducts that leak or lack insulation. A contractor can seal seams and joints and insulate sections of ductwork that run in spaces that aren't cooled or heated, such as attics or crawl spaces.

COST-CONSCIOUS COOLING

Time-honored steps keep cooling costs down and extend the life of a central-air system.

Keep up maintenance

♦ Clean or replace the air conditioner's filter frequently—monthly during heaviest use.

♦ Get annual, detailed equipment inspections.

♦ Keep fallen leaves, grass clippings, dryer lint, and other dirt and debris away from the system's outdoor condenser. And keep the condenser coils clean, following manufacturer's instructions.

♦ Cut back grass and foliage to permit easy airflow around the house and the condenser.

♦ See that leaks in ducts are sealed and that the ducts in uncooled spaces are insulated.

♦ Don't block vents or grills inside the house.

♦ Caulk and install weather stripping.

Work with the weather

♦ Raise the thermostat setting as much as you can without overly sacrificing comfort. For every degree you raise the setting, you can expect to cut your cooling bills by 3 percent or more.

♦ Keep sunlight out, especially in the afternoon in rooms facing west.

♦ Keep exterior doors and windows closed when running the air conditioner during the day. At night, turn it off and open the windows to draw in cooler air.

♦ Plant trees and shrubs to keep the house and the air conditioner's outdoor component in the shade, yet still allowing air to circulate. Deciduous trees in particular provide effective and attractive climate control by letting sunlight through in the winter but blocking it in the summer.

Keep heat down

♦ Ceiling fans can keep air moving in the rooms you occupy and allow you to comfortably cut back air-conditioner use. To conserve electricity, avoid running a fan in an unoccupied room.

♦ Use the oven sparingly; avoid baking in midday. Run the dishwasher, washing machine, or dryer in the evening, when electricity rates may be lower and heat from those appliances won't increase the demands on central air conditioning.

♦ Lamps, TVs, and other appliances produce some heat, so turn them off when not in use. Position them away from the air conditioner's thermostat. Use compact fluorescent lights if possible; they generate less heat and use less electricity than incandescents.

Along with your climate and the size of the space you need to cool, consider your existing heating and cooling equipment. If you have a central cooling system or a forced-air heating system, you already have the ductwork; all you may need a contractor to do is replace or add the basic hardware components of the central-air system. That's a significant savings, since installing ducts in a typical new home or retrofitting them to an existing one can add thousands of dollars to the bill. Adding ducts to a very old house may require significant construction costs. Ducts that already serve a heating system may have to be upgraded to accommodate the higher airflow that a central-cooling system requires. Because they may not have the best air-supply locations in each room, they can compromise cooling-system performance.

If you have an ailing split cooling system more than a decade old, consider total replacement of inside and outside units, rather than a major repair. (This is also a good time to consider the addition of a whole-house air cleaner. See page 180.) While only one of these system's major components typically fails, replacing the whole system at once usually is more cost-effective. What's more, unmatched major components can compromise efficiency and lead to additional repairs.

You can also take several steps to ensure a quality installation. For starters, be wary of contractors who base estimates merely on house size or vague rules of thumb. A contractor who bids on your job should calculate required cooling capacity by using a recognized method such as the Air Conditioning Contractors of America's Residential Load Calculation Manual—also called Manual J. An additional reference for assessing ductwork needs is Manual D. The result will be a detailed, room-by-room analysis of your cooling needs. Ask for a printout of all calculations and assumptions, including ductwork design. Finally, try to negotiate an overall price that includes a service plan with regular inspections, discounts on repairs, and a labor warranty.

HEATING SYSTEMS
Size, efficiency, and the contractor's competence are more important than brand names. A new unit could cut your heating bills, but don't count on a fast return on your investment.

Efficient heating will do more than just save on fuel bills. Properly installed, a new furnace can distribute heat more evenly and continuously than an old one, making your home a cozier place. Because new furnaces burn less fuel than their predecessors, they produce less carbon dioxide—and have less impact on the environment.

Despite the improved efficiency and comfort of most new furnaces, it is generally more cost-effective to repair a furnace than to replace it. An exception is when a key component such as the heat exchanger or control module fails. Then you're probably better off replacing the furnace, especially if the unit is more than about 15 years old. The average furnace typically lasts about 18 years.

What's available
Most new central-heating systems across the country use a gas furnace. Heat pumps, predominantly electric appliances, are the preferred way to heat in the South and Southwest, where winters are mild and electricity is relatively cheap. Oil furnaces are mostly used in older homes in the Northeast and Midwest.

GAS FURNACES. A gas furnace heats air and uses a blower to circulate it through ductwork. How efficiently a furnace converts gas into heat is reflected in its annual fuel-utilization efficiency (AFUE) rating, which is measured as a percentage. The higher that percentage, the more heat the furnace can wring from each therm (100,000 Btu) of gas—and the lower the environmental impact of its emissions. Gas furnaces generally have become more efficient. A unit made in the early 1970s typically has an AFUE of about 65 percent. Today the lowest efficiency allowed by federal law for new gas furnaces is 78 percent; the most efficient models have an AFUE as high as 97 percent. The major brands of gas furnaces are Amana, American Standard, Armstrong, Bryant, Carrier, Comfortmaker, Goodman, Heil, Janitrol, Lennox, Rheem, Ruud, Tempstar, and Trane. All offer units in a range of rated capacities and efficiencies.

HEAT PUMPS. Most units wring heat from outdoor air and pump it into your home using a blower. When it gets hot outside, they run in reverse and act as an air conditioner, drawing heat from indoor air and pumping it outdoors. When the temperature drops, heat pumps can't produce as much heat and must be supplemented, often with built-in electric elements that kick in automatically and provide expensive, less-efficient heating. Size (or capacity) is measured in British thermal units per hour (Btu/hr.). Efficiency is reflected in the unit's heating seasonal performance factor. HSPF ratings for new heat pumps range from 6.8, the minimum allowed, to about 10. Models that use the ground outside as a place to extract or dissipate heat are more efficient but more expensive to install. Higher-efficiency models cost more. The major brands of heat pumps are Bryant, Carrier, Heil, Janitrol, Lennox, Rheem, Ruud, Trane, and York.

OIL FURNACES AND BOILERS. These oil-fired counterparts to gas furnaces draw oil from a tank located in the basement or underground. Only homeowners who already own an oil unit and who live in a region where oil is widely distributed are likely to consider this option. It's safest to install the tank in the basement; in-ground models may eventually leak, posing an environmental hazard and requiring an expensive cleanup. Some oil dealers sell insurance against tank leakage; CONSUMER REPORTS recommends it if you have an older underground tank.

> ### HIRING A CONTRACTOR
>
> In the end, it's the contractor who will make the biggest difference in how well the installation of a furnace, heat pump, or central-air system goes. Seek referrals from neighbors, family, or business associates. It's wise to get price quotes from at least three contractors. Some utilities install and maintain furnaces themselves.
>
> Contractors who bid on your installation should show you proof of bonding and insurance, plus any required contractor's licenses. Check with your local Better Business Bureau and consumer-affairs office for complaint records. It's a plus if technicians are certified by North American Technician Excellence (NATE), a trade organization, and have several years' experience.

IN-FLOOR RADIANT HEATING SYSTEMS. These systems turn a home's floors into radiators. Water from a boiler or other heat source is routed through special plastic tubing installed on the subfloor and covered with concrete, gypsum-based concrete, or built-up finished flooring. Alternately, an electric heating grid can be used in lieu of the water piping. While radiant heating systems are relatively slow to warm up and cool down, they provide even heat with no drafts or noise. And they're an efficient way to warm large room areas—especially those with high ceilings. These systems also offer flexible energy options that include an oil- or gas-fired boiler, a solar water heater, or, in some regions, the home's hot-water system. Electric heating grids are less efficient than a heat pump—and electricity is more than three times as expensive than other heating fuels, based on national heating prices.

Key features

With gas furnaces, **variable-speed blowers** can deliver air more slowly (and often more quietly) when less heat is needed. Heat can then be delivered more continuously, with fewer uncomfortable swings in temperature and airflow. **Variable heat output,** available on some furnaces that have variable blower speed, can further increase efficiency and comfort by automatically varying the amount of heat the furnace delivers, usually between two levels. The furnace can then deliver heat more continuously than a fixed heat output allows.

A relatively recent refinement on that idea is infinitely variable air speed and heat output. Also referred to by the heating industry as "full modulation," a system so equipped is said to maintain a clean burn and proper fuel-air ratios across a spectrum of operating conditions. Rheem, for one, offers a fully modulating gas furnace.

Another option is **zone heating,** which employs a number of thermostats, a central controller, and a series of dampers that control airflow to deliver more or less heating or cooling to meet the different "loads" in various parts of the home. The larger the home, as a rule, the more useful zone heating is. That's especially true if sections of the home vary a lot in their heating or cooling needs. But contractors have told CONSUMER REPORTS that furnaces connected to zoned ductwork require more repair than furnaces connected to single-zone systems. An alternative is to install multiple independent heating/cooling systems. For instance, separate systems can be installed on the first and second floors of a large home.

In older gas furnaces, a continuously burning **pilot light** ignites the burners. But that design has largely been supplanted by more efficient alternatives such as **intermittent, direct-spark,** or **hot-surface ignition.**

To draw more heat from the air they burn, furnaces with an AFUE of 90 percent or higher have a **second heat exchanger**—the component that draws heat from the burned gas. Because the exhaust is cooler when it leaves that second exchanger, it may yield acidic condensation. To prevent acid from causing corrosion, the second exchanger is made of stainless steel, lined with plastic or otherwise protected. **Air filters** trap dust and reduce air-

WHEN IT'S TIME TO REPLACE YOUR HOT-WATER HEATER

A water heater isn't something you buy on impulse or upgrade as new features become available. Odds are, you don't think about it at all until it breaks or dies completely. That's when virtually all replacement purchases are made. Water heaters are fairly long-lived—most are warranted for a decade or more. When they do give out, it usually happens suddenly as water leaks out through corrosion in the tank.

Most water heaters are gas or electric. Electric water heaters are far more efficient when it comes to storing water. But because electricity is relatively expensive, gas heaters are cheaper to operate. Oil-fired water heaters are also available in locales such as the Northeast and Midwest, but they are comparatively expensive and represent a small fraction of the total number installed in homes. Solar- and heat-pump-operated water heaters make up a small part of the market. These use gas or electricity as a backup heat source.

American, A.O. Smith, Bradford, Rheem, State, and White are among the major manufacturers of hot-water heaters. In major retail stores, you'll find brands such as GE, Hotpoint, and Kenmore (Sears). There is some variety in the different models, though the brands compete mainly on warranty and price. Plumbers who buy direct from wholesale suppliers may offer to install water heaters branded by one of the manufacturers. Often, these are utilitarian, no-frills units, but they too offer a range of storage capacity and warranty options. If the unit breaks or needs service, your only recourse is the plumber, who may refer you to the supplier or the manufacturer for satisfaction. That may not be a problem if you deal with the same plumber for all your home's needs. Service warranties for appliances are also available through third-party repair providers such as Sears Home Central—at a price.

When you need to replace your hot-water heater, start by determining whether your old unit is big enough for your needs now and in the future. A typical, 40-gallon unit ranges from $175 to $350, depending on warranty and efficiency. That size may be fine for most families, but if yours may grow—or you're planning to install a hot tub or whirlpool bath—consider stepping up to a 50-gallon or an even larger model. While you'll pay more initially, a larger water heater costs about the same per year to operate as a smaller unit. Conversely, empty nesters probably don't need extra capacity. Opting for a smaller unit will only save a little on installation costs—and it may mean you'll run out of hot water.

In areas where the water is corrosive or has a high mineral content, choosing a model with a longer warranty may make sense (most warranties are divided between service, parts, and tank). And whichever heater you buy, ask if the service warranty includes in-home repairs.

borne particles. When installing a new heating or cooling system, it is a good time to think about upgrading your system's air cleaner.

How to choose

PERFORMANCE DIFFERENCES. Size can make a difference. A furnace that is too small won't keep the house comfortable during extreme cold. Partly to avoid that possibility, contractors sometimes sell furnaces that are too large for the home they're installed in. Unfortunately, a unit that's too large will cost more and may not work properly. Also, upgrading to a larger or high-efficiency furnace may require the installation of larger ducts. Without the larger ducts, the increased air flow needs of the furnace can create a noisy system.

The more efficient a furnace, generally, the lower your energy bill for heating. But you also have to figure in other costs. For instance, the electricity to run its blowers and other components is not considered in the AFUE rating, but the cost can be significant. Higher-efficiency models may have special installation requirements, such as new, revised, or special vents (needed for a furnace with an AFUE of 90 percent or more or if other appliances such as a gas-fired water heater share a vent or chimney with the furnace). All this can easily add several hundred dollars to the installed cost of a new furnace.

Some contractors we surveyed said the most efficient gas furnaces (those with, say, an AFUE of 90 percent or more) tend to need more repair than other models. These high-efficiency furnaces tend to have more components that can break down and are more likely to use new designs that are not yet tried-and-true. (More than half of the contractors we surveyed also cited new furnace designs as more repair-prone.)

RECOMMENDATIONS. Choosing a competent contractor is more important than considering brand. To be sure of correct capacity, choose a contractor who will take the time to calculate heating demand by using an industry-standard calculation such as the Air Conditioning Contractors of America's Manual J. Such a calculation accounts for climate as well as your home's size, design, and construction.

Generally the more efficient the gas furnace, the more expensive it will be. A gas furnace with an AFUE of 90 percent can cost $1,000 more than a similarly sized unit with an AFUE of 80 percent. That additional cost can generally be recouped over the lifetime of the furnace. Just how quickly the expenditure is recovered depends not only on the unit's AFUE but also on its electrical consumption, how well your home retains heat, and your region's climate. In regions where winters are especially harsh, the payback time may be only a decade or so.

When comparing models, make sure the contractor's estimate for each choice considers the cost of any changes to venting. And insist that the contractor estimate annual operating costs by basing them on the unit's AFUE and electrical consumption, information on your home, and the region where you live. Salespeople have the information needed to make these calculations easily and accurately. Then weigh the differences in operating costs against the prices for various units, along with their features. If a model that fits your needs and priorities has an AFUE in the mid-90-percent range or above, ask the contractor about any reliability problems that might exist. Some manufacturers' basic (usually low-efficiency) models may have less generous warranties than their premium models. Consider a service contract that includes an annual inspection of your furnace.

THERMOSTATS

Electronic setback thermostats offer far more flexibility and energy-saving potential than the electromechanical models they are replacing.

You can cut your energy costs by as much as 20 percent by lowering your home's thermostat 5° F at night and 10° during the day when no one is home—or raising it comparably when cooling. Setback thermostats can take much of the hassle out of doing that by handling the adjusting for you. While you'll still find a few electromechanical models with a 24-hour timer, they can't match the control and flexibility of today's electronic models. Many models let you program different temperatures for different days.

What's available

The major brands are Honeywell, Hunter, Lux, and White Rodgers. Some programmable electromechanical and electronic thermostats allow only two daily temperature periods. Others models let you set one schedule for weekdays, another for weekends, usually with four temperature periods each day. Seven-day electronic models let you pick different programs for different days, with four possible temperature periods per day. Price range: $30 to $150.

Key features

All electronic thermostats have a **liquid crystal display** that shows time of day and room temperature. Some also display the temperature you've programmed, whether the heating or cooling system is supposed to be on, and which programmed period is in effect. Some models can be briefly **illuminated,** handy in a dark room. Another feature on some displays is an **indicator** that tells you when the filter of a forced-air system should be replaced, based on operating time.

Most models come with a **factory-set program** you can adjust to your needs. This feature also makes programming easier, since you're refining an existing program, rather than creating one from scratch. Some models are **detachable** from the wall mount, allowing you to punch in your preferences from your sofa or another location. Many models include **abbreviated instructions** on their outer case. All models have **temperature-adjustment buttons** that also allow you to temporarily override the programmed temperature until the next programmed temperature period, when the temporary setting is automatically cancelled. A **hold button** allows you to override the programmed temperature until you cancel it. A variation allows you to set the temperature override for up to a month or more—handy when you go on business trips or vacations.

Most thermostats prevent frequent on/off cycling of the cooling system. A few models provide **secondary automatic backup switches** for turning the heat off if the house is in danger of overheating—or on if temperatures drop far enough for the pipes to freeze, for example. While most units are **battery-powered** and use one, two, or three AA alkaline batteries, some White Rodgers models draw power from the heating or cooling system and continue working even if their batteries die. But a **low-battery indicator** for battery models should generally provide ample warning.

How to choose

PERFORMANCE DIFFERENCES. Most of the thermostats that CONSUMER REPORTS has tested have been quite good at responding to changes in room temperature. Factory-installed set-back programs, logical dials and buttons, and helpful prompts on the display make programming intuitive with most units. Indeed, you should be able to program most electronic thermostats without checking the manual.

RECOMMENDATIONS. A unit that allows one schedule for weekdays and another for weekends is probably fine for most people. Consider a seven-day model if your daily schedule tends to vary—say, if children are at home earlier on some days than others. If you're replacing a thermostat that has a mercury switch, be careful not to break the tube that holds the mercury, a toxic substance. Contact your local recycling or hazardous-materials center for advice on proper disposal of the thermostat.

Also, be sure to change the thermostat's batteries once a year, even if they're still good, to prevent your heating or cooling system from shutting down in case the batteries die. You can always pop the old ones into another device to use whatever battery life that remains.

WATER FILTERS

Many are good at removing pollutants such as lead and chlorination byproducts. They can also remove off-tastes and odors.

Most drinking water in the U.S. is safe. But if you have any qualms about the quality of your tap water—or simply don't like its taste—you may want to consider getting a water filter. While boiling your tap water can protect against some organisms, it won't remove stable compounds that can affect water's taste; nor will it remove lead.

Facts about your water supply can help you decide. A federal law requires water utilities to send an annual "Consumer confidence report" to their customers before July 1 each year that explains what's in the water when it leaves the treatment plant. Some states have required such reports for years. If you don't find such a report in your mail, you may find the information online at a public library or in a local newspaper. People with a well must have testing done on their own.

What's available

The two major water-filter brands are Brita and Pur. Culligan, GE, Kenmore (Sears), Omni, and Teledyne/Water Pik round out the market. There are several different types, some cost less to maintain than others.

CARAFES. Generally made of plastic, these are simple to use and typically come in a half-gallon size or larger. Many can fit in the door of a fridge. Filter changes are usually required after processing 40 gallons—the equivalent of about two months of typical use. Price range: half-gallon size, $20. Annual cartridge cost: $50 to $110.

FAUCET-MOUNTED FILTERS. Models that attach to your faucet are compact and easy to install. The filter should generally be changed at least every two to three months. Price range: $20 to $45. Annual filter cost: $50 to $120.

UNDERSINK SYSTEMS. These attach to the cold-water line beneath a sink. The housing can

POLLUTANTS TO WATCH OUT FOR

A few pollutants can pose a risk even if they're under the government's legal limit. They are especially dangerous to vulnerable groups such as pregnant women and people with cancer or AIDS. Be especially alert for the following:

Arsenic. The Environmental Protection Agency (EPA) is moving ahead with plans to lower the safety limit for arsenic. At the current maximum level of 50 micrograms per liter, arsenic carries a lifetime cancer risk of at least 1 in 1,000 and perhaps as high as 1 in 100, according to a recent assessment by the National Research Council.

The element occurs naturally in the earth's crust and shows up mainly in water supplies drawn from wells. If your water supply has an arsenic level higher than 10 micrograms per liter—the World Health Organization safety limit—use a distiller or a reverse-osmosis filter.

Chlorination byproducts. Chlorination kills germs, but it also reacts with organic matter in water to form chloroform and other trihalomethanes, which are suspected carcinogens, and have been recently linked to an increased risk of miscarriage. If the level of trihalomethanes in your water is higher that 75 micrograms per liter, drink filtered water, especially if you're pregnant or planning a pregnancy.

Cryptosporidium. This tough microscopic parasite was responsible for the single largest outbreak of disease from a contaminated public water supply in U.S. history. Healthy adults generally recovered from infection, but the parasite was fatal to about half of those with cancer or AIDS. If your water system is required to test for cryptosporidium, your water report will note that. The cysts can be filtered out or killed by boiling water that you use for drinking or cooking.

Lead. Water that leaves the treatment plant relatively free of lead can pick up hazardous amounts from lead or lead-soldered pipes and some brass faucets by the time it emerges from your tap. The only way to be sure your own water is lead-free is to have it tested. (To find a certified testing laboratory in your area, call the EPA's Safe Drinking Water Hotline, 800-426-4791, or go to *www.epa.gov/safewater*. If the lead level is more than 15 parts per billion, consider filtering your water. We have found that most filters effectively remove lead.

be attached to a wall or cabinet back. Filtered water is drawn through a separate faucet. Some systems include that faucet; with others, you may need to buy one. Their cartridges last long, generally six months. Some have multiple cartridges. Professional installation is recommended. Price range: $55 to $180. Annual cartridge cost: about $45 to about $170.

REVERSE-OSMOSIS SYSTEMS. These undersink models use a special membrane to remove contaminants. Larger and more expensive than other undersink systems, they can take up most of the space beneath a sink. Removing dissolved minerals is their strength. Their cartridges last long, generally six months. But they require maintenance, including periodic sanitizing with bleach. Aside from distillers, these are the only units certified to filter out arsenic. Professional installation is recommended. Average price: about $235. Annual cartridge cost: from about $45 to $80.

WHOLE-HOUSE (POINT-OF ENTRY) SYSTEMS. These hook up to your home's water main, so you can use filtered water for bathing, laundry, and dishes. If your tap water contains sediment, a whole-house system can protect your appliances and eliminate periodic cleaning clogged faucet aerators. Professional installation is recommended. Price range: $35 to $55. Annual cartridge cost: About $15 to $50.

Key features

Some carafe, faucet-mounted, and undersink filters have a **flashing light**, **color indicator**, or other device signaling the need for a new filter cartridge. Slower-than-usual water flow may also tell you that it's time to replace the cartridge, since flow tends to slow or stop as impurities collect in the filter. Faucet-mounted, undersink, and reverse-osmosis filters allow you to choose unfiltered water for cleaning or washing.

How to choose

All tested filters made removal claims. Those claims are certified by National Sanitation Foundation International (NSF), a nonprofit testing lab. To ensure that the filter you buy will remove a contaminant, its label should specify that the filter is NSF-certified for that substance. Some manufacturers offer replacement cartridges, each designed to remove different contaminants. You can use those interchangeably, if they're the same size and brand as the cartridge included with the filtering system. If no model in our Ratings handles the claim you're concerned about, check NSF's Web site, *www.nsf.org*, for models that do.

PERFORMANCE DIFFERENCES. In CONSUMER REPORTS tests, all models except for the whole-house filters are fine for removing both lead and chloroform, which is sufficient for most people's needs. Most models were good, very good or excellent at removing off-tastes.

Most undersink models delivered water more quickly and were less prone to clog than faucet-mounted models and carafes. Slowest were the reverse-osmosis systems; they delivered water at about 50 minutes per half-gallon—too slow more most households. They also wasted about 5 gallons for each gallon purified.

While whole-house filters can provide filtered water to every tap in the house, CONSUMER REPORTS found there are probably better choices when significant taste or contamination issues exist.

RECOMMENDATIONS. Consider your daily water use to help determine the filtering equipment you need. A carafe filter might be fine if you need to filter only a relatively small amount of water at a time. Also determine how often you'll have to change filters, which affects annual costs; follow the manufacturer's recommended replacement schedule, since bacteria can thrive inside a filter. Also consider the type and degree of contamination; severe contamination will likely require more protection than the filters discussed here.

Beyond this, compare notes with neighbors and notify the water utility and local health officials if you suspect a contamination. The latter can help locate the problem and eliminate it at its source.

WATER FILTERS ♦ **Ratings:** Page 292

Reference

Pages 197-293 Ratings

HOW TO USE THE RATINGS

To find out important information on making your choice, read the buying-advice article on the product you're interested in. The Overall Ratings table gives the big picture on how well the product performed in CONSUMER REPORTS tests. "Recommendations & Notes" gives model-by-model details. Use the handy key numbers to move quickly from table to details.

Availability for most products is verified especially for this book. Some tested models may no longer be available. Models similar to the tested models, when they exist, are listed in "Recommendations and Notes." Such models differ in features, not essential performance, according to manufacturers.

Page 294 Finding Reliable Brands

Page 303 Index

Air cleaners, room

If you have a forced-air heating/cooling system, choose a whole-house air cleaner. Otherwise, look for a room model that will cover the size room you need to treat. The top models treat 450 to 500 square feet. Many cost little more than lower-rated models designed to treat areas half the size. The high-scoring Friedrich C-90A, $475, performs impressively at Low speed and has a filter that can be washed.

KEY NO	BRAND & MODEL	PRICE	ANNUAL COST ENERGY/FILTER	OVERALL SCORE	DUST		SMOKE		NOISE		COVERAGE (SQ. FT.)
				P F G VG E	HIGH SPEED	LOW SPEED	HIGH SPEED	LOW SPEED	HIGH SPEED	LOW SPEED	
1	**Friedrich** C-90A	$475	$55/ $72	▬▬▬	●	◑	◑	○	◑	◑	480
2	**Whirlpool** AP45030H0	250	63/130	▬▬	●	○	◑	○	◑	◑	500
3	**Bionaire** BAP-1300	220	62/132	▬▬	◑	○	◑	◑	●	○	490
4	**Holmes** HAP675	200	63/120	▬▬	◑	○	◑	◑	●	◑	460
5	**Honeywell** 13520	180	94/169	▬▬	◑	◑	◑	◑	◑	○	450
6	**Hunter** HEPATech 30375	170	105/128	▬▬	◑	◑	◑	◑	●	◑	440
7	**Honeywell** Enviracaire 17400	170	68/147	▬▬	◑	◑	◑	◑	●	◑	340
8	**Holmes** HAP650	160	44/95	▬	○	◑	◑	◑	◑	⊙	340
9	**Hunter** 30170	170	56/88	▬	○	◑	○	◑	○	◑	290
10	**Kenmore** (Sears) 83353	220	25/105	▬	○	◑	○	◑	○	◑	240
11	**Panasonic** F-P20HU1	200	80/77	▬	○	●	○	◑	◑	◑	320
12	**Honeywell** Enviracaire 18150	160	42/100	▬	◑	●	◑	◑	◑	◑	230
13	**Holmes** HAP625	120	24/60	▬	◑	●	◑	●	○	◑	210
14	**Honeywell** Enviracaire 17000	130	53/125	▬	◑	●	◑	●	◑	◑	200
15	**Sharper Image** SI637 Ionic Breeze Quadra Silent Air Purifier	350	4/–		●	●	●	●	⊙	⊙	NA [1]

Overall Ratings · In performance order

Legend: Excellent ● · Very good ◑ · Good ○ · Fair ◑ · Poor ●

[1] *Not AHAM-certified.*

See report, page 179. Based on tests published in Consumer Reports in February 2002, with updated prices and availability.

The tests behind the Ratings

Overall score is based on an air cleaner's ability to remove fine dust and cigarette-smoke particles from our test chamber, as well as on noise and on ease of use. Scores are based on performance when new. **Dust** and **smoke** scores reflect the ability to clear air of those particles at High and at Low speed. **Noise** is based on instrument measurements and panelists' judgments at the highest and lowest speeds. **Coverage** is given to the nearest 10 square feet, based on guidelines of the Association of Home Appliance Manufacturers (AHAM) for the largest sealed room each model can handle effectively. Performance should be better in a smaller room. **Price** is approximate retail. **Annual cost** is our estimate of the yearly energy consumed, calculated from an average of High- and Low-speed operation based on the national average electricity rate of 8 cents/kilowatt-hour, as well as on the annual cost of filter replacement, assuming the machine runs constantly and using the minimum recommended interval for replacing filters.

Recommendations and notes

Most models: Weigh 10 to 20 pounds. Are freestanding and can be placed anywhere in a room, including against a wall. Have Low, Medium, and High speeds. Turn off if filter cover is removed. Can be turned on with an external timer. Have disposable HEPA filters with prefilters or carbon filters designed to trap large particles and reduce odors. Have a handle. Have a one- to two-year warranty. Are AHAM-certified. Ease of use, which reflects ease of controls and of changing filters and moving the machine was good for most models. Exceptions are noted in the paragraphs.

1> **FRIEDRICH** C-90A **Electronic precipitator.** Heavier than most. Washable filter. Based on our tests, regular replacement of this model's carbon filter is unnecessary.

2> **WHIRLPOOL** AP45030HO **Heavier than most.** Similar: Kenmore 83355.

3> **BIONAIRE** BAP-1300 Heavier than most. **Can't be turned on with external timer.** Remote control. Four speeds. Similar: Holmes HAP675RC.

4> **HOLMES** HAP675 **Heavier than most.** Four speeds. 5-year warranty.

5> **HONEYWELL** 13520 **Can't be placed against wall.** Doesn't turn off when filter cover is removed.

6> **HUNTER** HEPATech 30375 **Has timer for automatic shutoff.** Can't be turned on with external timer. 5-year warranty. Similar: 30377.

7> **HONEYWELL** Enviracaire 17400 **Can't be placed against wall.** Can't be turned on with external timer. Doesn't turn off when filter cover is removed. 5-year warranty. Ease of use better than most.

8> **HOLMES** HAP650 **Four speeds.** 5-year warranty. Similar: GE (Wal-Mart) 106653.

9> **HUNTER** 30170 **Programmable.** 5-year warranty.

10> **KENMORE** (Sears) 83353 **Has usual features and warranty.** Discontinued, but similar Whirlpool AP25030HO is available.

11> **PANASONIC** F-P20HU1 **Four speeds.** Dust sensor and air-quality monitor. Can't be turned on with external timer. Ease of use better than most.

12> **HONEYWELL** Enviracaire 18150 **Can't be placed against wall.** Can't be turned on with external timer. Doesn't turn off when filter cover is removed. 5-year warranty.

13> **HOLMES** HAP625 **Four speeds.** 5-year warranty. Similar: GE (Wal-Mart) 106643.

14> **HONEYWELL** Enviracaire 17000 **Can't be placed against wall.** Can't be turned on with external timer. Doesn't turn off when filter cover is removed. 5-year warranty. Ease of use better than most. Similar: 17005.

15> **SHARPER IMAGE** SI637 Ionic Breeze Quadra Silent Air Purifier **Electronic precipitator, but has no fan.**

Air cleaners, whole-house

If you have a forced-air heating/cooling system, you can make a noticeable improvement in air quality by simply installing a filter. The 3M Filtrete Ultra Allergen Reduction 1250, $15, tops the Ratings for filters. If someone in your home smokes or has a chronic breathing problem, consider adding an electronic precipitator to your system. The three electronic models tested were 30 times more effective than conventional fiberglass furnace filters. But they cost between $400 and $500 plus installation.

Overall Ratings	In performance order		Excellent ● Very good ◐ Good ○ Fair ◑ Poor ●				
BRAND & MODEL, SIMILAR MODELS IN SMALL TYPE	**PRICE**	**ANNUAL COST OF REPLACEMENT FILTERS**	**OVERALL SCORE** 0 P F G VG E 100	**TECHNOLOGY**	**DUST**	**SMOKE**	**AIRFLOW**
PROFESSIONALLY INSTALLED MODELS							
Aprilaire 5000 ①	$500	$42		Electronic precipitator/ Extended media	●	●	◑
Trion SE1400 ①	400	Washable		Electronic precipitator	●	●	◑
Honeywell F50 ① ② F300	400	Washable		Electronic precipitator	●	◑	◑
INSTALL-IT-YOURSELF FILTER							
3M Filtrete Ultra Allergen Reduction 1250	15	60		Pleated electrostatic	●	◑	○
Precisionaire NaturalAire Microparticle	8	30		Pleated electrostatic	◑	◑	◑
3M Filtrete Micro Allergen Reduction 1000	14	56		Pleated electrostatic	◑	◑	◑
3M Filtrete 600	10	40		Pleated electrostatic	◑	◑	◑
Puralator PuroPleat Ultra (PPD)	5	21		Pleated electrostatic	○	●	◑
American Air Filter Dirt Demon UltraPleat	8	31		Pleated electrostatic	○	●	○
Precisionaire NaturalAire	5	20		Pleated	◑	●	○
American Air Filter Dirt Demon Pleated	5	20		Pleated	◑	●	○
Precisionaire EZ Flow	1	11		Fiberglass	●	●	◑
American Air Filter StrataDensity Premium	1	11		Fiberglass	●	●	◑
Purolator PuroPleat (Pur 40)	5	20		Pleated	◑	●	◑
American Air Filter ElectroKlean ①	25	Washable		Electrostatic	◑	●	○

① *Warranted for two or more years.* ② *Available in various sizes.*

See report, page 179. Based on tests published in Consumer Reports in February 2002, with updated prices and availability.

The tests behind the Ratings

Overall score is based mainly on the ability to remove dust and cigarette-smoke particles from a test chamber equipped with ductwork to simulate one room within a multiroom home with forced-air heating and cooling. **Technology** denotes the basic types of filters. **Dust** and **smoke** scores reflect the ability to clear the air of those particles. **Airflow** reflects how freely each product allows air to pass through. Lower-scoring products tend to impede airflow more than conventional filters, which can reduce heating or cooling performance. **Price** is approximate retail. **Annual cost of replacement filters** is based on replacement according to the manufacturer's minimum recommended schedule and is calculated from the suggested retail price.

Barbecue grills

Most grills tested were very good or even excellent. The Weber Summit 450, $2,200, and the Broilmaster P3, $840, performed superbly and offer the style and durability of stainless steel. But the Weber Genesis Silver-B, $450—**a CR Best Buy**—did almost as well and has premium features for less money. Superb performance helps the Weber Genesis Silver-A, $350—another **CR Best Buy**—stand out among less expensive grills. Key features for these models are listed in the table. See the product guide for an explanation of the features.

Excellent ● Very good ◕ Good ○ Fair ◐ Poor ●

Overall Ratings In performance order

KEY NO.	BRAND & MODEL	PRICE	OVERALL SCORE	EVENNESS	GRILLING	FEATURES AND CONVENIENCE
			0 P F G VG E 100			
1	**Weber** Summit 450 26[1]101	$2,200		Excellent	Excellent	Excellent
2	**Broilmaster** P3[BL]	840		Excellent	Excellent	Excellent
3	**Coleman** 4000 HG49810S	500		Excellent	Very good	Excellent
4	**Weber** Genesis Silver-B 228[1]001 **A CR Best Buy**	450		Very good	Excellent	Excellent
5	**Ducane** 1605SHLPE [1]	800		Very good	Very good	Very good
6	**Weber** Genesis Silver-A 227[1]001 **A CR Best Buy**	350		Very good	Very good	Very good
7	**Ducane** 1305SHLPE [1]	700		Very good	Very good	Very good
8	**Ducane** 804SHLP [1]	550		Very good	Very good	Very good
9	**Kenmore** (Sears) 15227 [1]	550		Very good	Excellent	Excellent
10	**Kenmore** (Sears) 15221 [1]	300		Very good	Very good	Very good
11	**Holland** Tradition BH421SG4 [1]	650		Excellent	Good	Good
12	**Fiesta** Advantis 3000 EZT34545	170		Very good	Good	Good
13	**Fiesta** Advantis 1000 EZH30030	120		Very good	Very good	Fair

[1] Price does not include tank ($25 to $30).

See report, page 92. Based on tests published in Consumer Reports in June 2002, with updated prices and availability.

The tests behind the Ratings

Overall score is based on a gas grill's performance, features, and convenience. We tested **evenness** of heating at high and low settings using temperature sensors, then combined the performance scores. Results were verified by searing 15 burgers on the worst and best grills' high setting for 1½ minutes. **Grilling** measures the ability to cook chicken and fish on the low setting. **Features and convenience** evaluates construction and materials, accessory burners and shelves, rack space, and ease of use. **Price** is approximate retail. For similar models, empty brackets indicate a color code.

Recommendations and notes

All grills: Are mounted on patio carts. Have side shelves. **Most grills:** Have a thermometer on the lid. Have a warming rack. Have warranties ranging from 25 years to life for the castings, 3 to 5 years for the burners, 1 or 2 years for other parts. Have a 370- to 425-square-inch cooking area and 300 to 500 square inches of shelf space. Require significant assembly. Have dual burner controls. Use a steel rack full of ceramic or charcoal-like briquettes, or steel triangles or plates, to distribute heat. Have a rotary or push-button igniter, porcelain-coated wire cooking grates and warming rack, a side burner, and four casters. Have spider protectors on the gas-line venturi tubes.

1 ▷ WEBER Summit 450 26[1]101 **Superb performance-but you pay for it.** The most shelf space of tested models. Less assembly than most. Wider than most. Knobs and removable thermometer got hot.

2 ▷ BROILMASTER P3[BL] **A premium grill at a premium price.** Lots of shelf space.

3 ▷ COLEMAN 4000 HG49810S **Excellent for entertaining large groups.** Extra-large cooking area. Lots of shelf space. Less assembly than most. Discontinued, but similar LG40811E is available.

4 ▷ WEBER Genesis Silver-B 228[1]001 **A CR Best Buy Excellent overall.** Lots of shelf space. Removable thermometer got hot. Similar: 228[ ]411, 228[ ]398.

5 ▷ DUCANE 1605SHLPE **Very good, but lower-priced models performed as well.** Extra-large cooking area. Lit-burner indicator. Less assembly than most. No thermometer. Inner handle got hot during use.

6 ▷ WEBER Genesis Silver-A 227[1]001 **A CR Best Buy Similar in appearance to #4,** but narrower. Less cooking area than most. Removable thermometer got hot. Similar: 227[ ]411, 227[ ]398

7 ▷ DUCANE 1305SHLPE **Very good. Lit-burner indicator.** Less assembly than most. Inner handle got hot during use. No thermometer.

8 ▷ DUCANE 804SHLP **Similar in appearance to #10, but smaller and only one burner.** Less cooking area than most. Must use match to light grill. Discontinued, but similar 1005SHLPE with igniter and spider protector is available.

9 ▷ KENMORE (Sears) 15227 **More shelf space than most but less warming-rack space.** No spider protector. Smoker tray. Infrared rotisserie burner. Warranty shorter than most.

10 ▷ KENMORE (Sears) 15221 **Very good.** More shelf space than most, but smaller cooking area and less warming-rack space. No spider protector. Warranty shorter than most. Similar: 15223.

11 ▷ HOLLAND Tradition BH421SG4 **Can steam and smoke as well as grill.** Smaller cooking area than most. Only one temperature setting. Smoker-drawer knob got hot. No warming rack. Similar: Heritage BH421SG5.

12 ▷ FIESTA Advantis 3000 EZT34545 **Very good, but smaller cooking area than most and less shelf space.** Cart judged less sturdy than others. No thermometer. Similar: EZA34545.

13 ▷ FIESTA Advantis 1000 EZH30030 **Good.** Smaller cooking area than most. Flared up more than others. Cart judged less sturdy than others. No thermometer. Similar: EZA30030.

Features at a glance — Barbecue grills

Tested products (keyed to the Ratings) Key no. / Brand	Burners			Grates		Fuel gauge	Electronic ignitor
	Long warranty	3 or 4	Side	Porcelain-cast iron	Stainless		
1 ▷ Weber		•			•	•	
2 ▷ Broilmaster	•				•		•
3 ▷ Coleman		•			•	•	•
4 ▷ Weber	•	•				•	
5 ▷ Ducane	•				•		
6 ▷ Weber	•					•	
7 ▷ Ducane	•				•		
8 ▷ Ducane	•				•		
9 ▷ Kenmore		•	•	•			•
10 ▷ Kenmore		•					•
11 ▷ Holland	•				•		
12 ▷ Fiesta			•				
13 ▷ Fiesta							

Camcorders

If you want to try video editing or downloading to the web, invest in a digital camcorder. The Sony DCR-TRV25, $900, Sony DCR-TRV240, $600, and Canon ZR45MC, $700, are worthy choices. Most analog models were rated good and cost hundreds of dollars less. Picture quality, though generally a notch below digital, is still perfectly fine. Consider the Hi8 Sony CCD-TRV608, $400, or the CCD-TRV308, $350.

KEY NO.	BRAND AND MODEL	PRICE	FORMAT	OVERALL SCORE	PICTURE QUALITY	EASE OF USE	IMAGE STABILIZER	WEIGHT (LBS)
DIGITAL MODELS								
1	**Sony** DCR-TRV25	$900	MiniDV		◉	◒	◒	1.6
2	**Sony** DCR-PC120BT	2,000	MiniDV		◒	○	◉	1.5
3	**Panasonic** PV-DV402	800	MiniDV		◉	◒	●	1.4
4	**Panasonic** PV-DC152	800	MiniDV		◉	○	◔	1.2
5	**Sony** DCR-TRV240	600	D8		◒	○	○	2.1
6	**Sony** DCR-TRV140	500	D8		◒	◒	●	2.2
7	**Canon** ZR45MC	700	MiniDV		◒	◒	○	1.4
8	**JVC** GR-DVL920U	900	MiniDV		◒	○	◔	1.5
9	**Canon** Optura 100MC	1,500	MiniDV		◒	○	○	1.7
10	**Panasonic** PV-DV52	500	MiniDV		◒	○	●	1.4
11	**Panasonic** PV-DV102	600	MiniDV		◒	○	●	1.4
12	**JVC** GR-DVL120U	500	MiniDV		◒	○	◔	1.5
13	**Sony** DCR-IP7BT	1,700	MicroMV		◒	◔	●	0.8
14	**Hitachi** DZ-MV200A	900	8cm DVD-RAM, 8cm DVD-R		○	○	◒	1.8
15	**JVC** GR-DVM76U	750	MiniDV		○	○	◔	1.2
16	**Samsung** SC-D80	475	MiniDV		○	◒	○	1.4
17	**Sharp** VL-NZ50U	500	MiniDV		○	○	●	1.2
ANALOG MODELS								
18	**Sony** CCD-TRV608	400	Hi8		○	◒	○	2.2
19	**Sony** CCD-TRV308	350	Hi8		◒	◒	●	2.2
20	**JVC** GR-SXM240U	300	SVHS-C		○	◔	○	2.4
21	**Sony** CCD-TRV108	300	Hi8		○	◒	NA	2.1
22	**Samsung** SC-L700	270	Hi8		○	◒	NA	2.0
23	**Panasonic** PV-L352	280	VHS-C		◔	○	◔	2.6
24	**Sharp** VL-AD260U	360	Hi8		○	○	◔	2.0
25	**Canon** ES75	230	Hi8		◔	○	NA	1.9
26	**Sharp** VL-AH131U	280	Hi8		◔	○	NA	1.9

Overall Ratings — In performance order

Excellent ● Very good ◒ Good ○ Fair ◔ Poor ●

Overall score scale: 0 — P F G VG E — 100

See report, page 55. Based on tests published in Consumer Reports in November 2002, with updated prices and availability.

The tests behind the Ratings

Format lists the recording format used. **Overall score** mainly reflects SP picture quality and ease of use. **Picture quality** is based on the judgments of trained panelists, who viewed still images shot at standard (SP) tape speed. **Ease of use** takes into account ergonomics, weight, how accurately the viewfinders framed the scene being shot, and measurements of the LCD's contrast. **Image stabilizer** scores reflect how well the circuitry worked, for models that have it. "NA" in a column means the camcorder lacks it. **Weight** is our measurement. **Price** is the approximate retail.

Recommendations and notes

Models listed as similar should offer performance comparable to the tested model's, although features may differ.

Most of these camcorders have: Rechargeable battery pack. AC adapter/battery charger. A/V cable. Playpack adapter (VHS-C and S-VHS-C models only). Ability to load tape, plug in power, or change battery when mounted on tripod. 10x optical zoom. 2.5-inch color LCD viewer. Selection of built-in autoexposure programs. Audio and video fade. Backlight compensation. High-speed manual shutter. Image stabilizer. LCD viewer. Brightness control. Manual aperture, shutter speed, focus, and white balance controls. Quick review. S-video output jack (not on VHS-C). Tape counter. **Most digital camcorders also have:** FireWire or iLink connection, digital still feature.

Optical zoom is as stated by the manufacturer. Audio frequency response, when recording with the built-in microphone, was very good and relatively noise-free for most camcorders. Most camcorders with LP/EP mode yielded same picture quality as in SP mode. In dim lighting, most camcorders yielded a tolerable picture quality.

DIGITAL MODELS

1> **SONY** DCR-TRV25 **Feature-laden, with the least audio noise among tested models.** Includes medium-resolution digital still. Similar DCR-TRV27 has a large LCD. Can't load tape if mounted on tripod.

2> **SONY** DCR-PC120BT **Excellent image stabilization in a feature-laden model, but poor performance in low light.** Includes Bluetooth wireless interface and novel communications capability to send video clips, stills, or e-mail over the Internet without a computer. Includes medium-resolution still feature. Can't load tape if mounted on tripod. Similar DCR-TRV27 has a large LCD.

3> **PANASONIC** PV-DV402 **Excellent in performance in good lighting, but poor image stabilization and zoom is noisy.** Barely adequate in low light, but very good if built-in light and manual controls are used. Includes a very large LCD viewer (3.5 in.) and medium-resolution digital-still feature. Similar PVDV-202 has typical 2.5 in. LCD. CCD and battery warranties on the short side (6 mo. and 10 days, respectively).

4> **PANASONIC** PV-DC152 **Very good overall and lightweight, but LCD viewer hard to see in bright light.** Short warranties for image sensor and battery (6 mo. and 10 days, respectively). Poor picture quality in low light but using manual controls helps. Lacks digital-still feature (similar PV-DC252 has it).

5> **SONY** DCR-TRV240 **Moderately priced and very good overall, with a 25x zoom that's among the longest.** Can play back analog tapes in Hi8 and 8mm formats. But LCD viewer hard to see in bright light. No manual white balance. Can't load tape if mounted on tripod. Lacks digital-still feature (similar DCR-TRV340 has it).

Features at a glance — Camcorders

Tested products (keyed to the Ratings) Key no. / Brand	LCD viewer size, in.	Battery life, min.	Full auto switch	Quick review	Video light	A/V input	Microphone jack
CONVENTIONAL DIGITAL MODELS							
1> Sony	2.5	145/115		•		•	•
2> Sony	2.5	130/110		•		•	•
3> Panasonic	3.5	N.S.		•	•		•
4> Panasonic	2.5	130/95		•			•
5> Sony	2.5	100/80		•		•	•
6> Sony	2.5	110/85		•	•		
7> Canon	2.5	90/75	•	•		•	•
8> JVC	3.5	70/55	•		•		•
9> Canon	2.5	120/100	•	•		•	•
10> Panasonic	2.5	N.S.		•	•		
11> Panasonic	2.5	NA		•	•		
12> JVC	2.5	75/60	•				
13> Sony	2.5	80/65		•		•	
14> Hitachi	2.5	115-130/100-115				•	•
15> JVC	2.5	65/50	•				
16> Samsung	2.5	120/90	•	•			•
17> Sharp	3.0	-/90	•				
ANALOG MODELS							
18> Sony	3.0	165/100		•	•		
19> Sony	2.5	165/120		•	•		
20> JVC	2.5	95/80	•	•	•		
21> Sony	2.5	165/120		•			
22> Samsung	2.5	130/90	•	•	•		
23> Panasonic	2.5	70/55			•		
24> Sharp	3.5	-/90					
25> Canon	-	150/-	•	•	•		
26> Sharp	3.0	-/95	•				

Recommendations and notes

6 ▷ **SONY** DCR-TRV140 **Very good, with 20x zoom.** Good in low light, and easy to use overall, but poor image stabilization and noisy audio. Cannot play back analog tapes. Lacks digital-still feature, manual white balance.

7 ▷ **CANON** ZR45MC **Lightweight, with no major flaws.** Very good and easy to use, with large controls, 18x zoom, good low-light performance (on manual setting), and flutter-free audio. ZR45MC and similar ZR50MC have low-resolution digital still. ZR40 lacks digital still. Tape-head warranty on the short side (3 mo.). Can't load tape if mounted on tripod. No backlight compensation switch.

8 ▷ **JVC** GR-DVL920U **Very good overall.** Poor in low light but becomes good if video light and manual settings are used. This and similar DVL820U have large LCD viewer (3.5 in.), but it's hard to view in bright light. DVL725U has 2.5 in. LCD. Has medium-resolution digital-still feature. Battery life is under one hour. No quick review. Short warranties for image sensor and battery (3 mo.).

9 ▷ **CANON** Optura 100MC **Very good overall, with medium-resolution digital-still feature.** Includes features advanced users might want (microphone jack, hot shoe, A/V input), which bring up the price. Tape-head warranty on the short side (3 mo.). Poor low-light picture quality, but using its low-light program helps. Can't load tape if mounted on tripod. No backlight compensation switch.

10 ▷ **PANASONIC** PV-DV52 **Similar to the PV-DV102 but without the digital-still camera feature.**

11 ▷ **PANASONIC** PV-DV102 **Very good overall, and good in low light if built-in light and manual settings used.** Includes medium-resolution digital-still feature. But image stabilizer is poor, and its zoom is noisy. Short warranties for image sensor and battery (6 mo. and 10 days, respectively). LCD viewer hard to view in bright light. No S-video jack.

12 ▷ **JVC** GR-DVL120U **Low-light performance improves if manual settings are used.** Short warranty on image sensor and battery. No audio fade. Can't load tape if mounted on tripod. Similar GR-DVL520U and GR-DVL720U have medium-resolution digital still. GR-DVL720U has a large LCD viewer. Has 16x zoom. Similar models have video light, 10x zoom.

13 ▷ **SONY** DCR-IP7BT **Good overall and very compact, but with cumbersome menu system and uses new recording format (MicroMV tape).** Includes Bluetooth wireless interface and novel communications capability to send video clips, stills, or e-mail over the Internet without a computer. Poor low-light performance and image stabilizer. Can't load tape if mounted on tripod.

14 ▷ **HITACHI** DZ-MV200A **Records directly onto disks.** You can navigate a disk randomly via thumbnail previews. No backlight-compensation switch. Fair picture quality in standard mode.

15 ▷ **JVC** GR-DVM76U **There are better digital choices.** Short warranty on image sensor and battery.

16 ▷ **SAMSUNG** SC-D80 **There are better digital choices.** Can't load tape if mounted on tripod. SC-D86 adds digital still.

17 ▷ **SHARP** VL-NZ50U **Lacks an eyepiece, quick review, and S-video jack.** Good overall, with a larger 3-inch LCD viewer but otherwise few frills. Poor image stabilizer. Zoom is noisy. High-speed manual shutter. Battery warranty on the short side (1 mo.). Lacks digital-still feature (similars VL-NZ100U and VL-NZ150U have it).

ANALOG MODELS

18 ▷ **SONY** CCD-TRV608 **Good, very easy to use, with 20x zoom and a larger 3-inch LCD viewer.** Good in low light. Picture quality drops a notch at LP speed. No manual white balance.

19 ▷ **SONY** CCD-TRV308 **Good, very easy to use, with 20x zoom.** Good in low light. This model offers poorer image stabilization, but better picture at SP speed than on the CCD-TRV608. No manual white balance.

20 ▷ **JVC** GR-SXM240U **A good, basic unit with 16x zoom and good low-light performance.** VHS playback on a VCR is a plus, but has inferior audio. LCD viewer hard to see in bright light, and camcorder not as easy to use as many. Short warranties for image sensor and battery (3 mo.). Similar SXM340U has 2.5 in. LCD; SXM740U has 3.5 in. LCD.

21 ▷ **SONY** CCD-TRV108 **A good and basic camcorder with 20x zoom.** Lack of image stabilizer and video light help hold the price. Picture quality drops a notch at LP speed. No manual white balance.

22 ▷ **SAMSUNG** SC-L700 **Good, basic, easy to use, and very inexpensive as camcorders go, with a 22x zoom.** No image stabilizer, slow recording speed, or manual aperture control.

23 ▷ **PANASONIC** PV-L352 **Good overall, with 20x zoom.** VHS playback on a VCR is a plus, but background noise and flutter mar audio quality, and battery life is under one hour. Eyepiece not too accurate at framing scenes. Short warranties for image sensor and battery (6 mo. and 10 days, respectively). No quick review, tape counter, manual aperture, or white balance controls. Similar: PV-L4S2, PV-L552, PV-L652.

24 ▷ **SHARP** VL-AD260U **There are better choices.** No slow speed, eyepiece, S-video jack. Short battery warranty.

25 ▷ **CANON** ES75 **There are better choices.** No slow speed, LCD viewer, image stabilizer. Short warranty on image sensor.

26 ▷ **SHARP** VL-AH131U **Has 16x zoom, but lacks an eyepiece and S-video jack.** Has a hard-to-use menu and no image stabilizer or slow recording speed. Fair performance overall, and battery warranty on the short side (1 mo.).

Chain saws

Gasoline-powered saws offer greater mobility and better cutting performance than their electric counter-parts. If you're willing to pay a premium for the fastest cutting, consider the Husqvarna 345, $270, or Husqvarna 350, $300. But several **CR Best Buys** also performed well and cost less. For lighter-duty sawing, consider an electric, which costs and weighs less than gas saws and starts with the squeeze of a trigger. The Poulan Handyman Plus ES300, $90 is competent and easy to use. Key features for all these models are listed in the table on page 206. See the product guide for an explanation of features.

Overall Ratings — In performance order

Rating legend: Excellent, Very good, Good, Fair, Poor

KEY NO.	BRAND & MODEL	PRICE	WEIGHT (LB.)	OVERALL SCORE	CUTTING SPEED	HANDLING	SAFETY	EASE OF USE	EASE OF SERVICE
	GASOLINE MODELS								
1	**Echo** CS-4400	$320	15.0		Very good	Excellent	Very good	Very good	Fair
2	**Husqvarna** 345	270	14.0		Excellent	Very good	Very good	Very good	Fair
3	**Husqvarna** 350	300	14.5		Excellent	Very good	Very good	Very good	Fair
4	**Craftsman** (Sears) Gray Chassis 35046 **A CR Best Buy**	150	13.5		Very good	Very good	Excellent	Very good	Good
5	**Poulan Pro** 295 **A CR Best Buy**	200	14.5		Very good	Very good	Very good	Excellent	Fair
6	**Husqvarna** 136 **A CR Best Buy**	180	12.5		Very good	Very good	Excellent	Very good	Fair
7	**Solo** 636	260	11.5		Very good	Very good	Very good	Good	Poor
8	**Poulan Pro** 260	190	14.0		Very good	Good	Excellent	Good	Good
9	**Poulan** Wood Master 2550	160	13.5		Very good	Good	Fair	Very good	Good
10	**Poulan** Woodsman 2150	130	13.0		Very good	Very good	Fair	Very good	Fair
11	**Poulan** Wild Thing 2375	150	13.5		Very good	Good	Very good	Very good	Fair
12	**Poulan** Wood Shark 1950	110	13.0		Very good	Very good	Fair	Very good	Fair
	ELECTRIC MODELS								
13	**Poulan** Handyman Plus ES300	90	10.5		Good	Very good	Good	Excellent	Excellent
14	**Remington** 100089-05	60	7.0		Good	Very good	Good	Good	Poor
15	**Remington** 075762J	40	7.0		Fair	Fair	Good	Good	Poor
16	**Remington** Limb N' Trim 099178H	40	5.5		Poor	Fair	Good	Good	Poor

See report, page 94. Based on tests published in Consumer Reports in May 2001, with updated prices and availability.

The tests behind the Ratings

Overall score is based on cutting speed, handling, safety, convenience, ease of service, and noise. **Cutting speed** denotes how quickly a saw cut through a maple beam with a 10-inch-square cross section. **Handling** reflects lack of vibration and ease of vertical and horizontal sawing, balance, weight, and handle comfort. **Safety** denotes resistance to kickback, protection from muffler contact, and safety equipment. **Ease of use** denotes ease of adjusting chain tension and, for gas saws, securing when starting. **Ease of service** denotes how easy it is to add and check bar oil and refuel gas models. **Price** is the estimated average, based on a national survey. The Recommendations and notes includes cubic centimeters (cc) of engine displacement for gas models and motor amperage for electrics, based on manufacturer specifications, as well as bar length.

Recommendations and notes

Models listed as similar should offer performance comparable to the tested models, although features may differ.

Most chain saws: Are claimed to conform to an American National Standards Institute (ANSI) safety standard (for gas saws) or an Underwriters Laboratory standard (for electrics), which includes a measurement of kickback intensity. Showed relatively mild kickback intensity in our tests. Have labels claiming compliance with at least EPA/CARB Tier I emissions requirements. (EPA/CARB Tier II began appearing in 2002.) Registered between 90 and 106 dBA at the operator's ear. Have a one-year warranty against defects in material and workmanship.

GASOLINE MODELS

1> ECHO CS-4400 **Easy vertical and horizontal cuts.** Kickback moderate without tip guard. Hard-to-use ignition switch. 43.6 cc/16 in.

2> HUSQVARNA 345 **Fast and impressive.** Inconvenient choke location. Kickback greater than most, but acceptable. 45 cc/16 in.

3> HUSQVARNA 350 **Impressive overall.** Kickback greater than most, but acceptable. Inconvenient choke location. 50 cc/18 in.

4> CRAFTSMAN (Sears) Gray Chassis 35046 **A CR Best Buy Strong performance at a low price.** Extra-large filler caps. 36 cc/16 in.

5> POULAN Pro 295 **A CR Best Buy Competent, and more convenient than most.** Kickback moderate. 46 cc/20 in.

6> HUSQVARNA 136 **A CR Best Buy A light, impressive saw at a low price.** Hard-to-use ignition switch. 36 cc/14 in.

7> SOLO 636 **Less convenient than most.** Foot room tight in rear handle. Bar-oil and fuel caps hard to grasp. Kickback moderate. No ANSI label. 36.3 cc/16 in.

8> POULAN Pro 260 **Competent overall.** Extra-large filler caps. Inconvenient choke location. 42 cc/18 in.

9> POULAN Wood Master 2550 **Competent overall.** Extra-large filler caps. Hard-to-use ignition switch. Inconvenient choke location. 42 cc/18 in.

10> POULAN Woodsman 2150 **Competent and low-priced.** Extra-large filler caps. Hard-to-use ignition switch. 36 cc/16 in.

11> POULAN Wild Thing 2375 **Competent and low-priced.** Extra-large filler caps. Lots of vibration. Hard-to-use ignition switch. 42 cc/ 18 in.

12> POULAN Wood Shark 1950 **Competent and low-priced, but few features.** Extra-large filler caps. Hard-to-use ignition switch. 36 cc/ 14 in.

ELECTRIC MODELS

13> POULAN Handyman Plus ES300 **More convenient than most, though motor makes horizontal sawing awkward.** Kickback moderate. 12 amp/16 in.

14> REMINGTON 100089-05 **Less convenient than most.** Lacks wraparound top handle. Kickback moderate. Hard-to-use trigger lockout. Small bar-oil filler. 11.5 amp/16 in.

15> REMINGTON 075762J **Less convenient than most.** Lacks wraparound top handle. Hard-to-use trigger lockout. Small bar-oil filler. Kickback moderate. 11.5 amp/14 in.

16> REMINGTON Limb N' Trim 099178H **Less convenient than most.** Lacks wraparound top handle. Kickback moderate. Hard-to-use trigger lockout. Small bar-oil filler. 8 amp/14 in. Similar: 34125.

Features at a glance Chain saws

Tested products (keyed to the Ratings) Key no. Brand	Chain brake	Reduced-kickback bar	Case or sheath	Effective bucking spikes	Choke/on-off switch	Easy chain adjuster	Anti-vibration	Visible bar-oil level	Filler-cap retainers
GASOLINE MODELS									
1> Echo	•			•			•		•
2> Husqvarna	•		•	•	•	•	•		•
3> Husqvarna	•		•	•	•	•	•		•
4> Craftsman	•	•	•		•	•			•
5> Poulan Pro	•			•		•	•		•
6> Husqvarna	•	•					•		•
7> Solo	•	•							•
8> Poulan Pro	•	•							•
9> Poulan		•							•
10> Poulan		•			•				
11> Poulan		•							•
12> Poulan		•			•				
ELECTRIC MODELS									
13> Poulan		•	•		•			•	
14> Remington		•	•		•			•	
15> Remington		•	•		•			•	
16> Remington	•	•			•			•	

Circular saws

If you're a serious do-it-yourselfer, look for a top-rated circular saw. But for occasional use, you can get a fine saw for as little as $60. Two **CR Best Buys** represent an excellent combination of performance and good price: the Makita 5740NB, $90, and the Craftsman 10842, $80. Among lower-priced saws, consider the Skil 5275-05 Classic, and the Craftsman 10841, both $60. Battery-powered saws such as the DeWalt DW939K, $260, lack the power for tough jobs but might do for occasional light work. For heavy-duty use, consider a top-rated model such as the Milwaukee 6390-21, $140, or the Porter-Cable 347K, $120. The worm-drive DeWalt DW378GK, $155, outperformed the others in its class, but was noticeably slower than the best of the regular saws.

Overall Ratings — In performance order

Ratings key: Excellent ● · Very good ◕ · Good ○ · Fair ◑ · Poor ◔

KEY NO	BRAND & MODEL	PRICE	OVERALL SCORE (0–100, P F G VG E)	CUTTING SPEED	POWER	EASE OF USE	CONSTRUCTION	WEIGHT (LB.)	AMPS
REGULAR SAWS									
1	Milwaukee 6390-21	$140		●	●	●	●	11	15
2	Porter-Cable 347K	120		●	◕	●	●	10½	13
3	DeWalt DW369CSK	140		●	●	◕	●	11	15
4	DeWalt DW364K	160		●	●	◕	●	12½	15
5	Makita 5740NB A CR Best Buy	90		●	○	●	◕	8½	10.5
6	Hitachi C7SBK	110		●	◕	◕	●	10½	13
7	Makita 5007NBK	130		●	●	○	●	11	13
8	Craftsman (Sears) 10842 A CR Best Buy	80		●	●	◕	◕	11	13
9	Craftsman (Sears) Professional 27108	100		◕	●	◕	◕	11	15
10	Bosch 1658K	110		●	◕	○	◕	11	13
11	Skil 5275-05 Classic	60		◕	○	○	○	11	12
12	Craftsman (Sears) 10841	60		◕	◕	○	○	10½	12
13	Black & Decker CS1000	40		○	◕	○	○	11	11
14	Black & Decker CS1010K	50		○	◕	○	○	11	12
BATTERY-POWERED SAWS									
15	DeWalt DW939K	260		◕	●	○	○	8½	18
16	Craftsman (Sears) Professional 27119	200		○	●	◕	○	10	18
17	Makita BSS730SHK	480		○	●	○	◕	9½	24
18	Bosch 1659K	300		○	●	○	○	9	18
WORM-DRIVE SAWS									
19	DeWalt DW378GK	155		◕	●	◕	●	13	15
20	Skil HD77	160		◔	●	○	◕	16	13
21	Craftsman (Sears) Professional 2761	140		◔	●	○	◕	16	13

See report, page 125. Based on tests published in Consumer Reports in August 2002, with updated prices and availability.

The tests behind the Ratings

Overall score is based mainly on cutting speed, power, and ease of use. **Cutting speed** is how fast each saw crosscut and ripped a series of 2x12 pine and a 24-inch sheet of ¾-inch-thick hardboard; the best were up to four times as fast as the slowest. **Power,** measured with a dynamometer, indicates how well a saw can handle thick or hard wood. **Ease of use** shows how easy it was to use the cutting guide, adjust depth and bevel, and change blades, as well as our judgment of the saw's balance and handle comfort. **Construction** includes our assessment of bearings, access to motor brushes, and ruggedness of the base, housing, and adjustments. **Weight** is to the nearest half-pound with blade and, for cordless models, battery. **Price** is approximate retail.

Recommendations and notes

All models have: Blade guard that retracts when you push the saw forward. Cutting depth adjustable to at least 3½ inches. Cutting angle adjustable to 45 degrees. Most have: Carbide 7¼-inch blade. Blade lock to make blade changes easier. One-year warranty.

REGULAR SAWS

1 **MILWAUKEE** 6390-21 **Excellent.** Adjustable handle. Heavy-duty base.

2 **PORTER-CABLE** 347K **Excellent.** Heavy-duty base. Blade-wrench storage. Extra-long cord. Left-handed version readily available.

3 **DEWALT** DW369CSK **Excellent.** Blade brake. Heavy-duty base. Earlier version of saw was subject of safety recall.

4 **DEWALT** DW364K **Excellent.** Blade brake. Heavy-duty base.

5 **MAKITA** 5740NB **A CR Best Buy Excellent.** Heavy-duty base. Safety interlock button. Attached wrench for blade change. Newest version has different front handle.

6 **HITACHI** C7SBK **Excellent.** Heavy-duty base. Small front handle. Additional backside cutting-line guide adds accuracy.

7 **MAKITA** 5007NBK **Excellent.** Heavy-duty base. Sharp bevel-angle guide can contact fingers on front handle.

8 **CRAFTSMAN** (Sears) 10842 **A CR Best Buy Excellent.** Blade-wrench storage.

9 **CRAFTSMAN** (Sears) Professional 27108 **Very good.** Heavy-duty base. Extra-long cord. Padded switch.

10 **BOSCH** 1658K **Very good.** Blade-wrench storage.

11 **SKIL** 5275-05 Classic **Good.** Safety interlock button, but it's awkward to use. Blade-wrench storage. Short cord. No blade lock. 2-yr. warranty.

12 **CRAFTSMAN** (Sears) 10841 **Good.** Not supplied with carbide blade. Short cord. Blade-wrench storage.

13 **BLACK & DECKER** CS1000 **Good.** Not supplied with carbide blade or blade lock. Short cord. Base less substantial. Blade-wrench storage. 2-yr. warranty.

14 **BLACK & DECKER** CS1010K **Good.** Not supplied with carbide blade. Short cord. No blade lock. Base less substantial. Blade-wrench storage. 2-yr. warranty.

BATTERY-POWERED SAWS

15 **DEWALT** DW939K **Good.** Safety interlock button. Blade-wrench storage.

16 **CRAFTSMAN** (Sears) Professional 27119 **Good.** Safety interlock button. Blade-wrench storage.

17 **MAKITA** BSS730SHK **Good.** Blade brake. Heavy-duty base. Safety interlock button, but it's awkward to use. Blade-wrench storage. Bevel adjustment has fasteners front and rear.

18 **BOSCH** 1659K **Good.** Blade brake. Safety interlock button, but it's awkward to use. Blade-wrench storage.

WORM-DRIVE SAWS

19 **DEWALT** DW378GK **Excellent.** Heavy-duty base. Not double-insulated.

20 **SKIL** HD77 **Good.** Extra-long cord. Not supplied with carbide blade. Poor dust ejection. Not double-insulated.

21 **CRAFTSMAN** (Sears) Professional 2761 **Good.** Not supplied with carbide blade. Not double-insulated. Poor dust ejection.

Coffeemakers

Most automatic drip coffeemakers are capable of brewing good coffee, so focus on convenience features such as clear cup markings and easy-to-read displays and controls. The top-ratedBraun Flavor Select KF 187, $75, and Cuisinart Brew Central DCC-1200, $100, have a host of handy features. For less money, consider any of the four **CR Best Buys:** the Black & Decker Smart Brew Plus DCM2500, $35, Black & Decker Smart Brew DCM2000, $25, Braun Aromaster KF 400, $20, and Mr. Coffee AR12, $20. Among thermal-carafe models, the programmable Mr. Coffee URTX83, $65, was easiest to use.

Overall Ratings
In performance order

KEY NO.	BRAND & MODEL	PRICE	OVERALL SCORE	AUTO ON/OFF
	REGULAR MODELS			
1	**Braun** Flavor Select KF 187	$75		✔
2	**Cuisinart** Brew Central DCC-1200	100		✔
3	**Black & Decker** Smart Brew Plus DCM2500 A CR Best Buy	35		✔
4	**Krups** ProAroma 12 Plus Time 453-71	100		✔
5	**Black & Decker** Smart Brew DCM2000 A CR Best Buy	25		
6	**KitchenAid** Pro 12 KCM400WH	100		✔
7	**Braun** Aromaster KF 400 A CR Best Buy	20		
8	**Mr. Coffee** AR12 A CR Best Buy	20		
9	**Kenmore** (Sears) KCM12WR	45		✔
10	**Hamilton Beach** Flavor Plus 43421	40		✔
11	**Proctor-Silex** Easy Morning 41331	20		
12	**Black & Decker** Spacemaker ODC325	75		✔
13	**Mr. Coffee** AD10	25		
14	**Mr. Coffee** PL12	20		
15	**Mr. Coffee** PLX20	30		✔
16	**Proctor-Silex** Simply Coffee 46871	20		✔
17	**Proctor-Silex** Simply Coffee 46801	20		
	THERMAL-CARAFE MODELS			
18	**Mr. Coffee** Thermal Carafe URTX83	65		✔
19	**Capresso** MT500 440	160		✔
20	**Krups** AromaControl Therm Time 199-73	100		✔
21	**Mr. Coffee** Thermal Gourmet TC80	43		
22	**Black & Decker** Thermal Select TCM300	35		

See report, page 16. Based on tests published in Consumer Reports in December 2002.

The tests behind the Ratings

Overall score is based on convenience. Tests included ease of filling, loading grounds, pouring, cleaning, and using controls. **Auto on/off** models are programmable, have a clock, and shut off after two hours. Thermal models shut off immediately. **Price** is approximate retail.

Recommendations and notes

Models listed as similar should offer performance comparable to the tested model, although features may differ.

Except as noted, all: Have drip-stop, "on" light, one-year warranty, clear cup markings in reservoir and/or on front-facing fill tube, or have removable reservoir with markings. Load without removing basket. Glass carafes have markings; most have flip-top lid.

REGULAR MODELS

1> **BRAUN** Flavor Select KF 187 **Excellent and feature-rich, but a bit expensive.** 12 cups. Adjustable hotplate. Brew-strength/small-batch controls. Water filter. Markings on side, but easy to read. Harder to program. Discontinued, but may still be available.

2> **CUISINART** Brew Central DCC-1200 **Excellent, with many features and unusual design, but expensive.** 12 cups. Adjustable hotplate. Small-batch control. Water filter. Cleaning cycle. Remove lid to fill carafe. Three-year warranty.

3> **BLACK & DECKER** Smart Brew Plus DCM2500 **A CR Best Buy Very good, with good price and features.** 12 cups. Long cord; storage. But markings on side. Tested model sold only at Kmart. Similar: DCM 2575, DCM 2550.

4> **KRUPS** ProAroma 12 Plus Time 453-71 **Very good and feature-rich, but expensive.** 12 cups. Adjustable hotplate. Brew-strength/small-batch controls. Water filter. Long cord; storage. Remove lid to fill carafe. Harder to program. Similar: 453-42.

5> **BLACK & DECKER** Smart Brew DCM2000 **A CR Best Buy Inexpensive and very good, if very basic. 12 cups.** But markings on side. Tested model sold only at Kmart and Target. Similar: DCM2050, DCM2075.

6> **KITCHENAID** Pro 12 KCM400WH **Very good and feature-rich, but expensive.** 12 cups. Brew-strength/small-batch controls. Water filter. Shows time elapsed since brewing. Carafe lid harder to clean than most. Filter basket over flowed with some coffee and filter combinations. Three-prong plug. Similar: KCM4000B.

7> **BRAUN** Aromaster KF 400 **A CR Best Buy Inexpensive and very good, if very basic.** 10 cups.

8> **MR. COFFEE** AR12 **A CR Best Buy Inexpensive and very good, if very basic.** 12 cups. Similar: AR13, ARX20, ARX23.

9> **KENMORE** (Sears) KCM12WR **Very good, with small footprint, but inconveniences.** 12 cups. Small-batch control. Long cord, with storage. But must hunt for on/off button. "On" light not easily visible; display hard to read. Similar: KCM12BLKR.

10> **HAMILTON BEACH** Flavor Plus 43421 **Very good.** 10 cups. Brew-strength control. Long cord; storage. Two-year warranty. Similar: 43424, 43425,43321

11> **PROCTOR SILEX** Easy Morning 41331 **Very good, but inconveniences.** 12 cups. Brew-strength control. But carafe harder to control when full. Two-year warranty. Similar: 41334.

12> **BLACK & DECKER** Spacemaker ODC325 **Very good if a bit expensive; mounts under cabinet.** 12 cups. Basket, reservoir pull out. Long cord; storage. But less brew than other 12-cup models. Sold only at Kmart, Target, Wal-Mart. Similar: ODC325N.

13> **MR. COFFEE** AD10 **Inexpensive and very good, if very basic.** 10 cups. Basket harder to open/close properly.

14> **MR. COFFEE** PL 12 **A basic, low-cost model.** 12 cups. Basket harder to close (overflowed when not closed securely) and harder to replace on hinges. Similar: PL 13.

15> **MR. COFFEE** PLX20 **Very good and reasonably priced, but inconveniences.** 12 cups. Basket harder to close (overflowed when not closed securely) and harder to replace. Display hard to read. Auto setting not obvious. Similar: PLX23.

16> **PROCTOR-SILEX** Simply Coffee 46871 **Basic model.** 12 cups. Brew-strength control. But basket won't sit upright on counter. Carafe harder to control when full. Six-month warranty. Similar: 46831.

17> **PROCTOR-SILEX** Simply Coffee 46801 **Inexpensive, but lacks conveniences.** 12 cups. But basket won't sit upright on counter. Carafe harder to control when full. Must remove basket to load. No drip-stop or "On" light. Uncoated hotplate. Markings on carafe only. Six-month warranty.

THERMAL-CARAFE MODELS

18> **MR. COFFEE** Thermal Carafe URTX83 **Very good, with helpful features.** 8 cups. Removable reservoir. Cleaning cycle.

19> **CAPRESSO** MT500 440 **Very good, but expensive; sleek silver-metal-and-black design and many features.** 10 cups. Small-batch setting. Water filter. Carafe easier to handle than other thermals. Long cord; storage. Fill tube with markings on side.

20> **KRUPS** AromaControl Therm Time 199-73 **Very good, but expensive; with contemporary rounded design.** 10 cups. Long cord; storage. Similar: 199-46, 197-46, 197-73, 229-45, 229-46, 229-70.

21> **MR. COFFEE** Thermal Gourmet TC80 **Very good, and reasonably priced for a thermal-carafe model.** 8 cups. Long cord; storage. Similar: TC81.

22> **BLACK & DECKER** Thermal Select TCM300 **Reasonably priced for a thermal-carafe model, but inconveniences.** 8 cups. "On" light not easily visible. Basket hard to open/close. Sold only at Target. Similar: TCM508, TCM500.

Cooktops

Electric smoothtops offer quick heating and easy-to-clean glass surfaces. The top-rated Frigidaire Gallery GLEC30S8A, $500, is the lowest-priced model and also a **CR Best Buy.** At the other end of the price spectrum, the GE Profile JP938WC, $1,200, offers features such as touch controls, pan sensors, a timer, and a child lockout. Gas cooktops provide easily adjustable flame controls and choices ranging from basic to pro-style. Among gas models, a fine choice is the Jenn-Air CCG2523, $750, a **CR Best Buy.** You can get a stylish, stainless-steel look from the top-rated GE Monogram ZGU375NSD, but it'll cost you $1,300. The lowest-priced gas cooktop, the Frigidaire Gallery GLGC36S8A, $600, offers good performance overall.

KEY NO	BRAND & MODEL	PRICE	OVERALL SCORE	SPEED OF HEATING	SIMMER
30-INCH ELECTRIC SMOOTHTOPS					
1	**Frigidaire** Gallery GLEC30S8A[S] **A CR Best Buy**	$500		◖	◉
2	**GE** Profile JP930TC[WW]	790		◖	◉
3	**GE** Profile JP938WC[WW]	1,200		◖	◉
4	**Kenmore** (Sears) Elite 4402[2]	600		◖	◉
5	**Maytag** CSE9000A[CE]	500		◖	◉
6	**Amana** AKT3040[WW]	540		◖	◖
7	**KitchenAid** KECC502G[WH]	650		◖	○
36-INCH GAS COOKTOPS					
8	**GE** Monogram ZGU375NSD[SS]	1,300		◖	◉
9	**Jenn-Air** CCG2523[W] **A CR Best Buy**	750		◖	◖
10	**Dacor** SGM365[R]	1,100		◖	◖
11	**GE** Profile JGP962TC[WW]	1,050		◖	○
12	**Kenmore** (Sears) Elite 3303[2]	750		◖	○
13	**KitchenAid** KGCC566H[WH]	900		◖	◖
14	**Frigidaire** Gallery GLGC36S8A[B]	600		○	◖
15	**Viking** VGSU161-6B[SS]	1,750		○	◖

Overall Ratings — In performance order

Excellent ◉ Very good ◖ Good ○ Fair ◖ Poor ●

See report, page 34. Based on tests published in Consumer Reports in August 2002, with updated prices and availability.

The tests behind the Ratings

Under **brand & model,** brackets show a tested model's color code. **Overall score** includes cooktop speed and simmer performance. **Speed of heating** is how quickly the highest powered burner or element heated 6⅓ quarts of room-temperature water to a near boil. **Simmer** shows how well the least powerful burner or element melted and held chocolate without scorching it and whether the most powerful, set to Low, held tomato sauce below a boil. **Price** is approximate retail.

Recommendations and notes

All 30-inch electric smoothtops have: Four burners. Glass cooktop. Hot surface indicator lights. **Most have:** Control knobs. Expandable element. Limited five-year warranties on glass and burner units. "On" light and four "hot" indicator lights. No rim to contain spills. **Most need:** 40-amp circuit.

All 36-inch gas cooktops have: Control knobs. Sealed burners. Lift-off burner base and cap for cleaning. Burner-cap covers. **All need:** 120-volt electrical connection. **Most have:** Five burners. Propane conversion kit. Has bridge element (small heating element inside a larger one that lets you heat various-sized pots).

30-INCH ELECTRIC SMOOTHTOPS

1> **FRIGIDAIRE** Gallery GLEC30S8A[S] **A CR Best Buy Excellent.** Has bridge element but no "on" light. Elements: 1@1,200, 2@1,800, 1@1,000/2,500 watts. Similar: GLEC36S8A[ ].

2> **GE** Profile JP930TC[WW] **Excellent.** Bridge element. Elements: 1@1,200, 2@1,800, 1@1,000/2,500 watts. Similar: JP960TC[ ].

3> **GE** Profile JP938WC[WW] **Excellent.** Touchpad controls. Bridge. Pan sensors. Timer. Child lockout. Warming feature on regular element. Not as hot as others with all burners on. Elements: 1@1,200, 2@1,800, 1@1,000/2,500 watts. Similar: JP968WC[ ].

4> **KENMORE** (Sears) Elite 4402[2] **Excellent.** Bridge element. Elements: 1@1,200, 2@1,800, 1@1,000/2,500 watts.

5> **MAYTAG** CSE9000A[CE] **Excellent.** No expandable element. Spill-guard rim, but seam with cooktop could trap soil. Only one "hot" light indicator. Needs only 30-amp circuit. Elements: 2@1,200, 2@2,200 watts. Warranties: 2-yr. on parts, limited 5-yr. on electronics. Similar: CSE9600A[ ].

6> **AMANA** AKT3040[WW] **Very good.** Install knobs to left or to right. Large element unable to simmer. Warranty: 2-yr. on parts. No 5-yr. electronics warranty. Elements: 1@1,200, 1@1,500, 1@2,000, 1@1,000/2,500 watts. Similar: AKT3020[ ], AKT3630[ ], AKT3650[ ].

7> **KITCHENAID** KECC502G[WH] **Very good.** Two expandable elements. But two largest elements unable to simmer. No 5-yr. burner warranty. Elements: 1@1,200, 1@1,500, 1@1,000/1,800, 1@1,000/2,500 watts.

36-INCH GAS COOKTOPS

8> **GE** Monogram ZGU375NSD[SS] **Excellent.** Auto reignition. Stainless–steel cooktop. "On" lights on each control knob. Wok ring. Simmer setting. Continuous, double-long, cast-iron grates. But tomato sauce stained burner. Not convertible to propane. Burners: 4@10,000, 1@14,000 Btu/hr. Similar: ZGU375LSD[SS] is propane.

9> **JENN-AIR** CCG2523[W] **A CR Best Buy Very good.** Easy to clean. Auto reignition. Glass cooktop. Enamel grates. No rim for spills. Warranty: 2-yr. on parts. Burners: 1@6,500, 2@9,100, 1@10,500, 1@12,000 Btu/hr. Similar: JGC7536A[ ].

10> **DACOR** SGM365[R] **Very good.** Auto reignition. Enamel cooktop. Simmer plate. Continuous, double-long cast-iron grates. Tomato sauce stained burner. Burners: 1@6,000, 2@8,500, 1@12,500, 1@14,000 Btu/hr. Propane conversion kit not included. Similar: SGM304[ ].

11> **GE** Profile JGP962TC[WW] **Very good.** Easy to clean. Glass cooktop. Continuous, double-long enamel grates. Available wok ring. No rim for spills. Burners: 2@6,000, 1@9,100, 1@11,000, 1@12,000 Btu/hr.

12> **KENMORE** (Sears) Elite 3303[2] **Very good.** Easy to clean. Glass cooktop. Double-long enamel grates. Wok ring. No rim for spills. Burners: 1@5,000, 1@9,500, 1@11,000, 1@14,200 Btu/hr. One electric/radiant warming element.

13> **KITCHENAID** KGCC566H[WH] **Good.** Easy to clean. Glass cooktop. Continuous, double-long enamel grates. Tomato sauce stained burner. No rim for spills. Burners: 2@6,000, 1@9,100, 1@12,500, 1@14,000 Btu/hr.

14> **FRIGIDAIRE** Gallery GLGC36S8A[B] **Good.** Glass cooktop. Enamel grates. Cooktop has wells but no rim for spills. Burners: 2@5,000, 2@9,100, 1@13,000 Btu/hr. Similar: PLGC36S9A[ ], GLGC30S8A[ ].

15> **VIKING** VGSU161-6B[SS] **Good.** Auto reignition. Stainless cooktop. Continuous cast-iron grates. Not as hot as others with all burners on. Scorched melted chocolate. Tomato sauce stained burner. Propane conversion kit not included. Burners: 1@6,000, 1@9,000, 3@12,000, 1@14,000 Btu/hr.

Cookware

You don't have to pay top-dollar to get even heating, comfortable handles, easy cleaning, and durability.

Among nonstick sets, the Calphalon Commercial Nonstick, $500 for 10 pieces, is great for a demanding cook who's willing to pay a premium. The two **CR Best Buys,** Simply Calphalon Nonstick, $200 for 8 pieces, and Cook's Essentials, $125 for 10 pieces, weigh less and are better choices for those on a budget. If you want an uncoated set, consider the Wolfgang Puck Bistro Collection. It has 20 pieces (including a 6-piece tool set and a nonstick frypan) and costs $150.

Overall Ratings — In performance order

Ratings key: Excellent, Very good, Good, Fair, Poor

KEY NO.	BRAND & MODEL (MATERIAL)	PRICE	OVERALL SCORE	PIECES	EVEN HEAT	DURABLE COATING	CLEANUP
NONSTICK SETS							
1	**Calphalon** Commercial (anodized aluminum)	$500		10	Very good	Very good	Very good
2	**Calphalon** Simply Calphalon A CR Best Buy (anodized aluminum)	200		8	Very good	Good	Very good
3	**Emerilware** by All-Clad (anodized aluminum)	350		10	Very good	Good	Very good
4	**Cook's Essentials** A CR Best Buy (stainless steel)	125		10	Good	Good	Very good
5	**Scanpan** Titanium New Tek Classic (aluminum)	330		8	Good	Very good	Very good
6	**Cuisinart** Stick Free (stainless steel)	200		7	Good	Very good	Very good
7	**Meyer** Anolon Titanium (anodized aluminum)	400		10	Good	Very good	Excellent
8	**Meyer** Circulon Steel (stainless steel)	150		8	Fair	Very good	Good
9	**Wearever** Soft Touch Handles (enamel on aluminum)	100		9	Fair	Good	Very good
10	**Farberware** Millennium Satin Enamel (enamel on aluminum)	150		12	Good	Fair	Very good
11	**Mirro** Series 500P (aluminum)	30		8	Fair	Good	Very good
12	**Regal** Easy Clean (aluminum)	50		18	Fair	Poor	Very good
13	**T-Fal** 4U Total (enamel on aluminum)	90		8	Fair	Good	Very good
14	**T-Fal** Encore Hard Enamel (enamel on aluminum)	80		8	Good	Good	Very good
15	**Nordic Ware** Rangeware Pro (aluminum)	100		8	Poor	Good	Very good
UNCOATED SETS							
16	**Wolfgang Puck** Bistro Collection (stainless steel)	150		20	Very good	Good	Good
17	**Farberware** Millennium (stainless steel, copper)	250		10	Very good	–	Good
18	**Tools of the Trade** Belgique Gourmet (stainless steel, copper)	250		12	Very good	–	Good
19	**Magnalite** Classic (aluminum)	115		8	Good	–	Good
20	**Wearever** Easy Pour and Strain (stainless steel)	80		8	Good	Good	Good
21	**Emerilware** by All-Clad (stainless steel)	150		7	Good	–	Good
22	**Calphalon** Simply Calphalon (stainless steel)	150		8	Good	–	Good
23	**Bialetti** Hi-Base (stainless steel)	70		8	Good	Good	Fair
24	**Cuisinart** Multiclad (stainless steel)	200		7	Fair	–	Good
25	**Revere** Copper Cuisine (stainless steel, copper)	60		7	Good	–	Poor

See report, page 32. Based on tests published in Consumer Reports in December 2002.

The tests behind the Ratings

Overall score is based on performance and convenience. Each set includes at least these pieces: one 9.5- to 11-inch frypan with no lid, a stockpot/Dutch oven (usually 5- to 6.5-qt.) with lid, and a 2- to 3-quart saucepan with lid. Exceptions and extras are listed in Recommendations and notes. To test for **even heat,** we cooked frypan-sized pancakes at 400° F on a gas cooktop and gauged how evenly they browned. To test for **durable coating** on nonstick sets, we had a mechanical arm rub a steel-wool pad over the frypan's surface. An excellent score means the pan's coating was intact after 2,000 strokes and still released fried eggs with relative ease. **Cleanup** scores are based on the ease of removing a baked-on sauce of flour, milk, and butter from saucepans. Recommendations and notes include judgments on handle sturdiness, which indicate how well the frypans fared when we tried to bend the handle with up to 75 lb. of force and to loosen it by moving the pan up and down with 1.5 times its own weight inside. **Price** is approximate retail for the set.

Recommendations and notes

All cookware sets: Can be used on gas, electric coil, and electric smoothtop ranges. **Except as noted all:** Are dishwasher-safe and oven-safe to at least 425° F. Have a limited lifetime warranty. Have riveted handles, which are strong but can be hard to clean. Have handles that did not come loose in our tests and that stayed cool enough to hold without a potholder even while boiling water. Offer additional open stock.

NONSTICK SETS

1> **CALPHALON** Commercial (anodized aluminum) **Excels at all tasks, including simmer.** But not dishwasher-safe, and saucepan handle not well balanced. Heavy. Lifetime warranty. 8-qt. stockpot. Extras: 3-qt. chef pan, 3-qt. sauté pan & lids, 8-in. frypan.

2> **CALPHALON** Simply Calphalon **A CR Best Buy** (anodized aluminum) **Almost as good as set above, but a fraction of the price and lighter weight.** Not dishwasher-safe. Handles uncomfortable. 10-year warranty. Extras: 1-qt. saucepan & lid, 8-in. frypan.

3> **EMERILWARE** (anodized aluminum) **Well equipped, simmers very well.** But not dishwasher-safe. Heavy. Extras: 3-qt. sauté pan & lid, 3.5-qt. casserole & lid, 8-in. frypan. Made by All-Clad.

4> **COOK'S ESSENTIALS A CR Best Buy** (stainless steel) **Very good, especially simmering.** But oven-safe only to 350º. Glass lids. Lifetime warranty. Extras: 1-qt. saucepan & lid, 12-in. sauté pan & lid, 8-in. frypan. No open stock. Available only from QVC.

5> **SCANPAN** Titanium New Tek Classic (aluminum) **Impressive overall.** But unriveted handles less comfortable and less well balanced than most. Heavy. Glass lids. Lifetime warranty. Extras: 1- qt. saucepan & lid, 8-in. frypan.

6> **CUISINART** Stick Free (stainless steel) **Very good value.** But saucepan handles got hot. Lifetime warranty. Extras: 2-qt. steamer insert, 8-in. frypan.

7> **MEYER** Anolon Titanium (anodized aluminum) **Very good.** But saucepan handles got hot. Heavy. Lifetime warranty. 8-qt stockpot. Extras: 3-qt. saucepan & lid, 5-qt. sauté pan & lid, 8-in. frypan.

8> **MEYER** Circulon Steel (stainless steel) **Commendable cooking.** But oven-safe only to 350º. Shallow ridges slightly impede cleaning. Lifetime warranty. 8-qt. stockpot. Extras: 1.5-qt. saucepan & lid, 8-in. frypan.

9> **WEAREVER** Soft Touch Handles (enamel on aluminum) **Very good performance and price.** Lifetime warranty. 8-qt. stockpot. Extras: 3.5-qt. saucepan & lid, steamer, 10-in. frypan lid.

10> **FARBERWARE** Millennium Satin Enamel (enamel on aluminum) **There are better values.** Stockpot couldn't hold simmer. Lifetime warranty. 8-qt. stockpot. Extras: 3- and 1-qt. saucepans & lids, 12-in. sauté pan & lid, 8-in. frypan. Limited open stock.

11> **MIRRO** Series 500P (aluminum) **Nice overall.** Comfortable, no-rivet handles. But oven-safe only to 350º. Glass lids. 20-yr. warranty. Extras: 1.5-qt. saucepan & lid, 8-in. frypan. Sold only at Wal-Mart.

12> **REGAL** Easy Clean (aluminum) **Lightweight, with comfortable handles.** But coating wore off quickly in tough tests. Oven-safe only to 350º. Glass lids. 25-yr. warranty. Extras: 1.5- and 1-qt. saucepans & lids, 8-in. frypan, big frypan lid, 7-piece tool set. Open stock sold only at Wal-Mart.

13> **T-FAL** 4U Total (enamel on aluminum) **Good.** Comfortable no-rivet handles. But not oven-safe, and stockpot couldn't hold simmer. Lifetime warranty. Small stockpot (4.6-qt.). Extras: 11-in. frypan, 2 spatulas.

14> **T-FAL** Encore Hard Enamel (enamel on aluminum) **There are better sets.** Lightweight, with comfortable, no-rivet handles. But oven-safe only to 350º. Lifetime warranty. Extras: 1-qt. saucepan & lid, 7.5-in. frypan, 3-piece tool set, recipe book.

15> **NORDIC WARE** Rangeware Pro (aluminum) **Choose another.** Stockpot couldn't hold simmer, stockpot handles got hot. Extras: 1.5-qt. saucepan & lid, 8-in. frypan. Limited open stock.

UNCOATED SETS

16> **WOLFGANG PUCK** Bistro Collection (stainless steel) **Well equipped, cooks well.** 8-in. frypan is nonstick. Glass lids. Lifetime warranty. 8-qt. stockpot. Extras: 3- and 4-qt.

Recommendations and notes

saucepans & lids, 10-in. casserole & lid, steamer insert, 11-in. frypan & lid, 6-piece tool set. Sold through Home Shopping Network. Open stock sold through www.wpcookware.com.

17▷ **FARBERWARE** Millennium (stainless steel, copper) **Impressive.** Saucepan handles got hot. Lifetime warranty. 8-qt. stockpot. Extras: 12-in. sauté pan & lid, 3-qt. saucepan & lid; 4.5-qt. steamer insert.

18▷ **TOOLS OF THE TRADE** Belgique Gourmet (stainless steel, copper) **Very good performance.** Comfortable handles. Lifetime warranty. 8-qt. stockpot. Extras: 1- and 3.5-qt. saucepans & lids, 12.5-inch frypan & lid, steamer insert. Sold only at Macy's and other Federated Department Stores. Nonstick frypan available in open stock.

19▷ **MAGNALITE** Classic (aluminum) **Very good overall.** But oven-safe only to 350º. Stockpot handles got hot. Uncomfortable, no-rivet handles. Some spouts. Heavy. 50-yr. warranty. Extras: 1-qt. saucepan & lid, meat rack. Limited open stock.

20▷ **WEAREVER** Easy Pour and Strain (stainless steel) **Good value for basic set.** But oven-safe only to 350º, frypan handle not well balanced. Some spouts. Glass lids. Frypan is nonstick. Heavy. Lifetime warranty. Extras: 1-qt. saucepan & lid, lid for frypan.

21▷ **EMERILWARE** (stainless steel) **Very good.** Handles uncomfortable. Glass lids. Can use in broiler. Heavy. Lifetime warranty. Extras: 3-qt. casserole & lid. Made by All-Clad.

22▷ **CALPHALON** Simply Calphalon (stainless steel) **Cooks evenly, but handles uncomfortable.** Can use in broiler. Glass lids. Heavy. 10-yr. warranty. Extras: 1-qt. saucepan & lid, 8-in. frypan.

23▷ **BIALETTI** Hi-base (stainless steel) **Good price, but not a standout.** Oven-safe only to 350º. Frypan handle unbalanced. No-rivet handle loosened in tough test. Slow to boil water. Frypan is nonstick. 10-yr. warranty. Extras: 1-qt. saucepan & lid, 8-in. frypan. Sold only at Target.

24▷ **CUISINART** Multiclad (stainless steel) **A princely sum for pauper performance.** Saucepan handles got hot. Can use in broiler. Lifetime warranty. Extras: 1.5-qt. saucepan & lid.

25▷ **REVERE** Copper Cuisine (stainless steel, copper) **Mediocre.** Stockpot couldn't hold simmer. Cleanup difficult. Glass lids. No-rivet handles. 25-year warranty. Extras: 1.5-qt. saucepan & lid. Limited open stock.

Countertops

Any of the tested materials can add a strong note of drama and luxury to a newly remodeled kitchen. And they aren't just for appearance—all except butcher block make practical countertops that can hold their looks even under heavy daily use. Let your budget and your own sense of style be your guide.

Overall Ratings — In performance order

Ratings key: Excellent, Very good, Good, Fair, Poor

Key No.	Product (common brands)	Price Range	Overall	Stains	Heat	Slicing	Abrasion	Impact	Chopping
1	Engineered stone (Silestone, Zodiaq)	$50 and up	Excellent	Excellent	Excellent	Very good	Excellent	Good	Fair
2	Granite	50 to 300	Excellent	Very good	Excellent	Very good	Excellent	Excellent	Excellent
3	Ceramic tile	4 to 80	Very good	Good	Excellent	Very good	Good	Fair	Excellent
4	Laminate (Wilsonart, Formica)	8 to 20	Good	Very good	Very good	Poor	Very good	Very good	Very good
5	Solid surface (Avonite, Corian, Gibraltar)	40 to 75	Good	Good	Very good	Very good	Very good	Very good	Poor
6	Butcher block	16 to 40	Very good	Very good	Fair	Poor	Poor	Poor	Poor

See report, page 154. Based on tests published in Consumer Reports in August 2002.

The tests behind the ratings

We tested the six leading types; differences from brand to brand (when there are brands) within a type are likely to be insignificant. **Overall** summarizes performance in all our tests. For **stains,** we used 20 common household products. For **heat,** we warmed a pot to 400° F and placed it on each material to check for discoloration. For **slicing,** 25 strokes with a weighted chef's knife. For **abrasion,** 25 back-and-forth swipes with a weighted sanding block. For **impact,** blunt and pointed weights dropped from heights of up to two feet. For **chopping,** impact from a weighted knife. **Price** is a range per square foot, installed.

Recommendations and notes

1 **ENGINEERED STONE** (Silestone, Zodiaq) **Needs professional installation and repair.** Provides a uniform, consistent appearance. Visible seams. Heavy.

2 **GRANITE Needs professional installation and repair, periodic sealing.** Visible seams. Heavy.

3 **CERAMIC TILE Fairly easy to install and repair.** Grout between tiles needs periodic cleaning or sealing. The uneven surface can make cleanup more difficult.

4 **LAMINATE** (Wilsonart, Formica) **Fairly easy to install.** Visible seams. Edge seams show as dark line. Heat and sharp edges can easily damage this material. Damage can't be repaired.

5 **SOLID SURFACE** (Avonite, Corian, Gibraltar) **Needs professional installation, but nicks and scratches can be sanded out.** Extensive damage is more easily repaired with solid-color countertops than with patterned ones. Available as solid countertop or as veneer over wood. Completely seamless, including integral sink.

6 **BUTCHER BLOCK Fairly easy to install and repair.** Needs periodic sealing and refinishing. This countertop choice shows its use.

Dishwashers

Most dishwashers do a very good or even excellent job. The costliest are not necessarily the best performers, although high-priced models may have desirable styling and extra soundproofing. The top-rated Bosch, Asko, and Viking models cost the most—from $900 to nearly $1,400. Some lower-priced models washed nearly as well, however. The GE Triton XL GSD6600G is excellent at washing and convenient to use. At $520, it's a **CR Best Buy.** Key features for these models are listed in the table on page 218. See the product guide for an explanation of features.

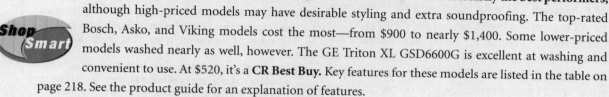

KEY NO.	BRAND & MODEL	PRICE	OVERALL SCORE	WASHING	ENERGY USE	NOISE	LOADING	EASE OF USE
1	**Bosch** SHV680[3]	$1,140		◕	◖	◕	◖	◖
2	**Bosch** SHU995[2]	900		◕	◖	◕	◖	◖
3	**Asko** D1996FI	1,250		◕	◕	◖	○	○
4	**Viking** DFUD140	1,375		◕	◕	◖	○	○
5	**Asko** D1716	800		◕	◕	◖	○	○
6	**Kenmore** (Sears) 1563[2]	420		◕	◖	◐	◐	◕
7	**Maytag** MDB9150AW[W]	920		◕	○	◖	◖	◕
8	**Miele** Novotronic G841SC Plus	900		◕	◖	◖	○	○
9	**Bosch** SHU330[2]	600		◕	◖	◖	○	◖
10	**GE** Profile PDW7800G[WW]	620		◕	○	○	◖	◕
11	**Fisher & Paykel** DD603[W]	1,200		◕	◖	◖	◖	◖
12	**Kenmore** (Sears) 1552[2]	350		◕	◖	◐	◐	◖
13	**GE** Triton XL GSD6600G[WW] **A CR Best Buy**	520		◕	○	◖	◖	◖
14	**Frigidaire** Gallery GLDB957J[S]	400		◕	○	◖	○	◖
15	**Maytag** MDB6650AW[W]	600		◖	◖	○	○	◖
16	**Jenn-Air** JDB9910[W]	800		◖	○	◖	◖	◖
17	**Maytag** PDB4600AW[E]	345		◕	◖	◐	○	◕
18	**Viking** Quiet Clean VUD141	1,575		○	◕	◖	○	◖
19	**Frigidaire** Gallery Ultra Quiet GLDB756A[S]	350		○	◕	○	◖	◖

See report, page 17. Based on tests published in Consumer Reports in May 2002, with updated prices and availability.

The tests behind the Ratings

Under **brand & model,** a bracketed letter or number is the color code. **Overall score** stresses washing but factors in noise, energy use, convenience, water use, and cycle time. **Washing** was tested using a full load of very dirty dishes, glasses, and flatware. **Energy use** is for a normal cycle. **Noise** was judged by a listening panel, aided by sound-level measurements. **Loading** reflects ability to hold extra place settings and oversized items. **Ease of use** considers convenience of controls and maintenance. **Recommendations and notes** cite long or short cycle length and high or low water use (8.5 gallons was average). Brand repair information is based on our most recent reader survey. **Price** is approximate retail.

Recommendations and notes

Models listed as similar should offer performance comparable to the tested model's, although features may differ.

All dishwashers: Are standard-sized, under-the-counter models that can wash a complete 10-piece place setting with two serving bowls and one serving platter. **Most models:** Have touchpad controls and at least three cycles (light, normal, pots-and-pans). Have rinse-and-hold, heated-water, and drain/cancel control for stopping midcycle. Have normal cycle times of 90 to 120 minutes. Have heated-dry and delay-start option. Use between 7 and 9 gallons of water during their normal cycle. Have 1-year warranty on parts and labor. Have 20-year or longer limited warranty on plastic tub and door liner.

1▷ **BOSCH** SHV680[3] **Excellent but expensive.** Among the quietest models tested. More loading flexibility than most, with adjustable upper rack. But heated-dry feature can't be turned off. Among the more water-efficient sensor models (about 7 gal.). Hidden controls; needs front panel (costs extra).

2▷ **BOSCH** SHU995[2] **Excellent; much like #1, but doesn't allow for custom door panel and has fewer wash options.**

3▷ **ASKO** D1996FI **Excellent but pricey.** Faster (85-min. cycle) and used less water than most (about 5 gal.). Hidden controls; needs front panel (costs extra). Full 3-yr. warranty. But has been among the more repair-prone brands. Similar: D1976[ ].

4▷ **VIKING** DFUD140 **Excellent but pricey.** Used less water than most (about 5.5 gal.). Hidden controls; needs front panel (costs extra).

5▷ **ASKO** D1716 **An excellent performer.** Efficient with energy and water (about 5.5 gal.). Full 3-yr. warranty. Has been among the more repair-prone brands. No delay start.

6▷ **KENMORE** (Sears) 1563[2] **A good buy, but not very flexible for special loading.** Noisier than most. Similar: 1663[ ] .

7▷ **MAYTAG** MDB9150AW[W] **Feature-laden.** More flexible loading than most, with adjustable upper rack. Long cycle time (130 min.).

8▷ **MIELE** Novotronic G841SC Plus **Very good performer.** Adjustable upper rack. But heated-dry option can't be turned off. No delay start.

9▷ **BOSCH** SHU330[2] **Among the more water-efficient sensor models (about 8 gal.).** Push-button controls. No light wash cycle. Similar: SHU332[ ], SHU333[ ].

10▷ **GE** Profile PDW7800G[WW] **Feature-laden.** More flexible loading than most. But high water use (10 gal.). Similar: PDW7300G[ ], PDW7700G[ ] .

11▷ **FISHER & PAYKEL** DD603[W] **Very good but expensive.** Has two separate drawers. More flexible loading than most.

Partially hidden controls. No heated-dry option. Full 2-yr. warranty.

12▷ **KENMORE** (Sears) 1552[2] **Good price, with adjustable upper rack, but not very flexible for special loading.** Dial and touchpad controls. But noisier than most. Similar: 1652[ ].

13▷ **GE** Triton XL GSD6600G[WW] **A CR Best Buy Good price for excellent cleaning, plenty of features.** More flexible loading than most. But high water use (about 10 gal.). 10-yr. tub and door liner warranty. Similar: GSD6200G[ ].

14▷ **FRIGIDAIRE** Gallery GLDB957J[S] **High water use (about 10.5 gal.).** Has been among the more repair-prone brands. Discontinued, but similar GLDB957A[ ] is available.

15▷ **MAYTAG** MDB6650AW[W] **Very good, with stainless-steel tub.** Short cycle time (85 min.).

16▷ **JENN-AIR** JDB9910[W] **Feature-laden.** More flexible loading than most, with adjustable upper rack. But long cycle time (130 min.). Similar: JDB8910[ ].

17▷ **MAYTAG** PDB4600AW[E] **Very good but basic.** Noisier than most.

Features at a glance Dishwashers

Key no.	Brand	Sensor	Self-cleaning filter	Stainless-steel tub	Child safety	Flatware slots
1	**Bosch**	•		•		•
2	**Bosch**	•		•		
3	**Asko**			•		
4	**Viking**			•		
5	**Asko**			•	•	
6	**Kenmore**		•		•	•
7	**Maytag**	•	•		•	
8	**Miele**			•	•	•
9	**Bosch**	•		•		•
10	**GE**	•	•		•	•
11	**Fisher & Paykel**			•		
12	**Kenmore**		•			
13	**GE**	•	•		•	•
14	**Frigidaire**	•	•	•		
15	**Maytag**		•	•	•	
16	**Jenn-Air**	•	•	•	•	
17	**Maytag**		•			
18	**Viking**			•		
19	**Frigidaire**		•			

Recommendations and notes

18▷**VIKING** Quiet Clean VUD141 **Pricey, but has some pluses: shorter cycle time than most (75 min.), low water use (about 5.5 gal.).** Stainless-steel exterior. Dial controls. No drain/cancel button.

19▷**FRIGIDAIRE** Gallery Ultra Quiet GLDB756A[S] **Good price, basic features.** But less flexible loading than most. Manual-control push buttons and cycle dial must be synchronized. Has been among the more repair-prone brands. 10-yr. tub and door liner warranty.

How to use the Ratings

• Read Shop Smart for recommendations on specific models.

• Note how the rated products are listed—in order of performance and convenience, price, or alphabetically.

• The overall score graph gives the big picture in performance. Notes on features and performance for individual models are listed in the Recommendations and notes.

• Use the key numbers to locate the details on each model.

• Before going to press, we verify model availability for most products with manufacturers. Some tested models listed in the Ratings may no longer be available. Discontinued models are noted. Such models may still be available in some stores for part of 2003. Models indicated as successors should perform similarly to the tested models, according to the manufacturer. Features may vary.

• Models similar to the tested models, when they exist, are indicated in Recommendations and notes.

• The original date of publication is noted for each Ratings.

Drills, cordless

Drills range from light-duty 6-volt models that start at about $50 to heavy-duty professional-grade 24-volt units than can top $300. The 24-volt Bosch 3960K, $330, delivers power and endurance, but the 18-volt Bosch 3860K, $200, did about as well, weighs less, and is a better value. For smaller projects, consider these two **CR Best Buys:** the 18-volt Craftsman 11334, $120, and Ryobi HP1802MK2, $100. Among 14.4-volt drills, the Skil 2584-04 is an inexpensive, lightweight choice. Consider a drill with less than 14.4 volts only if you value minimal weight and cost over performance.

Overall Ratings — In performance order

Ratings key: Excellent ● | Very good ◕ | Good ○ | Fair ◑ | Poor ●

Key No.	Brand & Model	Price	Weight (Lb.)	Overall Score (P F G VG E)	Overall Power	Run Time	Charge Time	Handling
	24-VOLT DRILL							
1	**Bosch** 3960K	$330	6.4		●	●	●	○
	18-VOLT DRILLS							
2	**Bosch** 3860K	200	5.6		●	◕	●	○
3	**Milwaukee** 0522-24	260	6.0		◕	●	◕	◕
4	**DeWalt** DW987K-2	270	6.0		●	◕	◕	◕
5	**Porter-Cable** 9884 (19.2 volts)	200	5.9		◕	◕	◕	◕
6	**Craftsman** (Sears) Professional 27124	200	6.5		◕	◕	●	○
7	**Makita** 6343DWAE	300	5.7		◕	◕	◕	○
8	**Craftsman** (Sears) 11334 **A CR Best Buy**	120	5.3		◕	○	◕	◕
9	**DeWalt** DW929K-2	200	4.6		◕	○	◕	◕
10	**Ryobi** HP1802MK2 **A CR Best Buy**	100	5.1		◕	○	●	◕
11	**Skil** 2884-04	105	4.2		◕	○	●	◕
12	**Black & Decker** FSD182K-2	110	5.2		◕	○	○	○
13	**Grizzly** G8596	70	4.2		○	◕	○	●
14	**Chicago Electric** 44849	40	3.8		◑	○	◑	●
	14.4-VOLT DRILLS							
15	**Panasonic** EY6431NQKW (15.6 volts)	220	4.5		◕	◕	●	◕
16	**Milwaukee** Power Plus 0516-22	190	5.5		◕	○	●	◕
17	**Porter-Cable** 9877	220	5.7		◕	○	●	◕
18	**DeWalt** DW928K-2	180	4.3		◑	◑	●	◕
19	**Milwaukee** Power Plus 0512-21	160	4.4		○	○	●	●
20	**Skil** 2584-04	85	3.9		◕	◑	●	◕
21	**Craftsman** (Sears) Professional 27123	160	4.7		○	○	●	○
22	**Makita** 6228DWAE	160	3.8		○	◑	●	●
23	**Ryobi** HP1442MK2	85	4.2		○	◑	○	◕
24	**Craftsman** (Sears) 11333	90	4.1		○	◑	○	◕
25	**Black & Decker** FSD142K-2	90	4.4		○	◑	○	○
26	**Grizzly** G8595	55	3.4		◑	◑	○	◕

Overall Ratings, cont.

Ratings key: Excellent ● · Very good ◖ · Good ○ · Fair ◖ · Poor ●

KEY NO.	BRAND & MODEL	PRICE	WEIGHT (LB.)	OVERALL SCORE (P F G VG E)	OVERALL POWER	RUN TIME	CHARGE TIME	HANDLING
	12-VOLT DRILLS							
27	**Porter-Cable** 9866	$140	4.5		○	○	●	●
28	**DeWalt** DW927K-2	140	4.0		◖	◖	●	◖
29	**Milwaukee** Power Plus 0502-26	150	3.8		○	◖	●	●
30	**Makita** 6227DWE	130	3.4		○	◖	●	●
31	**Craftsman** (Sears) 11332	70	3.8		○	◖	○	◖
32	**Hitachi** FDS12DVA	80	3.4		◖	●	○	◖
33	**Black & Decker** FSD122K	70	3.5		◖	◖	○	○
34	**Skil** 2468-02	40	3.2		◖	◖	○	◖
35	**Ryobi** HP1202MK2	70	3.4		◖	◖	◖	◖
	9.6 VOLT AND BELOW							
36	**DeWalt** DW926K-2	100	3.4		◖	◖	●	●
37	**Craftsman** (Sears) 11331	60	3.5		◖	◖	○	◖
38	**Ryobi** HP962K	40	3.2		◖	◖	◖	◖
39	**Black & Decker** CD9600K	60	2.9		◖	◖	◖	◖
40	**Black & Decker** 9099KB (7.2 volts)	40	2.3		●	●	●	◖
41	**Black & Decker** 9089KB (6 volts)	50	2.2		●	●	●	◖

See report, page 123. Based on tests published in Consumer Reports in January 2003.

The tests behind the ratings

Weight is to the nearest tenth of a pound for the drill and battery pack. **Overall score** is based on overall power, run time, charge time, and handling. **Overall power** denotes drilling speed and torque, or twisting force. **Run time** reflects work per battery charge, measured on a dynamometer. **Charge time** is how much time it took to fully recharge a discharged battery. **Handling** includes weight, balance, and effort needed to position the head. **Price** is approximate retail.

Recommendations and notes

All drills have: A keyless chuck. A reversible drive. **Most have:** A smart charger with 1-hour charge time. Two speed ranges: slow (0 to about 400 rpm) for driving screws, and fast (about 0 to 1,100-1,650 rpm) for drilling holes; single-speed models have a range of 0 to 600-800 rpm, which tends to compromise their driving and drilling performance. A variable clutch with at least 16 settings for limiting the tool's maximum torque. A ³/₈-inch chuck (¹/₂-inch for 18- and 24-volt models, except as noted). A trigger lockout for safety. Bit storage. Two NiCad battery packs. A carrying case. A one-year warranty.

24-VOLT DRILL
1 **BOSCH** 3960K **Powerful, well-equipped, but heavy and bulky.** Smart charger, 16 or more clutch adjustments, multiple speed ranges, easy bit changes, two batteries, electric brake.

18-VOLT DRILLS
2 **BOSCH** 3860K **Best of an impressive group.** Powerful and well-equipped. Smart charger, 16 or more clutch adjustments, multiple speed ranges, easy bit changes, two batteries, electric brake.

3 **MILWAUKEE** 0522-24 **Capable, but heavy.** Smart charger, 16 or more clutch adjustments, multiple speed ranges, two batteries, electric brake. Battery faces front or rear to ease handling. No bit storage. Discontinued, but similar 0622-24 is available.

4 **DEWALT** DW987K-2 **Powerful and well-equipped, but heavy.** Smart charger, 16 or more clutch adjustments, multiple speed ranges, easy bit changes, two batteries, electric brake.

5 **PORTER-CABLE** 9884 **Capable and well-equipped, but heavy.** Smart charger, 16 or more clutch adjustments, multiple speed ranges, two batteries, electric brake, soft handle grip. Discontinued, but similar 9984 is available.

6 **CRAFTSMAN** (Sears) Professional 27124 **Capable and well-equipped, but heavy.** Smart charger, 16 or more clutch adjustments, multiple speed ranges, easy bit changes, two batteries, electric brake, bubble level.

7 **MAKITA** 6343DWAE **Capable overall.** Smart charger, 16 or more clutch adjustments, multiple speed ranges, two batteries, electric brake. Removable brushes.

Recommendations and notes

8 ▷ **CRAFTSMAN** (Sears) 11334 **A CR Best Buy Lots of performance for the money.** Smart charger, 16 or more clutch adjustments, multiple speed ranges, two batteries, electric brake, bubble level.

9 ▷ **DEWALT** DW929K-2 **Capable and light.** Smart charger, 16 or more clutch adjustments, multiple speed ranges, two batteries, ⅜-inch chuck.

10 ▷ **RYOBI** HP1802MK2 **A CR Best Buy Lots of performance for the money.** Smart charger, 16 or more clutch adjustments, multiple speed ranges, Two batteries, electric brake, bubble level, magnetic screw holder. 2-year warranty.

11 ▷ **SKIL** 2884-04 **Capable and light.** Smart charger, multiple speed ranges, easy bit changes, two batteries, electric brake, bubble level, ⅜-inch chuck, magnetic screw holder. Clutch slipped in torque tests. 2-year warranty.

12 ▷ **BLACK & DECKER** FSD182K-2 **Capable, but charging takes 3 to 6 hours.** 16 or more clutch adjustments, multiple speed ranges, quick-connect bit changes, two batteries, level light, ⅜-inch chuck. 2-year warranty.

13 ▷ **GRIZZLY** G8596 **Light, though otherwise unimpressive.** 16 or more clutch adjustments, multiple speed ranges. Charging time takes 3 to 5 hours. Only one battery. Extra bits.

14 ▷ **CHICAGO ELECTRIC** 44849 **There are better choices.** Charging time takes 5 to 7 hours. Only one battery.

14.4-VOLT DRILLS

15 ▷ **PANASONIC** EY6431NQKW **Capable, light, and well-equipped.** Smart charger, 16 or more clutch adjustments, multiple speed ranges, easy bit changes, two NiMH batteries, electric brake, ½-inch chuck.

16 ▷ **MILWAUKEE** Power Plus 0516-22 **Capable and well-balanced.** Smart charger, 16 or more clutch adjustments, multiple speed ranges, two batteries, electric brake, ½-inch chuck. Similar: 0616-24.

17 ▷ **PORTER-CABLE** 9877 **Capable overall.** Smart charger, 16 or more clutch adjustments, multiple speed ranges, two batteries, electric brake, soft handle grip. Discontinued, but similar 9978 is available.

18 ▷ **DEWALT** DW928K-2 **Capable overall.** Smart charger, 16 or more clutch adjustments, multiple speed ranges, two batteries, electric brake.

19 ▷ **MILWAUKEE** Power Plus 0512-21 **Well-balanced, though otherwise mediocre.** Smart charger, 16 or more clutch adjustments, multiple speed ranges, two batteries, electric brake, ½-inch chuck.

20 ▷ **SKIL** 2584-04 **Inexpensive and light.** Smart charger, multiple speed ranges, easy bit changes, two batteries, magnetic screw holder. Clutch slipped in torque tests. 2-year warranty.

21 ▷ **CRAFTSMAN** (Sears) Professional 27123 **OK.** Smart charger, 16 or more clutch adjustments, multiple speed ranges, easy bit changes, two batteries, electric brake, ½-inch chuck, bubble level.

22 ▷ **MAKITA** 6228DWAE **Light and well-balanced.** Smart charger, 16 or more clutch adjustments, multiple speed ranges, two batteries. No bit storage.

23 ▷ **RYOBI** HP1442MK2 **OK.** Smart charger, 16 or more clutch adjustments, multiple speed ranges, two batteries, electric brake, bubble level, magnetic screw holder. 2-year warranty.

24 ▷ **CRAFTSMAN** (Sears) 11333 **OK.** 16 or more clutch adjustments, multiple speed ranges, two batteries, bubble level. Charging takes 3 to 5 hours.

25 ▷ **BLACK & DECKER** FSD142K-2 **OK, but charging takes 3 to 6 hours.** 16 or more clutch adjustments, multiple speed ranges, quick-connect bit changes, two batteries, electric brake, level light, ½-inch chuck. 2-year warranty.

26 ▷ **GRIZZLY** G8595 **There are better choices.** Charging takes 3 to 5 hours. Only one battery.

12-VOLT DRILLS

27 ▷ **PORTER-CABLE** 9866 **Best of a mediocre group.** Well-balanced. Smart charger, 16 or more clutch adjustments, multiple speed ranges, two batteries, electric brake, soft handle grip. Discontinued, but similar 9966 is available.

28 ▷ **DEWALT** DW927K-2 **Power offset by relatively short run time.** Smart charger, 16 or more clutch adjustments, multiple speed ranges, two batteries.

29 ▷ **MILWAUKEE** Power Plus 0502-26 **Well-balanced, but otherwise unimpressive.** Smart charger, 16 or more clutch adjustments, multiple speed ranges, two batteries, electric brake, flashlight.

30 ▷ **MAKITA** 6227DWE **Light and well-balanced, but otherwise unimpressive.** Smart charger, 16 or more clutch adjustments, multiple speed ranges, two batteries. No bit storage.

31 ▷ **CRAFTSMAN** (Sears) 11332 **OK, but charging takes 3-5 hours.** 16 or more clutch adjustments, multiple speed ranges, two batteries, bubble level.

32 ▷ **HITACHI** FDS12DVA **Light and well-balanced, but otherwise unimpressive.** Smart charger, 16 or more clutch adjustments, multiple speed ranges, two batteries, bubble level, extra bits, flashlight. No trigger lock. Discontinued, but similar DS12DVF is available.

Recommendations and notes

33 **BLACK & DECKER** FSD122K **There are better choices.** 16 or more clutch adjustments, easy bit changes, two batteries, bubble level. Charging takes 3 to 6 hours.

34 **SKIL** 2468-02 **There are better choices.** Charging takes 3 to 5 hours. One battery. Discontinued, but similar 2467-02 is available.

35 **RYOBI** HP1202MK2 **There are better choices.** 16 or more clutch adjustments, two batteries. Charging takes 3 to 6 hours.

9.6-VOLT AND BELOW

36 **DEWALT** DW926K-2 **Best of an uninspired group.** Well-balanced. Smart charger, 16 or more clutch adjustments, multiple speed ranges, two batteries.

37 **CRAFTSMAN** (Sears) 11331 **There are better choices.** 16 or more clutch adjustments, two batteries. Charging takes 3 to 5 hours.

38 **RYOBI** HP962K **There are better choices.** 16 or more clutch settings, bubble level. Charging takes 3 to 6 hours. One battery.

39 **BLACK & DECKER** CD9600K **There are better choices.** Charging takes 16 hours. One battery.

40 **BLACK & DECKER** 9099KB **There are better choices.** Charging takes 16 hours. One battery.

41 **BLACK & DECKER** 9089KB **There are better choices.** Charging takes 16 hours. One battery.

Dryers

Virtually all of the dryers we tested did a very good or excellent job and had ample capacity and convenient controls. Choosing the right one depends on which features you want. The Kenmore 6280, $410, and the Whirlpool LEQ8000J, $400, are **CR Best Buys.** When you pay more, you get a dryer loaded with conveniences, such as a porcelain top and touchpad controls. Key features for these models are listed in the table. See the product guide for an explanation of features.

Overall Ratings — In performance order

Rating key: ● Excellent ◖ Very good ○ Good ◗ Fair ● Poor

KEY NO.	BRAND & MODEL	PRICE	OVERALL SCORE (0–100)	DRYING	CAPACITY	NOISE
1	**Kenmore** (Sears) Elite 6393[2]	$540		Excellent	Very good	Good
2	**Kenmore** (Sears) 6280[2] **A CR Best Buy**	410		Excellent	Very good	Good
3	**GE** Profile Performance DPSE592EA[WW]	650		Excellent	Very good	Good
4	**Maytag** Neptune MDE7500AY[W]	800		Excellent	Very good	Very good
5	**GE** Profile DPSB519EB[WW]	520		Good	Very good	Good
6	**Kenmore** (Sears) Elite HE3 8282[2]	900		Good	Very good	Very good
7	**Whirlpool** Duet GEW9200L[W]	800		Good	Very good	Very good
8	**Whirlpool** LEQ8000J[Q] **A CR Best Buy**	400		Good	Very good	Very good
9	**Whirlpool** GEW9868K[Q]	700		Good	Very good	Very good
10	**Kenmore** (Sears) Elite 6283[2]	430		Good	Very good	Very good
11	**Kenmore** (Sears) Elite 6304[2]	730		Good	Very good	Very good
12	**Kenmore** (Sears) Elite 6206[2]	770		Good	Very good	Very good
13	**Whirlpool** Gold GEQ9858J[Q]	500		Good	Very good	Very good
14	**Frigidaire** Gallery GLER642A[S]	400		Good	Good	Good
15	**Amana** ALE866SA[W]	530		Good	Very good	Good
16	**GE** DPXH46EA[WW]	450		Good	Good	Very good
17	**Maytag** Atlantis MDE8600AY[W]	550		Good	Very good	Good
18	**Maytag** Performa PYE4500AY[W]	420		Good	Very good	Good
19	**GE** DWSR405EB[WW]	400		Good	Very good	Very good

See report, page 20. Based on tests published in Consumer Reports in July 2002, with updated prices and availability.

The tests behind the Ratings

In **brand & model,** the bracketed letter or number is a color code. **Overall score** is based primarily on drying performance, drum capacity, noise, and convenience. **Drying** combines performance on four types of laundry loads of different sizes and fabric mixes. **Capacity** varies from about 5.7 to 7.5 cubic feet. **Noise** reflects judgments by panelists. **Price** is approximate retail.

Recommendations and notes

Models listed as similar and gas equivalents should offer performance comparable to the tested model's, although features may differ.

Most full-sized dryers have: A moisture sensor. A dial with two or three automatic drying cycles. Separate start and temperature controls with at least three settings. Timed-dry and air-fluff (without heat) settings of at least one hour. An end-of-cycle signal. Raised edges to contain spills. A lint filter located in the drum opening. A drum light. A door that can be reversed to open left or right. Dimensions of about 44 inches high, 27 inches wide, and 28 inches deep. A full one-year warranty.

> 1 > **KENMORE** (Sears) Elite 6393[2] **Excellent overall.** Impressive on large loads and delicates. Similar: 6394[ ], 6395[ ]. Gas equivalent: 7393[ ], 7394[ ], 7395[ ].

2 ► **KENMORE** (Sears) 6280[2] **A CR Best Buy Superb drying for a good price.** But warmer than most on delicates. Fewer features than most. Similar: 6281[ ], 6282[ ]. Gas equivalent: 7280[ ], 7281[ ], 7282[ ].

3 ► **GE** Profile Performance DPSE592EA[WW] **Very good.** Impressive on large loads and delicates. 10-yr. warranty. Gas equivalent: DPSE592GA[ ].

4 ► **MAYTAG** Neptune MDE7500AY[W] **Strong performer.** Impressive on large loads and delicates. Similar: MDE5500AY[W]. Gas equivalent: MDG7500AW[ ], MDG5500AW[ ].

5 ► **GE** Profile DPSB519EB[WW] **Very good and feature-rich.** Impressive on large loads and delicates. Gas equivalent: DPSB519GB[ ].

6 ► **KENMORE** (Sears) Elite HE3 8282[2] **Very good, but pricey.** Performs better when paired with the Kenmore Elite 4292 HE3t washer. Feature-rich and exceptionally quiet. Has front window. Gas equivalent: HE3 9282[ ].

7 ► **WHIRLPOOL** Duet GEW9200L[W] **Much like #6.** Performs better when paired with the Whirlpool Duet HT GHW9200L washer. Exceptionally quiet. Gas equivalent: GGW9200L[ ].

8 ► **WHIRLPOOL** LEQ8000J[Q] **A CR Best Buy Very good performance for a good price.** But fewer features than most. Similar: LEQ9858L[ ]. Gas equivalent: LGQ8000J[ ].

9 ► **WHIRLPOOL** GEW9868K[Q] **Solid, feature-rich performer.** Very quiet. Gas equivalent: GGW9868K[ ].

10 ► **KENMORE** (Sears) Elite 6283[2] **Lots of performance for the price.** Simple, basic controls. Similar: 6284[ ], 6285[ ]. Gas equivalent: 7283[ ], 7284[ ], 7285[ ].

11 ► **KENMORE** (Sears) Elite 6304[2] **Very good. Lots of features.** Impressive on delicates. Similar: 6305[ ], 6306[ ]. Gas equivalent: 7304[ ], 7305[ ].

12 ► **KENMORE** (Sears) Elite 6206[2] **Lots of features.** Impressive on delicates. Similar: 6208[ ]. Gas equivalent: 7206[ ], 7208[ ]

13 ► **WHIRLPOOL** Gold GEQ9858J[Q] **A very good machine.** Gas equivalent: GGQ9858J[ ].

14 ► **FRIGIDAIRE** Gallery GLER642A[S] **A very good machine.** Gas equivalent: GLGR642A[ ].

15 ► **AMANA** ALE866SA[W] **Very good.** Stainless-steel drum. Gas equivalent: ALG866SA[ ].

16 ► **GE** DPXH46EA[WW] **Very good.** Impressive on large loads and delicates. Gas equivalent: DPXH46GA[ ].

17 ► **MAYTAG** Atlantis MDE8600AY[W] **Very good.** Moisture monitor shows load's dryness; use to get clothes damp-dry for ironing. Similar: MDE7600AY[ ]. Gas equivalent: MDG8600AW[ ], MDG7600AW[ ].

18 ► **MAYTAG** Performa PYE4500AY[W] **Very good machine.** Impressive on delicates. Drum opening smaller than most. Similar: PYE4057[ ], PYE4058[ ]. Gas equivalent: PYG4500AY[ ].

19 ► **GE** DWSR405EB[WW] **Not as good at drying as other sensor models.** Gas equivalent: DWSR405GB[ ].

Features at a glance — Dryers

Tested products (keyed to the Ratings) Key no. Brand	End-of-cycle signal	Drying rack	Express dry	Cool-down	Porcelain top	Touchpad controls
1 Kenmore	•	•				
2 Kenmore	•					
3 GE			•	•	•	
4 Maytag	•			•	•	
5 GE	•		•	•	•	
6 Kenmore	•	•	•	•		
7 Whirlpool	•	•	•		•	
8 Whirlpool					•	
9 Whirlpool	•	•		•		
10 Kenmore	•	•				
11 Kenmore	•	•	•	•	•	•
12 Kenmore	•	•	•	•	•	
13 Whirlpool	•			•		
14 Frigidaire		•		•		
15 Amana	•	•		•		
16 GE		•				
17 Maytag		•			•	
18 Maytag	•			•		
19 GE		•		•		

DVD players

Most models demonstrated a high level of performance across the board and would make a fine choice.

Check to see which features and connectivity options best suit your needs, and determine how much you want to spend. Among single-disc players, the Samsung DVD-S222 and Apex AD-2100, both $100, are excellent, inexpensive choices. If you plan to use your DVD player for back-to-back play of audio CDs as well as movies, consider a multidisc changer. All three players in this group are excellent. Progressive-scan players, which can also be used with a conventional TV, are a worthwhile option for those planning a digital TV purchase. Key features for these models are listed in the table. See product report for explanation of features.

Overall Ratings — In performance order

Rating key: Excellent ● | Very good ◖ | Good ○ | Fair ◗ | Poor ●

Overall score scale: 0 — P F G VG E — 100

KEY NO.	BRAND & MODEL	PRICE	OVERALL SCORE	PICTURE QUALITY	EASE OF USE
STANDARD SINGLE-DISC PLAYERS					
1	**Hitachi** DVP325U	$130		⊙	⊙
2	**Sony** DVP-NS315	130		⊙	◖
3	**Pioneer** DV-353-K	125		⊙	◖
4	**Toshiba** SD-2800	130		⊙	◖
5	**JVC** XV-S402SL	130		⊙	◖
6	**Samsung** DVD-S222	100		⊙	◖
7	**Yamaha** DVD-S520	200		⊙	◖
8	**Apex** AD-2100	100		⊙	◖
9	**Fisher** DVD-SL30	150		⊙	⊙
10	**Zenith** DVB211	100		⊙	○
11	**Sanyo** DWM-380	120		⊙	◖
STANDARD MULTIDISC PLAYERS					
12	**Toshiba** SD-2805	170		⊙	⊙
13	**Samsung** DVD-C621	150		⊙	◖
14	**Sony** DVP-NC615	180		⊙	◖
PROGRESSIVE-SCAN SINGLE-DISC PLAYERS					
15	**JVC** XV-S502SL	160		⊙	⊙
16	**Zenith** DVB216	130		⊙	⊙
17	**Samsung** DVD-P721M	200		⊙	◖
18	**Hitachi** DVP725U	180		⊙	⊙
19	**Denon** DVD-1600	500		⊙	◖
PROGRESSIVE-SCAN MULTIDISC PLAYERS					
20	**Sony** DVP-NC655P	230		⊙	◖
21	**Toshiba** SD-3805	200		⊙	⊙
22	**Yamaha** DVD-C920	450		⊙	◖

See report, page 64. Based on tests published in Consumer Reports in December 2002, with updated prices and availability.

The tests behind the Ratings

Overall score is based mainly on picture quality and ease of use. **Picture quality** indicates the sharpness and detail of video images. For progressive-scan models, score reflects performance with both conventional and HDTVs. **Ease of use** is our assessment of the remote control, console front panel, setup menu, basic playback functions, and features. **Price** is approximate retail.

Recommendations and notes

All models: Have parental-control function, multiple camera-angle options, resume-play function, multilingual setup menu, 12-month parts warranty. Played DVD-video and CD-audio discs. Played CD-R and CD-RW discs. Played DVD-R and DVD+R in our tests but could not play DVD-RAM discs. Output Dolby Digital and DTS multichannel digital audio. Have two-channel (stereo) analog-audio output. Let you program CD-track-play order. For multidisc models, have 5-disc, carousel-type changers that let you program the order of play from several CDs.

Most models: Have audio dynamic range control, virtual surround sound, coaxial and optical digital-audio output, video black-level control, screen saver, 3-month labor warranty. Played MP3-encoded audio files on CD. Played DVD-RW and DVD+RW discs in our tests.

STANDARD SINGLE-DISC PLAYERS

1▷ **HITACHI** DVP325U **Excellent performance at a modest price.**

2▷ **SONY** DVP-NS315 **An excellent player.** Allows order of play of DVD-video titles and chapters to be programmed. But no optical digital-audio output.

3▷ **PIONEER** DV-353-K **Excellent performance at a modest price.** Allows order of play of DVD-video titles and chapters to be programmed. But lacks video black-level control.

4▷ **TOSHIBA** SD-2800 **Excellent performance at a modest price.** But couldn't play DVD+RW discs in our tests. Has center-channel dialog enhancement. Allows order of play of DVD-video titles and chapters to be programmed.

5▷ **JVC** XV-S402SL **An excellent performer.** Has chapter-gallery feature to show first scene of several chapters at the same time. Allows order of play of DVD-video titles to be programmed. But lacks video black-level control. Similar model XV-S400BK, $150, is black instead of silver.

6▷ **SAMSUNG** DVD-S222 **Excellent performance at a low price.** Has chapter-gallery feature to show first scene of several chapters at the same time. Allows order of play of DVD-video chapters to be programmed. But failed to play CD-audio portion of hybrid SACD discs. 12-month labor warranty.

7▷ **YAMAHA** DVD-S520 **Excellent.** Has chapter-preview feature to show the first few seconds of each chapter in sequence. Allows order of play of DVD-video titles and chapters to be programmed. 12-month labor warranty.

8▷ **APEX** AD-2100 **Excellent and low priced.** Plays JPEG files on CDs. Allows order of play of DVD-video titles and chapters to be programmed. But no optical digital-audio output. Played back some older audio-CD discs with excessive treble. Lacks virtual surround sound and video black-level control.

9▷ **FISHER** DVD-SL30 **Excellent player.** But no coaxial digital-audio output. Lacks audio dynamic range control, video black-level control, and screen saver. Played back some older audio-CD discs with excessive treble. 12-month labor warranty.

10▷ **ZENITH** DVB211 **Very good and well priced.** Better than most at playing damaged CDs. But has no true console display. No optical digital-audio output. Lacks video black-level control. Discontinued, but may still be available.

11▷ **SANYO** DWM-380 **Very good and well priced.** But no coaxial digital-audio output. Lacks audio dynamic range control and video black-level control. Plays back some older audio-CD discs with excessive treble. 12-month labor warranty.

Features at a glance — DVD players

Tested products (keyed to the Ratings) Key no. — Brand	Coaxial output	Optical output	Surround sound	Screen saver	Chapter gallery
STANDARD SINGLE-DISC PLAYERS					
1▷ Hitachi	•	•	•	•	
2▷ Sony	•		•	•	
3▷ Pioneer	•	•	•	•	
4▷ Toshiba	•	•	•	•	
5▷ JVC	•	•	•	•	•
6▷ Samsung	•	•	•	•	•
7▷ Yamaha		•	•	•	•
8▷ Apex	•				
9▷ Fisher		•	•		
10▷ Zenith	•		•	•	
11▷ Sanyo			•	•	
STANDARD MULTIDISC PLAYERS					
12▷ Toshiba	•	•	•	•	
13▷ Samsung	•	•	•	•	
14▷ Sony	•		•	•	
PROGRESSIVE-SCAN SINGLE-DISC PLAYERS					
15▷ JVC	•	•	•	•	•
16▷ Zenith	•	•	•	•	•
17▷ Samsung	•	•	•	•	
18▷ Hitachi	•	•	•	•	
19▷ Denon		•	•	•	•
PROGRESSIVE-SCAN MULTIDISC PLAYERS					
20▷ Sony	•	•	•	•	•
21▷ Toshiba	•	•	•	•	
22▷ Yamaha	•	•	•		•

Recommendations and notes

STANDARD MULTIDISC PLAYERS

12▷ **TOSHIBA** SD-2805 **An excellent performer.** Better than most at playing damaged CDs. Has center-channel dialog enhancement. But doesn't allow order of play of DVD-video discs to be programmed. Discontinued, but may still be available.

13▷ **SAMSUNG** DVD-C621 **An excellent performer.** Has chapter-gallery feature to show first scene of several chapters at the same time. Has headphone jack with volume control. Allows order of play of DVD-video chapters to be programmed. Failed to play CD-audio portion of hybrid SACD discs. 12-month labor warranty.

14▷ **SONY** DVP-NC615 **An excellent performer.** Allows order of play of DVD-video titles and chapters to be programmed. But no optical digital-audio output.

PROGRESSIVE-SCAN SINGLE-DISC PLAYERS

15▷ **JVC** XV-S502SL **Excellent and modestly priced for this type of player.** Displays still pictures from JPEG files on CDs. Has chapter-gallery feature to show first scene of several chapters at the same time. But video in progressive-scan mode less detailed than that of other progressive-scan models. Similar model XV-S500BK, $170, is black instead of silver. Similar: XV-S500BK.

16▷ **ZENITH** DVB216 **Excellent and low priced for this type of player.** But lacks video black-level control. Discontinued, but may still be available.

17▷ **SAMSUNG** DVD-P721M **Excellent.** Displays still pictures from JPEG files on CDs and Memory Stick media, and can also play MP3 files on Memory Stick media. Has headphone jack with volume control. Allows order of play of DVD-video chapters to be programmed. But failed to play CD-audio portion of hybrid SACD discs. 12-month labor warranty.

18▷ **HITACHI** DVP725U **Excellent and modestly priced for this type of player.** Has headphone jack with volume control. But video in progressive-scan mode not as smooth and detailed as that of other progressive-scan models.

19▷ **DENON** DVD-1600 **Excellent.** High price gets you DVD-Audio playback and Dolby Digital and DTS decoders. Has center-channel dialog enhancement. Has chapter-preview feature to show the first few seconds of each chapter in sequence. Has headphone jack with volume control. Allows order of play of DVD-Audio titles and chapters to be programmed. But no coaxial digital-audio output or screen saver. 12-month labor warranty.

PROGRESSIVE-SCAN MULTIDISC PLAYERS

20▷ **SONY** DVP-NC655P **Excellent.** Has chapter-gallery feature to show first scene of several chapters at the same time. Allows order of play of DVD-video titles and chapters to be programmed. 12-month labor warranty.

21▷ **TOSHIBA** SD-3805 **Bargain price for an excellent progressive-scan multidisc player.** Has center-channel dialog enhancement. But doesn't allow order of play of DVD-video discs to be programmed.

22▷ **YAMAHA** DVD-C920 **Excellent.** High price gets you DVD-Audio playback and Dolby Digital and DTS decoders. Has center-channel dialog enhancement. Has chapter-preview feature to show the first few seconds of each chapter in sequence. Allows order of play of DVD-Audio discs, titles, and chapters to be programmed, but doesn't allow order of play of DVD-video discs to be programmed. 12-month labor warranty.

Flooring, wood

Prefinished solid-wood flooring offers authenticity and can be refinished over and over. But it's hard to install. Engineered-wood flooring costs about as much as solid wood and generally can't be refinished as often. Plastic-laminate flooring offers relatively easy installation and a tough surface. It can mimic stone, slate, and an array of other materials to fit many décors. The Pergo Select Concord Oak and the Formica Butterscotch Oak both performed excellently, though the Formica costs a bit less per square foot.

Overall Ratings — In performance order

Excellent ● Very good ◕ Good ○ Fair ◔ Poor ●

BRAND AND MODEL	PRICE PER PACKAGE	PRICE PER SQUARE FT.	OVERALL SCORE	STAINS	FOOT TRAFFIC	DENTS	SUNLIGHT (UV)
PREFINISHED SOLID-WOOD FLOORING							
Hartco Danville Strip Sahara	$95	$4.75		◕	◕	●	○
P.G. Hardwood Flooring Inc. Model Plus Oak	105	5.25		◕	◕	●	○
Bruce Laurel Strip	108	5.40		◕	◉	●	◔
Mirage Classic Red Oak	145	7.25		◕	◕	●	◕
Bruce Natural Reflections	172	4.30		◕	◕	●	◔
ENGINEERED-WOOD FLOORING							
Mannington American Classics Hudson Natural White Oak Plank	240	9.13		◕	◕	◔	◕
Harris-Tarkett Longstrip Everglades White Oak Natural	189	6.41		○	◕	●	○
Anderson Lincoln Plank Red Oak	146	4.79		◕	◕	◕	○
PLASTIC-LAMINATE FLOORING							
Formica Butterscotch Oak	79	3.71		◉	◉	◉	◉
Pergo Select Concord Oak PS 5280	67	4.32		◉	◉	◉	◉
Armstrong Princeton Oak Natural	75	3.47		◉	◉	◉	◉
Mannington Natural Oak	77	3.58		◉	◉	◕	◉
Wilsonart Classic Harvest Oak	80	4.00		◉	◉	○	◉
Congoleum Evermore	92	3.79		◉	◕	○	◉

See report, page 161. Based on tests published in Consumer Reports in February 2001, with updated prices and availability.

The tests behind the Ratings

Overall score is based primarily on foot traffic, and laboratory tests for resistance to dents, sunlight (UV), and stains, as well as the estimated number of times it can be refinished. **Stain resistance** shows how each product reacted to spilled water, wine, and other beverages; household cleaners such as ammonia; and stain-causing substances such as mustard. **Foot traffic** represents how well each product held up after being exposed to foot traffic for a year. **Dent resistance** denotes damage caused by a ½-pound steel ball dropped on its surface from heights of 1 to 48 inches. **Sunlight resistance** (UV) reflects color change after exposure to high levels of ultraviolet light. We also gauged slip resistance using an instrument that measures friction. All proved slippery enough to warrant caution. **Price per package** is the national average, rounded off to the nearest dollar, based on a survey. **Price per square foot** is the cost of each package of flooring divided by its coverage, which is estimated by the flooring manufacturer.

Most prefinished solid-wood flooring: Is ¾-inch thick. Has 36 to 46 pieces and covers 20 square feet per package. Has gloss finish. Has finish warranty of 15 to 25 years, though there are many limitations. **Most engineered-wood flooring:** Is ⅜- to 9/16-inches thick overall, with ¾₄- to 9/64-inch-thick veneer. Has 30 to 35 pieces and covers 26 to 30 square feet per package. Has finish warranty of 5 to 25 years, though there are many limitations. **Most plastic-laminate flooring:** Is 7⅝- to 8 inches wide. Has 6 to 9 pieces and covers 20 to 22 square feet per package. Has finish warranty of 15 to 25 years, but there are many limitations.

Home theater in a box

A home theater in a box, which consists of at least a receiver and six speakers, is an easy way to start a system.
 Make sure that the components you already own—DVD player, camcorder, and MP3 player—can connect to the system you're considering. Then look for a model that includes the features and capabilities you need. The top-rated Sony HT-DDW740 is very good, and is a **CR Best Buy** at $300. Key features for these models are listed in the table. See the product guide for an explanation of the features.

Excellent	Very good	Good	Fair	Poor
●	◒	○	◐	●

KEY NO.	BRAND & MODEL	PRICE	OVERALL SCORE	SOUND QUALITY	EASE OF USE	FEATURES
			0 P F G VG E 100			
1	**Sony** HT-DDW740	$300		◒	◒	◒
2	**Pioneer** HTD-510DV	400		●	○	◐
3	**Panasonic** SC-HT75	400		◒	○	○
4	**Yamaha** YHT-500	600		◒	○	◒
5	**Yamaha** YHT-300	400		◒	○	◒
6	**RCA** RT-DVD1	375		◒	○	○
7	**Sony** DAV-C450	500		◒	○	○
8	**JBL** Cinema ProPack 600II	900		○	○	◒

See report, page 70. Based on tests published in Consumer Reports in November 2002 with updated prices and availability.

The tests behind the Ratings

Overall score is based mostly on sound quality. **Sound quality** represents the accuracy of the front speakers, subwoofer, and center-channel speaker. **Ease of use** evaluates the console controls and remote control. We also judge models for useful features. **Recommendations and notes** include size (height by width by depth, in inches) and weight. **Price** is approximate retail.

Recommendations and notes

All tested models have: A receiver and six speakers: front left and right, center channel, rear left and right surround, and subwoofer. Decoders for Dolby Digital audio, Dolby Pro Logic or Pro Logic II surround audio, and other digital-signal processing (DSP) modes. At least 24 radio-station presets. Headphone jack. Mute button. Wiring and setup instructions. **Most tested models:** Have DTS decoder. Can play CD-RW discs and discs with MP3 files. Can't play SACD or DVD-Audio discs.

1> **SONY** HT-DDW740 **Very good and low-priced.** No DVD player. Front and rear surround 5.75x3.25x4.75 in., 1.7 lb. each; center channel 3.25x9.25x4.75 in., 2.1 lb.; subwoofer 13x10.75x16 in., 20 lb. Optical and coaxial digital-audio inputs. 2-yr. warranty.

2> **PIONEER** HTD-510DV **Excellent sound, but shy on features.** Front 10.75x6x7 in., 4.1 lb. each; rear surround 6x4.5x4 in., 1.6 lb. each; center channel 4.75x 14.5x5 in., 3.8 lb.; subwoofer

14.25x7.5x13 in., 10.6 lb. Coaxial digital-audio input. Bass-boost switch. Can't play CDs containing MP3 files. Discontinued, but may still be available.

3> **PANASONIC** SC-HT75 **Very good.** DVD player. Can play DVD-Audio discs. Front, center channel, and rear surround 5.5x3.5x4.5 in., 1.7 lb. each; subwoofer 12.5x6.5x12 in., 8.4 lb. No digital-audio input, bass/treble adjustment, or receiver-display dimmer.

4> **YAMAHA** YHT-500 **Very good.** DVD player. Front and rear surround 8.25x4x5 in., 2.7 lb. each; center channel 4x10.75x5 in., 3.8 lb.; subwoofer 14.5x8x14.5 in., 18.7 lb. 5.1 input for external digital-audio decoder. Has S-video and component-video outputs that can be used only with included DVD player. Optical and coaxial digital-audio inputs. 2-yr. warranty. Separate tone control for headphone jack.

5> **YAMAHA** YHT-300 **Very good.** No DVD player. Front, center channel, and rear surround 6.75x 4.25x4.75 in., 1.7 lb. each; subwoofer 14.5x8x14.5 in., 18.7 lb. 5.1 input for external digital-audio decoder. Optical and coaxial digital-audio inputs. 2-yr. warranty. Separate tone control for headphone jack.

6> **RCA** RT-DVD1 **Good.** DVD player. Can play DVD-Audio discs, but lacks standard audio input. Front, center channel, and rear surround 5.25x3.5x4.25 in., 1.1 lb. each; subwoofer 14x6.5x14 in., 10.8 lb. Optical and coaxial digital-audio inputs. No DTS decoder.

7> **SONY** DAV-C450 **Good.** DVD player. Front, center channel, and rear surround 4.5x4.5x4.5 in., 1.4 lb. each; subwoofer 14x7x14 in., 11.3 lb. Has S-video and component-video outputs that can be used only with included DVD player. No bass/treble adjustment or sleep timer. Can play SACD music discs but not CD-RW discs or CDs containing MP3 files.

8> **JBL** Cinema ProPack 600II **Good, and full-featured.** DVD player. Front and rear surround 4.5x3.25x3.75 in., 1.1 lb. each; center channel 3.25x7.75x3.75 in., 1.8 lb.; subwoofer 15x13x13 in., 20.1 lb. Only tested model with front-panel A/V input. Has S-video and component-video outputs that can be used only with included DVD player. 5.1 input for external digital-audio decoder. Optical and coaxial digital-audio inputs.

Features at a glance — Home theater in a box

Tested products (keyed to the Ratings) Key no. Brand	DVD player (no. of discs)	Powered subwoofer	Composite-video inputs	Composite-video outputs	S-video inputs	S-video outputs
1 Sony		•	3	1		
2 Pioneer	5					
3 Panasonic	5					
4 Yamaha	1	•	4	1		
5 Yamaha		•	4	1		
6 RCA	1		2	1	1	
7 Sony	5					
8 JBL	5		3	1	3	1

Irons

Even the least expensive steam irons on the market today come with plenty of convenient features, such as automatic shut-off and self-cleaning capabilities. The top-rated Rowenta Professional Luxe DM-880, $98, produced an impressive amount of steam, but it's heavy and expensive. For a fraction of the price, consider the Rowenta Powerglide 2 DM-273, $57, or either of the T-Fal models. Key features for these models are listed in the table. See the product guide for an explanation of features.

	Excellent	Very good	Good	Fair	Poor
	●	◒	○	◒	●

KEY NO.	BRAND & MODEL	PRICE	OVERALL SCORE	STEAM RATE	FILLING EASE	WATER GAUGE
1	**Rowenta** Professional Luxe DM-880	$98		●	○	○
2	**Krups** Intelligent V70	100		◒	○	○
3	**Rowenta** Powerglide 2 DM-273	57		○	○	◒
4	**T-Fal** Avantis 90	60		◒	○	◒
5	**T-Fal** UltraGlide Turbo 1664	52		○	○	◒
6	**Black & Decker** ProFinish X750	50		◒	◒	◒
7	**Rowenta** Powerglide DE-08	53		◒	●	○
8	**Black & Decker** ProFinish X747	50		○	◒	◒
9	**Black & Decker** SteamXpress S680	30		○	◒	●
10	**Black & Decker** Quick 'N Easy X380	20		◒	○	◒
11	**Kenmore** (Sears) Pro Steam KSR400	45		◒	◒	◒
12	**Black & Decker** Quick 'N Easy X340	16		◒	○	◒
13	**Toastmaster** 3302	11		○	◒	○

See report, page 24. Based on tests published in Consumer Reports in September 2001, with updated prices and availability.

The tests behind the Ratings

Overall score is based primarily on steam rate, ease of filling the reservoir, visibility of the water gauge, and setting ease. **Steam rate** reflects the amount of steam produced within the first ten minutes of ironing. **Filling ease** indicates how easy it is to fill and empty the water tank. **Water gauge** reflects how easy it is to see the water level in the gauge. In Recommendations and notes, weight is without water, rounded to the nearest quarter pound. **Price** is approximate retail.

Recommendations and notes

Models listed as similar should offer performance comparable to the tested model's although features may differ.
Most irons have: Spray, burst of steam, automatic shutoff, and self-cleaning. One or two indicator lights, adjustable or variable steam control, a temperature control and fabric guide under the handle, and a large water chamber (5 to 9¼ ounces) at the saddle area. A pivoting 7½- to 10½-foot cord that wraps around the iron for storage. A one-year warranty and draws 1,100 to 1,500 watts. Except as noted, setting ease was Very Good or Good.

1 ▷ **ROWENTA** Professional Luxe DM-880 **Outstanding steamer, but expensive and heavy.** Large tank capacity and antidrip feature. But fabric guide cluttered, cord may get in way, auto shutoff light hard to see. 3½ lb.

2 ▷ **KRUPS** Intelligent V70 **Illuminated temperature dial, heatproof carrying case, large tank capacity.** But fabric guide cluttered, cord may get in way. Spit or leaked from fill hole occasionally. 3¼ lb. Similar: V65.

3 ▷ **ROWENTA** Powerglide 2 DM-273 **Very good spray, temperature-ready light easy to see.** But fabric guide cluttered,

leaked from soleplate at low settings. Self-cleaning only so-so. 2¾ lb. Similar: DM-253.

4▷ T-FAL Avantis 90 **Very good spray, anticalcium feature.** But fabric guide cluttered, water level hard to see, and cord may get in way. 3¼ lb. Similar: Avantis 100.

5▷ T-FAL UltraGlide Turbo 1664 **Very good spray, anticalcium feature.** 2¾ lb.

6▷ BLACK & DECKER ProFinish X750 **Fabric guide easy to read, front temperature control easy to set.** But cord may get in way and steam/spray controls awkward Vertical steam. 3 lb.

7▷ ROWENTA Powerglide DE-08 **Very good spray.** But fabric guide cluttered and cord may get in way. Tank hard to fill, no indicator for auto shutoff. 2¾ lb.

8▷ BLACK & DECKER ProFinish X747 **Similar comments to X750, but steamed more lightly.** 3 lb. Sold only at Wal-Mart.

9▷ BLACK & DECKER SteamXpress S680 **Fabric guide easy to read, front temperature control easy to set.** But sprayed unevenly and too far, and cord may get in way. 2¼ lb. Similar: S650.

10▷ BLACK & DECKER Quick 'N Easy X380 **Fabric guide easy to read, front temperature control easy to set.** But steam/spray controls awkward, spit or leaked from fill hole occasionally. 2 lb. Similar: X360.

11▷ KENMORE (Sears) Pro Steam KSR400 **Beeps for auto shutoff.** Anticalcium, antidrip feature. Weighs more than most. 3½ lb.

12▷ BLACK & DECKER Quick 'N Easy X340 **Similar comments to X380 (above), but no spray, burst of steam, or auto shut-off.** 1¾ lb.

13▷ TOASTMASTER 3302 **There are better choices.** 1¾ lb.

Features at a glance — Irons

Key no.	Brand	Auto shutoff	Self-cleaning	Spray	Burst of steam	Vertical steam	Soleplate
1▷	**Rowenta**	•	•	•	•	•	SS
2▷	**Krups**	•	•	•	•	•	SS
3▷	**Rowenta**	•	•	•	•	•	SS
4▷	**T-Fal**	•	•	•	•	•	EN
5▷	**T-Fal**	•	•	•	•	•	EN
6▷	**Black & Decker**	•	•	•	•	•	NS
7▷	**Rowenta**	•	•	•	•	•	SS
8▷	**Black & Decker**	•	•	•	•	•	SS
9▷	**Black & Decker**	•	•	•	•		NS
10▷	**Black & Decker**	•	•	•	•		NS
11▷	**Kenmore**	•		•	•		SS
12▷	**Black & Decker**		•				NS
13▷	**Toastmaster**		•				AL

Soleplate surface material: AL=Aluminum; EN=Enamel nonstick; NS=Nonstick; SS=Stainless steel

Kitchen knives

If you frequently cook gourmet meals, you might appreciate the superior precision, control, and comfort afforded by the expensive knives that top the Ratings. You can get fine quality for far less, however. The two **CR Best Buys,** Farberware Pro Forged, $90 for nine pieces, and Chicago Cutlery Metropolitan, $60 for eight pieces, are very good choices. And, at $130 for seven pieces, the Oxo Good Grips MV55-PRO offers excellent performance and value. If you prefer no-maintenance knives, the Cutco Classic ($80 for two pieces) was very good overall. Much more economical is the Farberware Classic set ($20 for 12 pieces).

Overall Ratings In performance order

Rating key: Excellent ● | Very good ◖ | Good ○ | Fair ◑ | Poor ●

KEY NO.	BRAND & MODEL	PRICE	OVERALL SCORE	CUTTING PERFORMANCE	HANDLE COMFORT	BALANCE
			0 P F G VG E 100			
KNIVES THAT NEED HONING						
1	**Wüsthof** Trident Grand Prix	$300		●	●	●
2	**Henckels** Twin Select	500		●	●	●
3	**Wüsthof** Trident Classic	300		●	◖	●
4	**Henckels** Professional "S"	230		●	◖	●
5	**Wüsthof** Culinar 8169	450		●	●	●
6	**Henckels** Four Star	200		●	●	◖
7	**Tramontina** Professional L-400	70		◖	●	●
8	**LamsonSharp** Forged	200		◖	◖	●
9	**Chef's Choice** Trizor Professional 10X	200		●	◖	◖
10	**Oxo** Good Grips MV55-PRO	130		●	◖	●
11	**Farberware** Pro Forged **A CR Best Buy**	90		◖	◖	●
12	**Chicago Cutlery** Metropolitan **A CR Best Buy**	60		◖	◖	●
13	**Tupperware** Chef Series	440		◖	◖	◖
14	**Henckels** Five Star	230		●	○	◖
15	**Chicago Cutlery** Insignia	100		◖	◖	●
16	**Henckels** Twin Gourmet	100		●	◖	◖
17	**Chicago Cutlery** Walnut Tradition	60		●	○	◖
18	**KitchenAid** Epicurean	200		●	◖	○
19	**Farberware** Pro Stainless	70		○	●	●
20	**Pampered Chef** 1041	45		◖	○	○
NO-MAINTENANCE KNIVES						
21	**Cutco** Classic	80		●	◑	○
22	**Farberware** Classic	20		◑	○	○
23	**Henckels** Eversharp Pro	60		◑	○	●
24	**Oxo** Good Grips	10		◑	○	○

See report, page 26. Based on tests published in Consumer Reports in December 2002.

The tests behind the Ratings

Brand and model is line we tested; we judged only chef's, slicing, utility, and paring knives in a line. **Overall score** is based mainly on cutting performance and handle comfort and balance but factors in corrosion resistance and, for no-maintenance knives, blade-edge durability. Because we re-evaluated our assessment of overall score, some Ratings may differ from previous reports. **Cutting performance** reflects how well each type cut through foods. **Handle comfort** and **balance** are based on the chef's knife. **Price** is approximate retail for the smallest available set that includes all or most of the four tested knives and typically a block and steel. If sets do not include all four knives, we note missing ones and their approximate price. Recommendations and notes indicate number of pieces in the set, blade type, and handle material if not hard plastic or composite.

Recommendations and notes

Most knives tested in these sizes: chef's, 8 inches; slicing, 8 to 10 inches; utility, 4 to 6 inches; paring, 3 to 4 inches.

KNIVES THAT NEED HONING

1. **WÜSTHOF** Trident Grand Prix **Forged.** 8-piece set. Better for wet grip than most. Heavier than most.

2. **HENCKELS** Twin Select **Forged.** 7-piece set. Stainless-steel handles. Heavier than most.

3. **WÜSTHOF** Trident Classic **Forged.** 8-piece set.

4. **HENCKELS** Professional "S" **Forged.** 7-piece set.

5. **WÜSTHOF** Culinar 8169 **Forged.** 6-piece set (not included: utility, $65). Stainless-steel handles. Heavier than most.

6. **HENCKELS** Four Star **Forged.** 7-piece set (not included: slicer, $82).

7. **TRAMONTINA** Professional L-400 **Forged.** 3-piece set (not included: slicer, $35). Heavier than most.

8. **LAMSONSHARP** Forged **Forged.** 6-piece set. Wood handles; more prone to damage but offer better wet grip than most. Blade more likely to corrode than most. Maker will sharpen for free (you pay shipping).

9. **CHEF'S CHOICE** Trizor Professional 10X **Forged.** 3-piece set (not included: slicer, $125). Better for wet grip than most. Heavier than most.

10. **OXO** Good Grips MV55-PRO **Stamped.** 7-piece set. Rubber-coated steel handles are bulky but offer better wet grip than most. Blade more likely to corrode than most.

11. **FARBERWARE** Pro Forged **A CR Best Buy** **Forged.** 9-piece set. Handles are bulky. Utility knife too small and flexible.

12. **CHICAGO** Cutlery Metropolitan **A CR Best Buy** **Stamped.** 8-piece set. Handles are bulky. Lighter than most.

13. **TUPPERWARE** Chef Series **Forged.** 8-piece set (not included: slicer, $65). Heavier than most. Utility knife too small and flexible. Sold mainly through in-home parties.

14. **HENCKELS** Five Star **Forged.** 7-piece set. Handles are bulky. Blade more likely to corrode than most.

15. **CHICAGO CUTLERY** Insignia **Forged.** 10-piece set. Heavier than most.

16. **HENCKELS** Twin Gourmet **Stamped.** 7-piece set. Gap between handle and blade. Blade more likely to corrode than most.

17. **CHICAGO CUTLERY** Walnut Tradition **Stamped.** 6-piece set. Wood handles are bulky and more prone to damage but offer better wet grip than most. Gap between handle and blade. Lighter than most.

18. **KITCHENAID** Epicurean **Forged.** 5-piece set (not included: slicer, $90; utility, $60). Heavier than most. Utility knife too small and flexible.

19. **FARBERWARE** Pro Stainless **Forged.** 8-piece set. Stainless-steel handles. Utility knife is serrated.

20. **PAMPERED CHEF** 1041 **Stamped.** 2-piece carving set (not included: chef's knife, $26; utility, $19; paring, $15). Lighter than most. No sharpening steel; some knives come in a storage/sharpening case. Sold through sales representatives only.

NO-MAINTENANCE KNIVES

21. **CUTCO** Classic **Stamped.** 2-piece set (not included: chef's knife, $94; slicer, $69). Blade more likely to corrode than most. Chef's and paring knives are fine-edged; slicing and utility knives are serrated. Maker will sharpen for free (you pay shipping). Sold through sales representatives only.

22. **FARBERWARE** Classic **Stamped.** 12-piece set. Better for wet grip than most. Gaps between handle and blade. All tested knives are serrated. Lighter than most.

23. **HENCKELS** Eversharp Pro **Stamped.** 7-piece set. Gap between handle and blade. All tested knives are serrated. Lighter than most.

24. **OXO** Good Grips **Stamped.** 2-piece set (not included: chef's knife, $12; slicer, $9). Handles are bulky and have fins that can trap food. Lighter than most. Chef's and paring knives are fine-edged, slicing and utility knives are serrated.

Lawn mowers—push-type

Push-type power mowers are good for small yards and trimming around flower beds. There are many very good choices. Choose a rear-bagging model if you bag your clippings. Consider the top-rated Yard Machines by MTD 11A-439G129, $200, and 11A-549G129, $220—both **CR Best Buys.** Side-bagging models often cost less. The Yard Machines by MTD 11C-084C062, $140, and Poulan Pro 38618, $180, are **CR Best Buys.** Electric models are lighter, quieter, and run cleaner than gas models, but keep you tethered to an outlet. The Black & Decker MM675, $200, includes a reversible handlebar to help keep the cord from tangling.

Ratings legend: Excellent ◖ Very good ◐ Good ○ Fair ◑ Poor ●

KEY NO.	BRAND & MODEL	PRICE	OVERALL SCORE	EVENNESS	MULCH	BAG	SIDE	HANDLING	EASE OF USE
			0 P F G VG E 100						
REAR-BAGGING MODELS									
1	**Yard Machines** by MTD 11A-439G129 **A CR Best Buy**	$200		◐	◐	◐	○	◐	○
2	**Yard Machines** by MTD 11A-549G129 **A CR Best Buy**	220		◐	◐	◐	○	◐	○
3	**Craftsman** (Sears) 38880	310		◐	○	○	◖	○	○
4	**Murray** 205310x92	200		○	◐	○	○	○	●
5	**Craftsman** (Sears) 38875	270		○	◑	○	○	○	●
6	**Snapper** MR216015B	310		○	○	◐	◑	○	●
7	**Murray** Select 22315x8	199		◐	◑	○	◐	◑	○
SIDE-BAGGING MODELS									
8	**Yard Machines** by MTD 11C-084C062 **A CR Best Buy**	140		◐	◐	○	○	◐	○
9	**Poulan Pro** 38618 **A CR Best Buy**	180		◐	◐	◐	○	◐	○
10	**Craftsman** (Sears) 38762	200		◐	◐	◐	○	◐	○
11	**Yard Machines** by MTD 11A-509W300 Gold	230		◐	○	○	○	◐	○
12	**Honda** Harmony II HRS216PDA	300		◐	○	●	◖	○	○
13	**Yard-Man** by MTD 11B-106C401	280		○	○	●	◐	○	○
14	**Murray** Select 22415x8A	160		○	◑	◑	●	◐	○
15	**Murray** 22516x92	150		○	◑	●	●	○	○
SIDE-BAGGING ELECTRIC MODELS									
16	**Black & Decker** MM675	200		○	◐	○	○	◐	◐

See report, page 99. Based on tests published in Consumer Reports in June 2002, with updated prices and availability.

The tests behind the Ratings

Overall score is based mainly on cutting performance, handling, and ease of use. **Evenness** shows average cutting performance for three modes. **Mulch** reflects how completely clippings are distributed over the lawn's surface. **Bag** denotes how many clippings the bag held before it filled or the chute clogged. **Side** shows how evenly clippings were dispersed in that mode. **Handling** includes ease of pushing and pulling, making U-turns, and maneuvering in tight spots. **Ease of use** includes ease of starting the engine, operating the blade-stopping controls, and adjusting the cutting height. Bag convenience and ease of changing modes are separate judgments that contribute to the overall score. **Price** is approximate retail, and includes equipment for all three mowing modes unless noted in the Recommendations and notes.

Recommendations and notes

Most models have: A four-stroke engine with primer bulb instead of choke. An engine-kill safety system. No throttle control on handle. Stamped-steel deck. A two-year warranty on mower and engine.

REAR-BAGGING MODELS

1 > **YARD MACHINES** by MTD 11A-439G129 **A CR Best Buy Well-rounded performance at a good price.** Easy to push. Cut height hard to adjust. Engine: 6 hp. Swath: 21 in. Not sold in CA.

2 > **YARD MACHINES** by MTD 11A-549G129 **A CR Best Buy Well-rounded performance, and good handling for a high-wheel model.** Easy to push. Cut height hard to adjust. Engine: 6 hp. Swath: 21 in. Not sold in CA, though similar: 11A-546U724 is.

3 > **CRAFTSMAN** (Sears) 38880 **Very good overall performance.** Good choice for side-discharging. Throttle and choke. Engine: 5.5 hp. Swath: 21 in.

4 > **MURRAY** 205310x92 **An average performer at good price.** Good handling for a high-wheel model. Less noisy than most. Weak in tall grass. Engine: 5.5 hp. Swath: 20 in. Not sold in CA.

5 > **CRAFTSMAN** (Sears) 38875 **Good handling for a high-wheel model.** Noisier than most. Cut height hard to adjust. Chute $30. Engine: 6.5 hp. Swath: 21 in.

6 > **SNAPPER** MR216015B **Good.** Mediocre vacuuming. Bag inconvenient to empty. U-turns and jockeying side-to-side hard. Noisier than most. Engine: 6 hp. Swath: 21 in. Bag $65; mulch kit $36; chute $20.

7 > **MURRAY** Select 22315x8 **Good.** Weak in tall grass. U-turns and jockeying side-to-side hard. High rear wheels. Engine: 6 hp. Swath: 22 in. Bag $43. Not sold in CA.

SIDE-BAGGING MODELS

8 > **YARD MACHINES** by MTD 11C-084C062 **A CR Best Buy Well-rounded performer.** Easy to push. Bag inconvenient. Engine: 4 hp. Swath: 22 in. Bag $40. Not sold in CA.

9 > **POULAN PRO** 38618 **A CR Best Buy Very good performer at a good price.** Easy to push. High rear wheels. U-turns hard. Cut height hard to adjust. Bag $40. Engine: 4 hp. Swath: 22 in. Not sold in CA.

10 > **CRAFTSMAN** (Sears) 38762 **Fine for mulching and side-discharging.** Easy to push. U-turns hard. Cut height hard to adjust. High rear wheels. Bag $40. Engine: 6 hp. Swath: 22 in. Not sold in CA, though similar 38763 is. Discontinued, but may still be available.

11 > **YARD MACHINES** by MTD 11A-509W300 Gold **Very good, with good handling for a high-wheel model.** Easy to push. Bag inconvenient. Handle vibrates. Bag $40. Engine: 6 hp. Swath: 22 in.

12 > **HONDA** Harmony II HRS216PDA **Great for side-discharging, but pricey.** Throttle and choke. Weak in tall grass. Bagging requires blade change. Engine: 5.5 hp. Swath: 21 in. Bag $45.

13 > **YARD-MAN** by MTD 11B-106C401 **Competent performer.** Engine: 6 hp. Swath: 20 in. Bag $40. Not sold in CA.

14 > **MURRAY** Select 22415x8A **There are better choices.** Mediocre vacuuming. Weak in tall grass. Handle vibrates. Requires blade change for mulching. Engine: 4 hp. Swath: 22 in. Mulch kit $25; bag $39. Not sold in CA.

15 > **MURRAY** 22516x92 **Lackluster performer.** Mediocre vacuuming. Weak in tall grass. Noisier than most. U-turns and jockeying side-to-side hard. Mulching cover hard to remove. Engine: 4 hp. Swath: 22 in. Bag $39. Not sold in CA.

SIDE-BAGGING ELECTRIC

16 > **BLACK & DECKER** MM675 **Impressive-and pricey-for an electric.** Flip-over handle eases U-turns, but cord is still an inconvenience. Plastic deck. Engine: 12 amps. Swath: 18 in. Bag $40.

Lawn mowers—self-propelled

Self-propelled power mowers are good choices for larger yards. Rear-bagging models generally have more bagging capacity and maneuverability than side-baggers, though they usually cost more. All of the tested mowers cut competently. The top-rated John Deere JX75, $800, delivers carpetlike evenness and easy mode changes but it's pricey. For strong performance at a lower price, consider the Craftsman 37779, $500, or John Deere JS63C, $410. Both are **CR Best Buys.**

Overall Ratings — In performance order

Rating legend: Excellent, Very good, Good, Fair, Poor

KEY NO.	BRAND & MODEL	PRICE	OVERALL SCORE	EVENNESS	MULCH	BAG	SIDE	HANDLING	EASE OF USE
	REAR-BAGGING MODELS								
1	**John Deere** JX75	$800		◐	○	◐	○	○	●
2	**Craftsman** (Sears) 37779 **A CR Best Buy**	500		◐	○	◐	○	◐	●
3	**Honda** Masters HR215K1HXA	950		◐	◐	◐	○	○	●
4	**Honda** Harmony HRB216TDA	640		○	○	◐	◐	○	●
5	**John Deere** JS63C **A CR Best Buy**	410		◐	◐	◐	◐	◐	●
6	**Toro** Super Recycler 20037 Personal Pace	520		◐	◐	◐	◐	◐	◐
7	**Yard-Man** 12A-979L401	430		◖	◐	◉	○	◐	◐
8	**Ariens** LM21ST	560		○	○	◐	◐	○	●
9	**Toro** Recycler 20017	370		◐	○	◐	○	○	◐
10	**Snapper** ELP21602	600		○	◐	○	○	○	◐
11	**Snapper** P2167517B1	550		◐	◐	◐	○	○	◐
12	**Toro** Recycler 20016	320		◐	○	◐	○	○	◐
13	**Lawn-Boy** Silver Series 10360	258		◐	○	○	◉	◐	○
14	**Snapper** MRP216015B	400		○	○	◐	○	◐	◐
15	**Lawn-Boy** SilverPro 10324	380		○	◐	◐	○	◐	○
16	**Yard-Man** by MTD 12A569T401	400		◖	○	○	○	◖	○
17	**Husqvarna** Crown Series 6522CH	400		○	◖	◖	◉	●	○
	SIDE-BAGGING MODELS								
18	**Honda** Harmony II HRS216K2SDA	390		◐	◐	●	◐	○	○
19	**Yard Machines** by MTD 12A-288A300 Gold	250		◐	◐	◖	◐	○	○

See report, page 102. Based on tests published in Consumer Reports in June 2002, with updated prices and availabilty.

The tests behind the Ratings

Overall score is based mainly on cutting performance, handling, and ease of use. **Evenness** shows average cutting performance for three modes. **Mulch** reflects how completely clippings are distributed over the lawn's surface. **Bag** denotes how many clippings the bag held before it filled or the chute clogged. **Side** shows how evenly clippings were dispersed in that mode. **Handling** includes ease of operating the drive controls, pushing and pulling, making U-turns, and maneuvering in tight spots. **Ease of use** includes ease of starting the engine, operating the blade-stopping controls, shifting speeds, and adjusting the cutting height. Bag convenience and ease of changing modes are separate judgments that contribute to the overall score. **Price** is approximate retail, and includes equipment for all three mowing modes unless noted in the Recommendations and notes.

Recommendations and notes

Most models have: A four-stroke engine with primer bulb instead of choke. An engine-kill safety system. No throttle control on handle. Rear-wheel drive. Stamped-steel deck. A two-year warranty on mower and engine.

REAR-BAGGING MODELS

1> **JOHN DEERE** JX75 **Excellent, with blade-brake clutch.** Easy to use, with easy bag handling. Drive starts abruptly. Throttle and choke. Aluminum deck. Engine: 6 hp. Swath: 21 in. Mulch kit $29; chute $18.

2> **CRAFTSMAN** (Sears) 37779 **A CR Best Buy** Easy to use and moderately priced. Blade-brake clutch. Throttle and choke. Engine: 5.5 hp. Swath: 21 in.

3> **HONDA** Masters HR215K1HXA **Easy to use, with easy bag handling, though mulching requires a blade change.** Blade-brake clutch. Throttle and choke. Aluminum deck. Engine: 5 hp. Swath: 21 in. Mulch kit $20; chute $28.

4> **HONDA** Harmony HRB216TDA **Easy to use, with easy bag handling.** Less noisy than most. Front lifts with full bag. Throttle and choke. Plastic deck. Engine: 5.5 hp. Swath: 21 in. Chute $28.

5> **JOHN DEERE** JS63C **A CR Best Buy** Easy to use, and a good price. But hard to jockey side to side. Bag hard to empty. Engine: 6.5 hp. Swath: 21 in. Bag: $49.

6> **TORO** Super Recycler 20037 **Among the less repair-prone brands.** Less noisy than most. Hard to jockey side to side. Bag inconvenient to empty. 5-year mower warranty. Engine: 6.5 hp. Swath: 21 in.

7> **YARD-MAN** 12A-979L401 **Very good, but among the more repair-prone brands.** Hard to pull. Engine: 6.5 hp. Swath: 21 in.

8> **ARIENS** LM21ST **Very good.** U-turns and jockeying side to side hard. Bag hard to empty. Tools needed to change modes. Engine: 6.5 hp. Swath: 21 in.

9> **TORO** Recycler 20017 **Very good, and among the less repair-prone brands.** Engine: 6.5 hp. Swath: 22 in.

10> **SNAPPER** ELP21602 **Very good, with easy bag handling, but among the more repair-prone brands.** Mulching requires blade change. Front lifts with full bag. Aluminum deck. 3-year mower warranty. Engine: 6 hp. Swath: 21 in. Mulch kit $45; chute $28. Not sold in CA.

11> **SNAPPER** P2167517B1 **Very good, but among repair-prone brands.** U-turns and jockeying side to side hard. Noisier than most. Bag inconvenient to empty. Clippings may discharge at operator with bag off. Tools needed to change modes. 3-year mower warranty. Engine: 6.5 hp. Swath: 21 in. Mulch kit: $36.

12> **TORO** Recycler 20016 **Very good.** U-turns and jockeying side to side hard. Engine: 6.5 hp. Swath: 22 in.

13> **LAWN-BOY** Silver Series 10360 **Good for side-discharging.** Weak in tall grass. Hard to jockey side to side. Clippings may discharge at operator with bag off. Cut height hard to adjust. Engine: 5 hp. Swath: 21 in. Bag: $69. Not sold in CA.

14> **SNAPPER** MRP216015B **Among the more repair-prone brands.** Mediocre vacuuming. U-turns hard. Clippings may discharge at operator with bag off. Bag inconvenient to empty. Mode changes require tools, mulching requires a blade change. Inconvenient shift lever. 3-year mower warranty. Engine: 6 hp. Swath: 21 in. Bag $100; chute $20. Not sold in CA.

15▷ **LAWN-BOY** SilverPro 10324 **Good.** Weak in tall grass. Hard to jockey side to side. Clippings may discharge at operator with bag off. Cut height hard to adjust. Two-stroke engine. Engine: 6.5 hp. Swath: 21 in. Not sold in CA.

16▷ **YARD-MAN** by MTD 12A569T401 **Good, but among the more repair-prone brands.** Push-button starter. Hard to push and pull. U-turns, jockeying side-to-side, and bag emptying hard. Engine: 6 hp. Swath: 21 in. Not sold in CA.

17▷ **HUSQVARNA** Crown Series 6522CH **There are better choices.** Engine: 6.5 hp. Swath: 22 in.

SIDE-BAGGING MODELS

18▷ **HONDA** Harmony II HRS216K2SDA **Capable in all modes but bagging.** Drive starts abruptly. Bagging requires blade change. Throttle and choke. Engine: 5.5 hp. Swath: 21 in. Bag $37.

19▷ **YARD MACHINES** by MTD 12A-288A300 Gold **Among the more repair-prone brands.** Hard to pull. Bag inconvenient. Handle vibrates. Engine: 5 hp. Swath: 22 in. Bag: $40. Not sold in CA.

How to use the Ratings

- Read Shop Smart for recommendations on specific models.
- Note how the rated products are listed—in order of performance and convenience, price, or alphabetically.
- The overall score graph gives the big picture in performance. Notes on features and performance for individual models are listed in the Recommendations and notes.
- Use the key numbers to locate the details on each model.
- Before going to press, we verify model availability for most products with manufacturers. Some tested models listed in the Ratings may no longer be available. Discontinued models are noted. Such models may still be available in some stores for part of 2003. Models indicated as successors should perform similarly to the tested models, according to the manufacturer. Features may vary.
- Models similar to the tested models, when they exist, are indicated in Recommendations and notes.
- The original date of publication is noted for each Ratings.

Lawn tractors

Models with hydrostatic drive, which are replacing gear-drive tractors, allow you to infinitely adjust speed without shifting. The John Deere Spin-Steer SST-16, $4,300, has a zero-turn-radius, allowing the tractor to drive around trees and squeeze into tight spots. If you don't mind some extra maneuvering, consider the White Outdoor LT 1650, $1,800, a CR Best Buy. It cut more evenly than the Deere at a fraction of the price.

Overall Ratings — In performance order

Excellent ● Very good ◕ Good ○ Fair ◒ Poor ●

KEY NO.	BRAND & MODEL	PRICE	OVERALL SCORE	EVENNESS	SIDE	MULCH	BAG	HANDLING
1	**White Outdoor** LT 1650 A CR Best Buy	$1,800		◕	◕	◕	◕	●
2	**John Deere** Spin-Steer SST-16	4,300		○	●	○	◕	●
3	**Snapper** LT160H42FBV	2,500		○	●	●	○	●
4	**Husqvarna** YTH1542XP	2,000		○	◕	○	○	◕
5	**Toro** Wheel Horse 16-38 HXL	2,200		○	○	●	◕	●
6	**Cub Cadet** 2000 Series 2166	3,400		○	○	◕	◕	◕
7	**John Deere** LT155	2,500		○	◕	○	○	◕
8	**Craftsman** (Sears) 27208	1,750		○	◕	○	○	○
9	**Ariens** EZR 1742 915013	3,000		○	●	○	◕	◕
10	**Yard-Man** Revolution 624G	2,900		○	◕	○	●	◒

See report, page 99. Based on tests published in Consumer Reports in May 2002, with updated prices and availability.

The tests behind the Ratings

Overall score is based mainly on performance, handling, ease of use, and stability. **Evenness** is how close tractors came to even, carpetlike mowing in all modes. **Side** is how evenly clippings were dispersed from the side-discharge chute. **Mulch** is how finely and evenly clippings were cut and dispersed in this mode. **Bag** denotes effective capacity of the grass-catcher bags, measured when bags were filled or when chute clogged and collection stopped. **Handling** includes clutching or drive engagement, braking, steering, and turning radius. We also evaluated ease of use, including leg room, steering-wheel/lever comfort, getting on and off, and reaching and using controls. **Price** is approximate retail and does not include bagging, mulching, or other accessories, unless noted.

Recommendations and notes

Listed under each brand and model are the engine horse-power and the cutting swath in inches. Models listed as similar should offer performance comparable to the tested model's, although features may differ.

Most have: Single-cylinder, overhead-valve engine. Manual power takeoff (PTO) lever for blade-engagement. 2-year parts and labor warranty. No bag and mulching kits (they are extra-cost options). Performance: Most cut better on straight runs than in turns. Were easy to switch between side-discharge and bagging, but required at least a blade change for mulching. Can cut in reverse. Were reasonably stable on slopes.

HYDROSTATIC-DRIVE MODELS

1▷ **WHITE** Outdoor LT 1650 **A CR Best Buy Strong performance at a reasonable price.** Two-cylinder side-valve engine. Cruise control. No blade change needed for mulching. Clutch pedal too close. Won't cut in reverse. Mediocre vacuuming. Engine: 16.5 hp. Swath: 42 in. Bag $299. Mulch kit $55.

2▷ **JOHN DEERE** Spin-Steer SST-16 **Very good overall, with a steering wheel, but pricey.** Very smooth drive engagement and steering. Reverse safety switch allows cutting in reverse. Cut-height control inconvenient to use. Less noisy than most. Engine: 16 hp. Swath: 42 in. Bag kit: $390. Mulch kit: $46.

3▷ **SNAPPER** LT160H42FBV **Very good.** Electric PTO. Cut more evenly when side-discharging. Mediocre vacuuming. 3-year warranty on mower. Engine: 16 hp. Swath: 42 in. Bag $260. Mulch kit $75. Discontinued, but LT160H42FBV is available.

4▷ **HUSQVARNA** YTH1542XP **A competent, agile tractor with premium features.** Two-cylinder engine. Electric PTO. Front bumper. Comes with two sets of blades, but mulching set works best in all modes. Fuel level hard to check. Engine: 15 hp. Swath: 42 in. Bag: $239. Mulch kit included.

5▷ **TORO** Wheel Horse 16-38 HXL **Very good.** No blade change needed for mulching. Clutch pedal too close. PTO hard to engage. Catcher bags inconvenient to install. Weak in tall grass. Cut more evenly when bagging. Engine: 16 hp. Swath: 38 in. Bag $329. Mulch kit included.

6▷ **CUB CADET** 2000 Series 2166 **Very good.** Cruise control. Electric PTO. Clutch pedal too close. Won't cut in reverse. Wide turning. Fueling and fuel-level checks hard. Mediocre vacuuming. 3-year warranty on PTO clutch, 5 years on frame driveshaft, and drivetrain. Engine: 16 hp. Swath: 42 in. Bag $329. Mulch kit included.

7▷ **JOHN DEERE** LT155 **Very good, but some flaws.** Mulching conversion complicated. Cut more evenly when side-discharging, less evenly when mulching. Mediocre vacuuming. Fuel-level checks hard. Engine: 15 hp. Swath: 38 in. Bag $349. Mulch kit $89.

8▷ **CRAFTSMAN** (Sears) 27208 **Very good, but spending a little more buys a lot more features.** Similar design to #4, but has one-cylinder engine and fewer features. No blade change needed for mulching. Engine: 17 hp. Swath: 42 in. Bag: $260. Mulch kit included.

9▷ **ARIENS** EZR 1742 915013 **Very good overall, but difficult mode changes.** Evenness very good in mulching mode. Switching between mulching and side-discharge or bagging requires changing blade and other parts, using tools. Limited access to engine with cover raised. Noisier than most. Engine: 17 hp. Swath: 42 in. Bag kit: $499. Mulch kit: $99.

10▷ **YARD-MAN** Revolution 624G **Good, but has handling flaws.** Steering levers difficult to control precisely. Mediocre vacuuming in bagging mode. Cannot cut in reverse. Abrupt drive engagement. Parking brake hard to engage. Limited access to engine with cover raised. Engine: 17.5 hp. Swath: 42 in. Bag kit: $299. Mulch kit included.

Microwave ovens

Most microwave ovens tested, especially the larger sizes, did a very good job overall. If you're selecting a countertop model, buy the largest model that will comfortably fit in the space allowed to get more features and have more room for oversized dishes. If you can spare a bit more counter space, consider a midsized model with a sensor and more features. In this group, the Kenmore 6225, **a CR Best Buy,** was among the best and is only $95. In the large category, the Sharp Carousel R-420E and GE Profile JE1460, each $130, are **CR Best Buys.** Among over-the-range ovens, the Panasonic Genius NN-S262 and Samsung MO1650, $350 each, are very good and spacious. Both are **CR Best Buys.**

Overall Ratings In performance order

Excellent ● Very good ◑ Good ○ Fair ◔ Poor

KEY NO.	BRAND & MODEL	PRICE	WATTAGE	CAPACITY (CU. FT.)	OVERALL SCORE	COOK EVENLY	AUTO DEFROST	EASE OF USE
COMPACT COUNTERTOP OVENS *600-800 watts, 0.5-0.9 cu. ft. interior capacity*								
1	**GE** JE740[G]Y	$100	700	0.7		◑	●	◑
2	**Samsung** MW4699[S]	100	700	0.7		◑	–	◑
3	**Sharp** Half Pint R-120D[K]	95	600	0.5		◑	◑	◑
MIDSIZED COUNTERTOP OVENS *900-1,300 watts, 1.0-1.2 cu. ft.*								
4	**Kenmore** (Sears) 6225[9] **A CR Best Buy**	95	1,100	1.2		◑	◉	◑
5	**Sharp** Platinum Collection R-370E[K]	130	1,000	1.0		◑	◑	◑
6	**Sharp** Carousel R-330E[K]	120	1,200	1.2		◑	◑	◑
7	**GE** Profile JE1160[B]C	130	1,100	1.1		○	○	◑
8	**Sharp** Carousel R-320F[K]	110	1,200	1.2		◑	○	◑
9	**Samsung** MW1060[S]A	100	1,100	1.0		◑	○	◑
10	**Emerson** MW8107[W]A	80	1,000	1.1		◑	◑	◑
11	**Emerson** MW8102[SS]	100	1,100	1.0		◑	◑	○
12	**Emerson** Professional Series MW8108[P]	90	1,100	1.0		◑	◑	◑
13	**Panasonic** Genius NN-S562[B]F	130	1,300	1.2		○	●	○
LARGE COUNTERTOP OVENS *1,100-1,300 watts, 1.3-2.2 cu. ft.*								
14	**Goldstar** MA-1302S	150	1,150	1.3		◑	◉	◑
15	**Sharp** Carousel R-420E[K] **A CR Best Buy**	130	1,200	1.6		◑	◉	◑
16	**GE** Profile JE1460[B]F **A CR Best Buy**	130	1,150	1.4		◑	◑	◑
17	**Panasonic** Genius NN-S962[B]F	160	1,300	2.2		○	○	◉
18	**Kenmore** (Sears) Elite UltraWave 6236[9]	150	1,200	1.4		○	○	◉
19	**Goldstar** MA-2120[W]	140	1,200	2.1		◑	◉	◑
20	**Sharp** Carousel R-530E[K]	160	1,200	2.0		◑	◑	◑
21	**GE** Profile JE1360[B]C	100	1,100	1.3		○	◉	◑
22	**Panasonic** Inverter NN-S961[B]F	200	1,300	2.0		◑	◑	◑
23	**Whirlpool** MT4145SK[B]	130	1,100	1.4		◑	◑	◑
24	**Sharp** Carousel R-121[0]	265	1,100	1.5		◑	◑	◑
25	**Whirlpool** MT4140SK[B]	140	1,100	1.4		○	○	◑

Overall Ratings, cont.

			Excellent	Very good	Good	Fair	Poor
			●	◑	○	◑	●

KEY NO.	BRAND & MODEL	PRICE	WATTAGE	CAPACITY (CU. FT.)	OVERALL SCORE	COOK EVENLY	AUTO DEFROST	EASE OF USE
					P F G VG E (0–100)			
	OVER-THE-RANGE OVENS *900-1,200 watts, 1.4-1.9 cu. ft.*							
26	**Kenmore** (Sears) Elite 6168[9]	$450	1,100	1.8		○	◑	●
27	**Whirlpool** Gold GH8155XJ[B]	440	1,000	1.5		◑	◑	◑
28	**GE** Profile Spacemaker JVM1860[B]F	470	1,100	1.8		◑	◑	●
29	**Whirlpool** Gold GH9185XL[B]	500	1,100	1.8		○	◑	●
30	**KitchenAid** KHMS147H[BL]	700	1,000	1.4		○	◑	◑
31	**LG** Intellowave LMV-1915NV	600	1,000	1.9		○	○	◑
32	**Panasonic** Genius NN-S262[B]F **A CR Best Buy**	350	1,200	1.9		○	◑	◑
33	**Sharp** Carousel R-175[0]	400	1,100	1.6		◑	◐	◑
34	**Samsung** MO1650[B]A **A CR Best Buy**	350	1,000	1.6		○	◑	◑
35	**Amana** Radarange ACO1860A[B]	400	1,000	1.8		○	◑	◑
36	**GE** Spacemaker JVM1650[B]B	400	1,000	1.6		○	◐	◑
37	**Kenmore** (Sears) 6264[9]	350	1,000	1.6		○	○	●
38	**Frigidaire** Gallery GLMV168K[B]	350	1,000	1.6		○	○	◑
39	**Sanyo** EM-S9000	400	1,000	1.5		○	◐	●
40	**Maytag** MMV5186AA[S]	415	1,000	1.8		○	◑	◑
41	**Sharp** Carousel R-151[0]	300	1,000	1.5		◑	◐	○
42	**EWave** KOT-151S (Home Depot)	220	1,000	1.5		◑	◑	◑

See report, page 27. Based on tests published in Consumer Reports in January 2003.

The tests behind the Ratings

Overall score is based largely on evenness of cooking, ability to defrost, and ease of use. Space efficiency, window view, and features are also considered. **Wattage** and **capacity** are as listed on the product or packaging; our measurements of both were lower. Ability to **cook evenly** reflects how well a model heated a dish of cold mashed potatoes. **Auto defrost** is based on how well the automatic-defrost program defrosted 1 pound of frozen ground beef. **Ease of use** reflects how easily each model can be set without instruction. **Price** is approximate retail. Under brand & model, the color code is bracketed.

Recommendations and notes

Models listed as similar should offer performance comparable to the tested model, although features may differ.
All tested models: Operate on full power unless programmed otherwise. Stop operating when door is opened. Have electronic digital display with clock, removable glass turntable with rim, screened window, left-opening door, steel housing. Hold a 10-inch dinner plate or one large TV dinner on the turntable. **Most have:** Sensor. Automatic popcorn setting. Child-lock feature. Interior light that goes on when oven is in use or the door opens. Power level that can be checked. Reheat and automatic-defrost settings. 1-year parts-and-labor warranty; 4 to 10 years on magnetron, parts only.
All tested over-the-range models: Fit above a standard 30-inch range. Have an exterior light and a venting system with two or more settings. **Most:** Have a rack for bilevel cooking. Come with installation hardware and instructions included.

Recommendations and notes

COMPACT COUNTERTOP OVENS

1▷ **GE** JE740[G]Y **Good, but lacks a sensor.** Detailed user prompts on display. Shortcut keys. Audible signals can be made louder or quieter. For many keypad programs, oven starts as soon as pad is pressed.

2▷ **SAMSUNG** MW4699[S] **Good, but lacks a sensor, auto defrost, timer, and child lock.** Has door handle. Power level can't be checked. You may need instructions for some settings.

3▷ **SHARP** Half Pint R-120D[K] **Fair.** Lacks a sensor, child lock, auto reheat, and more. Plastic, iMac-style design and colors. Detailed user prompts on display. Has door handle. Oven light does not go on when door is opened. No automatic program for reheating a plate of food. Relatively shallow interior. Power level can't be checked. You may need instructions for some settings.

MIDSIZED COUNTERTOP OVENS

4▷ **KENMORE** (Sears) 6225[9] **A CR Best Buy Very good, and low-priced.** Detailed user prompts on display. Sensor-reheat feature accommodates different amounts of food. Has door handle. Shortcut keys.

5▷ **SHARP** Platinum Collection R-370E[K] **Very good, but window view so-so.** Detailed user prompts on display. Sensor-reheat feature accommodates different amounts of food. For many keypad programs, oven starts as soon as pad is pressed. Similar model R-360E[ ] lacks a sensor.

6▷ **SHARP** Carousel R-330E[K] **Very good across the board.** Sensor-reheat feature accommodates different amounts of food. Has door handle. Power level can't be checked. Must press "cook time" (or similar) before pressing numeric keypad for time. You may need instructions for some settings. Similar: R-310E[ ], R-320E[ ].

7▷ **GE PROFILE** JE1160[B]C **Very good, but auto reheat didn't work well.** Detailed user prompts on display. Sensor-reheat feature accommodates different amounts of food. Shortcut keys. Audible signals can be made louder or quieter. Must press "cook time" (or similar) before pressing numeric keypad for time. For many keypad programs, oven starts as soon as pad is pressed. Discontinued, but similar JE1160[ ]D is available. Similar JE1140[ ] lacks sensor.

8▷ **SHARP** Carousel R-320F[K] **Very good.** Sensor-reheat feature accommodates different amounts of food. Detailed user prompts on display. Has door handle. Shortcut keys. Power levels lower than full power set by multiple presses on "power" touchpad. Defrost weight can be entered only by multiple taps of 0.5 lb.

9▷ **SAMSUNG** MW1060[S]A **Very good.** Sensor-reheat feature accommodates different amounts of food. Detailed user prompts on display. Unique settings. Lacks child lock.

Shortcut keys. Defrost weight can be entered only by multiple taps of 0.5 lb. Can't cook small popcorn bags with auto feature.

10▷ **EMERSON** MW8107[W]A **Good, but lacks a sensor and auto reheat.** Some settings tedious to use. Detailed user prompts on display. No kitchen timer. Power level can't be checked. You may need instructions for some settings, such as popcorn. For many keypad programs, oven starts as soon as pad is pressed.

11▷ **EMERSON** MW8102[SS] **Good, but lacks a sensor.** Auto reheat didn't work well. Some settings confusing. Some dial controls. Has door handle. Oven light does not go on when door is opened. No kitchen timer. Power level can't be checked. Must press "cook time" (or similar) before pressing numeric keypad for time. You may need instructions for some settings. Can't cook small popcorn bags with auto feature. No instant-on settings: Must press "start" (or some sequence of keys) before oven will start.

12▷ **EMERSON** Professional Series MW8108[P] **Good, but lacks a sensor.** Has hidden controls. Oven light does not go on when door is opened. No kitchen timer. Must press "cook time" (or similar) before pressing numeric keypad for time. Can't cook small popcorn bags with auto feature. Auto popcorn feature left many kernels unpopped.

13▷ **PANASONIC** Genius NN-S562[B]F **Good, but no child lock.** Poor defrost. Sensor-reheat feature accommodates different amounts of food. Has door handle. Oven light does not go on when door is opened. Power levels lower than full power set by multiple presses on "power" touchpad. Keypad entry for popcorn tedious. Similar: NN-S592[S]F; NN-S542[ ]F, lacks a sensor.

LARGE COUNTERTOP OVENS

14▷ **GOLDSTAR** MA-1302S **Very good.** Defrost excellent only when using included plastic tray. Dial controls. Detailed user prompts on display. Sensor-reheat feature accommodates different amounts of food. Has door handle. For many keypad programs, oven starts as soon as pad is pressed. In-home warranty service for one year if oven is built in.

15▷ **SHARP** Carousel R-420E[K] **A CR Best Buy Very good.** Keypad entry for defrost tedious. Detailed user prompts on display. Sensor-reheat feature accommodates different amounts of food. Power levels lower than full power set by multiple presses on "power" touchpad. Defrost weight can be entered only by multiple taps of 0.5 lb. For many keypad programs, oven starts as soon as pad is pressed. Similar: R-430E[ ]F, R425E[ ].

16▷ **GE** Profile JE1460[B]F **A CR Best Buy Very good.** Detailed user prompts on display. Sensor-reheat feature accommodates different amounts of food. Shortcut keys. Audible signals can be made louder or quieter. Similar: JE1440[ ] lacks a sensor.

Recommendations and notes

17⊳ PANASONIC Genius NN-S962[B]F **Very good.** Turntable fits 9x15-in. dish. Detailed user prompts on display. Sensor-reheat feature accommodates different amounts of food. Displays power level being used. Can turn off touchpad beeps and end beeps. Power levels lower than full power set by multiple presses on "power" touchpad. Similar: NN-S990[ ]A; NN-S952[ ]F, lacks a sensor.

18⊳ KENMORE (Sears) Elite UltraWave 6236[9] **Very good.** Rounded interior cavity. Detailed user prompts on display. Sensor reheat feature accommodates different amounts of food. Controls on door. Has door handle. Shortcut keys. Turntable fits 9x15-in. dish. For many keypad programs, oven starts as soon as pad is pressed.

19⊳ GOLDSTAR MA-2120[W] **Very good.** Turntable fits 9x15-in. dish. Lacks a sensor. Detailed user prompts on display. Has door handle. Shortcut keys. Can turn off touchpad beeps and end beeps.

20⊳ SHARP Carousel R-530E[K] **Very good.** Turntable fits 9x15-in. dish. Detailed user prompts on display. Sensor-reheat feature accommodates different amounts of food.

21⊳ GE Profile JE1360[B]C **Very good.** Detailed user prompts on display. Audible signals can be made louder or quieter. For many keypad programs, oven starts as soon as pad is pressed. Discontinued, but similar JES1351[ ] is available.

22⊳ PANASONIC Inverter NN-S961[B]F **Very good.** Detailed user prompts on display. Sensor reheat feature accommodates different amounts of food. Turntable fits 9x15-in. dish. You may need instructions for some settings. No instant-on settings: must press "start" (or some sequence of keys) before oven will start. Keypad entry for popcorn tedious. Discontinued, but similar NN-T990[S]A is available.

23⊳ WHIRLPOOL MT4145SK[B] **Very good.** Window view so-so. Sensor-reheat feature accommodates different amounts of food. Built-in installation. Shortcut keys. Audible signals can be made louder or quieter. In-home warranty service for one year if oven is built in. Similar: MP2145SJ[ ].

24⊳ SHARP Carousel R-121[0] **Good.** Over-the-counter model. Controls across bottom of door. Window view so-so. Sensor-reheat feature accommodates different amounts of food. Shortcut keys. Power levels lower than full power set by multiple presses on "power" touchpad. In-home warranty service for one year. Similar: R120[ ].

25⊳ WHIRLPOOL MT4140SK[B] **Good, but lacks a sensor.** Very quiet. You may need instructions for some settings. For many keypad programs, oven starts as soon as pad is pressed.

OVER-THE-RANGE OVENS

26⊳ KENMORE (Sears) Elite 6168[9] **Very good, and roomy.** Vent fan very quiet, has 5 settings. Detailed user prompts on display. Has door handle. Has metal oven rack. Turntable on/off. Relatively quiet. For many keypad programs, oven starts as soon as pad is pressed. Touchpad beeps can be turned off, but not end beep.

27⊳ WHIRLPOOL Gold GH8155XJ[B] **Very good, and feature-laden.** Detailed user prompts on display. Has door handle. Has metal oven rack. Turntable on/off. Very quiet exhaust fan. For many keypad programs, oven starts as soon as pad is pressed. Touchpad beeps can be turned off, but not end beeps. In-home warranty service for one year. Similar: GH7155XH[ ], MH8150XJ[ ].

28⊳ GE Profile Spacemaker JVM1860[B]F **Very good.** Detailed user prompts on display. Has door handle. Has metal oven rack. Turntable on/off. Shortcut keys. Audible signals can be made louder or quieter. Night light can be set to turn on/off automatically. Must press "cook time" (or similar) before pressing numeric keypad for time. Can't cook small popcorn bags with auto feature. Has plastic defrost rack. Hidden vent cover. In-home warranty service for one year. Similar: JVM1850[ ].

29⊳ WHIRLPOOL Gold GH9185XL[B] **Very good.** Displays power level being used. Has door handle. Has metal oven rack. Turntable on/off. Shortcut keys. Must press "cook time" (or similar) before pressing numeric keypad for time. Comes with steamer pot. In-home warranty service for one year.

30⊳ KITCHENAID KHMS147H[BL] **Very good, and feature-laden.** Has door handle. Has metal oven rack. Dial controls. Turntable on/off. Shortcut keys. Very quiet exhaust fan. Exhaust fan has 5 level settings. Sensor night-light turns on and off automatically. In-home warranty service for one year. Similar: KHMS145J[ ].

31⊳ LG Intellowave LMV-1915NV **Very good, and roomy, with large turntable.** Vent fan noisy. Detailed user prompts on display. Displays power level being used. Has door handle. Has metal oven rack. Turntable on/off. No auto popcorn. Audible signals can be made louder or quieter. Very quiet. Has plastic defrost rack. In-home warranty service for one year.

32⊳ PANASONIC Genius NN-S262[B]F **A CR Best Buy Very good.** Detailed user prompts on display. Has metal oven rack. Turntable on/off. Power levels lower than full power set by multiple presses on "power" touchpad. In-home warranty service for one year. Similar: NN-S252[ ]F, lacks a sensor.

33⊳ SHARP Carousel R-175[0] **Very good, but among the more repair-prone brands of OTR ovens.** Has door handle. Has metal oven rack. Turntable on/off. Audible signals can be made louder or quieter. Night-light can be set to turn on/off automatically. You may need instructions for some settings. For many keypad programs, oven starts as soon as pad is pressed. In-home warranty service for one year.

Recommendations and notes

34 ▷ **SAMSUNG** MO1650[B]A **A CR Best Buy Very good.** Detailed user prompts on display. Has door handle. Has metal oven rack. Turntable on/off. Shortcut keys. Night-light can be set to turn on/off automatically. Defrost weight can be entered only by multiple taps of 0.5 lb. Has plastic defrost rack.

35 ▷ **AMANA** Radarange ACO1860A[B] **Very good.** Detailed user prompts on display. Has door handle. Has metal oven rack. Turntable on/off. Night-light can be set to turn on/off automatically. For many keypad programs, oven starts as soon as pad is pressed. Similar: ACO1840A[ ].

36 ▷ **GE** Spacemaker JVM1650[B]B **Very good.** Vent fan noisy. Detailed user prompts on display. Has door handle. Has metal oven rack. Turntable on/off. Shortcut keys. Audible signals can be made louder or quieter. Relatively quiet. Night-light can be set to turn on/off automatically. Must press "cook time" (or similar) before pressing numeric keypad for time. For many keypad programs, oven starts as soon as pad is pressed. In-home warranty service for one year. Similar: JVM1653[ ]; JVM1640[ ], lacks a sensor.

37 ▷ **KENMORE** (Sears) 6264[9] **Very good.** Vent fan has 5 settings. Detailed user prompts on display. Has door handle. Has metal oven rack. Turntable on/off. Shortcut keys. Similar: 6262[ ], lacks a sensor.

38 ▷ **FRIGIDAIRE** Gallery GLMV168K[B] **Very good.** Detailed user prompts on display. Has door handle. Has metal oven rack. Turntable on/off. Shortcut keys. Audible signals can be made louder or quieter. Temperature probe. Night-light can be set to turn on/off automatically. Must press "cook time" (or similar) before pressing numeric keypad for time. Similar: PLMV168K[ ].

39 ▷ **SANYO** EM-S9000 **Very good.** No 1-touch buttons. Detailed user prompts on display. Has metal oven rack. Turntable on/off. Shortcut keys. Temperature probe. Power level lower than full power set by multiple presses on "power" touchpad. Must press "cook time" (or similar) before pressing numeric keypad for time. No instant-on settings: must press "start" (or some sequence of keys) before oven will start. Touchpad beeps can be turned off, but not end beeps. Similar: EM-S8000[ ].

40 ▷ **MAYTAG** MMV5186AA[S] **Good.** Detailed user prompts on display. Has door handle. Has metal oven rack. Turntable on/off. Shortcut keys. 2-yr. parts and labor warranty.

41 ▷ **SHARP** Carousel R-151[0] **Good, but among the more repair-prone brands of OTR ovens.** Hidden controls. Window view so-so. Can't turn off turntable. Shortcut keys. Power level lower than full power set by multiple presses on "power" touchpad. In-home warranty service for one year. Similar: R-150[ ], lacks a sensor.

42 ▷ **EWAVE** KOT-151S **Good.** Detailed user prompts on display. Has door handle. Has metal oven rack. Turntable on/off. Shortcut keys. Must press "cook time" (or similar) before pressing numeric keypad for time. Noisy vent fan, even at low setting. Door Instructions are misprinted. Available only at Home Depot.

Minisystems

While the sound quality of a minisystem won't rival that of separate components, you can get good sound for just a few hundred dollars. Among models with a cassette deck, the **CR Best Buy** Philips MC-50, $150, is a standout with three-disc capacity and the ability to accept an external antenna to improve FM reception. Models without a cassette deck are generally more expensive, largely because of their miniaturization. The Yamaha MCR-E150, $400, and the Onkyo MC25TECH and PS-510, each $500, performed well except for AM tuning. The Yamaha TSX-15, $350, is especially compact. Key features for these models are listed in the table. See product report for explanation of features.

Overall Ratings — In performance order

Ratings key: Excellent ● | Very good ◓ | Good ○ | Fair ◒ | Poor ●

KEY NO.	BRAND & MODEL	PRICE	OVERALL SCORE (0 P F G VG E 100)	SOUND QUALITY	TAPING QUALITY	FM TUNING	CD HANDLING	EASE OF USE
	MODELS WITH CASSETTE DECK							
1	**Philips** MC-50 A CR Best Buy	$150		Very good	Good	Very good	Very good	Good
2	**Panasonic** SC-AK300	170		Good	Good	Very good	Very good	Good
3	**Rio** EX1000	275		Good	Good	Good	Very good	Good
4	**Panasonic** SC-PM12	170		Good	Good	Excellent	Very good	Good
5	**Panasonic** SC-PM07	150		Fair	Good	Excellent	Very good	Good
	MODELS WITHOUT CASSETTE DECK							
6	**Yamaha** MCR-E150	400		Very good	–	Excellent	Very good	Good
7	**Onkyo** MC25TECH	500		Very good	–	Very good	Very good	Good
8	**Onkyo** PS-510	500		Very good	–	Very good	Very good	Good
9	**JVC** FS-SD1000	450		Good	–	Very good	Very good	Good
10	**Yamaha** TSX-15	350		Very good	–	Excellent	Good	Fair
11	**JVC** FS-SD550	250		Very good	–	Excellent	Good	Poor
12	**Emerson** ES2	100		Good	–	Fair	Very good	Good
13	**Emerson** ES8	100		Very good	–	Fair	Good	Poor

See report, page 71. Based on tests published in Consumer Reports in January 2003, with updated prices and availability.

The tests behind the ratings

Overall score is based largely on the quality of sound. **Sound quality** is the accuracy of the two main speakers and the amplifier, with the tone controls set for the best sound performance. **Taping quality** combines frequency response, dynamic range, and freedom from flutter of the tape deck(s). **FM tuning** includes sensitivity to weak signals and selectivity among adjacent stations. **CD handling** is how well the player handled defective discs and how long it took the player to go from one track to another on the same disc. **Ease of use** rates each model on ergonomics and the controls on the main unit and remote. **Price** is approximate retail. Features and AM tuning are also part of the overall score, but they are not shown on the Ratings chart; all models were judged good at both unless otherwise noted.

Recommendations and notes

All tested models: Have a main console that contains an AM/FM tuner with 24 or more presets. Have a CD player that accepts one, three, or five discs at a time and displays CD track/time elapsed. Have two detached speakers. Have remote control and a headphone jack with volume control. Can't be turned on by an external timer. Can't control other A/V equipment using remote. Lack direct tuning of radio stations. **All models with a cassette deck:** Can record and play normal (Type I) tapes, have auto stop on fast-forward and rewind, and permit one-button CD/cassette sync recording. Lack recording-level control and high-speed dubbing. Do not claim ability to record onto Type II or Type IV (metal) tape.

Most tested models: Have one audio input for connecting components such as a TV, DVD player, or external cassette player. 75-ohm input for FM antenna. Bass-boost switch. CD shuffle/random play. Clock radio and sleep timer that can turn on/off at preset times. One-year warranty on unit and speakers. Lack speaker balance control and the ability to play MP3 files on CD. Don't display CD time remaining. **Most models with a cassette deck:** Have auto reverse. Let you set timer to record radio programs. Have a flip-out mechanism for loading tape. Lack a tape counter.

MODELS WITH CASSETTE DECK

1▷ **PHILIPS** MC-50 A **CR Best Buy Very good, compact system with attractive case and wood-grained-finish speakers.** Has bass/treble adjustment, DSP-mode presets, detachable AC cord. But lacks bass boost. Good for features.

2▷ **PANASONIC** SC-AK300 **Good overall.** Larger than most; flashy style. Has black-plastic case and speakers, detachable AC cord. Can display CD time remaining. But lacks auto reverse on cassette deck and bass/treble adjustment. Only fair for features.

3▷ **RIO** EX1000 **Good but pricey; only model tested that can play MP3 files on CD.** Has blond-veneer-finish speakers, hinged cassette compartment on top, DSP-mode presets, tape counter. But lacks bass/treble adjustment. Only fair for features.

4▷ **PANASONIC** SC-PM12 **Good and stylish, with black-veneer speakers; excels at FM reception.** Has DSP-mode presets, detachable AC cord. Good for features. But lacks bass/treble adjustment.

5▷ **PANASONIC** SC-PM07 **Fair overall.** Among smallest tested; excels at FM reception, but sound quality only fair. Has wood-grained-finish speakers, detachable AC cord. Headphone jack located on top, near rear of console. Lacks bass/ treble adjustment. Timer can't be set to record radio programs. Only fair for features.

MODELS WITHOUT CASSETTE DECK

6▷ **YAMAHA** MCR-E150 **Very good, with gold-finish console and black speakers.** Excels at FM reception. Has speaker balance control, bass/ treble adjustment, 3 analog-audio inputs, detachable speaker wires, 2-yr. warranty on console and speakers. Can display CD time remaining. But no bass boost. AM reception and features only fair.

7▷ **ONKYO** MC25TECH **Good overall, and lots of features for the price; console has separate tuner/amp and CD player.** Has wood-grained-finish speakers, bass/treble adjustment, DSP-mode presets, 5 analog-audio inputs, detachable speaker wires, 2-yr. warranty on console and speakers. Can display CD time remaining. Can accept and display Radio Data System (RDS) info, if available. Good for features. But couldn't play all CD-R and CD-RW test discs. AM reception only fair. No clock radio or bass boost.

8▷ **ONKYO** PS-510 **Much like # 7, with same console but different speakers.** Has 2-yr. warranty on console; 5-yr. on speakers. But couldn't play all CD-R and CD-RW test discs.

9▷ **JVC** FS-SD1000 **Good overall; slim, with transparent, hinged CD compartment on top.** Only model we tested to include external subwoofer. Has cylindrical silver speakers, bass/treble adjustment, detachable AC cord and speaker wires. But AM reception and features only fair.

Features at a glance   Minisystems

Tested products (keyed to the Ratings) Key no. Brand	CD capacity	Play exchange	Direct track access	Digital-audio output	Subwoofer out	Tape decks
MODELS WITH CASSETTE DECK						
1▷ Philips	3	•		•	•	1
2▷ Panasonic	5	•		•		2
3▷ Rio	1					1
4▷ Panasonic	5	•		•		1
5▷ Panasonic	1	•		•		1
MODELS WITHOUT CASSETTE DECK						
6▷ Yamaha	1		•	•	•	
7▷ Onkyo	3	•	•	•	•	
8▷ Onkyo	3	•	•	•	•	
9▷ JVC	1			•	•	
10▷ Yamaha	1			•	•	
11▷ JVC	1			•	•	
12▷ Emerson	1			•	•	
13▷ Emerson	1					

Recommendations and notes

10▷ YAMAHA TSX-15 **Good overall; slim, with top hatch that lifts to accept CDs.** Excels at FM reception. Has black case, bass/treble adjustment, detachable speaker wires, 2-yr. warranty on console and speakers. Console and speakers easy to wall-mount using included brackets. Can display CD time remaining. But AM reception and features only fair.

11▷ JVC FS-SD550 **Much like # 9, with same console but different speakers and no external subwoofer.** Has blond-veneer-finish speakers.

12▷ EMERSON ES2 **Fair; touch-screen console among smallest**

tested. Clock radio has alarm. Can display CD time remaining. But lacks bass/treble adjustment and bass boost. AM reception and features only fair. Can't connect external FM antenna. Short (90-day) warranty on console and speakers.

13▷ EMERSON ES8 **Fair; slim, with transparent, hinged CD compartment on top.** But lacks bass/treble adjustment, bass boost, CD shuffle/random play, audio input, clock radio, and sleep timer. Can't connect external FM antenna. Couldn't play all CD-R and CD-RW test discs. AM reception only fair. Short (90-day) warranty on console and speakers. Poor for features.

Power blowers

For yards that can be navigated with an extension cord, an electric blower is the best and cheapest choice. All the models tested were very good or excellent and cost $35 to $80. If you can't drag an extension cord around, consider the gasoline-powered Stihl BG45, $150. For an additional $40, you can upgrade to the BG55, which includes an accessory vacuum mode. For larger jobs that require more power, consider a backpack model. You'll find several excellent choices for around $400.

Overall Ratings In performance order

Key: Excellent, Very good, Good, Fair, Poor

KEY NO.	BRAND & MODEL	PRICE	PERFORMANCE: BLOWING	PERFORMANCE: HANDLING	PERFORMANCE: VACUUMING	NOISE: OPERATOR EAR	NOISE: FROM 50 FT.
	ELECTRIC HANDHELD BLOWERS						
1	**Weed Eater** 2595 Barracuda	$55	Excellent	Good	Very good	Good	Good
2	**Ryobi** 190r	65	Good	Excellent	Excellent	Good	Very good
3	**Black & Decker** Leaf Hog BV2500	70	Fair	Excellent	Excellent	Good	Excellent
4	**Ryobi** RESV1300	80	Good	Good	Good	Very good	Very good
5	**Ryobi** 160r	45	Fair	Excellent	NA	Very good	Excellent
6	**Weed Eater** 2540 Groundskeeper	40	Good	Very good	Good	Good	Good
7	**Weed Eater** 2510 Groundsweeper	35	Fair	Excellent	NA	Good	Very good
	GASOLINE HANDHELD BLOWERS						
8	**Stihl** BG45	150	Very good	Excellent	NA	Good	Very good
9	**Stihl** BG55	190	Very good	Excellent	Very good	Good	Good
10	**Weed Eater** BV1650	110	Very good	Very good	Good	Fair	Good
11	**Ryobi** RGBV3100	130	Good	Fair	Good	Fair	Good
12	**Weed Eater** FL 1500 Featherlite	80	Fair	Good	NA	Good	Very good
13	**Ryobi** 310BVr	105	Fair	Fair	Very good	Fair	Good
	GASOLINE BACKPACK BLOWERS						
14	**Husqvarna** 145BT	350	Excellent	Excellent	NA	Poor	Good
15	**Makita** RBL500	425	Excellent	Excellent	NA	Poor	Good
16	**Echo** PB-46LN Quiet 1	430	Excellent	Very good	NA	Poor	Very good
17	**Echo** Pro Lite PB260L	300	Very good	Excellent	NA	Fair	Very good
18	**John Deere** BP40	420	Excellent	Good	NA	Poor	Good

See report, page 103. Based on tests published in Consumer Reports in September 2001, with updated prices and availability.

The tests behind the Ratings

Overall score includes blowing performance, handling, and, where applicable, vacuuming. **Blowing** reflects the ability to move increasingly large piles of leaves. **Handling** gauges ease of maneuvering and moving from side to side in the blower mode. **Vacuuming** denotes how quickly the machines took in a measured pile of leaves and how easily they handled in that mode. "NA" means that model isn't designed to vacuum. **Noise** is as measured at the operator's ear and from 50 feet, using a decibel meter. Models judged Excellent from 50 feet are quieter than 65 dBA. Models judged Fair or Poor at operator's ear are louder than 90 dBA; we recommend using them with ear protection. **Weight** is based on our own measurements with a full fuel tank for gas models. **Price** is approximate retail.

Recommendations and notes

Models listed as similar should offer performance comparable to the tested model's, although features may differ.

Typical features for these models: Reduce leaf volume by about 4-to-1 or 6-to-1 when vacuuming. Switch without tools. 2-yr. warranty.

Most electric models: Aren't loud enough to require the use of hearing protection. On/off switch that can be reached only by the hand not holding the blower. Two speed settings.

Most handheld gas models: Are loud enough to warrant hearing protection. Require a firm hold when starting to avoid twisting. Ignition switch that can be reached by the same hand holding the blower. Trigger throttle. Translucent fuel tank.

Most backpack models: Require the use of hearing protection. Require a firm hold when starting to avoid twisting. Ignition switch that can be reached by the hand holding the main handle. Translucent fuel tank.

ELECTRIC HANDHELD BLOWERS

1> **WEED EATER** 2595 Barracuda **Excellent overall and most powerful electric.** Weight: 7 lb. Features: Better than most at reducing vacuumed volume. But: Control takes two hands. Similar: 695 Barracuda.

2> **RYOBI** 190r **Very good and excellent at vacuuming.** Weight: 7 lb. Features: Better than most at reducing vacuumed volume.

3> **BLACK & DECKER** Leaf Hog BV2500 **Easiest to convert to vacuuming, but unimpressive at blowing.** Weight 7 lb. Features: Excellent at vacuuming. Vacuum bag easy to remove for emptying. Quietest at 50 ft. Ergonomic molded handle. But: Only one speed.

4> **RYOBI** RESV1300 **Very good with unique design.** Weight: 9 lb. Features: Permanently mounted blower nozzle and vacuum tube; lever easily switches between the two. Vacuum bag easy to remove. But: Small bag.

5> **RYOBI** 160r **Very good, but unimpressive at blowing.** Weight: 6 lb. Only one speed. No vacuum mode.

6> **WEED EATER** 2540 Groundskeeper **Very good.** Weight: 7 lb. Optional $35 vacuum attachment.

7> **WEED EATER** 2510 Groundsweeper **Very good, but unimpressive at blowing.** Weight: 5 lb. But: Only one speed. No vacuum mode.

GASOLINE HANDHELD BLOWERS

8> **STIHL** BG45 **Best of the gas handheld models, and relatively quiet.** Weight: 10 lb. Features: Lightweight and easy to handle for a gas blower. Comfortable handle. But: No vacuum mode.

9> **STIHL** BG55 **Similar to #8, but with a vacuum mode; not as quiet.** Weight: 10 lb. Features: Strong performer in both modes, though conversion is complicated. Very good at grinding debris. Lightweight and easy to handle for a gas blower. Comfortable handle. Vacuum kit: $30.

10> **WEED EATER** BV 1650 **Very good and fairly quiet.** Weight: 11½ lb. Features: Easy to start without twisting. But: Inconvenient throttle. Small bag. Hard to tell when opaque fuel tank is full.

11> **RYOBI** RGBV3100 **An unimpressive performer.** Weight: 12½ lb. Features: A lever switches between blowing and vacuuming. But: Vacuum tube blocks view when blowing. Heavy. Throttle difficult to use.

12> **WEED EATER** FL 1500 Featherlite **Good, but intense handle vibration.** Weight: 7½ lb. Features: Easy to start without twisting. But: Inconvenient throttle. No vacuum mode.

13> **RYOBI** 310BVr **Good, but there are better choices.** Weight: 12 lb. Features: Easy to start without twisting. But: Complicated to convert from blower to vacuum. Hard to tell when opaque fuel tank is full. Choke hard to operate.

GASOLINE BACKPACK BLOWERS

14> **HUSQVARNA** 145BT **Excellent performer.** Weight: 22 lb. Features: Comfortable handle with presettable throttle on blower tube, a convenience. Large fuel-tank opening. But: Only 1-yr. warranty. Sliding shoulder straps.

15> **MAKITA** RBL500 **Excellent but pricey.** Weight: 24½ lb. Features: Comfortable handle with a presettable throttle on blower tube, a convenience. Straps easy to adjust. Large fuel-tank opening. Excellent ease of use. But: Only 1-yr. warranty. Models sold between March 1997 and January 2001 have been recalled because of a leaky fuel tank.

16> **ECHO** PB-46LN Quiet 1 **Excellent, but pricey.** Weight: 28½ lb. Features: Straps easy to adjust.

17> **ECHO** Pro Lite PB260L **Relatively inexpensive, though a bit less powerful than most backpacks.** Weight: 16 lb. Features: Carrying handle. Shoulder straps easy to adjust in use. Relatively quiet at 50 ft. Optional curved blower nozzle ($6) improves performance.

18> **JOHN DEERE** BP40 **Very good, but pricey.** Weight: 20½ lb. Features: Large fuel-tank opening. But: Short throttle arm; controls hard to reach. Sliding shoulder straps. Ease of use less than other tested models.

Ranges, electric

You can purchase a very good electric range without spending a fortune. Whether you're buying a smoothtop model or one with coil elements, look for a capacious oven and more than one large, fast burner. Smoothtops, while generally more expensive than coil models, are easier to clean and provide extra counter space when not in use. Tests of smoothtop models turned up two **CR Best Buys:** the Maytag Performa PER5710BA, $565, and the Frigidaire FEF366A, $600. If smoothtop styling isn't a must, any of the four coil ranges tested would be a fine choice.

Overall Ratings   In performance order

Excellent ● | Very good ◕ | Good ○ | Fair ◔ | Poor ●

KEY NO	BRAND & MODEL	PRICE	OVERALL SCORE	COOKTOP HIGH	COOKTOP LOW	OVEN CAPACITY	OVEN BAKE	OVEN BROIL
	SMOOTHTOP MODELS							
1	**Maytag** Accellis MER6750AA[W]	$1,050		◕	●	○	◕	●
2	**Maytag** Gemini MER6769BA[W]	1,000		◕	●	◕	◕	◕
3	**Kenmore** (Sears) 9559[2]	750		◕	●	◕	◕	◕
4	**Kenmore** (Sears) 9582[2]	1,050		●	●	◕	◕	○
5	**Maytag** Performa PER5710BA[W] **A CR Best Buy**	565		◕	●	◕	◕	●
6	**Frigidaire** FEF366A[S] **A CR Best Buy**	600		◕	●	◕	◕	◕
7	**Frigidaire** Gallery GLEF378A[S]	700		◕	◕	◕	◕	◕
8	**KitchenAid** KERC500H[WH]	750		●	●	○	◕	◕
9	**Maytag** MER5880BA[W]	1,200		◕	◕	◕	◕	◕
10	**Jenn-Air** JES8850AA[W]	1,600		◕	◕	○	○	○
11	**Whirlpool** Gold GR460LXK[P]	900		◕	●	◕	◕	◔
	COIL MODELS							
12	**GE** JBP35BB[WH]	500		●	●	●	●	●
13	**Kenmore** (Sears) 9375[1]	550		●	●	◕	◕	●
14	**Hotpoint** RB757WC[WW]	400		●	●	◕	◕	○
15	**Whirlpool** RF379LXK[Q]	550		●	●	◕	◕	◔

See report, page 34. Based on tests published in Consumer Reports in August 2002, with updated prices and availability.

The tests behind the Ratings

Under **brand & model,** brackets show a tested model's color code. **Overall score** includes cooktop high power and low power performance, oven capacity, baking, broiling, and self-cleaning. **Cooktop high power** is how quickly the highest powered burner or element heated $6\frac{1}{3}$ quarts of room-temperature water to a near boil. **Low power** shows how well the least powerful burner or element melted and held chocolate without scorching it and whether the most powerful, set to Low, held tomato sauce below a boil. **Oven capacity** is usable oven space. **Bake** shows baking evenness for cakes and cookies. **Broil** shows cooking and searing evenness for a tray of burgers. **Price** is approximate retail.

Recommendations and notes

Similar models have the same burners or elements, oven, and broiler; other details may differ.

All ranges: Are 30 inches wide. Have an oven light and anti-tip hardware. Most ranges have: Freestanding construction. Touchpad oven controls. A cooktop rim to hold spills. A self-cleaning oven. Two or three oven racks with five positions. An oven window with a reasonably clear view. A storage drawer. A warranty of one year for parts and labor, five years for smoothtop surfaces.

SMOOTHTOP RANGES

1> **MAYTAG** Accellis MER6750AA[W] **Very good.** Microwave feature. "Hot" light for each element. Expandable elements. Excelled at self-cleaning. Window view worse than most. Elements: 1@750/2,200, 1@2,200, 2@1,200 watts.

2> **MAYTAG** Gemini MER6769BA[W] **Very good.** Dual ovens. Excellent at self-cleaning. No storage drawer. Elements: 2@2,200, 2@1,200 watts.

3> **KENMORE** (Sears) 9559[2] **Very good.** Warming drawer and element. Expandable element. Elements: 1@1,000/2,500, 1@2,200, 2@1,200 watts. Discontinued, but may still be available.

4> **KENMORE** (Sears) 9582[2] **Very good.** Warming drawer and element. "Hot" light for each element. Expandable element. Split rack. Elements: 1@1,600/2,400, 1@2,500, 2@1,500 watts.

5> **MAYTAG** Performa PER5710BA[W] **A CR Best Buy Very good.** Excelled at self-cleaning. Window view worse than most. Elements: 2@2,200, 2@1,200 watts. Similar: PER5702BA[ ], PER5705BA[ ].

6> **FRIGIDAIRE** FEF366A[S] **A CR Best Buy Very good.** Elements: 1@2,500, 1@2,200, 2@1,200 watts.

7> **FRIGIDAIRE** Gallery GLEF378A[S] **Very good.** Convection option. Warming and expandable elements. Window view worse than most. Elements: 1@1,000/2,500, 1@2,200, 2@1,200 watts. Similar: FEF379A[ ].

8> **KITCHENAID** KERC500H[WH] **Very good.** Warming and expandable elements. "Hot" light for each element. Elements: 1@1,000/2,500, 2@1,800, 1@1,500 watts.

9> **MAYTAG** MER5880BA[W] **Very good.** Convection option. Warming drawer and element. Expandable element. Window view worse than most. Elements: 1@750/2,200, 1@2,200, 2@1,200 watts. Similar: MER5870BA[ ].

10> **JENN-AIR** JES8850AA[W] **Very good.** Among the more repair-prone brands. Slide-in design. Convection option. "Hot" light for each element. Expandable element. Split rack. Excelled at self-cleaning. Elements: 1@1,700/2,700, 1@2,200, 2@1,200 watts.

11> **WHIRLPOOL** Gold GR460LXK[P] **Very good.** Warming and expandable elements. "Hot" light for each element. Split rack. Window view worse than most. Elements: 1@1,000/2,400, 1@1,800, 2@1,200 watts. Similar: GR465LXK[ ], GR470LXK[ ], GR475LXK[ ].

COIL MODELS

12> **GE** JBP35BB[WH] **Excellent.** Elements: 2@2,600, 2@1,500 watts. Similar: JBP30BB[ ], JBP48WB[ ].

13> **KENMORE** (Sears) 9375[1] **Very good.** Warming drawer. Elements: 2@2,600, 2@1,500 watts.

14> **HOTPOINT** RB757WC[WW] **Very good.** Oven dial. Window view worse than most. Elements: 2@2,600, 2@1,500 watts.

15> **WHIRLPOOL** RF379LXK[Q] **Very good.** Window view worse than most. Elements: 2@2,600, 2@1,500 watts. Similar: RF367LXK[ ].

Ranges, gas

You can buy a very good gas range for $500 to $600. When you pay more than that, you typically get more features, such as sealed burners, cast-iron grates, and a self-cleaning oven. You also pay for styling. Three GE models top the Ratings, with prices from $800 to $1,250. Hotpoint models are also made by GE. The RGB745WEA, $550, is a **CR Best Buy.** Dual-fuel ranges, which combine a gas cooktop with an electric oven, are often pro-style with stainless-steel construction. The Jenn-Air JDS9860AA, $1,900, performed nearly as well overall as the top-scoring KitchenAid KDRP407H and costs much less.

Shop Smart

Overall Ratings — In performance order

Ratings key: Excellent ● · Very good ◔ · Good ○ · Fair ◑ · Poor ●

KEY NO	BRAND & MODEL	PRICE	OVERALL SCORE	COOKTOP HIGH	COOKTOP LOW	OVEN CAPACITY	OVEN BAKE	OVEN BROIL
	GAS RANGES							
1	**GE** Profile Performance JGB910WEC[WW]	$1,250		◔	◔	◔	●	●
2	**GE** Profile JGBP85WEB[WW]	950		○	●	◔	◔	●
3	**GE** JGBP35WEA[WW]	800		○	●	◔	◔	●
4	**Hotpoint** RGB745WEA[WW] **A CR Best Buy**	550		◔	●	◔	◔	◔
5	**Maytag** MGR5880BD[W]	1,075		○	●	◔	◔	○
6	**Maytag** Performa PGR5710BD[W]	565		○	●	◔	◔	○
7	**GE** Profile Performance JGB920WEC[WW]	1,350		○	○	◔	●	●
8	**Kenmore** (Sears) 7584[2]	1,050		○	◔	◔	◔	○
9	**Jenn-Air** JGS8750AD[W]	1,500		◔	◔	◔	◔	●
10	**Kenmore** (Sears) 7566[1]	700		◔	●	○	◔	○
11	**Kenmore** (Sears) 7575[1]	600		○	●	○	◔	○
12	**KitchenAid** KGRT607H[BS]	1,360		◔	○	○	◔	◔
13	**Whirlpool** Gold GS460LEK[Q]	830		○	◔	◔	○	◑
14	**Frigidaire** Gallery GLGF366A[S]	600		○	●	◔	◔	◔
15	**Dacor** PGR30[S]	2,650		○	◑	◔	◔	◑
	DUAL-FUEL RANGES							
16	**KitchenAid** KDRP407H[SS]	3,450		○	◔	◔	●	●
17	**Jenn-Air** JDS9860AA[W]	1,900		●	◔	○	◔	●
18	**Dacor** ERD30S06[BK]	3,800		◔	◔	○	◔	◑
19	**Viking** VDSC305B[SS]	3,800		◔	◔	◑	○	●
20	**GE** Monogram ZDP30N4D[SS]	3,600		○	◔	◔	◔	◔

See report, page 34. Based on tests published in Consumer Reports in August 2002, with updated prices and availability.

The tests behind the Ratings

Under **brand & model,** brackets show a tested model's color code. **Overall score** includes cooktop high power and low power performance, oven capacity, baking, broiling, and self-cleaning. **Cooktop high power** is how quickly the highest powered burner or element heated 6⅓ quarts of room-temperature water to a near boil. **Low power** shows how well the least powerful burner or element melted and held chocolate without scorching it and whether the most powerful, set to Low, held tomato sauce below a boil. **Oven capacity** is usable oven space. **Bake** shows baking evenness for cakes and cookies. **Broil** shows cooking and searing evenness for a tray of burgers. **Price** is approximate retail.

Recommendations and notes

Similar models have the same burners or elements, oven, and broiler; other details may differ.

All ranges: Are 30 inches wide. Have an oven light and anti-tip hardware. **Most ranges have:** Freestanding construction. Touchpad oven controls. A cooktop rim to hold spills. A self-cleaning oven. Two or three oven racks with five positions. An oven window with a reasonably clear view. A storage drawer. A warranty of one year for parts and labor. Sealed burners and cast-iron grates. Can be converted to LP fuel.

GAS MODELS

1> **GE** Profile Performance JGB910WEC[WW] **Convection option.** Warming drawer. Burners: 2@12,000, 1@9,500, 1@5,000 Btu/hr.

2> **GE** Profile JGBP85WEB[WW] **Warming drawer.** Window view worse than most. Burners: 2@12,000, 1@9,500, 1@5,000 Btu/hr. Similar: JGBP90MEB[ ], JGBP86WEB[ ].

3> **GE** JGBP35WEA[WW] **Window view worse than most.** Burners: 1@12,000, 2@9,500, 1@5,000 Btu/hr. Similar: JGBP79WEB[ ].

4> **HOTPOINT** RGB745WEA[WW] **A CR Best Buy Oven dial.** Window view worse than most. Steel grates. Burners: 1@12,000, 2@9,500, 1@5,000 Btu/hr.

5> **MAYTAG** MGR5880BD[W] **Among the more repair-prone gas-range brands.** Convection option. Warming drawer. Burners: 1@12,000, 2@9,200, 1@7,200 Btu/hr. Similar: MGR5870BD[ ].

6> **MAYTAG** Performa PGR5710BD[W] **Among the more repair-prone gas-range brands.** Steel grates. Window view worse than most. Burners: 1@12,000, 3@9,200 Btu/hr. Similar: PGR5705BD[ ].

7> **GE** Profile Performance JGB920WEC[WW] **Convection option.** Glass ceramic cooktop. Warming drawer and element. Burners: 2@12,000, 1@9,500, 1@5,200 Btu/hr.

8> **KENMORE** (Sears) 7584[2] **Warming drawer.** Split rack. Continuous grates. Burners: 1@13,500, 2@9,500, 1@5,000 Btu/hr.

9> **JENN-AIR** JGS8750AD[W] **Among the more repair-prone gas-range brands.** Slide-in design. Cooktop burners reignite. Continuous grates. Burners: 1@12,000, 1@10,500, 1@9,100, 1@6,500 Btu/hr.

10> **KENMORE** (Sears) 7566[1] **Warming drawer.** Burners: 1@14,200, 1@12,000, 1@9,500, 1@5,000 Btu/hr.

11> **KENMORE** (Sears) 7575[1] **Warming drawer.** Burners: 1@12,000, 3@9,500 Btu/hr.

12> **KITCHENAID** KGRT607H[BS] **Stainless-steel door and trim.** Convection option. Continuous grates. Burners: 1@14,000, 1@12,500, 2@6,000 Btu/hr. Discontinued, but may still be available. Similar: KGRT600H[ ].

13> **WHIRLPOOL** Gold GS460LEK[Q] **Continuous grates.** Window view worse than most. Split rack. Burners: 1@13,500, 2@9,500, 1@5,000 Btu/hr. Similar: SF387LEK[ ], GS465LEK[ ], GS470LXK[ ], GS475LXK[ ].

14> **FRIGIDAIRE** Gallery GLGF366A[S] Burners: 1@12,000, 3@9,500 Btu/hr. Similar: FGF366A[ ].

15> **DACOR** PGR30[S] **Pro-style features.** Slide-in design. Stainless-steel construction. Convection option. Continuous grates. Cooktop burners reignite. Burners: 2@12,500, 2@9,500 Btu/hr.

DUAL-FUEL MODELS

16> **KITCHENAID** KDRP407H[SS] **Pro-style.** Stainless-steel construction. Convection option. Continuous grates. Simmer plate. Oven dial. Burners: 4@15,000 Btu/hr.

17> **JENN-AIR** JDS9860AA[W] **Slide-in design.** Convection option. Continuous grates. Grill with downdraft vent. Burners: 2@10,000, 2@8,000 (grill) Btu/hr.

18> **DACOR** ERD30S06[BK] **Pro-style.** Stainless-steel construction. Convection option. Continuous grates. Simmer plate. Cooktop burners reignite. Excelled at self-cleaning. Burners: 4@15,000 Btu/hr.

19> **VIKING** VDSC305B[SS] **Pro-style.** Stainless-steel construction. Convection option. Continuous grates. Oven dial. Unsealed burners. Window view worse than most. Least effective at self-cleaning. Burners: 4@15,000 Btu/hr.

20> **GE** Monogram ZDP30N4D[SS] **Pro-style.** Stainless-steel construction. Convection option. Continuous grates. Unsealed burners. Oven dial. Three rack positions. Burners: 4@15,000 Btu/hr.

Receivers

Receivers are typically capable performers these days. Most of those rated offer a good selection of features. At $300, the Panasonic SA-HE100 is a **CR Best Buy.** The top performer in our tests, it's easy to use and has many useful features. It has the power to handle 4-ohm speakers—ideal if you have a very large room or if you like to play bass-heavy music. If you don't need that extra power and can settle for fewer features, consider the Panasonic SA-HE70, another very good performer priced at just $200. Key features for these models are listed in the table. See the product guide for an explanation of the features.

KEY NO.	BRAND & MODEL	PRICE	OVERALL SCORE	PERFORMANCE	EASE OF USE	FEATURES	WATTS PER CHANNEL		
							8 OHM	6 OHM	4 OHM
1	**Panasonic** SA-HE100 A CR Best Buy	$300		◓	◓	◓	85	112	45
2	**Onkyo** TX-SR600	500		◓	◓	○	109	127	—
3	**Harman Kardon** AVR 320	650		◓	○	○	88	105	—
4	**Onkyo** TX-SR500	300		◓	○	○	92	110	—
5	**Yamaha** RX-V430	300		◓	○	○	101	115	74
6	**Harman Kardon** AVR 120	350		◓	○	○	77	88	—
7	**Panasonic** SA-HE70	200		◓	○	◓	73	94	—
8	**Kenwood** VR-6060	500		◓	◓	◒	128	152	—
9	**Pioneer** VSX-D811S	400		○	○	○	140	157	—
10	**Pioneer** VSX-D511	200		○	○	○	135	149	—
11	**RCA** STAV-3990	250		○	○	○	139	152	—
12	**Sony** STR-DE685	250		○	◓	○	131	151	—
13	**JVC** RX-6020VBK	200		○	◓	◒	98	114	—
14	**Sony** STR-DE485	200		○	◓	◒	106	124	—

Overall Ratings — In performance order

Excellent ● Very good ◓ Good ○ Fair ◒ Poor ●

See report, page 76. Based on tests published in Consumer Reports in November 2002.

The tests behind the Ratings

Overall score is based on amplifier and AM/FM tuner performance, ease of use, and convenience features. **Performance** combines lack of noise and distortion in the amplifier, plus AM and FM reception. **Ease of use** reflects our judgments on the ergonomics of the front panel and remote control (including visibility and clarity of labeling); ease of operation; and, on the remote, button size and overall physical balance. **Features** reflects the presence or absence of convenience features. **Watts per channel** is our measure of power when the receiver is used with 8-ohm, 6-ohm, and 4-ohm speakers (a dash means the manufacturer does not recommend use with such speakers).

Recommendations and notes

All tested models: Can decode Dolby Digital and DTS sound-tracks. Have a 75-ohm FM-antenna connection. Have output jack for powered subwoofer. Have Dolby Pro Logic and other DSP modes besides Dolby Surround. Have test-tone function for setting sound level. Have remote control that can operate devices of the same brand. Have display dimmer. Lack direct tuning of frequency on console. Lack function to scan preset radio stations for a few seconds.

Most tested models: Have a two-year warranty for parts and labor. Lack center-channel pre-amp out jack. Have 5.1 inputs for external decoder. Lack bass-boost switch. Lack phono input. Have sleep-timer function. Have universal remote control to operate devices from other manufacturers. Have a good AM tuner. Have Dolby Pro Logic II mode. Lack tape monitor. Have one or two switched AC outlets. Have at least 30 AM or FM station presets.

Similar models should offer performance comparable to that of the tested model, although features may differ.

1▷ **PANASONIC** SA-HE100 **A CR Best Buy Best value among tested models.** FM tuner adjusts in full-channel increments. Troubleshooting "help" button. Tape monitor. Phono input. Lacks sleep timer. Warranty only 1 yr.

2▷ **ONKYO** TX-SR600 **Very good performer, though pricey.** Extra back-center channel for 6.1 surround. Mediocre AM performance. Similar: TX-SR700.

3▷ **HARMAN KARDON** AVR 320 **Very good, but pricey and lacking some features available in less expensive models.** Extra back-center channel for 6.1 surround. Center-channel pre-amp out jacks. Similar: AVR 520.

4▷ **ONKYO** TX-SR500 **Very good performer and very good value.**

5▷ **YAMAHA** RX-V430 **Good value.** FM tuner adjusts in full-channel increments. Mediocre AM performance. Similar: RX-V530.

6▷ **HARMAN KARDON** AVR 120 **Very good overall performer.** Lacks 5.1 inputs for external decoders like DVD players. Discontinued, but similar AVR 125 is available.

7▷ **PANASONIC** SA-HE70 **Very good value.** FM tuner adjusts in full-channel increments. Tape monitor. Troubleshooting "help" button. Lacks sleep timer. Warranty only 1 yr.

8▷ **KENWOOD** VR-6060 **Good overall, but lacking some features available in less expensive models.** Extra back-center channel for 6.1 surround. Phono input. Bass-boost switch. Mediocre AM performance. Lacks sleep timer. Similar: VR-6070.

9▷ **PIONEER** VSX-D811S **Good.** Extra back- center channel for 6.1 surround. Can program to display station call letters. Tape monitor. Lacks sleep timer. Warranty only 1 yr. Similar: VSX-D711.

10▷ **PIONEER** VSX-D511 **Good, basic model.** Can program to display station call letters. Lacks sleep timer and universal remote. Warranty only 1 yr. Similar: VSX-D411.

11▷ **RCA** STAV-3990 **Good value.** Tape monitor. Mediocre AM performance. Lacks sleep timer. Surround lacks Dolby Pro Logic II. Similar: STAV-4090.

12▷ **SONY** STR-DE685 **Good.** Can program to display station call letters. Mediocre AM performance. Similar: STR-DE885.

13▷ **JVC** RX-6020VBK **Good.** There are better choices. Mediocre FM and AM performance. Lacks universal remote and AC outlets. Similar: RX-7020VBK.

14▷ **SONY** STR-DE48 **Good.** There are better choices. Can program to display station call letters. Mediocre FM and AM performance. Lacks AC outlets. Surround lacks Dolby Pro Logic II.

Features at a glance   Receivers

Tested models (keyed to the Ratings) Key no. Brand	Front-panel input	S-video inputs/outputs	Component-video inputs	Direct AM/FM tuning	Onscreen display
1▷ **Panasonic**	•	3/0	•	•	
2▷ **Onkyo**	•	5/1	•		•
3▷ **Harman Kardon**	•	5/2	•	•	•
4▷ **Onkyo**	•	4/1			
5▷ **Yamaha**		0/0			
6▷ **Harman Kardon**	•	5/1		•	
7▷ **Panasonic**		3/0		•	
8▷ **Kenwood**	•	5/1	•		
9▷ **Pioneer**	•	4/1	•	•	
10▷ **Pioneer**		3/1			
11▷ **RCA**	•	4/1	•	•	
12▷ **Sony**	•	3/1	•	•	
13▷ **JVC**		0/0			
14▷ **Sony**		0/0		•	

Refrigerators

Choose the size and style, then look for the features you want, good performance, and a brand with a good track record for reliability. Among top-freezer models, the Maytag MTB1956GE, $825, is feature-laden and convenient. Nearly as good, and quieter, is the Kenmore 7118, $750. The GE GSS25JFM, $890, a **CR Best Buy,** is a real bargain among side-by-side refrigerators. Among built-in models with a freezer on the bottom, consider the GE Monogram ZIC360NM, $3,900. It scored nearly as well as the Sub-Zero, costs less, and it's quieter. Key features for these models are listed in the table on page 260. See the product guide for an explanation of the features.

Overall Ratings — In performance order

Legend: Excellent ● / Very good ◕ / Good ◑ / Fair ◔ / Poor ○

KEY NO	BRAND & MODEL	PRICE	OVERALL SCORE (P F G VG E, 0–100)	ENERGY COST/YR.	ENERGY EFFICIENCY	TEMP. TESTS	NOISE	EASE OF USE
	TOP-FREEZER MODELS (18-22 CU. FT.)							
1	**Maytag** MTB1956GE[W]	$825		$36	●	◑	○	◑
2	**Kenmore** (Sears) 7118[2]	750		43	●	◑	◑	○
3	**Maytag** MTB2156GE[W]	850		39	●	◑	◑	◑
4	**GE** GTS18KCM[WW]	600		40	●	◑	○	◑
5	**Kenmore** (Sears) 7198[2]	750		35	●	◑	●	○
6	**Frigidaire** Gallery GLHT216TA[W]	680		38	●	◑	◑	◑
7	**Kenmore** (Sears) 7285[2]	680		40	●	◑	○	○
8	**Whirlpool** Gold GR9SHKXK[Q]	940		37	●	◑	○	○
9	**Frigidaire** Gallery GLRT186TA[W]	680		40	●	◑	○	○
10	**GE** GTS22KCM[WW]	650		44	●	◑	○	◑
11	**Whirlpool** Gold GR2SHTXK[Q]	1,050		40	●	◑	○	◑
12	**Frigidaire** FRT18P5A[W]	510		40	●	◑	○	◑
	SIDE-BY-SIDE MODELS (20-28 CU. FT.)							
13	**Frigidaire** Gallery GLHS267ZA[W]	1,275		$54	◑	◑	○	◑
14	**Whirlpool** Gold GC5THGXK[Q]	2,300		53	◑	◑	○	◑
15	**KitchenAid** Superba KSRG27FK[WH]	1,700		55	◑	○	◑	◑
16	**Maytag** MSD2456GE[W]	1,210		52	◑	◑	◑	◑
17	**GE** GSS25JFM[WW] **A CR Best Buy**	890		60	◑	◑	○	◑
18	**Frigidaire** Gallery GLRS237ZA[W]	1,100		57	○	◑	○	○
19	**Kenmore** (Sears) 5106[2]	1,200		56	○	◑	◑	◑
20	**Whirlpool** ED2FHGXK[Q]	1,020		54	○	◑	○	◑
21	**Maytag** Plus MZD2766GE[W]	1,500		55	◑	◐	○	◑
22	**GE** GSS20IEM[WW]	800		54	○	○	○	○
	BUILT-IN BOTTOM-FREEZER MODELS (20-21 CU. FT.)							
23	**Sub-Zero** 650/F	4,600		42	●	●	○	○
24	**GE** Monogram ZIC360NM	3,900		47	◑	●	◑	○
25	**KitchenAid** KBRS36FKX[ ]	4,100		43	●	●	○	○
26	**Viking** DDBB363R[SS]	4,800		47	◑	●	○	○

See report, page 38. Based on tests published in Consumer Reports in August 2002, with updated prices and availability.

The tests behind the Ratings

Under **brand & model,** brackets indicate the tested model's color code. **Overall score** gives the most weight to energy efficiency and temperature performance. **Energy cost/year** is based on 2002 national average electricity rate, 8.3 cents per kilowatt-hour. **Expected annual usage** is based on model's EnergyGuide sticker. **Energy efficiency** reflects consumption per EnergyGuide and model's usable volume. **Temperature tests** combines the outcome of tests run at different room temperatures, including extreme heat; they judge how closely and uniformly the maker's recommended settings match our ideal temperatures for refrigerators. **Noise** was gauged with compressors running. **Ease of use** assesses more than 100 features, including controls and ice/water dispenser. **Price** is approximate retail; includes optional icemaker on some models.

Recommendations and notes

Models listed as similar should offer performance comparable to the tested model's, although features may differ.

Most models have: Ability to keep main space at 37° F and freezer at 0° with good temperature uniformity. Very good or excellent ability to handle heavy loads on hot days. Meatkeeper that reaches good storage temperature. Ability to make more than 3½ pounds of ice daily. Spillproof glass shelves. Slide-out bins or shelves. One-year full warranty on parts and labor, five years on refrigeration system.

All side-by-sides have: Icemaker with lighted, through-the-door dispenser for ice and water; selection for cubes or crushed ice. **Most side-by-sides have:** Water filter.

Most top- and bottom-freezers have: Half shelves.

TOP-FREEZER MODELS

1 MAYTAG MTB1956GE[W] **Very good performance, with features that make it more convenient than most top-freezers.** Crank-adjustable shelf. 67x30x29½ in. 18.5 cu. ft. (14.4 usable).

2 KENMORE (Sears) 7118[2] **Very good performer, though short on features.** 66x32½x29½ in. 20.8 cu. ft. (16.9 usable). Similar: 7119[ ].

3 MAYTAG MTB2156GE[W] **Very good overall with features that make it more convenient than most top-freezers.** Crank-adjustable shelf. 67x33x29 in. 20.7 cu. ft. (15.1 usable).

4 GE GTS18KCM[WW] **Well priced for very good performance, with features that make it more convenient than most top-freezers.** 66½x30x30½ in. 17.9 cu. ft. (14.0 usable). Similar: GTS18KBM[ ], GTH18KBM[ ].

5 KENMORE (Sears) 7198[2] **Very good and quiet, with attractive features.** Made more ice than the other top-freezers– about 4.5 lbs. per day. 66x30x31 in. 18.8 cu. ft. (14.1 usable).

6 FRIGIDAIRE Gallery GLHT216TA[W] **Well priced for very good performance.** But among the more repair-prone brands of top-freezers with icemakers. 69x30x32½ in. 20.6 cu. ft. (16.4 usable). Similar: PLHT217TAC[ ].

7 KENMORE (Sears) 7285[2] **Well priced for very good performance, though short on features.** 66x30x30 in. 18.1 cu. ft. (14.1 usable). Similar: 7286[ ].

8 WHIRLPOOL Gold GR9SHKXK[Q] **Very good overall.** Curved, smooth-surface doors. 66x30x32 in. 18.8 cu. ft. (14.1 usable).

Features at a glance — Refrigerators

Tested products (keyed to the Ratings) Key no. / Brand	Child lock-out	Energy Star	Ice/water dispenser	Ice Bin on Door	Pullout shelves/bins	Speed Ice
TOP-FREEZER MODELS						
1 Maytag		•			•	
2 Kenmore						
3 Maytag		•			•	
4 GE						
5 Kenmore		•			•	•
6 Frigidaire		•			•	
7 Kenmore						
8 Whirlpool		•			•	
9 Frigidaire						
10 GE						
11 Whirlpool	•	W			•	
12 Frigidaire						
SIDE-BY-SIDES						
13 Frigidaire		•	•		•	•
14 Whirlpool	•	•	•		•	
15 Kitchenaid		•	•		•	
16 Maytag		•	•			
17 GE		•				
18 Frigidaire		•			•	•
19 Kenmore		•				
20 Whirlpool		•				
21 Maytag	•	•	•			
22 GE		•				
BUILT-INS (BOTTOM-FREEZERS)						
23 Sub-Zero			•			
24 GE			•			
25 KitchenAid		•	•			
26 Viking			•			

Recommendations and notes

9▷ **FRIGIDAIRE** Gallery GLRT186TA[W] **Very good overall and well priced, but among the more repair-prone brands of top-freezers with icemakers.** 66½x30x31 in. 18.3 cu. ft. (14.3 usable). Similar: GLHT186TA[ ].

10▷ **GE** GTS22KCM[WW] **Well priced for very good performance, with features that make it more convenient than most top-freezers.** But manufacturer's recommended settings left fridge and freezer too cold. 67½x33x31½ in. 21.7 cu. ft. (16.5 usable). Similar: GTS22KBM[ ].

11▷ **WHIRLPOOL** Gold GR2SHTXK[Q] **Very good, with attractive features, though pricey.** Curved, smooth-surface doors. Water dispenser with filter. 66½x33x31½ in. 21.6 cu. ft. (15.9 usable). Similar: GR2SHKXK[ ].

12▷ **FRIGIDAIRE** FRT18P5A[W] **Very good overall and well priced.** No meatkeeper controls, pull-out shelves, or freezer light. Frigidaire has been among the more repair-prone brands of top-freezers with icemakers. 66½x30x30 in. 18.4 cu. ft. (14.5 usable). Similar: FRT18HP5A[ ].

SIDE-BY-SIDE MODELS

13▷ **FRIGIDAIRE** Gallery GLHS267ZA[W] **Very good overall and relatively inexpensive compared with similar performers.** Excellent at making ice—about 8.5 lbs. per day. But among the more repair-prone side-by-side brands. 69½x36x33½ in. 25.9 cu. ft. (17.5 usable). Similar: PLHS267ZA[ ].

14▷ **WHIRLPOOL** Gold GC5THGXK[Q] **Cabinet depth (requires door panels and 36-in.-wide opening).** 72x35½x27½ in. 24.5 cu. ft. (14.7 usable). Discontinued, but similar GC5THGXL[ ] is available.

15▷ **KITCHENAID** Superba KSRG27FK[WH] **Pricey but very good overall.** Ice bin located on the freezer door for easy access and removal. 70x36x32 in. 26.8 cu. ft. (16.8 usable). Similar: KSRD27FK[ ].

16▷ **MAYTAG** MSD2456GE[W] **Very good overall, but has been the most repair-prone side-by-side brand.** Crank-adjustable shelf. 69x33x32 in. 23.6 cu. ft. (13.3 usable).

17▷ **GE** GSS25JFM[WW] **A CR Best Buy Well priced for very good performance and fairly large capacity.** But freezer door was a bit too warm. 70x36x31 in. 24.9 cu. ft. (16.9 usable). Discontinued, but may still be available. Similar: GSS25JEM[ ].

18▷ **FRIGIDAIRE** Gallery GLRS237ZA[W] **Very good overall and excellent at making ice.** But among the more repair-prone brands and not as energy efficient as most. 69½x33x33 in. 22.6 cu. ft. (14.6 usable). Similar: GLHS237ZA[ ].

19▷ **KENMORE** (Sears) 5106[2] **Very good overall, but not as energy efficient as most.** 66½x33½x29 in. 20 cu. ft. (13.2 usable). Similar: 5104[ ].

20▷ **WHIRLPOOL** ED2FHGXK[Q] **Very good overall, but not as energy efficient as most.** 66½x33x31 in. 22 cu. ft. (13.3 usable).

21▷ **MAYTAG** Plus MZD2766GE[W] **Good overall and novel design holds wider items than most side-by-sides.** But warm spots throughout fridge, especially butter compartment, and has been the most repair-prone side-by-side brand. 70½x36x32 in. 26.8 cu. ft. (17.7 usable).

22▷ **GE** GSS20IEM[WW] **Good overall and well priced, but not as energy efficient as most.** Meatkeeper too warm. No spill-proof shelves or water filter. 67½x32x31½ in. 19.9 cu. ft. (13.3 usable). Discontinued, but may still be available.

BUILT-IN BOTTOM-FREEZER MODELS

23▷ **SUB-ZERO** 650/F **Very good overall and very energy efficient.** Bottom freezer opens like a drawer. Sub-Zero is among the most repair-prone brands. 2-yr. full warranty. 84x36½x25½ in. 20.6 cu. ft. (15.4 usable).

24▷ **GE** Monogram ZIC360NM **Very good overall and very quiet.** Bottom freezer opens like a drawer. 2-yr. full warranty. 84x36½x25½2 in. 20.6 cu. ft. (13.6 usable). Water filter. Similar: ZICS360NM[ ].

25▷ **KITCHENAID** KBRS36FKX[ ] **Very good overall and very energy efficient.** Bottom freezer opens like a drawer. 2-yr. full warranty. 83½x36x25½ in. 20.9 cu. ft. (14.4 usable).

26▷ **VIKING** DDBB363R[SS] **Very good, with stainless steel front.** Bottom freezer opens like a drawer. 2-yr. full warranty. 83½x36x24½ in. 20.3 cu. ft. (15.0 usable). Similar: DFBB363[ ], VCBB363[ ], DTBB363[ ].

Smoke alarms

Smoke alarms can detect either smoke or flame, but few excel at detecting both. Ionization alarms react quickly to fast-flaming fires, while photoelectric alarms are best at detecting smoke. Dual-detection alarms blend both technologies and are the best choice for a battery model. If your home is wired for alarms, install both kinds.

Overall Ratings — In performance order

Rating key: Excellent ⊙ Very good ◔ Good ○ Fair ◑ Poor ●

KEY NO.	BRAND & MODEL	PRICE	OVERALL SCORE (0 P F G VG E 100)	FLAME	SMOKE	FALSE ALARM
	DUAL-DETECTION ALARMS: BATTERY					
1	**Firex** Dual Sensor CCPB-04021	$22		⊙	⊙	◑
	IONIZATION ALARMS: BATTERY					
2	**First Alert** Smoke & CO SCO1N [CL]	45		⊙	●	◑
3	**Fire Sentry** Micro Profile 0914	6		⊙	●	○
4	**Kidde** Nighthawk Combination (CO) KN-COSM-B	50		⊙	●	◑
5	**First Alert** 10 Year Lithium Power SA10YR	32		⊙	●	○
6	**Kidde** Basic 0915K	10		⊙	●	○
7	**Lifesaver** 0915	10		⊙	●	○
8	**Firex** Basic Protection CB-04000	9		⊙	●	○
	PHOTOELECTRIC ALARMS: BATTERY					
9	**Kidde** Nighthawk Elite PE9N	22		●	⊙	○
10	**First Alert** Photoelectric Sensor SA203 [B/C]	22		●	⊙	○
	IONIZATION ALARMS: AC					
11	**Firex** 120V AC with Battery B/U 04518	13		⊙	●	◑
12	**First Alert** Strobe Light SA100B	125		⊙	●	◑
13	**Kidde** Professional Premium 1275K	18		⊙	●	○
14	**Firex** 120V Signaling Kit 0242	80		⊙	●	○
	PHOTOELECTRIC ALARMS: AC					
15	**Kidde** Professional Elite PE120	32		●	⊙	○

See report, page 128. Based on tests published in Consumer Reports in August 2001 with updated prices and availability.

The tests behind the Ratings

Overall score denotes performance for flaming and smoky test fires and includes convenience features and resistance to false alarms. **Flame** reflects the response to paper fires that generated flames but little smoke. **Smoke** reflects the response to wood-fed smoky, smoldering fires with no flames. **False alarm** measures how well alarms resisted being triggered by cooking. **Price** is approximate retail.

Recommendations and notes

All models have: A sufficiently loud alarm horn of a least 85 decibels. A chirp warning that sounds when batteries are weak (for battery models). A UL listing.

Most models have: A five- or ten-year warranty.

DUAL-DETECTION ALARMS: BATTERY
1▷ **FIREX** Dual Sensor CCPB-04021 **Hush button.**

IONIZATION ALARMS: BATTERY
2▷ **FIRST ALERT** Smoke & CO SCO1N [CL] **Hush button and carbon-monoxide detector.**

3▷ **FIRE SENTRY** Micro Profile 0914 **Compact size.** Test button hard to press with unit on ceiling. 3-year warranty. Similar: 0914E.

4▷ **KIDDE** Nighthawk Combination (CO) KN-COSM-B **Carbon-monoxide detector.**

5▷ **FIRST ALERT** 10 Year Lithium Power SA10YR **Built-in long-life battery.** Hush button. Test button hard to distinguish.

6▷ **KIDDE** Basic 0915K **Test button hard to press with unit on ceiling.** Similar: 0916K, 0918K.

7▷ **LIFESAVER** 0915 **Similar to Kidde Basic 0915K, but different housing.** Similar: 0916LL.

8▷ **FIREX** Basic Protection CB-04000 **Good overall.** Similar: 04003, 04009, 04015.

PHOTOELECTRIC ALARMS: BATTERY
9▷ **KIDDE** Nighthawk Elite PE9N **Test button hard to press with unit on ceiling.** Similar: PE9E.

10▷ **FIRST ALERT** Photoelectric Sensor SA203 [B/C] **Test button hard to press with unit on ceiling.**

IONIZATION ALARMS: AC
11▷ **FIREX** 120V AC with Battery B/U 04518 **Battery backup.** Hush button. Similar: 4618, 5000.

12▷ **FIRST ALERT** Strobe Light SA100B **Built-in strobe light for hearing-impaired.** Test button hard to press with unit on ceiling.

13▷ **KIDDE** Professional Premium 1275K **Battery backup.** Hush button. Test button hard to distinguish and press when on ceiling. Similar: 1275E, 1275EH.

14▷ **FIREX** 120V Signaling Kit 0242 **Separate strobe light for hearing-impaired.** Hush button.

PHOTOELECTRIC ALARMS: AC
15▷ **KIDDE** Professional Elite PE120 **Battery backup.** Test button hard to distinguish and press when on ceiling. Similar: Fyrnetics PE 120E.

Speakers

Paired with today's receivers, speakers—whether bookshelf, floor-standing, or three- or six-piece systems —can easily fill a large room with loud sound. Tests show that some are better than others at playing loud bass without buzzing or otherwise distorting the sound. Keep in mind that most speakers perform better with a little elbow room, so a corner, crowded bookshelf, or wall-mount is unlikely to be the ideal location. Paying more for speakers won't always get you better sound, but it may get you more stylish boxes.

Overall Ratings In performance order

Excellent ● Very good ◕ Good ○ Fair ◑ Poor ●

KEY NO	BRAND & MODEL	PRICE	OVERALL SCORE	ACCURACY	BASS HANDLING	IMPEDANCE (OHMS)
			0 P F G VG E 100			
BOOKSHELF MODELS						
1	**Pioneer** S-DF3-K	$350		89	●	4
2	**Bose** 301 Series IV	300		89	◕	7
3	**Cambridge Soundworks** Model Six	150		88	◕	7
4	**BIC** America Venturi DV62si	200		90	○	7
5	**Infinity** Entra One	300		87	●	4
6	**B&W** DM 602 S2	550		85	●	5
7	**Bose** 201 Series IV	200		88	◕	9
8	**Acoustic Research** 215PS	130		89	◕	4
9	**Mission** MS M72	350		88	○	4
10	**Pioneer** S-DF2-K	250		87	◕	5
11	**Sony** SS-MB300H	100		86	◕	9
12	**PSB** Image 2B	370		84	●	4
13	**Pioneer** S-H252B-K	100		85	◕	8
14	**Mission** 780	600		87	○	5
15	**Pioneer** S-DF1-K	200		85	◕	4
16	**Bose** 141	100		86	○	6
17	**Cerwin Vega** RL-16M	300		81	◕	4
18	**Acoustic Research** AR15	230		77	◕	4
19	**Klipsch** Synergy SB-3 Monitor	450		76	●	4
20	**KLH** 911B	70		79	○	7
21	**Acoustic Research** AR17	$180		79	◑	4
FLOOR-STANDING MODELS						
22	**Mission** MS M73	500		89	◕	5
23	**Cerwin Vega** E-710	360		84	●	3
24	**Yamaha** NS-A200XT	400		83	●	5
THREE-PIECE SYSTEMS						
25	**Cambridge Soundworks** Ensemble III	250		94	◑	4
26	**Bose** Acoustimass 3 Series IV	300		88	◕	5
27	**Bose** Acoustimass 5 Series III	600		86	◕	6
28	**Cambridge Soundworks** New Ensemble II	300		83	◕	4

See report, page 82. Based on tests published in Consumer Reports in November 2002, with updated prices and availability.

The tests behind the Ratings

Overall score is based primarily on the ability to reproduce sound accurately. For bookshelf and floor-standing speakers and for three-piece systems, it also considers the ability to play bass music loudly without distortion. We measured the **accuracy** with which a speaker reproduced test signals containing the range of frequencies appropriate to each type of speaker; 100 is the best possible score. **Bass handling** reflects the ability to play bass-heavy music loudly without buzzing or distortion. **Impedance,** measured in ohms, is an electrical characteristic you should consider when matching speakers to a receiver or amplifier. We list our measurement, which in almost all cases was lower than the manufacturer's rating (theirs was typically 8 ohms). **Price** is approximate retail for a pair of bookshelf, floor-standing, or rear-surround speakers; for one center-channel speaker; and for two satellites and a bass module in three-piece sets. Size is height by width by depth, in inches; weight is per speaker, in pounds. For three-piece systems, the size and weight shown are for satellites. Bass modules are about 14x8 inches, with depth of 13 to 19 inches; they weigh 12 to 21 pounds. **Recommendations and notes** include optimal placement and Audio Notes, a technical description of the sound profile.

Recommendations and notes

Most tested models have: A black veneer finish (some may be available in other colors). A five-year warranty. Magnetic shielding to prevent video interference when placed near a TV. No included wires.

BOOKSHELF MODELS

1▷ **PIONEER** S-DF3-K **Excellent.** Best placed 54 in. from side wall, 12 in. from back. Audio notes: Very smooth. 16.5x10x13 in., 18 lb.

2▷ **BOSE** 301 Series IV **Excellent speakers but rather wide.** Designed for left or right position. Best placed 18 in. from side wall, 24 in. from back. May cause video interference near a TV. Audio notes: Slight emphasis in midbass. 10.75x16.5x9.5 in., 12 lb.

3▷ **CAMBRIDGE SOUNDWORKS** Model Six **Very good and low-priced, with long (10-yr.) warranty.** Best placed 36 in. from side wall, 6 in. from back. May cause video interference near a TV. Audio notes: Not quite as smooth as other high-accuracy models. 18.25x11.25x7.5 in., 16 lb.

4▷ **BIC** America Venturi DV62si **Very good.** Best placed 36 in. from side wall, 6 in. from back. Long (7-yr.) warranty. Audio notes: Smooth and accurate, but shy in deep bass, strong in treble. 14.25x9x9.25 in., 13 lb.

5▷ **INFINITY** Entra One **Very good.** Best placed 48 in. from side wall, 18 in. from back. Audio notes: Smooth, with good extreme treble, slight dip in midrange. 15x8.5x9.25 in., 15 lb.

6▷ **B&W** DM 602 S2 **Very good but expensive.** Best placed 48 in. from side wall, 18 in. from back. May cause video interference near a TV. Audio notes: Good deep bass, noticeable weakness in upper midrange. 19.25x9.25x12 in., 23 lb.

7▷ **BOSE** 201 Series IV **Very good and compact.** Best placed 60 in. from side wall, 12 in. from back. Designed for left or right position. May cause video interference near a TV. Audio notes: Fairly smooth overall response, but lacks deep bass, overemphasizes midbass region. 9.5x15x6.75 in., 9 lb.

8▷ **ACOUSTIC RESEARCH** 215PS **Very good, light, and low-priced.** Best placed 30 in. from side wall, 18 in. from back. Audio notes: Somewhat uneven overall response. Emphasizes lower midrange and de-emphasizes upper midrange. 10.25x7x6.5 in., 7 lb.

9▷ **MISSION** MS M72 **Very good.** Best placed 24 in. from side wall, 12 in. from back. Short (2-yr.) warranty. Audio notes: Somewhat uneven overall response, with emphasis in lower midrange, de-emphasis in upper midrange. 13.25x7.75x12 in., 15 lb.

10▷ **PIONEER** S-DF2-K **Very good.** Best placed 48 in. from side wall, 12 in. from back. Audio notes: Fairly smooth response. Slight emphasis in midrange region, lacks extreme treble. 14x8.25x9.25 in., 13 lb.

11▷ **SONY** SS-MB300H **Very good and low-priced.** Best placed 48 in. from side wall, flush with rear. Removable grille. Audio notes: Fairly even overall response except for treble region. Slight de-emphasis in upper midrange but a peak in treble, lacks extreme treble. 21x9.5x10 in., 14 lb.

12▷ **PSB** Image 2B **Very good.** Best placed 48 in. from side wall, 18 in. from back. 5-yr. warranty only if card mailed in; otherwise 1-yr. Audio notes: Smooth, but slopes from strong midbass to weak treble. Moderate treble boost can improve accuracy. 15.25x8x12 in., 17 lb.

13▷ **PIONEER** S-H252B-K **Very good and low-priced.** Best placed 48 in. from side wall, 12 in. from back. May cause video interference near a TV. Audio notes: Somewhat uneven overall, with emphasis in lower midrange, severe de-emphasis in upper midrange. 21.5x11x10 in., 15 lb.

14▷ **MISSION** 780 **Very good and compact, but expensive.** Best placed 30 in. from side wall, 18 in. from back. May cause video interference near a TV. Audio notes: Extended treble, slightly weak deep bass, slightly strong midbass. 11x6.5x11 in., 11 lb.

Recommendations and notes

15▷ **PIONEER** S-DF1-K **Very good.** Best placed 48 in. from side wall, 18 in. from back. Audio notes: Somewhat uneven overall response, with lack of deep bass and overemphasized lower midrange. 12x7x9.75 in., 10 lb.

16▷ **BOSE** 141 **Very good overall.** Small, light, and low-priced. Shortest bookshelf model tested. Compact, gray vinyl cabinet. Best placed 24 in. from side wall, 18 in. from back. Designed for left or right position. May cause video interference near a TV. Audio notes: Smooth, but lacks deep bass and soft treble. Slight tone-control boost in both can improve accuracy. 6x10x6.25 in., 5 lb.

17▷ **CERWIN VEGA** RL-16M **Good choice.** Best placed 48 in. from side wall, 18 in. from back. Audio notes: Emphasized midbass, reduced midrange and treble. Moderate treble boost can improve accuracy. 14x8.5x11 in., 14 lb.

18▷ **ACOUSTIC RESEARCH** AR15 **Good.** Best placed 48 in. from side wall, 18 in. from back. Audio notes: Somewhat uneven overall response, with overemphasis across entire midrange region. 14.25x8.5x9 in., 16 lb.

19▷ **KLIPSCH** Synergy SB-3 Monitor **Good.** Best placed 36 in. from side wall, 24 in. from back. Audio notes: Emphasis on midbass, weak treble. Moderate treble boost can improve accuracy. 17x8.25x11.25 in., 18 lb.

20▷ **KLH** 911B **Good, lightweight speakers at a low price.** Best placed 18 in. from side wall, 12 in. from back. Short (1-yr.) warranty. Audio notes: Uneven response, with little bass, muted upper midrange, peak in treble. 11x6.5x6.75 in., 7 lb.

21▷ **ACOUSTIC RESEARCH** AR17 **Good, but avoid if you play bass-heavy music very loud.** Best placed 60 in. from side wall, 12 in. from back. Audio notes: Lacks deep bass and extreme treble, overemphasizes bass and lower midrange region. 13x8x8 in., 13 lb.

FLOOR-STANDING MODELS

22▷ **MISSION** MS M73 **Very good.** Short (2-yr.) warranty. Best placed 24 in. from side wall, 12 in. from back. Audio notes: Smooth overall, but lacks deep bass, de-emphasizes upper midrange. 33.5x8x12 in., 30 lb.

23▷ **CERWIN Vega** E-710 **Very good.** Among the best choices for playing bass-heavy music very loud. May cause video interference near a TV. Best placed 42 in. from side wall, 24 in. from back. Audio notes: Smooth overall, with strong midbass. Slight treble boost can help. 31.25x12.5x12 in., 40 lb.

24▷ **YAMAHA** NS-A200XT **Very good.** Short (2-yr.) warranty. Includes speaker wires. Best placed 48 in. from side wall, 24 in. from back. Audio notes: Somewhat uneven overall, with slight emphasis in bass, treble roll-off. 42.75x12x17.5 in., 44 lb.

THREE-PIECE SYSTEMS

25▷ **CAMBRIDGE SOUNDWORKS** Ensemble III **Excellent.** Very accurate and smooth. Black metal cabinet. Bass unit best placed 60 in. from side wall, 18 in. from back. Audio notes: Midrange de-emphasized, treble uneven. 6.5x4.25x3.5 in., 3 lb.

26▷ **BOSE** Acoustimass 3 Series IV **Excellent.** Black plastic cabinet. Includes speaker wires. Bass unit best placed 60 in. from side wall, 18 in. from back. Audio notes: Smooth, with slight reduction in treble and deep bass. 3x3.25x4 in., 1 lb.

27▷ **BOSE** Acoustimass 5 Series III **Very good.** Bass unit best placed 48 in. from side wall, 18 in. from back. Audio notes: Slight emphasis on bass, slight de-emphasis on treble. 6.25x3.25x4.25 in., 2 lb.

28▷ **CAMBRIDGE SOUNDWORKS** New Ensemble II **Very good.** Long (10-yr.) warranty. Gray plastic cabinet. Bass unit best placed 30 in. from side wall, flush with back. Audio notes: Midrange de-emphasized, treble uneven. 8.25x5.25x4.5 in., 4 lb.

String trimmers

You don't have to spend a lot of money to get a capable trimmer. Consider a corded electric trimmer for smaller yards or for lighter-duty trimming. The best among those we tested is the Ryobi 132r TrimmerPlus, $70, and the 105r, $60. Battery-powered models combine mobility with easy starting, but are only suitable for light trimming chores. Gasoline-powered string trimmers are your best bet for large properties or for clearing tall grass. Consider the top-performing John Deere S1400, $170—**a CR Best Buy.**

Overall Ratings — In performance order

Rating key: ◉ Excellent · ◕ Very good · ○ Good · ◔ Fair · ● Poor

KEY NO.	BRAND & MODEL	PRICE	WEIGHT	OVERALL SCORE (0–100)	TRIM	CUT	EDGE	HANDLING	EASE OF USE
	GASOLINE MODELS								
1	**John Deere** S1400 **A CR Best Buy**	$170	13 lb.		◉	◉	◉	◕	◕
2	**Stihl** FS 55R	200	12		◉	◉	◉	◕	○
3	**Stihl** FS 45 **A CR Best Buy**	150	10		◉	◉	◉	◕	○
4	**Stihl** FS 75	200	11		◉	◉	◕	◉	◕
5	**Ryobi** 775r EZ TrimmerPlus **A CR Best Buy**	140	14		◉	◉	◉	◕	○
6	**Husqvarna** 325CX E-tech	200	10		◉	◉	◕	◉	◕
7	**Stihl** FS 46	170	9		◉	◉	◕	◕	◕
8	**Ryobi** 875r TrimmerPlus	185	13		◉	◉	◕	◕	◕
9	**John Deere** C1200	150	11		◉	◕	◕	◕	○
10	**John Deere** T105C	170	9		◉	◕	◕	◕	◕
11	**Homelite** VersaTool	100	11		◉	◕	◕	◕	○
12	**Homelite** Trim N' Edge	85	10		◉	◕	◕	◕	◕
13	**Ryobi** 700r	75	11		◉	◉	◕	◕	○
14	**Weed Eater** FeatherLite 25 HO SST	95	9		◕	○	○	◕	○
15	**Weed Eater** FeatherLite Plus	85	9		◕	○	○	○	○
16	**Poulan** PP031	115	12		◕	◔	◕	◕	◕
	CORDED MODELS								
17	**Ryobi** 132r TrimmerPlus	70	10		◉	○	◕	◕	◕
18	**Ryobi** 105r	60	8		◉	○	○	◕	◕
19	**Black & Decker** Grass Hog GH400	55	5		◕	○	○	◕	◕
20	**Black & Decker** Grass Hog GH500	50	5		◕	○	○	◕	◕
21	**Weed Eater** YardMaster YM 600	65	8		◕	◔	○	◕	◕
22	**Weed Eater** Snap 'N Go SG14	40	5		○	○	◕	○	◕
23	**Weed Eater** XT110	30	5		◕	◔	○	◕	◕
24	**Weed Eater** Snap 'N Go SG12	30	4		◕	○	○	○	◕
25	**Weed Eater** XT112	30	4		◕	○	◔	○	◕
26	**Toro** 51353	45	5		○	◔	○	○	◕
27	**Toro** 51301	35	4		○	◔	◔	◕	◕
28	**Toro** 51332	35	4		○	◔	◔	◕	◕

				Excellent ●	Very good ◖	Good ○	Fair ◗	Poor ●

Overall Ratings, cont.

KEY NO.	BRAND & MODEL	PRICE	WEIGHT	OVERALL SCORE	TRIM	CUT	EDGE	HANDLING	EASE OF USE
29	**Weed Eater** ElectraLite EL 10 Type 1	20	3		◖	●	●	○	◗
30	**Weed Eater** ElectraLite EL8	20	4		●	◗	●	○	◗
31	**Black & Decker** ST1000	20	3		●	●	●	○	○
	BATTERY-POWERED MODELS								
32	**Ryobi** 155r	100	10		◖	◖	◖	○	◗
33	**Black & Decker** Grass Hog CST2000	100	10		◖	◖	●	○	◗

See report, page 104. Based on tests published in Consumer Reports May 2002, with updated prices and availability.

The tests behind the Ratings

The **overall score** is based mainly on trimming near a wall, cutting weeds and tall grass, edging, handling, and ease of use. **Weight** is rounded to the nearest pound and includes a full spool of string but not fuel, which can add one-half pound to gas models. **Trim** indicates how quickly and neatly models cut grass. **Cut** measures cutting power in overgrown weeds. **Edge** reflects the ability to quickly trim a neat, vertical line along the lawn's border on a walkway or other hard surface. **Handling** assesses responsiveness and balance. **Ease of use** is the ease of starting the engine and feeding out more line, along with handle comfort and ease of accessing controls. **Price** is approximate retail.

Recommendations and notes

GASOLINE MODELS

1 > **JOHN DEERE** S1400 **A CR Best Buy Straight shaft.** Can also power blower and other tools. Heavier than most. Adjusting front handle requires tools.

2 > **STIHL** FS 55R **Straight shaft.** Adjusting front handle requires tools.

3 > **STIHL** FS 45 **A CR Best Buy Curved shaft.** Better balance and less vibration than most.

4 > **STIHL** FS 75 **Curved shaft.** Adjusting front handle requires tools.

5 > **RYOBI** 775r EZ TrimmerPlus **A CR Best Buy Straight shaft.** Can also power blower and other tools. Heavier than most.

6 > **HUSQVARNA** 325CX E-tech **Curved shaft.** Tall grass wrapped around head.

7 > **STIHL** FS 46 **Curved shaft.** Lighter than most. Rear handle more comfortable than most.

8 > **RYOBI** 875r TrimmerPlus **Straight shaft.** Can power other tools. 4-stroke engine. Heavier than most. Starting harder than most.

9 > **JOHN DEERE** C1200 **Curved shaft.** Can power blower and other optional tools. Adjusting front handle requires tools.

10 > **JOHN DEERE** T105C **Curved shaft.** Inconvenient choke. Lighter and better balanced than most.

11 > **HOMELITE** VersaTool **Curved shaft.** Can also power blower and other tools. Head rotates for edging. Tall grass wrapped around head.

12 > **HOMELITE** Trim N' Edge **Curved shaft.** Starting harder than most.

13 > **RYOBI** 700r **Curved shaft.**

14 > **WEED EATER** FeatherLite 25 HO SST **Straight shaft.** Lighter than most. Quick-release spool. Starting harder than most. Only one cutting line.

15 > **WEED EATER** FeatherLite Plus **Curved shaft.** Lighter than most. Quick-release spool. Only one cutting line.

16 > **POULAN** PP031 **Curved shaft.** Only one cutting line. 1-year warranty.

Recommendations and notes

CORDED MODELS

17▷ **RYOBI** 132r TrimmerPlus **Curved shaft.** Dual cutting lines. Motor on top, improving balance. Can also power blower and other tools.

18▷ **RYOBI** 105r **Curved shaft.** Dual cutting lines. Motor on top, improving balance.

19▷ **BLACK & DECKER** Grass Hog GH400 **Curved shaft.** Quick-release spool. Lighter than most.

20▷ **BLACK & DECKER** Grass Hog GH500 **Curved shaft.** Quick-release spool. Lighter than most.

21▷ **WEED EATER** YardMaster YM 600 **Straight shaft.** Motor on top, improving balance. Quick-release spool. No cord retainer.

22▷ **WEED EATER** Snap 'N Go SG14 **Curved shaft.** Lighter than most. Quick-release spool.

23▷ **WEED EATER** XT110 **Curved shaft.** Lighter than most. Quick-release spool.

24▷ **WEED EATER** Snap 'N Go SG12 **Curved shaft.** Lighter than most. Quick-release spool.

25▷ **WEED EATER** XT112 **Curved shaft.** Lighter than most. Quick-release spool.

26▷ **TORO** 51353 **Curved shaft.** Lighter than most. Quick-release spool.

27▷ **TORO** 51301 **Curved shaft.** Lighter than most. Quick-release spool.

28▷ **TORO** 51332 **Curved shaft.** Lighter than most. Quick-release spool.

29▷ **WEED EATER** ElectraLite EL 10 Type 1 **Curved shaft.** Lighter than most. Quick-release spool.

30▷ **WEED EATER** ElectraLite EL8 **Curved shaft.** Lighter than most. Quick-release spool.

31▷ **BLACK & DECKER** ST1000 **Curved shaft.** Lighter than most. Quick-release spool.

BATTERY-POWERED MODELS

32▷ **RYOBI** 155r **Straight shaft.** Awkward start safety button.

33▷ **BLACK & DECKER** Grass Hog CST2000 **Straight shaft.** Quick-release spool. Automatic line feed. Shield contacts ground during trimming.

Toasters & toaster ovens

If you want the best toast, choose a toaster over a toaster-oven/broiler. Just about any of the toasters CONSUMER REPORTS tested would be a fine choice. A toaster-oven/broiler toasts adequately but is handy for many other kitchen chores. The Cuisinart TOB-175, $205, performed best and has features such as electronic touchpad controls and convection. But it's big and expensive. The Kenmore KTES8, **a CR Best Buy** at $70, is more basic but performed well.

Excellent	Very good	Good	Fair	Poor
●	◗	○	◖	●

Overall Ratings — In performance order

KEY NO.	BRAND & MODEL	PRICE	OVERALL SCORE	COLOR RANGE	FULL BATCH	EASE OF USE
			0 P F G VG E 100			
TOASTERS						
1	**West Bend** 6220	$45		○	◗	◗
2	**Proctor-Silex** 2247[5]	13		○	○	◗
3	**Proctor-Silex** 2220[5]	10		○	○	◖
4	**Proctor-Silex** 2444[5]	24		○	◗	◖
5	**Toastmaster** T2030[W]	20		◗	◗	○
6	**Proctor-Silex** 2241[5]	17		◖	○	◗
7	**Toastmaster** T2050[W]	27		◗	◗	○
8	**Rival** TT9264	10		○	○	○
9	**Krups** 156	45		○	○	○
The following two models were downrated because they didn't shut off when the carriage was jammed, as is required by a new UL standard.						
10	**Sunbeam** 6225	29		◗	●	●
11	**Oster** 6322	55		○	○	●
TOASTER-OVEN/BROILERS						
12	**Cuisinart** TOB-175	205		◗	◗	●
13	**Kenmore** (Sears) KTES8 **A CR Best Buy**	70		◖	◗	◗
14	**Krups** F286-45	80		◖	○	◗
15	**Black & Decker** TRO 3000	55		◖	◖	◗

See report, page 42. Based on tests published in Consumer Reports in December 2001, with updated prices and availability.

The tests behind the Ratings

Overall score blends performance, ease of use, and safety. **Color range** is the ability to make toast ranging from very light to dark. **Full batch** is the ability to evenly toast full batches. **Ease of use** is based on ease of setting controls. Overall score also reflects ability to make one slice and successive batches, plus ease of cleaning. All models were good or very good in all three areas, except as noted. Toaster-oven/broiler scores also reflect baking and broiling ability. **Price** is approximate retail. Brackets indicate a color code.

Recommendations and notes

Models listed as similar should offer performance comparable to the tested model's, although features may differ.

All toasters: Have wide slots, with "jaws" that adjust to fit item being toasted. Except as noted all have: Two slots. White, stay-cool plastic body. Hinged crumb tray. Auto shutoff if toast gets jammed. One-year warranty.

All toaster-oven/broilers: Were rated at least good for baking and broiling. Have a removable rack. Have oven pan.

Most toaster-oven broilers have: Room for four large slices of bread. A timer. Hinged crumb tray. Metal body that gets hot in use. One-position rack. Broiler-rack insert for pan. One-year warranty.

TOASTERS

1 > **WEST BEND** 6220 **Very good overall.** Toast slides down onto removable crumb tray. One elongated slot. Cord wrap. Couldn't make dark English muffins; only 90-day warranty.

2 > **PROCTOR-SILEX** 2247[5] **Very good overall and inexpensive.** Two-year warranty.

3 > **PROCTOR-SILEX** 2220[5] **Inexpensive and very basic, but very good overall.** Has plastic end panels, but sides are metal and get hot in use. Two-year warranty. Similar: 22225, 22315.

4 > **PROCTOR-SILEX** 2444[5] **Very good performance.** Four slots. Two-year warranty. Similar: Hamilton Beach 24505, 24507, 24508.

5 > **TOASTMASTER** T2030[W] **Inexpensive and good overall.** Removable crumb tray.

6 > **PROCTOR-SILEX** 2241[5] **Good overall, but only fair at making full range of shades.** Removable crumb tray. Two-year warranty. Similar: Hamilton Beach 22416.

7 > **TOASTMASTER** T2050[W] **Good overall.** Four slots. But shade dial is mostly unmarked.

8 > **RIVAL** TT9264 **Basic, but good overall.** Similar: TT9222-W.

9 > **KRUPS** 156 **Good overall, though only fair at making single slice (one side of bread darker).** Cord wrap.

10 > **SUNBEAM** 6225 **Good overall, but did not shutoff when the carriage was jammed, as is required by a new UL standard.** Removable crumb tray with rounded edges. Audible signal when toast is done. Similar: 6223, 6220.

11 > **OSTER** 6322 **Good overall, but did not shutoff when the carriage was jammed, as is required by a new UL standard.** Electronic touchpad controls and digital display. Removable crumb tray with rounded edges. Cord wrap. Audible signal when toast is done. Two-year warranty. Similar: 6320.

TOASTER-OVEN/BROILERS

12 > **CUISINART** TOB-175 **Very good overall and feature-laden, but big and pricey.** Convection option, electronic touchpad controls, digital display, three-position rack, removable crumb tray. Three-year warranty. Similar: TOB-165, TOB-160.

13 > **KENMORE** (Sears) KTES8 **A CR Best Buy Very good performance and value, though fewer features than some.** Two-position rack. Removable crumb tray. Cord wrap.

14 > **KRUPS** F286-45 **Good overall, but burned bottoms of corn muffins.** Electronic touchpad controls and digital display. Rack advances when door is opened. Cord wrap.

15 > **BLACK & DECKER** TRO 3000 **Similar in performance to more-expensive brandmates:** Good overall, but just fair at toasting consecutive batches. Similar: TRO3200, TRO2000, TRO2100, TRO2200.

Toilets

Toilets are available in three main types: gravity flush, vacuum assist, and pressure assisted. Gravity-flush models, the traditional type, cost least but are least effective. The Kohler Wellworth 3422, $150, and American Standard Cadet 2798.012, $170, are both good performers for the type. The pricier Toto Carlyle MS874114SG, $460, offers a more stylized one-piece design with a plastic trapway. The top-rated Briggs Vacuity 4200, $220 is a very good choice, but may be difficult to find. The pressure-assisted models we tested performed reliably, but they are all noisy.

Overall Ratings — In performance order

Rating key: Excellent / Very good / Good / Fair / Poor

KEY NO	BRAND & MODEL	PRICE	OVERALL SCORE	TYPE	SOLID WASTE	WASH DOWN	DRAINING	DILUTION	NOISE
1	**Briggs** Vacuity 4200	$220		Vacuum	Very good	Excellent	Excellent	Excellent	Very good
2	**American Standard** Cadet PA 2333.100	450		Pressure	Very good	Very good	Excellent	Excellent	Good
3	**Gerber** Ultra Flush 21-302	280		Pressure	Excellent	Very good	Excellent	Excellent	Good
4	**Crane** Vacuum Induced Power FlushVIP 3999	250		Vacuum	Very good	Excellent	Excellent	Very good	Very good
5	**Gerber** Ultra Flush 21-312	300		Pressure	Excellent	Very good	Excellent	Excellent	Good
6	**Kohler** San Raphael Power Lite K-3398	600		Pressure	Excellent	Very good	Very good	Excellent	Good
7	**Crane** Economiser 3834	200		Pressure	Very good	Very good	Good	Very good	Good
8	**Mansfield** Quantum 150-100	230		Pressure	Very good	Good	Excellent	Fair	
9	**Toto** Carlyle MS874114SG	460		Gravity	Very good	Good	Very good	Excellent	Poor
10	**Kohler** Wellworth 3422	150		Gravity	Very good	Good	Very good	Very good	Poor
11	**American Standard** Cadet 2798.012	170		Gravity	Good	Very good	Very good	Excellent	Very good
12	**Eljer** Aqua Saver 091-7025	420		Pressure	Very good	Fair	Very good	Very good	Fair
13	**Kohler** Wellworth K-3423	120		Gravity	Good	Good	Good	Very good	Very good
14	**Eljer** Canterbury 081-1625	505		Gravity	Good	Good	Very good	Very good	Poor
15	**Eljer** Patriot 091-2125	185		Gravity	Very good	Good	Excellent	Poor	Very good
16	**Eljer** Patriot 091-2175 17"	285		Gravity	Good	Fair	Excellent	Good	Very good
17	**American Standard** Cadet 2898.012	210		Gravity	Fair	Good	Very good	Very good	Very good
18	**American Standard** Colony 2399.012	170		Gravity	Fair	Good	Very good	Very good	Very good
19	**Eljer** Patriot 091-2120	160		Gravity	Fair	Good	Excellent	Good	Very good
20	**Toto** Ultramax MS853113S3	60		Gravity	Fair	Good	Excellent	Very good	Very good
21	**Universal-Rundle** Atlas 4191	240		Gravity	Fair	Good	Very good	Very good	Very good
22	**Crane** Galaxy Elite II 3792	100		Gravity	Poor	Very good	Very good	Very good	Very good
23	**American Standard** Antiquity 2464.019	370		Gravity	Poor	Good	Good	Good	Excellent
24	**Gerber** Aqua Saver 21-702	100		Gravity	Poor	Good	Good	Good	Very good
25	**Kohler** Gabrielle Comfort Height K-3322	400		Gravity	Poor	Good	Very good	Very good	Excellent
26	**American Standard** Cadet One Piece 2100.016	400		Gravity	Poor	Good	Excellent	Excellent	Excellent
27	**Kohler** Portrait K-3591	300		Gravity	Poor	Good	Excellent	Excellent	Excellent
28	**Gerber** Aqua Saver 21-712	140		Gravity	Poor	Good	Good	Excellent	Very good

See report, page 173. Based on tests published in Consumer Reports in October 2002, with updated prices and availability.

The tests behind the Ratings

Overall score is based on performance with water pressure of 35 pounds per square inch (psi). **Solid waste** includes how well each model moved sponges, plastic balls, latex cylinders, and baby wipes through the bowl and trap. This test carried by far the greatest weight. **Wash down** is a measure of how well the toilets cleaned the sides of the bowl with each flush. **Draining** shows how well each toilet could move solid material through a drainline. **Dilution** shows how well the toilets flushed liquid waste. **Noise** characterizes how loudly the toilets flush, with the lid up. **Price** is the estimated average.

Recommendations and notes

Models listed as similar should offer performance comparable to the tested model's, although features may differ.

Most of these toilets: Have an elongated bowl and are two-piece designs. Require 12 inches of clearance from the wall to the center of the drain hole. Have rim that's 14 to 15 inches from floor. Complete a flush cycle in 75 seconds or less. Work with water pressure of 20 to 80 psi. Have a basic warranty of one to five years, some have a lifetime warranty on china.

1> **BRIGGS** Vacuity 4200 **Very good overall.**

2> **AMERICAN STANDARD** Cadet PA 2333.100 **Very good overall.** Mold and mildew can grow in stagnant water below pressure-assist tank. Very good at minimizing soil and odor in bowl.

3> **GERBER** Ultra Flush 21-302 **Very good overall.** Mold and mildew can grow in stagnant water below pressure-assist tank. Round-front bowl. Very good at minimizing soil and odor in bowl.

4> **CRANE** Vacuum Induced Power FlushVIP 3999 **Very good overall.** Taller than most; designed for the elderly and disabled. Very good at minimizing soil and odor in bowl.

5> **GERBER** Ultra Flush 21-312 **Very good overall.** Mold and mildew can grow in stagnant water below pressure-assist tank.

6> **KOHLER** San Raphael Power Lite K-3398 **Very good overall.** One-piece design. Seat included. Uses electric pump.

7> **CRANE** Economiser 3834 **Very good overall.** Mold and mildew can grow in stagnant water below pressure-assist tank. Round-front bowl.

8> **MANSFIELD** Quantum 150-100 **Very good overall.** Mold and mildew can grow in stagnant water below pressure-assist tank. Discontinued but may be available.

9> **TOTO** Carlyle MS874114SG **Very good overall.** One-piece design. Seat included. Similar: MS874114S.

10> **KOHLER** Wellworth 3422 **Very good overall.** As received, used more than 2 gal. per flush. Similar: 3438, 3448, 3479, 3480.

11> **AMERICAN STANDARD** Cadet 2798.012 **Very good overall.** Round-front bowl. Very good at minimizing soil and odor in bowl. Similar: 2319.015, 2321.018.

12> **ELJER** Aqua Saver 091-7025 **Good overall.** Mold and mildew can grow in stagnant water below pressure-assist tank. Poor at minimizing soil and odor in bowl.

13> **KOHLER** Wellworth K-3423 **Good overall.** As received, used more than 2 gal. per flush. Round-front bowl. Similar: 3449, 3480, 3433.

14> **ELJER** Canterbury 081-1625 **Good overall.** One-piece design. Seat included.

15> **ELJER** Patriot 091 **Good overall.** Poor at minimizing soil and odor in bowl. Similar: 2125 091-2195, 091-2127, 091-2135, 091-2155, 091-0225, 091-0228, 091-0227, 091-0245, Preserver II 091-4835, 091-2136.

16> **ELJER** Patriot 091-2175 17" **Good overall.** Taller than most. Designed for the elderly and disabled. Poor at minimizing soil and odor in bowl. Similar: Laguna 17" ER 091-3385.

17> **AMERICAN STANDARD** Cadet 2898. 012 **Good overall.** Similar: 2898.014, 2316.019, 2323.011, 2898.010.

18> **AMERICAN STANDARD** Colony 2399.012 **Good overall.** Similar: 2399.010, 2399.014.

19> **ELJER** Patriot 091-2120 **Good overall.** Round-front bowl. Similar: Preserver II 091-4830, 091-2150, 091-2190, 091-0220, 091-0240, 091-2130, 091-0223, 091-2122.

20> **TOTO** Ultramax MS853113S **Good overall.** Round-front bowl. One piece. Seat included.

21> **UNIVERSAL-RUNDLE** Atlas 4191 **Good overall.** Round-front bowl. Similar: 4190, 4192, 4193, 4290.

22> **CRANE** Galaxy Elite II 3792 **Fair overall.** Similar: Radcliffe II 3852, 3793, 3972, Galaxy II 3790.

23> **AMERICAN STANDARD** Antiquity 2464.019 **Fair overall.** Similar: 2483.019.

24> **GERBER** Aqua Saver 21-702 **Fair overall.** Round-front bowl.

25> **KOHLER** Gabrielle Comfort Height K-3322 **Fair overall.** Seat included. Taller than most; designed for the elderly and disabled. One- piece design.

26> **AMERICAN STANDARD** Cadet One Piece 2100.016 **Fair overall.** Seat included.

27> **KOHLER** Portrait K-3591 **Fair overall.** Poor at minimizing soil and odor in bowl.

28> **GERBER** Aqua Saver 21-712 **Fair overall.**

TV sets

Shopping for a TV requires balancing the space the set occupies, features you want, and price. Our tests turned up very good choices in each size category. For a 27-inch set, consider the flat-screen Toshiba 27AF42, $500. It was among the easiest sets to use. Among 32-inch TVs, the standout is the pricey Sony KV-32FV300, $1,200. For a fraction of the price, look to the Zenith C32A26, $450, and JVC AV-32D303, $550. A good value among 36-inch sets is the Toshiba 36A42, $750. You might want to consider an HD-ready TV if you have a high-definition satellite receiver or watch lots of movies on DVD. All the HD sets tested were fine performers. Key features for these models are listed in the table on page 276. See product report for explanation of features.

Overall Ratings In performance order

Rating legend: ◉ Excellent ◕ Very good ○ Good ◔ Fair ● Poor

KEY NO.	BRAND & MODEL	PRICE	OVERALL SCORE (0–100: P F G VG E)	PICTURE QUALITY — ANTENNA/CABLE INPUT	PICTURE QUALITY — S-VIDEO INPUT	SOUND QUALITY	EASE OF USE
27-INCH CONVENTIONAL SETS							
1	Toshiba 27AF42	$500	▬▬▬▬	◕	◉	◕	◕
2	Sony KV-27FV300	750	▬▬▬▬	◕	◕	◉	○
3	JVC AV-27D303	330	▬▬▬	○	◕	○	○
4	Sharp 27U-F500	450	▬▬▬	○	◕	◕	○
5	Akai CFT2791	380	▬▬▬	○	◕	◉	○
6	Sharp 27U-S600	290	▬▬▬	○	◕	◕	○
7	Toshiba 27A62	380	▬▬▬	○	◕	○	○
8	Samsung TXM2790F	450	▬▬▬	○	◕ [1]	○	○
9	Samsung TXL2767	300	▬▬▬	○	◕	◕	○
10	Philips 27PS60S	330	▬▬▬	○	○	◕	◕
11	Quasar SP-2725	230	▬▬	◕	○	●	○
12	Samsung TXM2756	270	▬▬	○	◕ [1]	●	○
13	Haier HTF27R11	480	▬▬	◕	○	○	◕
32-INCH CONVENTIONAL SETS							
14	Sony KV-32FV300	1,200	▬▬▬▬	◕	◕	◉	○
15	Zenith C32A26	450	▬▬▬	○	○	◉	◕
16	JVC AV-32D303	550	▬▬▬	○	◕	◕	○
17	Quasar SP-3235	400	▬▬▬	○	◕	◕	○
18	Sharp 32U-F500	700	▬▬▬	○	◕	◕	○
19	Panasonic CT-32D32	530	▬▬▬	○	◕	◕	◕
20	Sharp 32U-S60	375	▬▬	◕	◕	●	○
36-INCH CONVENTIONAL SETS							
21	Sony KV-36FV300	1,500	▬▬▬▬	◕	◕	◉	○
22	Toshiba 36A42	750	▬▬▬	○	◕	◕	◕
23	Toshiba 36AX61	850	▬▬▬	○	◕	○	◕
24	JVC AV-36330	750	▬▬▬	○	◕	◉	○
25	JVC AV-36D503	900	▬▬▬	○	◕	◕	◕
26	Sharp 36U-S60	600	▬▬	◕	◕	●	○

Overall Ratings, cont.

Legend: Excellent ● | Very good ◕ | Good ○ | Fair ◔ | Poor ●

KEY NO.	BRAND & MODEL	PRICE	OVERALL SCORE (0 P F G VG E 100)	PICTURE QUALITY ANTENNA/CABLE INPUT	PICTURE QUALITY S-VIDEO INPUT	SOUND QUALITY	EASE OF USE
	HD-READY SETS						
27	**Sony** KV-32HV600 (32-in.)	$1,700	▬▬▬▬	◔	◑	◑	◔
28	**Samsung** TXM2797HF (27-in.)	900	▬▬▬	◔	◑	◑	○
29	**Samsung** TXM3298HF (32-in.)	1,500	▬▬▬	◔	◑	◑	◔
30	**Hitachi** 36UDX10S (36-in.)	1,600	▬▬▬	◔	◑	◐	◔

① *Model lacks S-video input. Component-video input performance shown.*

See report, page 84. Based on tests published in Consumer Reports in December 2002, with updated prices and availability.

The tests behind the Ratings

Overall score is based primarily on picture quality; sound quality and ease of use also figured in. Expert panelists evaluated **picture quality** based on clarity and color accuracy. **Sound quality** is for the built-in speakers. **Ease of use** assesses the remote control, onscreen menu, labeling of the rear-jack panel, and useful features. **Price** is approximate retail.

Recommendations and notes

All tested models have: Sleep (or "off") timer. 12-month warranty on parts. Most tested models have: A comb filter. Virtual surround sound. Front A/V inputs. Audio tone controls. Clock. Alarm (or "on") timer. Universal remote. 24-month warranty on picture tube, 3 months on labor. No fleshtone adjustment, channel block-out, EnergyStar compliance, headphone jack, switchable video-noise reduction, or auto clock set. Most cannot receive Extended Data Services (XDS) program information and do not permit you to lock video inputs.
Dimensions: Most 27-inch sets are no more than 32 inches wide and 24 inches high. Most 32-inch sets are no more than 36 inches wide and 31 inches high. Most 36-inch sets are no more than 39 inches wide and 31 inches high. All tested sets are between 19 and 29 inches deep.

27-INCH CONVENTIONAL SETS

1> TOSHIBA 27AF42 **A flat-screen set with outstanding picture and sound—and it's easy to use.** A good value. Can select different color temperatures. Has channel block-out and front A/V inputs. Can lock all video inputs. Very good remote control; easy to use in low light. Very good onscreen menu. But lacks clock and alarm ("on") timer. Rear jacks are poorly labeled. 23 x 30¾ x 19½ in.

2> SONY KV-27FV300 **A very good and feature-laden flat-screen set.** But pricey, even for dual-tuner PIP. Can select different color temperatures. EnergyStar compliance claimed. Has contrast control and front A/V inputs. Can receive Extended Data Services (XDS) program information, if available. Rear jacks are poorly labeled. Short (3-month) labor warranty. 23¾ x 31 x 20½ in.

3> JVC AV-27D303 **A good set at a low price.** Can select different color temperatures. Has channel block out, auto clock set, and front A/V inputs. Can receive Extended Data Services (XDS) program information, if available. But only 2 composite-video inputs. Rear jacks are poorly labeled. 23¼ x 29¾ x 23 in.

4> SHARP 27U-F500 **Flat-screen set delivers solid performance.** Has "viewtimer" for restricting viewing and front A/V inputs. Can select different color temperatures. Remote control easy to use in low light. EnergyStar compliance claimed. Lacks virtual surround sound, clock, and alarm ("on") timer. Rear jacks are poorly labeled. 23¾ x 25¾ x 20 in.

5> AKAI CFT2791 **Lowest-priced flat-screen set in this size, with excellent sound.** But onscreen menu harder to use than others. Can select different color temperatures. Remote control easy to use in low light. Front A/V jacks located on side. Has headphone jack. Has switchable video noise reduction and auto clock set. Rear jacks are poorly labeled. Short (3-month) labor warranty. Twelve-month picture-tube warranty. 23¾ x 31¾ x 19¼ in.

6> SHARP 27U-S600 **Single-tuner PIP and solid performance at a low price.** Can select different color temperatures. Remote control easy to use in low light. Has front A/V inputs. EnergyStar compliance claimed. But lacks virtual surround sound, clock, and alarm ("on") timer. Rear jacks are poorly labeled. 23¾ x 25¾ x 21¼ in.

7> TOSHIBA 27A62 **Decent performance at a reasonable price for dual-tuner PIP and flat screen.** Remote control easy to use in low light. Has channel block-out, auto power-off, and front A/V inputs. Can lock all video inputs. But lacks virtual surround sound, clock, and alarm ("on") timer. Rear jacks are poorly labeled. Cannot select different color temperatures.

Recommendations and notes

Short (3-month) labor warranty. Similar model 27A42, $330, has no PIP; has "game timer" to limit game-playing. 22¼ x 29¼ x 19¾ in.

8▷ **SAMSUNG** TXM2790F **Good performance, but lacks S-video input.** Basic remote is very good, though not universal type; easy to use in low light. Can select different color temperatures. Has headphone jack, front A/V inputs, switchable video noise reduction, and auto clock set. EnergyStar compliance claimed. Onscreen menu only fair. Rear jacks are poorly labeled. Short (3-month) labor warranty. 23 x 26½ x 20½ in.

9▷ **SAMSUNG** TXL2767 **A good value.** Excellent remote control. Has headphone jack, switchable video noise reduction, "compressed" and "16:9" image modes, and auto clock set. EnergyStar compliance claimed. But cannot select different color temperatures. Short (3-month) labor warranty. 23½ x 26 x 21 in. Discontinued, but may still be available.

10▷ **PHILIPS** 27PS60S **A good price for single-tuner PIP, but remote control is so-so.** Can select different color temperatures. Has headphone jack, switchable video noise reduction, contrast control, channel block-out, and front A/V inputs. Rear jacks are poorly labeled. Short (3-month) labor warranty. Similar model 27PS55S has no PIP. 23 x 28¾ x 20¼ in.

11▷ **QUASAR** SP-2725 **Low-priced, but compromises include picture and sound quality.** Lacks some inputs (including front) and convenience features. EnergyStar compliance claimed. But lacks audio tone controls and virtual surround sound. Onscreen menu only fair. Rear jacks are poorly labeled. Short (3-month) labor warranty. 23½ x 26¼ x 21¾ in.

12▷ **SAMSUNG** TXM2756 **Low-priced, but no bargain.** There are better choices. Can select different color temperatures. Very good remote control, though not universal type; easy to use in low light. Has front A/V inputs. Rear jacks are clearly labeled. EnergyStar compliance claimed. But lacks S-video input. Onscreen menu is only fair. Short (3-month) labor warranty. 20 x 25 x 22½ in.

13▷ **HAIER** HTF27R11 **There are better choices, especially at this price.** Has switchable video noise reduction and front A/V inputs. But lacks a comb filter (thus reducing picture quality when using antenna/cable or composite-video input), audio tone controls, and virtual surround sound. Only 2 composite-video inputs. Cannot select different color temperatures. Remote control is not universal type and is poorly designed. Onscreen menu only fair. Rear jacks are poorly labeled. Short (3-month) labor warranty. 20½ x 26½ x 24½ in.

Features at a glance TV sets

Tested products (keyed to the Ratings) Key no. Brand	Flat screen	PIP (# of tuners)	Composite video	S-video	Component video	Auto volume leveler
27-INCH CONVENTIONAL SETS						
1▷ Toshiba	•		3	2	1	
2▷ Sony	•	2	3	2	1	•
3▷ JVC			2	1	1	
4▷ Sharp	•		3	1	1	
5▷ Akai	•		3	1	1	•
6▷ Sharp		1	3	1	1	
7▷ Toshiba		2	3	1	1	•
8▷ Samsung	•		3		1	•
9▷ Samsung			3	1	1	•
10▷ Philips		1	3	1	1	•
11▷ Quasar			1	1		•
12▷ Samsung			2		1	•
13▷ Haier	•		2	1		
32-INCH CONVENTIONAL SETS						
14▷ Sony	•	2	3	2	1	•
15▷ Zenith		2	2	2		•
16▷ JVC			3	1	1	

Features at a glance TV sets

Tested products (keyed to the Ratings) Key no. Brand	Flat screen	PIP (# of tuners)	Composite video	S-video	Component video	Auto volume leveler
32-INCH CONVENTIONAL SETS						
17▷ Quasar			2	1	1	•
18▷ Sharp	•		3	1	1	
19▷ Panasonic		2	3	1	1	•
20▷ Sharp			2	1		
36-INCH CONVENTIONAL SETS						
21▷ Sony	•	2	3	2	1	•
22▷ Toshiba			3	1	1	
23▷ Toshiba		2	3	2	1	
24▷ JVC			2	1	1	
25▷ JVC		2	3	1	1	
26▷ Sharp			2	1		
HD-READY SETS						
27▷ Sony	•	2	4	3	2	•
28▷ Samsung	•		4	1	2	•
29▷ Samsung	•	2	4	1	2	•
30▷ Hitachi		2	3	3	1	•

Recommendations and notes

32-INCH CONVENTIONAL SETS

14 **SONY** KV-32FV300 **A very good flat-screen set with features galore, like dual-tuner PIP and wireless headphones.** But pricey. Can select different color temperatures. Remote control easy to use in low light. Has front A/V inputs. EnergyStar compliance claimed. Can receive Extended Data Services (XDS) program information, if available. Rear jacks are poorly labeled. Short (3-month) labor warranty. 27 x 35½ x 23 in.

15 **ZENITH** C32A26 **Good picture, excellent sound, and dual-tuner PIP.** Stands out for clear labeling of rear inputs. But lacks component-video input, and has only 2 composite-video inputs. Can select different color temperatures. Very good remote control; easy to use in low light. Displays channel ratings when switching channels. Has front A/V inputs and auto clock set. Can lock all video inputs. Can receive Extended Data Services (XDS) program information, if available. Short (3-month) labor warranty. 27 x 30¼ x 22 in.

16 **JVC** AV-32D303 **A solid performer.** Can select different color temperatures. Has front A/V inputs, auto clock set and channel block-out. Can receive Extended Data Services (XDS) program information, if available. Rear jacks are poorly labeled. 27 x 34 x 21¾ in.

17 **QUASAR** SP-3235 **Decent and low-priced, but onscreen menu harder to use than others.** No front A/V inputs. Can select different color temperatures. Displays channel ratings when switching channels. Has channel block-out. Remote control easy to use in low light. Rear jacks are poorly labeled. 27 x 30½ x 21½ in.

18 **SHARP** 32U-F500 **Good flat-screen, but has few features to justify price.** Can select different color temperatures. Remote control easy to use in low light. Has front A/V inputs and "viewtimer" to restrict viewing. EnergyStar compliance claimed. Lacks virtual surround sound, clock, and alarm ("on") timer. Rear jacks are poorly labeled. 26¾ x 30 x 23½ in.

19 **PANASONIC** CT-32D32 **Good dual-tuner PIP set.** But onscreen menu harder to use than others. Can select different color temperatures. Has front A/V inputs, headphone jack, and channel block-out. Very good remote control, but difficult to use in low light. Displays channel ratings when switching channels. Rear jacks are poorly labeled. 30¼ x 27½ x 22 in.

20 **SHARP** 32U-S60 **Low-priced, but compromises include picture and sound quality.** Lacks some inputs and convenience features. Can select different color temperatures. Has front A/V inputs. Remote control easy to use in low light, though not universal type. EnergyStar compliance claimed. Lacks audio tone controls, virtual surround sound, clock, and alarm ("on") timer. Rear jacks are poorly labeled. 27x30x21½ in.

36-INCH CONVENTIONAL SETS

21 **SONY** KV-36FV300 **Flat-screen set has very good picture and excellent sound and features, like dual-tuner PIP and wireless headphones.** But pricey. Among widest 36-inch sets at 401/4 inches. Can select different color temperatures. Has front A/V inputs and contrast control. Remote control easy to use in low light. EnergyStar compliance claimed. Can receive Extended Data Services (XDS) program information, if available. Rear jacks are poorly labeled. Short (3-month) labor warranty. 30 x 40¼ x 25¼ in.

22 **TOSHIBA** 36A42 **Very good performance at a modest price.** Can select different color temperatures. Has front A/V inputs and channel block-out. Very good remote control; easy to use in low light. Lacks clock and alarm ("on") timer. Rear jacks are poorly labeled. 30¼ x 38¼ x 25¼ in.

23 **TOSHIBA** 36AX61 **Very good performance and dual-tuner PIP at a modest price.** Can select different color temperatures. Has channel block-out and front A/V inputs. But onscreen menu and remote control difficult to use. Lacks clock and alarm ("on") timer. 30¼ x 38¼ x 25¼ in.

24 **JVC** AV-36330 **Good picture quality and excellent sound at a modest price.** Has front A/V inputs and auto clock-set, but only 2 composite-video inputs. Can receive Extended Data Services (XDS) program information, if available. Rear jacks are clearly labeled. 30¼ x 34 x 23¾ in.

25 **JVC** AV-36D503 **A solid performer, with dual-tuner PIP.** Stands out for clear labeling of rear inputs. Has channel block-out, front A/V inputs, front-panel lock feature, and auto clock set. Can select different color temperatures. EnergyStar compliance claimed. Can receive Extended Data Services (XDS) program information, if available. 30½ x 38 x 24½ in.

26 **SHARP** 36U-S60 **Low-priced, but compromises include picture and sound quality** Lacks some inputs and convenience features. Can select different color temperatures. Remote control easy to use in low light, though not universal type. EnergyStar compliance claimed. Lacks audio tone controls, virtual surround sound, clock, and alarm ("on") timer. Rear jacks are poorly labeled. 30 x 34¾ x 24¾ in.

HD-READY SETS

27 **SONY** KV-32HV600 (32-in.) **The best HD picture, plus excellent sound. Has flat screen, dual-tuner PIP, and features galore.** Can select different color temperatures. Rear jacks are clearly labeled. Front A/V inputs. Has Memory Stick input for viewing still images from Sony digital cameras and camcorders, Digital Visual Interface (DVI) for use with copy-protected HD content, and scrolling index that displays previews of four other channels simultaneously. EnergyStar compliance claimed. Can receive Extended Data Services (XDS) program information, if available. Short (3-month) labor warranty. 27¼ x 35½ x 24 in.

Recommendations and notes

28 **SAMSUNG** TXM2797HF (27-in.) **A very good flat-screen set with fine picture and sound.** Reasonably priced for HD-ready. But onscreen menu is so-so. Can select different color temperatures. Very good remote control; easy to use in low light. Front A/V jacks located on side. Rear jacks are clearly labeled. Has audio equalizer, BBE audio processing (boosts bass and treble to enhance sound), switchable video noise reduction, auto clock set, and headphone jack. EnergyStar compliance claimed. Short (3-month) labor warranty. Similar model TXM2796HF does not include BBE. 19³/₄ x 29½ x 22½ in.

29 **SAMSUNG** TXM3298HF (32-in.) **A very good flat-screen set with dual-tuner PIP and subwoofer.** But onscreen menu is so-so. Can select different color temperatures. Rear jacks are clearly labeled. Has audio equalizer, BBE audio processing (boosts bass and treble to enhance sound), switchable video noise reduction, auto clock set, and headphone jack. Front A/V jacks located on side. EnergyStar compliance claimed. Remote control difficult to use in low light. Short (3-month) labor warranty. Twelve-month picture-tube warranty. 23 x 32³/₄ x 28½ in.

30 **HITACHI** 36UDX10S (36-in.) **Dual-tuner PIP model is only one tested to offer fleshtone adjustment; excellent remote.** But mediocre sound. Can select different color temperatures. Has front A/V inputs, switchable video noise reduction, and channel block-out. 29 x 35 x 25 in.

Vacuum cleaners

There are many very good choices among uprights and canisters. Uprights tend to be the best choice for wall-to-wall carpeting. Most are less expensive and easier to store than canister vacs. High scores for carpet and floors make the upright Kenmore Progressive 31912, $330, a top pick. Nearly as good: the upright Hoover WindTunnel Self-Propelled Ultra U6430-900, $300, and the Eureka Boss Smart Vac 4870, $160, a **CR Best Buy**. Canisters tend to be more stable on stairs and are better for hard-to-reach areas. There are several very good models for under $400. Key features for these models are listed in the table on page 281. See the product guide for an explanation of features.

Shop Smart

Overall Ratings In performance order

Excellent ● Very good ◒ Good ○ Fair ◓ Poor ●

KEY NO.	BRAND & MODEL	PRICE	OVERALL SCORE (0–100: P F G VG E)	CLEANING: CARPET	CLEANING: BARE FLOOR	CLEANING: TOOLS	EASE OF USE	NOISE	EMISSIONS
	UPRIGHTS								
1	**Kenmore** (Sears) Progressive with Direct Drive 31912	$330		Very good	Excellent	Very good	Very good	Good	Excellent
2	**Hoover** WindTunnel Self-Propelled Ultra U6430-900	300		Excellent	Excellent	Excellent	Good	Fair	Excellent
3	**Eureka** Boss Smart Vac 4870 **A CR Best Buy**	160		Excellent	Excellent	Good	Good	Good	Excellent
4	**Panasonic** Dual Sweep MC-V7515	170		Very good	Excellent	Very good	Good	Fair	Excellent
5	**Kenmore** (Sears) Progressive 33612	180		Very good	Excellent	Very good	Good	Good	Excellent
6	**Hoover** WindTunnel Bagless Self-Propelled U6630-900	400		Very good	Excellent	Good	Good	Fair	Excellent
7	**Eureka** Ultra Whirlwind 4885	240		Very good	Excellent	Very good	Good	Good	Excellent
8	**Hoover** Wind Tunnel Bagless U5720-900	200		Excellent	Excellent	Good	Good	Fair	Excellent
9	**Bissell** ProLite 3560-2	200		Very good	Excellent	N/A[3]	Very good	Fair	Excellent
10	**Dirt Devil** Platinum Force 091210	190		Excellent	Excellent	Good	Fair	Fair	Very good
11	**Oreck** XL21-600	700		Very good	Excellent	N/A[3]	Very good	Good	Excellent
12	**Kirby** Ultimate G G7d	1,330		Very good	Excellent	Very good	Good	Fair	Excellent
13	**Dyson** DC07	400		Good	Excellent	Very good	Fair	Fair	Excellent
14	**Eureka** Whirlwind Litespeed 5843	160		Good	Very good	Very good	Good	Fair	Excellent
15	**Hoover** Bagless U5290-900	170		Very good	Excellent	Fair	Good	Poor	Excellent
16	**Dirt Devil** Featherlite Bagless 088500	100		Very good	Excellent	Fair	Fair	Poor	Excellent
17	**Hoover** Preferred U5061-900	80		Very good	Excellent	Good	Good	Poor	Excellent
18	**Panasonic** Dual-Sweep MC-V7581	200		Very good	Very good	Fair	Good	Fair	Excellent
19	**Dirt Devil** Featherlite Plus 085550	60		Very good	Excellent	Fair	Very good	Poor	Very good
20	**Aerus** Lux 3000 U147A[1]	700		Good	Excellent	Fair	Good	Fair	Very good
21	**GE** 106585	120		Good	Very good	Good	Good	Good	Excellent
22	**Hoover** WindTunnel V2 U8134-900	260		Very good	Good	Good	Fair	Poor	Good
23	**Eureka** Whirlwind Plus 4686	150		Good	Excellent	Good	Good	Fair	Excellent
24	**Sharp** Multi-Floor EC-T5180	$200		Good	Excellent	Good	Good	Good	Poor
25	**Dirt Devil** Swivel Glide Vision 086925	150		Good	Very good	Fair	Good	Fair	Excellent
26	**Eureka** The Boss Power 2270	70		Fair	Excellent	Good	Good	Good	Very good

Overall Ratings

Rating legend: Excellent ◉ | Very good ◕ | Good ○ | Fair ◒ | Poor ●

KEY NO.	BRAND & MODEL	PRICE	OVERALL SCORE (0–100, P F G VG E)	CLEANING – CARPET	CLEANING – BARE FLOOR	CLEANING – TOOLS	EASE OF USE	NOISE	EMISSIONS
UPRIGHTS *continued*									
27	**Bissell** Powerforce 3522	50		○	◉	○	○	◒	◒
28	**Kenmore** (Sears) Quick Clean 33720 33721	80		◒	◒	○	◒	◒	◉
29	**Bissell** Cleanview Power Trak 3591	115		○	◉	○	○	●	◒
30	**Bissell** Cleanview Bagless 8990	95		○	◉	○	○	●	●
31	**Eureka** Whirlwind Lite 4388	100		◒	◒	◒	○	◒	○
32	**Hoover** PowerMax U5344-900	130		◒	○	●	○	◒	N/A[2]
33	**Kenmore** (Sears) Progressive Intuition 32920	330		○	◒	○	○	◒	N/A[2]
CANISTERS									
34	**Kenmore** (Sears) Progressive 22612	380		◒	◉	◒	◉	○	◉
35	**Miele** Plus S251	425		○	◉	◒	◉	○	◉
36	**Eureka** The Home Cleaning System 6984	240		◒	◒	○	○	○	◉
37	**Samsung** Quiet Jet VAC-9048R	250		◒	◒	◒	◒	◒	◉
38	**Aerus** Lux 5000 C101K [1]	750		◒	◉	●	◒	○	◉
39	**Hoover** Wind Tunnel Plus S3639	350		◒	◉	◒	◒	○	◒
40	**Miele** Solaris Electro Plus S514	700		○	◉	○	◒	◒	◒
41	**Oreck** DutchTech DTX1300C	900		◒	◉	◒	◒	◒	◒
42	**Kenmore** (Sears) eVo 22822	380		◒	◉	◒	○	○	◒
43	**Panasonic** Dirt Sensor MC-V9635	275		○	◒	◒	○	◒	◒
44	**Sanyo** High Power SC-800P	300		○	◉	◒	◒	◒	◒
45	**Hoover** PowerMax Deluxe S3607	200		◒	◉	○	○	○	●
46	**Hoover** PowerMax Runabout S3614	200		◒	◉	○	◉	◒	●

[1] Formerly Electrolux. [2] Inconsistent small-particle results and presence of large-particle emissions made rating impossible. [3] Comes with minicanister for cleaning with tools. Performance was fair for #9, poor for #11.

See report, page 132. Based on tests published in Consumer Reports in February 2003.

The tests behind the Ratings

Overall score reflects mainly cleaning performance, ease of use, and emissions. **Cleaning for carpet** denotes how much embedded talc and sand models lifted from a medium-pile carpet. Scores for **bare floor** show how well models vacuumed sand without dispersing it, while those for **tools** reflect airflow through the hose with increasing amounts of dust-simulating wood "flour." **Ease of use** evaluates how easy machines were to push, pull, carry, and use beneath furniture, as well as the capacity of the dust bag or bin. **Noise** denotes results using a decibel meter. **Emissions** is our measure of how much wood flour is released while vacuuming. In Recommendations and notes, comments on brand-repair history are based on our most recent reader survey. Weight is noted in the Recommendations and notes and is rounded to the nearest pound. **Price** for vacuums and equipment is approximate retail.

Recommendations and notes

Most vacuums have: A disposable microfiltration bag. Upholstery and crevice tools and a brush. A flexible hose at least 5 feet long. A warranty of at least one year on parts and labor. **Most uprights have:** A 30- to 35-foot cord with quick-release, wrap-around storage. Protection for the motor in case of jamming, overheating, or electrical overload. **Most canisters have:** A 20- to 30-foot retractable power cord. A detachable power nozzle.

UPRIGHTS

1▷ **KENMORE** (Sears) Progressive with Direct Drive 31912 **Very good all around.** Weight: 20 lb. Bag: $4 to $5. HEPA filter: $21. Similar: 31913.

2▷ **HOOVER** WindTunnel Self-Propelled Ultra U6430-900 **Excelled at cleaning, but noisy.** May not fit on some stairs. Weight: 21 lb. Bag: $2. Similar: U6432-900, U6435-900, U6446-900.

3▷ **EUREKA** Boss Smart Vac 4870 **A CR Best Buy Highest performance for the dollar.** Excelled at most cleaning, but hard to pull. Weight: 21 lb. Bag: $2.30. HEPA filter: $20. Similar:

4▷ **PANASONIC** Dual Sweep MC-V7515 **Very good, but noisy and hard to push and pull.** More stable than most on stairs. Weight: 17 lb. Bag: $1.65. HEPA filter: $12. Similar: MC-V7521.

5▷ **KENMORE** (Sears) Progressive 33612 **Very good, but prone to tip with hose extended.** Weight: 18 lb. Bag: $4 to $5. HEPA filter: $21. Similar: 32212, 32213, 33613.

6▷ **HOOVER** WindTunnel Bagless Self-Propelled U6630-900 **Very good, but noisy, heavy, and tippy on stairs.** Weight: 24 lb. HEPA filter: $20. Similar: U6625-900, U6655-900, U6660-900.

7▷ **EUREKA** Ultra Whirlwind 4885 **A very good bagless vac, but small capacity.** Weight: 23 lb. HEPA filter: $20. Similar: 4880.

Features at a glance — Vacuums

Tested products (keyed to the Ratings) Key no. / Brand	Bag-equipped	Brush on/off switch	Cord retract	Easy on/off switch	Full-bag/bin alert	Manual pile adjust	Suction control
UPRIGHTS							
1▷ Kenmore	•	•		•	•	•	
2▷ Hoover	•	•		•			
3▷ Eureka	•	•		•			
4▷ Panasonic	•	•		•			•
5▷ Kenmore	•	•		•	•		
6▷ Hoover	•			•			
7▷ Eureka		•		•			
8▷ Hoover				•	•	•	
9▷ Bissell	•			•			
10▷ Dirt Devil		•		•	•	•	
11▷ Oreck	•						
12▷ Kirby	•			•		•	•
13▷ Dyson		•			•		
14▷ Eureka		•			•	•	
15▷ Hoover				•	•		
16▷ Dirt Devil				•	•	•	
17▷ Hoover	•		•			•	
18▷ Panasonic		•			•	•	
19▷ Dirt Devil	•			•			
20▷ Aerus	•	•		•			•
21▷ GE				•	•		
22▷ Hoover		•		•	•	•	
23▷ Eureka				•	•	•	
24▷ Sharp		•		•	•		

Features at a glance — Vacuums

Tested products (keyed to the Ratings) Key no. / Brand	Bag-equipped	Brush on/off switch	Cord retract	Easy on/off switch	Full-bag/bin alert	Manual pile adjust	Suction control
25▷ Dirt Devil					•	•	
26▷ Eureka	•		•				
27▷ Bissell	•	•				•	
28▷ Kenmore				•	•	•	
29▷ Bissell		•					
30▷ Bissell		•			•		•
31▷ Eureka				•	•	•	
32▷ Hoover		•			•		
33▷ Kenmore				•	•	•	
CANISTERS							
34▷ Kenmore	•	•	•	•	•	•	•
35▷ Miele	•	•	•	•	•	•	
36▷ Eureka	•	•	•	•	•	•	
37▷ Samsung	•	•	•	•	•		
38▷ Aerus	•	•	•	•	•		
39▷ Hoover	•	•	•	•	•		
40▷ Miele	•	•	•	•	•	•	
41▷ Oreck	•	•	•		•		
42▷ Kenmore	•	•	•	•	•	•	
43▷ Panasonic	•	•	•	•	•	•	
44▷ Sanyo	•	•		•			
45▷ Hoover	•	•	•	•	•	•	
46▷ Hoover	•	•	•	•	•		

Recommendations and notes

8 ▷ HOOVER Wind Tunnel Bagless U5720-900 **Excelled at most cleaning, but noisy.** Small capacity. Weight: 21 lb. HEPA filter: $30. Similar: U5720-990, U5721-900, U5750-900, U5755-900, U5757-900.

9 ▷ BISSELL ProLite 3560-2 **Very good, but noisy and awkward to carry.** No overload protection. Weight: 9 lb. Bag: $2.

10 ▷ DIRT DEVIL Platinum Force 091210 **Excelled at most cleaning, but noisy and tippy on stairs.** Bagless. Hose longer than most. Hard to push and pull. Weight: 21 lb. HEPA filter: $25.

11 ▷ ORECK XL21-600 **Very good, but no overload protection.** Filter on tested models wasn't a HEPA, despite label. Weight: 11 lb. Bag: $3.

12 ▷ KIRBY Ultimate G G7d **Very good, but pricey and noisy.** Among the more reliable upright brands. Works as an upright, canister, rug shampooer, or floor polisher. Tools don't stow onboard. Weight: 24 lb. Bag/HEPA filter: $9.50.

13 ▷ DYSON DC07 **A very good bagless vac, but has confusing controls.** Hose longer than most. Noisy. Hard to push and pull. No headlamp. Weight: 19 lb. HEPA filter (washable): $17.50.

14 ▷ EUREKA Whirlwind Litespeed 5843 **A good bagless vac, but noisy.** Hose longer than most. No upholstery tool. Weight: 19 lb. HEPA filter: $20. Similar: 5740, 5840, 5846, 5847.

15 ▷ HOOVER Bagless U5290-900 **Good, but noisy.** No overload protection. Cord shorter than most. Weight: 18 lb. HEPA filter: $30. Similar: U5296-900, U5298-900, U5280-940.

16 ▷ DIRT DEVIL Featherlite Bagless 088500 **A good bagless vac, but noisy. Hard to push and pull.** No upholstery tool or overload protection. Weight: 16 lb. HEPA filter: $12.50. Similar: 088520.

17 ▷ HOOVER Preferred U5061-900 **Good, but noisy.** Tippy on stairs. Hard to push and pull. Hose and cord shorter than most. Weight: 15 lb. Bag: $2. Similar: U5062-900, U5074-900.

18 ▷ PANASONIC Dual-Sweep MC-V7581 **A good bagless vac, but noisy and hard to push.** Tippy with hose extended. Weight: 18 lb. HEPA filter: $9. Similar: MC-V7571.

19 ▷ DIRT DEVIL Featherlite Plus 085550 **Good.** No overload protection or upholstery tool. Hose and cord shorter than most. Weight: 13 lb. Standard bag: $1. Microfilter bag: $3.30. Discontinued, but similar 085560 is available.

20 ▷ AERUS Lux 3000 U147A **Good, but pricey and noisy.** Tippy with hose extended. Unstable on stairs. Tools don't stow onboard. Weight: 17 lb. Bag: $18.

21 ▷ GE 106585 **A good bagless vac, but small capacity and poor furniture clearance.** Weight: 18 lb. HEPA filter: $16. Wal-Mart only.

22 ▷ HOOVER WindTunnel V2 U8134-900 **A good bagless vac, but noisy.** Hard to push and pull. Tippy with hose extended. Hose longer than most. Weight: 21 lb. HEPA filter: $8. Similar: U8126-900, U8130-900, U8140-900, U8142-900, U8146-900.

23 ▷ EUREKA Whirlwind Plus 4686 **A good bagless vac, but noisy.** Tippy on stairs and with hose extended. Small capacity. Cord shorter than most. Weight: 19 lb. HEPA filter: $20. Discontinued, but similar 4684 is available.

24 ▷ SHARP Multi-Floor EC-T5180 **A good bagless vac, but high emissions.** Tippy on stairs and with hose extended. Hose longer than most. No upholstery tool. Weight: 17 lb. Main foam filter: $7. HEPA filter: $10. Similar: EC-T5170.

25 ▷ DIRT DEVIL Swivel Glide Vision 086925 **Good, but noisy and tippy on stairs.** Weight: 14 lb. Bag: $1. Similar: 086935.

26 ▷ EUREKA The Boss Power 2270 **Good.** Hose longer than most. Cord shorter than most. Weight: 17 lb. Bag: $1.30. Motor filter: $2. Exhaust filter: $3. Similar: 2271.

27 ▷ BISSELL Powerforce 3522 **Good, but noisy.** Tippy with hose extended and unstable on stairs. Hard to push. Hose and power cord shorter than most. No overload protection. Weight: 15 lb. Bag: $3. Filter: $3.

28 ▷ KENMORE (Sears) Quick Clean 33720 **A good bagless vac, but noisy.** Tippy on stairs and with hose extended. Hose and cord shorter than most. No upholstery tool. Weight: 16 lb. Tower filter: $20. Exhaust filter: $14. Similar: 33721.

29 ▷ BISSELL Cleanview Power Trak 3591 **A good bagless vac, but noisy.** Tippy with hose extended and unstable on stairs. Hard to push. No upholstery tool. Weight: 17 lb. HEPA filter: $10.

30 ▷ BISSELL Cleanview Bagless 8990 **There are better choices.** Weight: 16 lb. Upper-tank filter: $4. Premotor filter: $1.50. Postmotor filter: $3. Similar: 3590.

31 ▷ EUREKA Whirlwind Lite 4388 **There are better choices.** Bagless. Weight: 16 lb.

32 ▷ HOOVER PowerMax U5344-900 **Poor overall because of visible dust emissions.** Bagless. Weight: 18 lb. Similar: U5348-900, U5349-900, U5462-900, U5464-900, U5465-960, U5347-960.

33 ▷ KENMORE (Sears) Progressive Intuition 32920 **Poor overall because of visible dust emissions.** Bagless. Weight: 19 lb. HEPA filter: $14. Similar: 32921.

CANISTERS

34 ▷ KENMORE (Sears) Progressive 22612 **Very good, but noisy and heavy.** Hose longer than most. Weight: 24 lb. Bag: $4. HEPA filter: $21. Similar: 22613, 22812, 22813.

35 ▷ MIELE Plus S251 **Very good. Less bulky, and heavy than most.** Cord shorter than most. Weight: 20 lb. Bag: $2.60.

36 ▷ EUREKA The Home Cleaning System 6984 **Very good, but among the more repair-prone canister brands.** Hose longer than most. Cord shorter than most. Weight: 23 lb. Bag: $1.70. HEPA filter: $20. Similar: 6983.

Recommendations and notes

37> **SAMSUNG** Quiet Jet VAC-9048R **Very good, and quieter than most, but hard to push.** No overload protection. Weight: 22 lb. Bag: $2. Limited availability. Similar: 9069G.

38> **AERUS** Lux 5000 C101K **Fine for most cleaning, but tippy on stairs.** Cord shorter than most. Weight: 21 lb. Bag: $2. Filter: 2 for $7. Similar: 5500.

39> **HOOVER** Wind Tunnel Plus S3639 **A very good, well-rounded vac.** Weight: 22 lb. Bag: $2.

40> **MIELE** Solaris Electro Plus S514 **Very good, and quieter than most, but hard to push and pull.** Cord and hose shorter than most. Weight: 21 lb. Filters and 5-bag set: $12.

41> **ORECK** DutchTech DTX1300C **Very good, but hard to push and pull.** Quieter than most. Weight: 20 lb. Bag: $2.80. HEPA filter: $40.

42> **KENMORE** (Sears) eVo 22822 **A very good bagless vac, but noisy and heavy.** Unstable on stairs. Hose longer than most. Weight: 29 lb. HEPA filter: $15.50.

43> **PANASONIC** Dirt Sensor MC-V9635 **Very good.** No overload protection. Weight: 24 lb. Bag: $2.

44> **SANYO** High Power SC-800P **Good, but spartan for the price.** Noisy. No overload protection. Cord shorter than most. Weight: 22 lb. Bag: $4. Electrostatic micron filter: $9.95.

45> **HOOVER** PowerMax Deluxe S3607 **A good, inexpensive canister for most cleaning, but high emissions.** Weight: 21 lb. Bag: $2.

46> **HOOVER** PowerMax Runabout S3614 **A good, inexpensive canister for most cleaning, but high emissions.** Noisy. No overload protection. Weight: 21 lb. Standard bag: $1.30. Allergen filtration bag: $2.90.

VCRs

Most VCRs provide a very good picture at SP speed. Choose based on features and whether you'll mostly record programs or play tapes. If recording and saving TV programs is a priority, consider the top-ranked Toshiba W-727, $100, or the Sony SLV-N55, $90. The Toshiba offers conveniences such as VCR Plus+ and automatic speed switching. If you use a VCR mostly to play prerecorded tapes, you can buy one with fewer features and a lower price. The midranked Toshiba W-522, $70, is an economical choice. Key features for these models are listed in the table. See product report for explanation of features.

Shop Smart

Overall Ratings In performance order

Excellent / Very good / Good / Fair / Poor

KEY NO.	BRAND & MODEL	PRICE	OVERALL SCORE (0–100: P F G VG E)	VHS PICTURE QUALITY		EASE OF USE
				SP	EP	
1	**Toshiba** W-727	$100		Good	Good	Very good
2	**RCA** VR648HF	90		Good	Fair	Very good
3	**Go-Video** DDV3110	200		Good	Fair	Very good
4	**Panasonic** PV-V4612S	100		Good	Fair	Very good
5	**Sony** SLV-N55	90		Good	Good	Very good
6	**Toshiba** W-522	70		Good	Fair	Very good
7	**Sony** SLV-N99	150		Good	Fair	Very good
8	**Samsung** VR8260	80		Good	Fair	Very good
9	**Mitsubishi** HS-U448	80		Good	Fair	Very good
10	**Sharp** VC-H965U	80		Fair	Fair	Very good
11	**Sanyo** VWM-710	70		Good	Fair	Good
12	**Zenith** VRE4222	75		Good	Fair	Good
13	**JVC** HR-A591U	70		Good	Fair	Good

See report, page 88. Based on tests published in Consumer Reports in December 2002.

The tests behind the Ratings

Overall score is based mainly on VCR picture quality and ease of use. **Picture quality** reflects sharpness and freedom from video noise for material recorded by and played back on the model. **SP** and **EP** scores reflect high-speed/standard-play and low-speed/extended-play modes. **Ease of use** includes usability of remote and front-panel controls, ease of programming and other functions, fast-forward and rewind speeds, and key features. **Price** is approximate retail.

Recommendations and notes

All tested models have: Stereo. Composite-video output but no S-video outputs. Auto channel set. Multilingual menu. Slow motion. Daily and weekly recording. Front-panel A/V jacks. Ability to program tape speed in record-timer mode. 12-month warranty on parts, 3 months on labor. **Most tested models have:** Time remaining on tape displayed. Zero search. Manual commercial skip. Tape counter displayed on console. Auto clock set. Universal remote control. Frame-by-frame advance. One-month time-shift programming.

1> TOSHIBA W-727 **Good, with lots of useful features.** Warns of time-shift conflicts. Fast tape handling, but overshoots. Jog/shuttle. Multispeed slow motion.

2> RCA VR648HF **Good, but fewer features.** Warns of time-shift conflicts. Auto commercial skip. Fast tape handling, but overshoots. Has 365-day advance programming. Memory backup. Similar: VR637HF.

3> GO-VIDEO DDV3110 **Good dual-deck model, but expensive.** Has 365-day, 16-event advance programming. Fast tape handling, but overshoots. Programmable from console. Auto commercial skip. Similar: DDV3120.

4> PANASONIC PV-V4612S **Good, and can record in LP speed.** Auto commercial skip. Similar: PV-V4622, PV-V462, PV-V4522.

5> SONY SLV-N55 **Good, especially for time-shifting in EP mode.** Warns of time-shift conflicts. Fast tape handling, but overshoots.

6> TOSHIBA W-522 **Good, and inexpensive.** Lacks universal remote. Warns of time-shift conflicts. Fast tape handling, but overshoots. Multispeed slow motion.

7> SONY SLV-N99 **Good, with many useful features, but expensive.** VCR Plus+ Gold simplifies setup. Memory backup. Programmable from console.

8> SAMSUNG VR8260 **Good, with several useful features.** Warns of time-shift conflicts. Fast tape handling, but overshoots. Multispeed slow motion. Memory backup. Programmable from console. Lacks universal remote. Similar: VR9260.

9> MITSUBISHI HS-U448 **Good.** Warns of time-shift conflicts. Fast tape handling, but overshoots. Delay-start one-touch recording. Memory backup.

10> SHARP VC-H965U **Good.** Has 365-day advance programming. Fast tape handling, but overshoots. Multispeed slow motion. Programmable from console.

11> SANYO VWM-710 **Fair; there are better choices.** No universal remote. No front-console display. Has TV Guardian. Slow tape handling. Has 365-day advance programming.

12> ZENITH VRE4222 **Fair; there are better choices.** No universal remote. Multispeed slow motion. Slow tape handling. No automatic clock set. Has 365-day advance programming.

13> JVC HR-A591U **Fair; there are better choices.** No universal remote. Slow tape handling. No commerical skip.

Features at a glance VCRs

Tested products (keyed to the Ratings) Key no. Brand	VCR Plus+	Auto speed	Cable/satellite	Lighted remote	Index search	Plug and play
1> Toshiba	•	•	•	•		•
2> RCA					•	
3> Go-Video			•		•	•
4> Panasonic	•			•	•	•
5> Sony		•			•	•
6> Toshiba		•				•
7> Sony	•	•		•	•	
8> Samsung		•		•	•	
9> Mitsubishi		•		•		
10> Sharp				•	•	•
11> Sanyo		•				
12> Zenith		•				
13> JVC						

VCR/DVD combos

Combination players save space and simplify hooking up equipment, but have fewer features than many stand-alone units. If convenience and saving space are paramount, choose from the models that require the fewest compromises. The top-rated Samsung DVD-V2000, $215, was among the easiest to use, has an auto speed switch on the VCR side, and a universal remote. The Hitachi DV-PF2U was very good overall, among the easiest to use, and costs about $35 less. Key features for these models are listed in the table. See product report for explanation of features.

Shop Smart

				Excellent ●	Very good ◔	Good ○	Fair ◑	Poor ●

| | | | | PICTURE QUALITY | | | EASE OF USE | |
KEY NO.	BRAND & MODEL	PRICE	OVERALL SCORE	DVD	SP	EP	DVD	VCR
1	**Samsung** DVD-V2000	$215		●	○	◑	●	◑
2	**Panasonic** PV-D4752	300		●	○	◑	○	◑
3	**Hitachi** DV-PF2U	180		●	○	◑	●	○
4	**Zenith** XBV243	250		●	○	◑	◑	○
5	**Go-Video** DVR4250	200		●	○	○	◑	○
6	**JVC** HR-XVC1U	280		●	○	◑	○	◑
7	**Sanyo** DVW-5000	230		●	○	◑	◑	○
8	**Toshiba** SD-V280U	230		●	◑	◑	◑	◑

Overall Ratings — In performance order. Overall score scale: 0 (P F G VG E) 100.

Based on tests published in Consumer Reports in December 2002.

The tests behind the Ratings

Overall score is based mainly on DVD and VCR picture quality and ease of use. **DVD picture quality** reflects sharpness and freedom from video "noise" for material played on the model's DVD player. **SP** and **EP** scores reflect similar judgments of recordings made in the high-speed/standard-play and low-speed/extended-play modes for the model's VCR. **Ease of use** includes usability of remote and front-panel controls, ease of setup and programming time-shift recording and other functions, fast-forward and rewind speeds, and key features listed above. **Price** is approximate retail.

Recommendations and notes

All tested models have: Stereo. Composite and RF output for VCR and DVD. S-video and component-video output, parental controls, and Dolby Digital 5.1 audio output for DVD. Onscreen and console displays. Auto channel set. Multilingual menu. Slow motion. Daily and weekly recording. Ability to play CD-R, CD-RW, and MP3-format discs as well as commercial audio CDs, but not DVD-RAM discs. Single-disc DVD player. Virtual surround sound. Front-panel A/V jacks. **Most tested models have:** Display of time remaining on tape. Zero search. Manual commercial skip. Tape counter displayed on console. Auto clock set. Ability to play DVD-R, DVD-RW, DVD+R, and DVD+RW discs and CD-audio portion of hybrid SACD discs. Audio dynamic range control. Screen saver. 12-month warranty on parts, 3 months on labor.

1> **SAMSUNG** DVD-V2000 **Very good and easy to use.** Universal remote. Full 1-yr. warranty. VCR: Warns of time-shift conflicts. Fast, but overshoots. Multispeed slow motion. Memory backup. DVD: Shows first scene of several chapters. Failed to play CD-audio portion of hybrid SACD discs. Can't copy from DVD to tape.

2> **PANASONIC** PV-D4752 **Very good.** Universal remote. VCR: Can record in LP speed. Fast, but overshoots. Auto commercial/movie-preview skip. Poor console display. DVD: Excellent progressive-scan performance. Played some older audio CDs with excessive treble. Can't copy from DVD to tape. Similar: PV-D4762.

3> **HITACHI** DV-PF2U **Very good, and inexpensive for a combination model.** Universal remote. VCR: Slow tape handling. Lacks zero search, commercial skip, and auto clock setting. Can't copy from DVD to tape.

4> **ZENITH** XBV243 **A good, basic player.** Failed to play DVD+R and DVD+RW discs.

5> **GO-VIDEO** DVR4250 **A good, basic player.** 3-mo. warranty. DVD: Failed to play DVD+R and DVD+RW discs.

6> **JVC** HR-XVC1U **Good, but expensive.** Remote control works with same-brand TV. Poor console display. DVD: Lacks audio dynamic range control. Lacks screen saver.

7> **SANYO** DVW-5000 **Good, and a good price.** VCR: Few features. DVD: No screen saver. Failed to play DV+R and DVD+RW discs.

8> **TOSHIBA** SD-V280U **A good, basic player.** DVD: Center-channel dialog enhancement to improve clarity of DVD movie dialog.

Features at a glance VCR/DVD combos

Tested products (keyed to the Ratings) Key no. Brand	Auto speed	Lighted remote	Index search	Plug and play	Coaxial digital-audio output	Optical digital-audio output	Progressive-scan DVD
1> Samsung	•		•	•	•	•	
2> Panasonic			•	•		•	•
3> Hitachi			•		•		
4> Zenith	•				•		
5> Go-Video	•				•		
6> JVC		•	•		•		
7> Sanyo	•				•		
8> Toshiba			•		•	•	

Wall ovens

The wall ovens tested performed well and were convenient to use. The Frigidaire Gallery GLEB30S8A, though slightly smaller inside than most, is a relative bargain at $700, and it is a **CR Best Buy.** The top-rated Thermador SC301T, $1,600, is a capacious model that baked very well and broiled excellently. Any of the top seven in our Ratings are very good, though pricey choices.

KEY NO	BRAND & MODEL	PRICE	OVERALL SCORE	BAKE	BROIL
	ELECTRIC CONVECTION WALL OVENS				
1	**Thermador** SC301T[W]	$1,600		◒	●
2	**Jenn-Air** JJW9530BA[W]	1,380		◒	◒
3	**Dacor** PCS130[R]	1,700		◒	◒
4	**GE** Profile JTP18WD[WW]	1,300		◒	◒
5	**Kenmore** (Sears) Elite 4902[2]	1,450		◒	◒
6	**Frigidaire** Gallery GLEB30S8A[S] **A CR Best Buy**	700		●	○
7	**KitchenAid** Superba KEBC107K[WH]	1,500		◒	◒
8	**Whirlpool** Gold GBS307PD[Q]	1,180		◒	⊖
9	**Viking** DESO100-[SS]	2,150		○	●

Overall Ratings — In performance order

Ratings scale: Excellent ● Very good ◔ Good ○ Fair ◓ Poor ●

Overall score scale: 0 — P F G VG E — 100

See report, page 34. Based on tests published in Consumer Reports in August 2002, with updated prices and availability.

The tests behind the Ratings

Under **brand & model,** brackets show a tested model's color code. **Overall score** includes oven capacity, baking, broiling, and self-cleaning. **Bake** shows baking evenness for cakes and cookies. **Broil** shows cooking and searing evenness for a tray of burgers. **Price** is approximate retail.

Recommendations and notes

Similar models have the same burners or elements, oven, and broiler; other details may differ.

1 **THERMADOR** SC301T[W] **Excellent window view.** Larger capacity than most. Two timers. No temperature probe. Similar: SC301Z[ ].

2 **JENN-AIR** JJW9530BA[W] **Excellent window view.** Excellent at self-cleaning, and door and window not as hot as others in this mode. Two timers. Offset shelf. Four rack positions. One oven light. Warranties: 2-yr. on parts; 5 yr. on controls, element. Discontinued, but similar nonconvection oven JJW8530CA[ ] is available.

3 **DACOR** PCS130[R] **Excellent window view.** Two timers. Needs 30-amp circuit. 2-yr. warranty.

4 **GE** Profile JTP18WD[WW] **Excellent window view.** Auto shut-off. Covered bottom element, removable floor. Rack for broiling pan. One oven light.

5 **KENMORE** (Sears) Elite 4902[2] **Excellent window view.** Auto shutoff. Covered bottom element, removable floor. But no temperature probe.

6 **FRIGIDAIRE** Gallery GLEB30S8A[S] **A CR Best Buy Smaller capacity than most.** Excellent window view. Excellent at self-cleaning. Offset shelf. Rack for broiling pan. Four rack positions. One oven light. No temperature probe. Similar: PLEB30S8A[ ], FEB30S5A[ ].

7 **KITCHENAID** Superba KEBC107K[WH] **Larger capacity than most.** Covered bottom element. Convection broil. Rack for broiling pan. But needs 30-amp circuit. Warranty: 5-yr. limited.

8 **WHIRLPOOL** Gold GBS307PD[Q] **Larger capacity than most.** Rack for broiling pan. Two rack positions. Needs 30-amp circuit. Similar: RBS305PD[ ].

9 **VIKING** DESO100-[SS] **Knobs for controls.** Convection-broil, defrost, convection-defrost modes. But no temperature display or probe. No child lockout. Manual light switch. Needs 40-amp circuit. Stainless steel. Least effective at self-cleaning. Warranties: 5-yr. on element; 10-yr. on rust-through. Similar: VESO105[ ].

Washing machines

Most machines do a fine job of washing. Top-loaders use the most energy and water, but typically cost less.

Two high-priced but excellent top-loaders are the Kenmore Elite Calypso 2206 and the Whirlpool Calypso GVW9959K, both $1,250. You can get excellent performance for less money with the Maytag Performa PAV2300A, **a CR Best Buy** at $370, but you will sacrifice some water and energy efficiency. Front-loaders are efficient and quiet, but they usually cost more. If money is no object, consider the top four models, excellent choices for $1,000 and up. Less expensive and very good alternatives: the Kenmore, Frigidaire, and GE models priced at $750 to $800. Key features for these models are listed in the table on page 290. See the product guide for an explanation of the features.

Overall Ratings — In performance order

Ratings key: E = Excellent, VG = Very good, G = Good, F = Fair, P = Poor

KEY NO.	BRAND & MODEL	PRICE	OVERALL SCORE (0–100, P F G VG E)	WASHING	EFFICIENCY — ENERGY	EFFICIENCY — WATER	CAPACITY	NOISE
TOP-LOADERS								
1	**Kenmore** (Sears) Elite Calypso 2206[2]	$1,250		E	VG	VG	E	E
2	**Whirlpool** Calypso GVW9959K[Q]	1,250		E	VG	VG	E	E
3	**Fisher & Paykel** GWL10 US	680		E	E	VG	G	VG
4	**Kenmore** (Sears) Elite Catalyst 2203[2]	920		E	F	VG	G	VG
5	**Whirlpool** Catalyst GSX9885J[Q]	680		E	G	VG	VG	VG
6	**GE** Profile WHSB9000B[WW]	600		VG	VG	G	VG	VG
7	**Maytag** Performa PAV2300A[WW] **A CR Best Buy**	370		E	G	G	VG	VG
8	**Frigidaire** Gallery GLWS1749A[S]	450		VG	VG	VG	VG	VG
9	**Kenmore** (Sears) 2381[2]	460		E	VG	G	VG	VG
10	**Kenmore** (Sears) Elite 2303[2]	590		E	VG	G	VG	G
11	**Maytag** Performa PAV5000A[WW]	500		VG	VG	G	G	G
12	**GE** Profile Performance WPSE7003A[WW]	745		VG	VG	VG	G	VG
13	**Hotpoint** VWSR4150B[WW]	370		VG	VG	G	G	G
14	**Amana** ALW480DA[W]	530		VG	VG	G	G	VG
15	**Amana** ALW895SA[W]	650		VG	G	G	F	VG
16	**GE** WWSE6260B[WW]	450		VG	VG	G	G	G
17	**KitchenAid** Superba KAWS850J[Q]	480		VG	VG	G	G	VG
18	**Haier** XQJ100-96	500		VG	VG	G	G	G
FRONT-LOADERS								
19	**Kenmore** (Sears) Elite 4292[2] HE3t	1,450		E	E	E	E	E
20	**Whirlpool** Duet HT GHW9200L[W]	1,300		E	E	E	E	E
21	**Kenmore** (Sears) Elite 4282[2] HE3	1,100		E	VG	E	E	E
22	**Whirlpool** Duet GHW9100L[Q]	1,000		E	VG	E	E	E
23	**Maytag** Neptune MAH7500A[WW]	1,370		E	E	VG	G	E
24	**Kenmore** (Sears) 4204[2]	800		VG	E	E	G	E
25	**Frigidaire** Gallery GLTR1670A[S]	750		VG	E	VG	G	E
26	**GE** Profile WPXH214A[WW]	750		VG	E	VG	G	E

See report, page 44. Based on tests published in Consumer Reports in July 2002, with updated prices and availability.

The tests behind the Ratings

In **brand & model,** the bracketed letter or number is a color code. **Overall score** is based primarily on washing ability, efficiency, capacity, and noise; gentleness and ease of use also figure in. For **washing,** machines were loaded with 8 pounds of cotton items, run on their most aggressive cycle, and judged on soil removed from test items. **Energy efficiency** is based on electricity needed to run the washer, energy needed to heat the water for a warm wash, and amount of water extracted (since that reduces drying time). **Water efficiency** denotes how much water per pound of clothing it took to wash an 8-pound load and each model's maximum load. **Capacity** denotes how large a load each machine could wash effectively. **Noise** reflects judgments by panelists. **Price** is approximate retail.

Recommendations and notes

TOP-LOADERS

1▷ **KENMORE** (Sears) Elite Calypso 2206[2] **An excellent, efficient washer without usual agitator.** Especially large capacity, gentle on clothes, and quiet.

2▷ **WHIRLPOOL** Calypso GVW9959K[Q] **Much like #1; some minor differences.**

3▷ **FISHER & PAYKEL** GWL10 US **A well-equipped machine that was the most energy efficient in this category.**

4▷ **KENMORE** (Sears) Elite Catalyst 2203[2] **Fully featured, with numerous wash/spin speed combinations.** Similar: 2205[ ], 2204[ ].

5▷ **WHIRLPOOL** Catalyst GSX9885J[Q] **A very good performer with lots of features.**

6▷ **GE** Profile WHSB9000B[WW] **A very good performer.**

7▷ **MAYTAG** Performa PAV2300A[WW] **A CR Best Buy Strong performance for the price.** But fewer features than most. Similar: PAV3300A[ ].

8▷ **FRIGIDAIRE** Gallery GLWS1749A[S] **Good.**

9▷ **KENMORE** (Sears) 2381[2] **Good basic machine.** Numerous wash/spin speed combinations. But only fair at handling unbalanced loads, and fewer features than most. Similar: 2383[ ], 2382[ ].

10▷ **KENMORE** (Sears) Elite 2303[2] **Good.** Numerous wash/spin speed combinations. But fewer features than most.

11▷ **MAYTAG** Performa PAV5000A[WW] **Numerous wash/spin speed combinations.** But only fair at handling unbalanced loads. Similar: PAV5157[ ], PAV5158[ ].

12▷ **GE** Profile Performance WPSE7003A[WW] **A good performer.**

13▷ **HOTPOINT** VWSR4150B[WW] **Excellent washing.** Lots of features. But less gentle than most.

14▷ **AMANA** ALW480DA[W] **A good performer.** Similar:

Features at a glance — Washing machines

Tested products (keyed to the Ratings) Key No.	Brand	Auto. dispensers	Auto. temp. control	End-of-cycle signal	Porcelain top and lid	Stainless-steel tub	Touchpad controls	Two-direction dials	Cycle time (in min.)
TOP-LOADERS									
1▷	Kenmore	•	•	•	•	•	•		70
2▷	Whirlpool	•	•	•	•	•	•		65
3▷	Fisher & Paykel		•	•		•	•		50
4▷	Kenmore	•	•	•		•	•		50
5▷	Whirlpool	•	•	•		•	•		50
6▷	GE		•	•				•	45
7▷	Maytag								50
8▷	Frigidaire		•	•					50
9▷	Kenmore								40
10▷	Kenmore		•						45
11▷	Maytag		•	•					50
12▷	GE		•	•				•	40
13▷	Hotpoint								45
14▷	Amana					•		•	40
15▷	Amana		•			•		•	55
16▷	GE		•					•	45
17▷	KitchenAid		•	•	•				45
18▷	Haier					•			50
FRONT-LOADERS									
19▷	Kenmore	•	•	•			•	•	70
20▷	Whirlpool	•	•	•			•	•	•	60
21▷	Kenmore	•	•	•		•	•		70
22▷	Whirlpool	•	•	•		•	•		70
23▷	Maytag	•	•	•		•	•		75
24▷	Kenmore	•	•	•		•	•		60
25▷	Frigidaire	•	•	•		•			60
26▷	GE	•	•	•		•			55

Recommendations and notes

ALW540RA[ ], ALW432RA[ ].

15▷ **AMANA** ALW895SA[W] **Good.** Numerous wash/spin speed combinations. But only fair capacity.

16▷ **GE** WWSE6260B[WW] **Good.** Numerous wash/spin speed combinations. Similar: WWSE5200B[ ].

17▷ **KITCHENAID** Superba KAWS850J[Q] **Good.** But less gentle than most. Discontinued, but similar 850L[Q] is available.

18▷ **HAIER** XQJ100-96 **There are better choices.** Being phased out; may be hard to find in stores.

FRONT-LOADERS

19▷ **KENMORE** (Sears) Elite 4292[2] HE3t **Top performance, at a top price.** Exceptional capacity: 20 lb. Similar: 4293[ ] HE3t.

20▷ **WHIRLPOOL** Duet HT GHW9200L[W] **Strong performer with handy two-direction dial controls.** Exceptional capacity: 20 lb.

21▷ **KENMORE** (Sears) Elite 4282[2] HE3 **Excellent overall.** Exceptional capacity: 20 lb.

22▷ **WHIRLPOOL** Duet GHW9100L[Q] **Much like #20; some minor differences.** Exceptional capacity: 20 lb.

23▷ **MAYTAG** Neptune MAH7500A[WW] **Strong performer.** But Maytag front-loaders have been the least reliable brand.

24▷ **KENMORE** (Sears) 4204[2] **Strong performer.** Similar: 4214[ ], 4205[ ].

25▷ **FRIGIDAIRE** Gallery GLTR1670A[S] **A very good machine.** Similar: GLTF1670A[ ].

26▷ **GE** Profile WPXH214A[WW] **Much like #24; some minor differences.**

Water filters

Carafes and faucet-mounted filters are a simple solution but installed models provide more water with less effort. Among carafes, the Brita Classic, 0B01, $20, was best at removing off-tastes. The undersink Kenmore 38460, $80, is an excellent choice and **a CR Best Buy.**

Shop Smart

Overall Ratings — In performance order

Legend: Excellent / Very good / Good / Fair / Poor

KEY NO.	BRAND & MODEL	PRICE	OVERALL SCORE	REMOVAL EFFECTIVENESS			FLOW RATE	ANNUAL COST (CARTRIDGE MODEL)
			P F G VG E	OFF-TASTES	LEAD	CHLOROFORM		
CARAFES *(Filter cartridges last 2 months)*								
1	**Pur** Advantage CR-1500R	$18		Good	Very good	Excellent	Excellent	$54 (CRF-1550)
2	**Brita** Classic 0B01	20		Very good	Excellent	Excellent	Fair	48 (0B03)
3	**Pur** Ultimate Small CR-800	23		Fair	Excellent	Very good	Poor	72 (CRF-950)
4	**GE** SmartWater XPL03D	19		Very good	Good	Very good	Good	108 (FXPL3D)
FAUCET-MOUNTED MODELS *(Filter cartridges last 2 to 3 months)*								
5	**GE** SmartWater GXFM03C	22		Excellent	Very good	Excellent	Good	52 (FXMLC)
6	**Pur** Ultimate Horizontal FM-4700L	43		Excellent	Very good	Excellent	Poor	80-120 (RF4050L)
UNDERSINK MODELS *(Filter cartridges last 6 months, except where noted)*								
7	**Kenmore** 38460 **A CR Best Buy**	80		Excellent	Excellent	Excellent	Very good	54 (34370; 34377)
8	**Omni** CBF-20	170		Excellent	Excellent	Excellent	Good	120 (CB20)
9	**Culligan** SY-2500	180		Excellent	Excellent	Excellent	Good	44 (D-25)
10	**GE** SmartWater (rev. 2) GXSL03C	105		Excellent	Very good	Excellent	Very good	56 (FXSLC rev. 2)
11	**Omni** OT32	150		Excellent	Excellent	Excellent	Good	168 (RS2; CB3)
12	**GE** SmartWater (rev. 2) GX1S15C	70		Very good	Excellent	Very good	Very good	34 (FXULC)
13	**Kenmore** 38465	150		Fair	Excellent	Excellent	Very good	90 (38466)
14	**Culligan** SY-1000	55		Very good	Very good	Excellent	Good	45 (1000R)
15	**Kenmore** 38455	100		Poor	Very good	Excellent	Excellent	54 (38456)
REVERSE-OSMOSIS MODELS *(Filter cartridges last 6 months)*								
16	**Kenmore** 38470	230		Excellent	Excellent	Very good	Poor	44 (34370; 34373)
17	**GE** SmartWater GXRV10ABL01	240		Excellent	Excellent	Very good	Poor	80 (FX12PA; FX12M)
WHOLE-HOUSE (POINT-OF-ENTRY) MODELS *(Filter cartridges last at least 3 months)*								
18	**Kenmore** 38440	35		Very good	Excellent	Fair	Very good	14-21 (34370)
19	**Omni** U-25	55		Poor	Poor	Good	Very good	52 (T01SS)

See report, page 192. Based on tests published in Consumer Reports in January 2003.

The tests behind the Ratings

Overall score is based mainly on the cartridges' effectiveness in removing chloroform, lead, and off-tastes, as well as flow rate and resistance to clogging. Sensory panelists judged removal of **off-tastes.** To test **lead** and **chloroform** we measured the chloroform and lead levels in water entering and leaving the filters. Except as noted, filters are National Sanitation Foundation International (NSF) certified for parasite and chlorine removal. **Flow rate** measures the performance of the filters with a new filter cartridge. It typically slows with continued use. **Annual cost** is based on the number of cartridges required per year and their cost as estimated by the manufacturers. **Cartridge model** is the replacement cartridge. **Price** is approximate retail.

Recommendations and notes

Most models included cartridges; for others, the price includes the additional cost of one. Undersink models include parts needed for someone with plumbing skills to install. In paragraphs, "other metals" means other than lead and mercury; "organics" refers to a variety of organic compounds; "VOCs" means volatile organic compounds. MTBE (methyl tert-butyl ether) is a gasoline additive.

CARAFES

1▷ **PUR** Advantage CR-1500R **Very good.** Fills quickly. Life indicator. But no covered spout. Doesn't remove cysts. Two quarts. Certified for mercury, lindane/atrazine, 0.5-1 micron particles, organics.

2▷ **BRITA** Classic OB01 **Economical, but relatively slow.** Doesn't remove cysts. Two quarts. Certified for mercury, 0.5-1 micron particles, organics, other metals.

3▷ **PUR** Ultimate Small CR-800 **Very good, but slow.** Filter tends to clog. Two quarts. Life indicator. Certified for lindane/ atrazine, mercury, 0.5-1 micron particles, organics, MTBE, other metals, cysts.

4▷ **GE** SmartWater XPL03D **A good choice.** Fills quickly. Two quarts. Doesn't remove cysts. Certified for mercury, other metals.

FAUCET-MOUNTED MODELS

5▷ **GE** SmartWater GXFM03C **Very good, but processed water lever must be reset with each use.** Certified for 0.5-1 micron particles, sediment, cysts.

6▷ **PUR** Ultimate Horizontal FM-4700L **A good choice.** But clogged prematurely. Life indicator. Certified for lindane/atrazine, mercury, asbestos, 0.5-1 micron particles, organics, MTBE, cysts.

UNDERSINK MODELS

7▷ **KENMORE** 38460 **A CR Best Buy An excellent choice.** Less likely than others to clog. Filter is hard to change. Certified for 0.5-1 micron particles, sediments, cysts.

8▷ **OMNI** CBF-20 **Excellent performer.** Less likely than others to clog. Includes tools. But hard to change filter. Certified for lindane/atrazine, mercury, asbestos, MTBE, VOCs, cysts.

9▷ **CULLIGAN** SY-2500 **Excellent, with long-lasting (12 mos.) double-filter set.** Life indicator. Includes tools. Certified for lindane/atrazine, mercury, asbestos, 0.5-1 micron particles, sediment, organics, cysts.

10▷ **GE** SmartWater (rev. 2) GXSL03C **An excellent, double-filter choice.** Includes tools. But hard to change filter. Certified for lindane/atrazine, mercury, chlorine, asbestos, 0.5-1 micron particles, cysts.

11▷ **OMNI** OT32 **Very good double-filter model.** Includes tools. But hard to change filter. Clogging worse than most. Certified for 0.5-1 micron particles, sediment, cysts. Cartridges last 3 and 4 months.

12▷ **GE** SmartWater (rev. 2) GX1S15C **Very good value.** Includes tools. Certified for lindane/atrazine, mercury, asbestos, 0.5-1 micron particles, cysts.

13▷ **KENMORE** 38465 **Very good double-filter model, but falters removing off-tastes.** Hard to change filter even with tools. Life indicator. Certified for lindane/atrazine, asbestos, MTBE, organics, VOCs, cysts.

14▷ **CULLIGAN** SY-1000 **A very good choice.** No filter housing. Certified for lindane/ atrazine, 0.5-1 micron particles, sediment, cysts.

15▷ **KENMORE** 38455 **Very good against contaminants, but poor at removing off-tastes.** Hard to change filter, even with tools. Life indicator. Certified for lindane/atrazine, asbestos, organics, MTBE, cysts.

REVERSE-OSMOSIS MODELS

16▷ **KENMORE** 38470 **Excellent filtering, but slow.** Hard to change filter. Certified for sediment, total dissolved solids. Does not claim to remove lead. Doesn't remove parasites.

17▷ **GE** SmartWater GXRV10ABL01 **Excellent filtering, but slow.** Less likely than others to clog. Hard to change filters, even with provided tools. Certified for mercury, 0.5-1 micron particles, sediment, total dissolved solids, other metals, cysts.

WHOLE-HOUSE (POINT-OF-ENTRY) MODELS

18▷ **KENMORE** 38440 **A very good choice, except for chloroform removal.** Hard to change filter. Certified only for sediment. Doesn't remove parasites.

19▷ **OMNI** U-25 **Not a good choice.** Poor at removing off-tastes. Doesn't remove parasites. Includes tools.

Finding Reliable Brands

In general, products today are pretty reliable. But CONSUMER REPORTS surveys have found that some brands have been more reliable than others. By buying the brands that have been the most reliable, you can improve your chances of getting a less repair-prone product. We know about trends in product reliability because, every year, CONSUMER REPORTS asks its readers to report on repairs and problems they encounter with household products. From responses to the Annual Questionnaire, we are able to derive the percentage of each brand's products that have been repaired or suffered a serious problem.

Products with complicated mechanisms typically need more repairs than simpler devices. Gas ranges break down more than electric ranges. Self-propelled lawn mowers fail more often than push models. The presence of an icemaker or a water dispenser in a refrigerator increases the chance of needing a repair.

These reliability findings can shed light on the dilemma that you face when a product breaks. Should you fix it or replace it? Two factors conspire to make obtaining repairs difficult. Prices are plummeting for many products, notably electronics and computers, often making repair the more expensive option. Also, repairs may be harder to obtain—parts and repairers may be scarce, their fees are high, and repair times are long.

Many people decide to get a model with new features when a product breaks. And you can sometimes get a lot more for less. Electronics products are the best example. For instance, a typical 27-inch TV set currently costs about $400 and has more features than did TVs that cost $560 five years ago. With appliances, you might reap cost savings due to newer models' greater efficiency. Appliances are more efficient today, especially refrigerators and washers. The most frugal cost the most, but they can save enough in energy over the long term to make replacing a broken older model a smarter option than repairing it.

Should you repair it?

Here's a way to assess whether or not to repair something. Consider its original cost, repair cost, and the technology velocity—the speed of improvement and innovation. Thus, replacing a broken product may be worthwhile if a new model brings major new technology and if the cost of repair is high. With many electronic products, a repair often involves replacing an entire circuit board—a costly proposition. Complexity and proprietary parts can be a disincentive to fixing a laptop computer, for example.

You should probably fix nearly anything in its first year—especially if it's under warranty. Items such as pro-style ranges, lawn tractors, and projection TVs are usually worth repairing long into their lives because new ones are so expensive. Otherwise consider replacing products if their repair cost exceeds 50 percent of replacement.

When something breaks, a few simple steps can help make the repair process easier. First, determine if you can fix it yourself. Most owners' manuals have a troubleshooting section, and manufacturers' web sites sometimes include repair instructions.

If the item is still not working, you may have to call the manufacturer. This can be frustrating: In a reader survey, about one quarter of those who tried had difficulty getting through, and almost half found the assistance wanting. Persistence can sometimes pay: Nearly 10 percent of those who called the manufacturer got an offer to fix or replace an out-of-warranty item for free.

Manufacturers generally train authorized service technicians on the latest equipment and hold them to certain standards—but repairs by these technicians may cost more. Independent repairers can be a viable choice, especially for products out of warranty. Ask if the repairer belongs to a trade association such as the Professional Service Association or the International Society of Certified Electronics Technicians (ISCET). While membership doesn't guarantee integrity, it may mean repairers have had special training.

If you feel victimized by a repairer, you can file a complaint with your local community affairs department, the Better Business Bureau (*www.bbb.org*), or your state's attorney general's office. You can also take the repairer to small-claims court. Keep all receipts and records. And ask to keep any parts that are replaced.

If you replace it

Disposing of broken products may make economic sense for the individual consumer, but the environmental costs for communities include burdening landfills and the risk that hazardous materials will enter the waste stream. Examples of dangerous waste include lead in circuit boards and picture tubes; mercury in laptops and digital cameras; and cadmium in some rechargeable batteries. Repositories for batteries and other potentially hazardous products are available. Look on page 301 for a list of web sites that provide information on where to recycle these items.

Brand Repair Histories

To help you gauge reliability, the graphs that follow give brand repair rates for 26 product categories. CONSUMER REPORTS has been asking about brands' reliability for more than 30 years. The findings have been quite consistent, though they are not infallible predictors. A brand's repair history includes data on many models, some of which may have been more or less reliable than others. And surveys of past products can't anticipate design or manufacturing changes in new products.

Product categories include appliances such as refrigerators and vacuum cleaners, electronic products such as TV sets and camcorders, as well as lawn mowers and tractors. Histories for different kinds of products aren't directly comparable because they cover products of different ages, and older products tend to break more often than newer ones. In addition to the guidance provided by our survey, CONSUMER REPORTS engineers have noted the kinds of problems likely to occur.

Camcorders, compact analog and digital models

Camcorders are used only about 12 hours per year, which may influence their repair rate. Things that go wrong include temporary problems caused by moisture condensation or clogged heads and more serious problems involving the motors or loading mechanism. Differences of 4 or more points are meaningful.

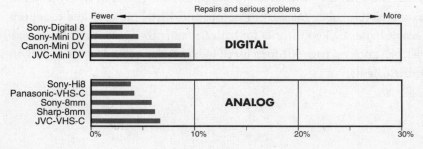

BASED ON MORE THAN 24,000 RESPONSES ON COMPACT ANALOG AND DIGITAL CAMCORDERS PURCHASED IN 1999 TO 2002. DATA HAVE BEEN STANDARDIZED TO ELIMINATE DIFFERENCES BETWEEN BRANDS DUE TO AGE AND USAGE.

Dishwashers

Asko and Frigidaire were the most repair-prone brands. In general, things that go wrong include door-lock assembly problems, excessive water in unit (pump assembly), and no water or overflow (water valve). Differences of 4 or more points are meaningful.

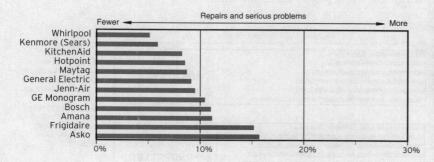

BASED ON MORE THAN 108,000 RESPONSES ON BUILT-IN DISHWASHERS PURCHASED IN 1996 TO 2001. DATA HAVE BEEN STANDARDIZED TO ELIMINATE DIFFERENCES BETWEEN BRANDS DUE TO AGE AND USAGE.

Dryers

Clothes dryers are simpler machines than washers. Gas and electric models have been equally reliable. Things that go wrong include motor failure, problems with the igniter or heating element causing the dryer not to heat, and problems with rollers or belts. Differences of 4 or more points are meaningful.

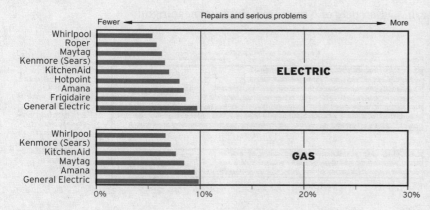

BASED ON NEARLY 95,000 RESPONSES ON GAS AND ELECTRIC DRYERS PURCHASED IN 1996 TO 2001. DATA HAVE BEEN STANDARDIZED TO ELIMINATE DIFFERENCES BETWEEN BRANDS DUE TO AGE AND USAGE.

SITES THAT CAN HELP YOU FIX IT

◆ **www.repairclinic.com.** This site is primarily a source for appliance parts–available overnight if needed. It covers nearly 90 brands and includes troubleshooting hints, care tips, and a "RepairGuru" you can query via e-mail.

◆ **www.livemanuals.com.** Included are simulations of how appliances and electronics equipment work, along with lists of manufacturers' addresses, phone numbers, and web links. Some of the web links allow you to e-mail the manufacturer for help with a problem.

Lawn mowers Push and self-propelled

Push models have been generally more reliable than self-propelled ones because they're less complex. Things that go wrong include problems with starting, cables, controls, wheels, belts and drive systems. We don't have sufficient data to give reliability for electric models. Differences of 4 or more points are meaningful.

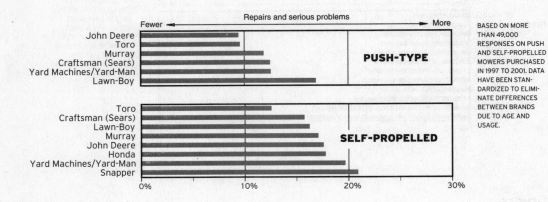

BASED ON MORE THAN 49,000 RESPONSES ON PUSH AND SELF-PROPELLED MOWERS PURCHASED IN 1997 TO 2001. DATA HAVE BEEN STANDARDIZED TO ELIMINATE DIFFERENCES BETWEEN BRANDS DUE TO AGE AND USAGE.

Lawn tractors and riding mowers

These products, which have many moving parts, have typically been very repair-prone. Things that go wrong include problems with starting, batteries, cables, controls, pulleys, belts, and drivetrain. Differences of 6 or more points are meaningful.

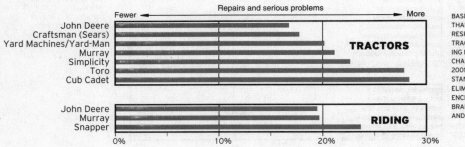

BASED ON MORE THAN 17,000 RESPONSES ON LAWN TRACTORS AND RIDING MOWERS PURCHASED IN 1997 TO 2001. DATA HAVE BEEN STANDARDIZED TO ELIMINATE DIFFERENCES BETWEEN BRANDS DUE TO AGE AND USAGE.

Microwave ovens Over the range

Microwave ovens have historically shown low repair rates; we have found no meaningful differences among major brands of countertop models. A simple failure to operate can be caused by a power surge. (Restart by unplugging and plugging back in.) Differences of 4 or more points are meaningful. The chart doesn't include Kenmore or Whirlpool because of an unusual situation. Certain over-the-range models of these brands were recalled last year, resulting in extraordinarily high repair rates: 52 percent for Kenmore and 38 percent for Whirlpool—much higher than the repair rates for those brands from our last Annual Questionnaire.

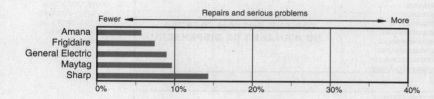

BASED ON MORE THAN 22,600 RESPONSES ON MICROWAVE OVENS OR COMBINATION MICROWAVE/CONVECTION OVENS PURCHASED IN 1998 TO 2002. DATA HAVE BEEN STANDARDIZED TO ELIMINATE DIFFERENCES BETWEEN BRANDS DUE TO AGE AND USAGE.

Ranges Electric models

In general, electric ranges have required fewer repairs than gas ranges. Smoothtop models have been about as reliable as conventional coil-burner models. Things that do go wrong include failed heating elements. Differences of 3 or more points are meaningful.

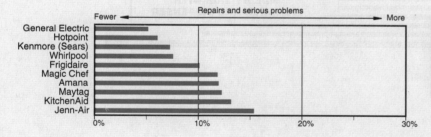

BASED ON MORE THAN 55,000 RESPONSES ON COIL AND SMOOTHTOP ELECTRIC RANGES PURCHASED IN 1996 TO 2001. DATA HAVE BEEN STANDARDIZED TO ELIMINATE DIFFERENCES BETWEEN BRANDS DUE TO AGE.

Ranges Gas models

In general, gas ranges have required more repairs than electric ranges. Things that go wrong include failed igniters. Differences of 5 or more points are meaningful.

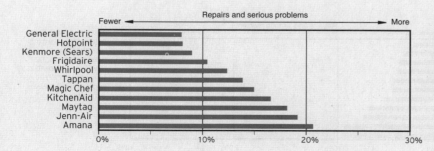

BASED ON MORE THAN 29,000 RESPONSES ON GAS RANGES PURCHASED IN 1996 TO 2001. DATA HAVE BEEN STANDARDIZED TO ELIMINATE DIFFERENCES BETWEEN BRANDS DUE TO AGE.

Refrigerators

Regardless of configuration—top-freezer, bottom-freezer, and side-by-side—the presence of an icemaker increases the chance of needing a repair. All side-by-side models included an outside ice and water dispenser, features that also increase the chance of needing a repair. Of models so equipped, Maytag has been the least reliable. In general, things that go wrong with all types of refrigerators include cooling problems caused by the compressor or motor. Differences of 3 or more points are meaningful.

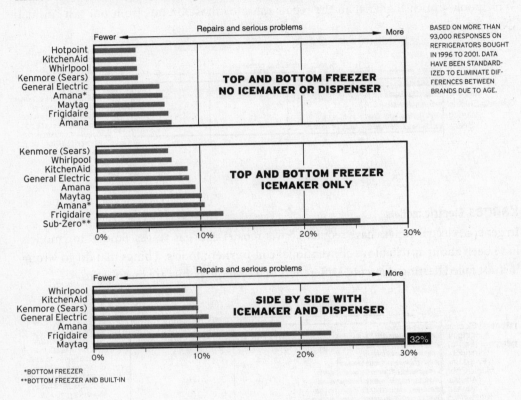

BASED ON MORE THAN 93,000 RESPONSES ON REFRIGERATORS BOUGHT IN 1996 TO 2001. DATA HAVE BEEN STANDARDIZED TO ELIMINATE DIFFERENCES BETWEEN BRANDS DUE TO AGE.

*BOTTOM FREEZER
**BOTTOM FREEZER AND BUILT-IN

TV sets 25- to 27-inch

These models tend to be a bit older than sets in the 31- to 36-inch range. GE and RCA have been among the more troublesome brands. In general, things that go wrong with this size set are no picture or sound (which may be related to the power supply), deteriorating picture quality (picture tube or tuner), and inability to get channels (tuner). Differences of 3 or more points are meaningful.

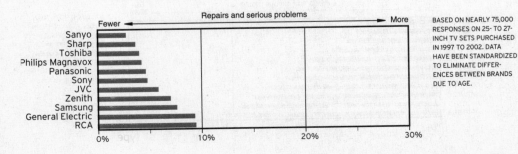

BASED ON NEARLY 75,000 RESPONSES ON 25- TO 27-INCH TV SETS PURCHASED IN 1997 TO 2002. DATA HAVE BEEN STANDARDIZED TO ELIMINATE DIFFERENCES BETWEEN BRANDS DUE TO AGE.

TV sets 31-, 32-, 35-, and 36-inch

Most models in our survey were fairly new and were used more often than smaller-sized TVs. RCA has been significantly more troublesome than other brands. In general, things that go wrong with this size set are much the same as with smaller sets. Differences of 3 or more points are meaningful.

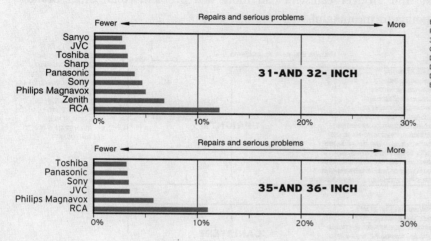

Fewer ← Repairs and serious problems → More

31-AND 32- INCH

Sanyo, JVC, Toshiba, Sharp, Panasonic, Sony, Philips Magnavox, Zenith, RCA
0% 10% 20% 30%

BASED ON NEARLY 41,000 RESPONSES ON 35- AND 36-INCH TV SETS PURCHASED IN 1998 TO 2002. DATA HAVE BEEN STANDARDIZED TO ELIMINATE DIFFERENCES BETWEEN BRANDS DUE TO AGE.

Fewer ← Repairs and serious problems → More

35-AND 36- INCH

Toshiba, Panasonic, Sony, JVC, Philips Magnavox, RCA
0% 10% 20% 30%

TV sets Projection

Beyond the types of things that generally go wrong with TV sets, projection sets tend to have problems with the projection and lens systems. Because of these sets' high price tag, it's usually worth repairing them—even sets as old as 6 years. Differences of 3 points are meaningful.

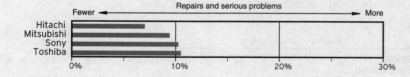

Fewer ← Repairs and serious problems → More

Hitachi, Mitsubishi, Sony, Toshiba
0% 10% 20% 30%

BASED ON MORE THAN 5,600 RESPONSES ON PROJECTION TV SETS PURCHASED IN 1996 TO 2001. DATA HAVE BEEN STANDARDIZED TO ELIMINATE DIFFERENCES BETWEEN BRANDS DUE TO AGE AND USAGE.

SITES THAT HELP YOU SAFELY DISPOSE OF THINGS

These sites provide information on recycling:

◆ *www.iaer.org* (International Association of Electronics Recyclers). A searchable database on this site allows you to look up the location of recyclers of large-screen TV sets, cell phones, and other electronics products.

◆ *www.eiae.org* (Electronic Industries Alliance). This site connects you with charities, needy schools, and recycling programs that collect electronics products.

◆ *www.recycle-steel.org/database/main.html* (The Steel Alliance Steel Recycling Institute). A searchable database of 30,000 listings helps you track down local appliance recyclers.

◆ *www.rbrc.org* (Rechargeable Battery Recycling Corp.) This site has information on a nationwide recycling program for all types of rechargeable batteries.

Vacuum cleaners

Things that go wrong include inability to run (motor), unusually loud noise or vibration (impeller, rotating brush, or bearing), and self-propelling problems. The results shown here don't include broken belts—a frequent but inexpensive problem. Broken belts were more common for Eureka, Panasonic, and Dirt Devil as compared with other brands of uprights. Eureka and Hoover canisters had more belt problems than other brands. Differences of 4 points are meaningful.

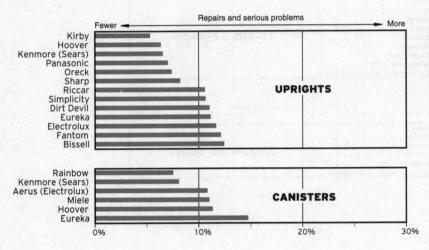

BASED ON MORE THAN 119,000 RESPONSES ON FULL-SIZED UPRIGHT AND CANISTER VACUUM CLEANERS PURCHASED IN 1997 TO 2001. DATA HAVE BEEN STANDARDIZED TO ELIMINATE DIFFERENCES BETWEEN BRANDS DUE TO AGE AND USAGE.

Washing machines Top and front loaders

Things that go wrong with washing machines included problems with the timer, pump, valves, motor, transmission, and drive belt. Differences of 4 points or more are meaningful. Maytag front loaders were the most trouble-prone washing machines.

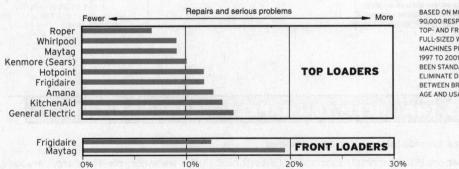

BASED ON MORE THAN 90,000 RESPONSES ON TOP- AND FRONT-LOADING FULL-SIZED WASHING MACHINES PURCHASED IN 1997 TO 2001. DATA HAVE BEEN STANDARDIZED TO ELIMINATE DIFFERENCES BETWEEN BRANDS DUE TO AGE AND USAGE.

Index